DOING QUALITATIVE RESEARCH IN SOCIAL WORK

DOING QUALITATIVE RESEARCH IN SOCIAL WORK

IAN SHAW & SALLY HOLLAND

Los Angeles | London | New Delhi
Singapore | Washington DC

Los Angeles | London | New Delhi
Singapore | Washington DC

SAGE Publications Ltd
1 Oliver's Yard
55 City Road
London EC1Y 1SP

SAGE Publications Inc.
2455 Teller Road
Thousand Oaks, California 91320

SAGE Publications India Pvt Ltd
B 1/I 1 Mohan Cooperative Industrial Area
Mathura Road
New Delhi 110 044

SAGE Publications Asia-Pacific Pte Ltd
3 Church Street
#10-04 Samsung Hub
Singapore 049483

Editor: Katie Metzler
Assistant editor: Lily Mehrbod
Production editor: Ian Antcliff
Copyeditor: Jen Hinchliffe
Proofreader: Chris Bitten
Marketing manager: Camille Richmond
Cover design: Shaun Mercier
Typeset by: C&M Digitals (P) Ltd, Chennai, India
Printed and bound by CPI Group (UK) Ltd,
Croydon, CR0 4YY

Library of Congress Control Number: 2013950322

British Library Cataloguing in Publication data

A catalogue record for this book is available from
the British Library

MIX
Paper from
responsible sources
FSC® C013604
www.fsc.org

ISBN 978-1-4462-5282-6
ISBN 978-1-4462-5287-1 (pbk)

For
Maria Lau
Jonathan Scourfield

Table of Contents

About the authors

Ian Shaw

I arrived in York (England) as Professor of Social Work in the Spring of 2003, following a long career in the School of Social Sciences at Cardiff University (Wales). I presently hold positions at the University of York and the Department of Sociology and Social Work at Aalborg University, Denmark.

I have written and researched extensively. My next book, body and soul permitting, will be *Social Work and Science* for Columbia University Press, followed by a four-volume 'Major Work' for SAGE Publications on *Social Work Research*, with Jeanne Marsh and Mark Hardy. I am involved, alone or with others, at various stages of four research projects: an extended historical project on the relationship of sociology and social work, partly through the Special Collections at the University of Chicago; a historical study of the *British Journal of Social Work*; a study of the nature of research networks in social work; and a systematic review of practitioner research in adult social care. I hope to develop the notion of 'sociological social work' to the point where I will write a further book.

I co-founded the journal *Qualitative Social Work*. I envisioned and led to fruition in 2011 the European Conference for Social Work Research, and have worked with others to consolidate that initiative through a new European Social Work Research Association.

Sally Holland

I am a Reader in Social Work in Cardiff University's School of Social Sciences. Previously I was a social worker in the field of child and family social work, working in the voluntary and statutory sectors. I have extensive experience of conducting qualitative research projects in social work and have investigated issues related to looked after children, assessment of parenting, family group conferences, child neglect, involving fathers in child protection work, adoption and community safeguarding. I have used a range of qualitative methods to explore these topics, including participative research with children, ethnography, mobile methods, life history interviews and documentary analysis. I facilitate a research advisory group for young people who are care experienced and am deputy chair of my departmental research ethics committee. I am the author of *Child and Family Assessment in Social Work Practice* (SAGE, 2nd edition, 2011).

Introduction

Doing Qualitative Research in Social Work endeavours to provide a one-stop reference point for all the deliberations, decisions and practices that are entailed in qualitative research in social work. A scan of the contents page will demonstrate how the book covers each interwoven stage of the research process, broader methodological questions, and the fields where the social work context gives qualitative research special character. Perhaps needless to say, some readers will need to look elsewhere for more information on specialist or arcane qualitative interests, or for detailed skills advice on, for example, particular data analysis packages.

The book has faint echoes of an earlier book (Shaw and Gould, 2001) – a synergy of authored and invited exemplars. We acknowledge the generosity of Nick Gould and some of the contributors to that book in enabling us to draw here and there on some passages in that book. But *Doing Qualitative Research in Social Work* is a very different project.

As two authors we have some commonalities and some differences. A shared part of our histories is that we have both spent substantial parts of our careers in the School of Social Sciences in Cardiff University, overlapping by seven years. Cardiff's rich tradition of qualitative research methods has been a clear influence, with references to the work of current and former colleagues such as Delamont, Atkinson, Bloor, Coffey, Pithouse, Scourfield, Renold and Hall appearing throughout the book.

Ian Shaw's recent and continuing interests within social work and social science focus on several themes, including the practice/research relationship, understanding the nature of social work as an applied social science in relation to disciplines like sociology, qualitative methodology, practitioner research, developing social work research strategies, the history of social work and research, and technology and professional practice. He co-founded the journal *Qualitative Social Work* – a resource to which this book is much indebted. His general stance is perhaps best captured in an essay reflecting on his back catalogue (Shaw, 2012d).

Sally Holland has a background in child and family social work and much of her methods expertise is practical, arising from experience of conducting qualitative and mixed methods projects using approaches such as ethnography, case studies, life history and participative research. Despite her main expertise and experience being with qualitative research, she is perhaps less critical of other positions and approaches than Ian, and this has led to constructive debates as the book has progressed, particularly when from time to time we make statements such as 'our position is ... '. Our way of managing this mutual trust and difference has been that all of the chapters were first fully drafted by one of the authors, then critically responded to by the other, before further re-drafting. Just as peer reviewing of journal articles probably leads to a better final product, we hope that this critical collaboration has produced a sounder, more thoughtful and comprehensive book than each of us might have produced individually.

We have tried to sustain a, sometimes delicate, fusion of audiences. We were asked to write a 'textbook'. While acute readers may detect somewhat fluctuating ways in which each of us understands that requirement, we have gone to some lengths, through many exemplifications of research practice and 'Taking it further' tasks, to make a strong reality of that aim. However, we also have tried throughout to interest those van Maanen calls 'collegial readers' (2011: 26), yet without the use of unexplained collegial language. We have steered clear of heavily digested, pre-packaged textbook writing forms, although that *genre* is itself in flux, as well as varying significantly between, for example, the USA and Europe. While one expectation the reader will reasonably bring is for clarity, we have tried to write with a modest degree of literary quality. We have also sought to balance abstraction and concrete example – to 'be empirical enough to be credible and analytical enough to be interesting', and artfully evocative in addition to being factual and truthful (van Maanen, 2011: 29, 34).

Contents of the book

The book is in three parts.

In **Part I** we ask **What is distinctive about qualitative social work research?** The first chapter begins with an exploration of what characterises qualitative research, then places this in the context of qualitative research in social work. In Chapter Two we review the connections between social work and research, examining the people, problems and domains that are the foci of both fields. In Chapter Three we continue to map qualitative social work research with a historical and contemporary review of methods and innovations, ending this section with a query as to what is good social work research, and who decides the answer to that question?

Part II is devoted more explicitly to the ***Doing*** **of qualitative social work research.** This is the largest part of the book with nine chapters devoted to research methods and processes. In sequencing the chapters in this section we do not necessarily claim that they represent an order for doing research. Literature reviewing, for example, will take place at several points, and in particular before and after key decisions are made about research design. Analysis is a process that is embedded in qualitative research from the start. Nonetheless, the format of a book requires sequencing and we start this section with Chapter Four on reviewing research – a process that may be an end in itself or as part of a primary research project. Chapter Five is a relatively pragmatic chapter on qualitative research design, where major designs are critically reviewed and the process of designing a qualitative project is outlined. Chapter Six explores research ethics, situating debates about ethics particularly within qualitative social work research. We then include four chapters devoted to data generation methods. In these we have chosen those we think are particularly pertinent to social work research and we include long established methods alongside newer forms. The chapter titles are deliberate, in that, rather than refer directly to a method, we consider research practice at a more abstract level in terms of the underlying form of inquiry that is involved. Chapters Seven and Eight introduce, compare and contrast various forms of asking questions and telling stories in qualitative social work research. Chapter Nine examines ways of researching written texts, while Chapter Ten is about researching social work contexts, through ethnography, and through the lenses of place, time, sounds and smells. Part II ends with two chapters on qualitative analysis – how analysis is anticipated and prepared for (Chapter Eleven) and how it is conducted (Chapter Twelve).

Part III contains the final four chapters and covers the outworking of **the purposes and consequences of qualitative social work research.** We sustain a focus on the doing of research in the first two chapters. In Chapter Thirteen we explore evidence for practice, through the qualitative evaluation of interventions and outcomes. Chapter Fourteen considers social justice in social work research, and we review the concept of standpoints and designs and methods associated with research that has aims of furthering social justice. The final two chapters are concerned with the relationships between research and what we may call 'outer-science' influences and concerns. Chapter Fifteen is about research and practice, and in it we particularly challenge the notion that there is a linear, unidirectional relationship of research informing practice. In Chapter Sixteen we look at the consequences of social work research – impact and research utilisation. We also open up one of the most interesting developments, that of forms of writing research.

PART I
What is Distinctive about Qualitative Social Work Research?

PART I
What Is Distinctive about Qualitative Social Work Research?

ONE
Qualitative Research and the Social Work Context

We open the book by inviting you to consider an example of qualitative social work research. Extending from this, we consider two general questions during the chapter. First, what is entailed in a commitment to qualitative research? Second, how does social work frame and infuse the practice of qualitative research? In response to the first question we examine how qualitative research has developed an understanding of subjective meanings and also the routines of everyday life. We introduce three areas of debate within qualitative methods: whether qualitative methods should be seen as a paradigm position; the relationship between numbers and qualities; and the kinds of knowledge claims that may be made from different methods. The *social work* character of qualitative research comes under scrutiny throughout this opening section of the book. In this chapter we take up the significance of social work contexts.

Through their personal memory people give meaning to what has happened to them. When people are involved in traumatic events, they are faced with questions regarding their identity and relation with others and the world. On the one hand, they have the need to recollect and process those memories; on the other hand, they feel a need to distance themselves and forget or detach from the pain and threat involved in such memories.

Seeking to understand these issues, several different researchers – men and women – interviewed twenty couples who had been involved in domestic violence. Guy Enosh and Eli Buchbinder say that

> In the process of remembering, the interviewee might recall a sensitive event in detail, reliving it to the fullest and re-experiencing the feelings felt during the event. At other times, interviewees might narrate events at various levels of distance, taking the position of an outsider or of an observer witnessing the experience … To describe this range of ways of reconstructing experience, from full reliving of the experience to its disowning, we use the terms 'knowledge', 'focus of awareness' and 'alienation'. (Enosh and Buchbinder, 2005: 14)

There is little knowledge regarding the processes by which such memories are constructed. They suggest an understanding of 'approaching and distancing' (remembering and forgetting) around the axes of emotional involvement and linguistic abstraction. Analysis of the data yielded four broad categories:

- 'Knowledge', defined as direct remembering and reliving, with complete details of the event.
- 'Awareness of mental processes', including awareness of emotions and of cognitive processes.
- 'Awareness of identity', including awareness of values and the construction of personal characteristics of each partner and of the couple as a unit.
- 'Alienation', characterised by a refusal to observe, reflect or remember.

Enosh and Buchbinder's article exemplifies much of what is characteristic of qualitative research. For example, we suggest in Chapter Three that more than 70 percent of qualitative social work research relies on some form of interview as its primary method of collecting data. The authors of this article were aware of one possible limitation of that approach and so modify it by focusing their attention on the reconstruction of narrative memory as a means of remedying the inconsistency of methods that rely on self-report in domestic violence.

More unusually, they carried out joint interviews with couples. In the later chapter on 'Asking Questions' we show that there is considerable diversity in forms of interviewing, and some important recent developments of the method. In the 'Telling Stories' chapter we give considerable space to narrative methods.

An obvious feature of the article is how the authors are endeavouring to understand things that we may think of as largely 'internal' – memories and how people sort and manage them. In a way that is strikingly different from, for example, a questionnaire or a measurement scale, the understanding of behaviour is mediated through a primary emphasis on what things *mean* to people, and also on how that meaning emerges from the research process – in this case by talking to two people simultaneously. Meaning is, we might say, 'co-constructed'. They talk in the article about how this influenced the analysis of the data. They searched for themes in the data, but did so in a way that inserted those themes back into their context, rather than treating them as abstract 'variables'. We unpack methods of analysing qualitative data towards the end of the book.

They are not writing *any* qualitative study, but one that is about social work. This comes over in different ways. For example, domestic violence is centrally, though not exclusively, a social work concern. In Chapter Two we analyse the range of research problems that characterise qualitative *social work* research. Interviewing couples where at least one of them has been violent towards the other is a sensitive topic. In the next chapter we ask whether social work research is especially sensitive, and what we mean when we talk about doing 'sensitive' research. Finally, although they emphasise how to *understand* memory, there is an undercurrent of concern about applications of their work. We talk during this book about how the explicitness of the applied agenda of social work research varies considerably from one study to another.

The article poses a further issue. Interviewing couples about domestic violence may be regarded as ethically complex and even controversial. Qualitative research poses ethical and political problems. We take these up in Chapter Six, and elsewhere in discussions of 'false consciousness' and 'standpoints'.

To enable us to get inside the book we treat this chapter as setting out how to approach qualitative research in social work. We do this by considering two broad questions. First, what is entailed in a commitment to qualitative research? Second, how, in general terms, does 'social work' frame and infuse the practice of qualitative research?

Qualitative research

We have taken for granted so far that we can refer to qualitative research without undue ambiguity. However, any attempt to list the shared characteristics of qualitative research will fall short of universal agreement, and some think the effort itself is misguided. We say more about these challenges of diversity and delusion in a few paragraphs' time. Nonetheless, most qualitative researchers would appeal to and identify with the majority of the following descriptors.

- It involves immersion in situations of *everyday life*. 'These situations are typically "banal" or normal ones, reflective of the everyday life of individuals, groups, societies and organizations' (Miles and Huberman, 1994: 6). It involves 'looking at the ordinary in places where it takes unaccustomed forms', so that 'understanding a people's culture exposes their normalness without reducing their particularity' (Geertz, 1973: 14).
- The researcher's role is to gain an overview of the *whole* of the culture and context under study.
- Holism is pursued through inquiry into the *particular*. This contrasts with methods where '[t]he uniqueness of the particular is considered "noise" in the search for general tendencies and main effects' (Eisner, 1988: 139). Grand realities of Power, Faith, Prestige, Love, etc. are confronted 'in contexts obscure enough ... to take the capital letters off' (Geertz, 1973: 21). Qualitative research studies 'make the case palpable' (Eisner, 1991: 39).
- The whole and the particular are held in tension. 'Small facts speak to large issues' (Geertz, 1973: 23), and 'in the particular is located a general theme' (Eisner, 1991: 39). Patrick Kavanagh, the Irish poet, wrote 'parochialism is universal. It deals with the fundamentals'.

    All great civilisations are based on parochialism. To know fully even one field or one land is a lifetime's experience. In the world of poetic experience it is depth that counts, not width. A gap in a hedge, a smooth rock surfacing a narrow lane, a view of woody meadows, the stream at the junction of four small fields – these are as much as a man can fully experience.

    Robert Macfarlane, from whose essay we have taken this quotation,[1] says that for Kavanagh, 'the parish was not the perimeter, but an aperture: a space through which the world could be seen'.

---

[1] In an essay in *The Guardian* newspaper, 30 July 2005.

- 'The researcher attempts to capture data on the perceptions of local actors "from the inside", through a process of deep attentiveness, of empathic understanding (*verstehen*), and of suspending or "bracketing" preconceptions about the topics under discussion' (Miles and Huberman, 1994: 6). Stanley Witkin talks in this context about the need for us to have 'a theory of noticing', and to look for rich points (Witkin, 2000a).

- This stance is sometimes referred to as one of 'ethnomethodological indifference' (after Garfinkel). However, 'bracketing' preconceptions, even if it is possible, need not preclude taking a normative position – 'you do not have to be neutral to try to be objective' (Wolcott, 1990: 145). 'Appreciation does not necessarily mean liking something ... Appreciation ... means an awareness and an understanding of what one has experienced. Such an awareness provides the basis for judgement' (Eisner, 1988: 142). Indeed, qualitative approaches 'can effectively give voice to the normally silenced and can poignantly illuminate what is typically masked' (Greene, 1994: 541).

- Respondent or *member categories* are kept to the foreground throughout the research. This is linked to a strong inductive tradition in qualitative research – a commitment to the imaginative production of new concepts, through the cultivation of openness on the part of the researcher. One of the most difficult challenges for the qualitative researcher is how to develop a convincing account of the relationship between the language, accounts and everyday science of those to whom she has spoken and her own analytic categories.

- When it comes to those analytic categories, qualitative research is characteristically *interpretive*. 'A main task is to explicate the ways people in particular settings come to understand, account for, take action, and otherwise manage their day-to-day situations' (Miles and Huberman, 1994: 7). For qualitative researchers, subjectivity is *created* by culture, and does not simply *display* it. This is partly what is meant when the word 'constructivist' is used.

- The researcher is essentially the main instrument in the study, rather than standardised data collection devices. It is here that the word 'reflexive' often occurs – referring to the central part played by the subjectivities of the researcher and of those being studied. Qualitative fieldwork is not straightforward. 'The features that count in a setting do not wear their labels on their sleeve' (Eisner, 1991: 33). The part played by the self in qualitative research also raises the special significance of questions of ethics in qualitative research, and renders the relationship between researcher and researched central to the activity.

- Finally, most analysis is done in words. This is true – perhaps even more so – with the advent of increasingly sophisticated software for analysing qualitative data. There are frequent references in this connection to 'texts'. Judgement and persuasion by reason are deeply involved, and in qualitative research the facts never speak for themselves.

Is there a central organising idea behind this characterisation of qualitative research? Maybe not, and anyway the question is not very interesting. But we like, for example, Elliot Eisner's comment that qualitative research slows down the perception and invites exploration, and releases us from the stupor of the familiar, thus contributing to a state of wide-awakeness (Eisner, 1991). He compares this to what happens when we look at a painting. If there is a core – a qualitative eye – it has been expressed in different ways. For Riessman, it is 'Scepticism about universalising generalisations; respect for particularity and context; appreciation of reflexivity and standpoint; and the need for empirical evidence' (Riessman, 1994: xv).

Qualitative research is not a unified tradition. The term qualitative 'refers to a family of approaches with a very loose and extended kinship, even divorces'

(Riessman, 1994: xii). These differences of research *practice* stem from diverse *theoretical* positions. While there have been numerous cross-currents that muddy the waters of these differences, it is helpful to think of them as following two general lines.

Subjective meanings

The first of these different traditions starts with the subjective meanings that people attribute to their actions and environments, and follows through to the work of Norman Denzin on interpretive interactionism, much of the work on the sociology of knowledge and on subjective theories, and some of the influences from feminist research and postmodernism. *Symbolic interactionism* lies behind most approaches that stress studying subjective meanings and individual ascriptions of meaning. Symbolic interactionist research is founded on the premises that

- People act towards things on the basis of the meanings such things have for them.
- The meaning is derived from interactions one has with significant members of one's social networks.
- Meanings are handled in, and modified through, an interpretive process used by the person in dealing with the things encountered (Flick, 2006).

These processes form the starting point for empirical work. Is culture people's beliefs or material artifacts (subjective or objective)? In Geertz's much alluded to essay on thick description, he said 'Once human behavior is seen as … symbolic action … the question as to whether culture is patterned action or a frame of mind or even the two somehow mixed together, loses sense' (Geertz, 1973: 10). For him the meaning of culture 'is the same as that of rocks on the one hand and dreams on the other – they are things of this world. The thing to ask is what their import is … what is being said' (ibid., p. 10).

This position developed out of American philosophical traditions of pragmatism, and the work of people in Chicago early in the twentieth century, and was given its fullest early statements in the writings of George Herbert Mead and Herbert Blumer. The reconstruction of such subjective viewpoints becomes the instrument for analysing social worlds. There has been a major research interest in the forms such viewpoints take. These include subjective theories about things (e.g., lay theories of health, education, counselling or social work), and narratives such as life histories, autobiographies and deviant careers.

One of the most famous encapsulations of this position was found in W.I. Thomas and Dorothy Thomas' famous aphorism that if men (*sic*) define situations as real they are real in their consequences (Thomas and Thomas, 1928). There were those with a social work identity who had as sophisticated an understanding of the issues as anyone in sociology. Ada Sheffield is a foremost example, and her 1922 book on *Case-study Possibilities* stands as a forgotten classic. She anticipated a symbolic interactionist stance when she says of the case worker that 'selection of facts amounts to an implicit interpretation of them' (Sheffield, 1922: 48). In a remarkably strong passage, she says that 'the traditions and training of the observer more or less condition the *nature* of the fact-items that make their appearance … In this sense the subject-matter of much social study is unstable. Not only do two students perceive different facts, they actually in a measure make different facts to be perceived.' Example 1.1 illustrates how a symbolic interactionist position moulded a study of social work practitioners engaged in their own research.

EXAMPLE 1.1	Practitioners Doing Research

A British project drew on a case study evaluation of two networked cohorts of practitioner researchers in a children's services national social work agency in Scotland. The aim of this study was to understand the meaning of practitioner research for social work professionals through an exploration of how language, ascriptions of meaning and interpretation provide a social environment through which the nature and meaning of practitioner research emerge.

The authors say

> 'In doing so we pursue a moderate symbolic interactionist position, in exploring how language, ascriptions of meaning, and interpretation provide a social environment through which the nature and meaning of practitioner research emerge. To express this through a familiar statement, the distinctive character of interaction as it takes place between human beings consists in the fact that human beings interpret or 'define' each other's actions instead of merely reacting to each other's actions. Their 'response' is not made directly to the actions of one another but instead is based on the meaning which they attach to such actions. Thus, human interaction is mediated by the use of symbols, by interpretation, or by ascertaining the meaning of one another's actions. (Blumer, 1969: 180 quoted in Shaw and Lunt, 2012: 198)

The authors conclude that:

- Practitioner researchers engage with a language and culture that is strange yet potentially rewarding for practice and research. They find themselves located in a culture that lies between 'practice' and 'research' but is fundamentally shaped by and challenges both.
- Practitioner researchers are typically engaged in negotiating an uncertain world, which is at its heart an effort to learn what it's about.
- The location of practitioner research as lying both within and outside of core professional work poses difficult challenges of moral accountability for their work within their practice cultures.
- Involvement in practitioner research stirs reflection on the meaning and value of professional work. For some practitioners this may be overly demanding in the context of the perceived constraints of their core work.
- Networked initiatives inevitably raise questions of ownership.
- The nature of practitioner research is something that emerges from the experience, rather than something that prescribes it in advance. It is only in the doing of practitioner research that its critical identity takes shape.

Shaw and Lunt (2012)

The routines of everyday life

The second diffuse tradition in qualitative research is concerned with how people produce social reality through interactive processes. Broader traditions of social anthropology and ethnography are often best understood in this way, but it has been most marked in the writing of Harold Garfinkel on what he called ethnomethodology. For him the 'central concern is with the study of the methods used by members to produce reality in everyday life' (Flick, 2006: 68). The focus is not the subjective meaning for the participants of an interaction and its contents but how this interaction is organised. The research topic becomes the study of the routines of everyday life. Interaction is assumed by ethnomethodologists to be structurally organised, and to be both shaped by and in turn shape the context. Hence, interaction repays detailed attention, because it is never disorderly, accidental or irrelevant.

One important strand of this emphasis has been through the analysis of conversation, and how something is made a certain kind of conversation, whether it be talk over coffee in a social work team room, a GP consultation, or a parent–teacher evening exchange. It is characteristically seen as constituted through turn-by-turn organisation of talk in an institutional context. Conversation is looked at as comprising 'speech acts' rather than grammatical word strings or statements. It proceeds by looking at 'turns' and treating each utterance as *displaying an interpretation* of the previous utterance, and thus looks at the understanding displayed by the participants. This line of research has often focused on studies of work in organisational contexts. Take, for example, this example of a supervision session between a team manager (TM) and a social worker (SW) (Example 1.2).

EXAMPLE 1.2	Social Work Supervision
Social Worker (SW):	… She's got a lot of positives. She's a personable girl, pleasant, bright girl. One odd quality is an incredible neatness – her schoolwork is absolutely immaculate. You can't tell the difference between one page and another. Every word the same.
Team Manager (TM):	Sort of obsessional?
SW:	Erm, well tidy. Very tidy people. I don't know what she's got. She's certainly got it up there for the application of graphics – she's a bright girl. Although she's a problem in school behaviour-wise, she's likely to blow up. She does reasonably well in examinations, she's got many positives, she's not a negative girl altogether.
TM:	The criminal. It doesn't fit in with this part of Jackie does it?
SW:	Well she's a well-known shoplifter – to the extent that a note comes to the house saying "Jackie, can you pinch me a pair of trousers, will pay five pounds for them". She's well known in her circle at school as being the top shoplifter.
TM:	She's not far from becoming a labelled criminal?

(Continued)

(Continued)

SW: She er yes. But her criminality is in (*pause*) er strange really, it's almost a mania. It has a quality about it that is almost psychologically driven. I don't know if that's the proper use of the term 'psychology' but – you know – the drive is there, er because of an abnormal psychology, there's something there all right.

TM: Um how long has she been doing it? ...

Pithouse and Atkinson (1988)

This is part of a discussion about a 'case' where they are discussing a family where the daughter Jackie has been caught for shoplifting – not for the first time. They are discussing how the family lulls social workers into a false sense of security 'and then they blow' (Pithouse and Atkinson, 1988). The form and structure of the conversational turns communicate that this is a social work supervision session.

Two caveats are in order. First, we should not, however, assume that forms of language, discourse and conversation are predictable. The example just given illustrates *this* well. The team manager introduces a series of possible explanations, which could be seen either as efforts to bring in the lessons of experience and expertise, or possibly as efforts to bring closure to this phase of the session. But the social worker seems to resist this, as seen in her responses of 'well ... ' and 'but ... ', each of which points up the risks of assuming a naïve model of managerialist power. Second, not all talk takes the form of conversation. There are various forms of talk that are in the form of lectures, speeches, newscasts, media reports or monologues.

This approach – together with the wider traditions of ethnography – emphasises that 'social practices constitute real objects and subjects ... embodied know-how' and points to the priority of the study of practical activity (Packer, 2011: 11). As Packer subsequently expresses it, 'Ethnomethodology sees human activity as skilled, intelligent and improvisatory. Like good jazz, social action is artfully made up on the spot' (ibid., p. 190).

Power, philosophy and paradigms

The positions we have sketched out raise three related questions. First, if qualitative research is committed to constructivist epistemology, does this entail rejecting realist understanding and explanation of the world? Second, does qualitative research entail a paradigmatic worldview, such that the philosophy and subsequent practice of research are incommensurable with mainstream quantitative research, or should these be seen as complementary perspectives? Third, do the traditions of research we have outlined culpably neglect the operation of power that operates to oppress others?

These are complex and much rehearsed questions. Our position is best conveyed through the cumulative positions we take during the book. For the moment we want to ask a deceptively simple question that immediately leads us into the first and third of these questions. What if we suspect participants *mis*understand their form of life? To misunderstand implies that there is a correct and incorrect way of understanding something, and thus challenges relativist epistemology. It also leads us to acknowledge the circumstances in which such misunderstanding might occur. 'This is the troubling suggestion made most powerfully by Karl Marx' (Packer, 2011: 271). Marx had much to say about *alienation* – the process whereby workers are separated from one another, from the products of their labour, and from the activity of work itself. Alienation exerts power such that workers are unaware they are being exploited, thus producing *false consciousness*. Down through the work of the Frankfurt School, most versions of feminism, and the critical theorising of Habermas, Bourdieu and Foucault, the consequent vision for research has been an emancipatory one. Packer's conclusion to the 'what if' question is that we 'still need to take their understanding into account. We do not need to accept the understanding that participants display in an interaction, and our analysis does not need to stop there. But it does need to *start* there … We cannot *critique* participants' understanding unless we first figure out what it is' (ibid., p. 267). For some writers this includes a more general scepticism about methodology of any kind. Once again we are in deep water, and face to face with how we see both the limits and limitations of science.

Numbers and qualities

While our position on paradigms is not cut and dried, it has four key elements, which we elaborate in this section. These are:

- A commitment to a strongly fallibilist version of realism (while things are real, our understanding or representation of them will always be incomplete and probably flawed).
- The constructed character of social reality.
- The central role of political and individual interests.
- The real but imperfect and partial relationship between paradigms and methodology.

A stance such as this combines elements of relativity of meaning, realism and power. One possible way of seeing paradigms is to view them as including 'regulative ideals' (Phillips, 1990: 43), entailing normative rather than always achievable standards (McKay, 1988), and as more akin to Weber's concept of ideal types, where we should expect few studies to reflect 'pure' versions of paradigm-led research. We should take an empirical interest in paradigms as much as a philosophical interest. For example, 'study of notions of bias, error, mistakes and truth as used in ordinary practice might be a profitable way to gain a sense of the actual epistemologies used by social workers' (Reid, 1994: 469). We should also note the relevance of these debates for social work practice.

Debates surrounding values and philosophical positions in social work are often conducted in similar ways to debates about paradigms and pragmatism in research. This should not be surprising. At their philosophical and moral roots they are more or less the same problems.

Like the qualitative health researchers, Miller and Crabtree, we are prepared to 'hold quantitative objectivisms in one hand and qualitative revelations in the other' (Miller and Crabtree, 2005: 613) – 'hold' not as something to possess but as better enabling a close inspection and understanding. Critical understanding of the merits of this or that research methodology requires being insider and outsider, member and stranger, white coat thought and purple coat experience and action.[2] It demands the cultivation of 'anthropological strangeness' (Lofland and Lofland, 2006), and the avoidance of sentimentality, which we are guilty of

> when we refuse, for whatever reason, to investigate some matter that should properly be regarded as problematic. We are sentimental, especially, when our reason is that we would prefer not to know what is going on, if to know would be to violate some sympathy whose existence we may not even be aware of. (Becker, 1970c: 132–3)

Yet the ways in which such debates have been conducted are in large part unhelpful. Not that there is nothing to debate, or that we stand as neutral bystanders (e.g., Shaw 2012a, 2012b), but our concern is that social workers have tended to adopt entrenched positions which make it difficult to get fully inside or outside the arguments. Hence positivism, for example, becomes 'a swearword by which no-one is swearing' (Williams, 1976),[3] or we are sometimes left with the impression that if only we were courageous enough to 'deconstruct' a problem or take a 'postmodern' position, we would be more than half way to its solution. For both positivists and committed advocates of humanist alternatives the comment often attributed to Augustine is apposite – 'total abstinence is easier than perfect moderation'.

'Paradigm' is a thorny word. Indeed, it has become a 'bucket word' (Popper, 1989) to hold diverse meanings. If we take it in a general sense of 'a basic set of beliefs that guides action' (Guba, 1990: 17) we are only a little further forward. It would give even a mildly tendentious philosopher a heyday with each of the five key words in this definition! How many such 'basic sets of beliefs' are there?

For example, Hammersley, while discussing ways in which quantitative and qualitative methods have been distinguished in paradigmatic terms, convincingly argues that characteristics of each paradigm element in every case can be identified in examples of research conducted under the alternative paradigm (Hammersley, 1992: Chapter 10). Perhaps the most well-known ethnographic voice on this issue is that of Howard Becker. Writing of epistemological issues, he says, 'I think it is

---

[2]The reference is to the Welsh doctor–poet Dannie Abse's poem 'Song for Pythagoras', which can be found in his *New and Collected Poems* published by Hutchinson.

[3]Not quite 'no-one' of course.

fruitless to try to settle them ... These are simply the commonplaces, in the rhetorical sense, of scientific talk in the social sciences, the framework in which the debate goes on. So be it ... There's nothing tragic about it' (Becker, 1993: 219). We should take an empirical perspective on such matters, treating them as 'a topic rather than an aggravation' (ibid., p. 222). But we should beware the paralysing effect of too much methodological discussion. 'We still have to do theoretical work, but we needn't think we are being especially virtuous when we do' (ibid., p. 221). Rather than regard such theoretical work as the responsibility of all qualitative researchers, he is content to view it as a specialism – the profession of 'philosophical and methodological worry' (ibid., p. 226)!

Yet we should not underestimate the relationship between epistemology, values and methods. People's actions, in research as much as in any other activity, *are* shaped by values and worldviews, and paradigm positions do *not* inevitably tend to intolerance of others. We agree with Greene when she dissents from the methodological pragmatism that avers epistemological purity does not get research done. Rather, 'epistemological integrity does get meaningful research done right' (Greene, 1990: 229).

Knowledge claims and mixing qualitative methods

A helpful way of laying out one's own preconceptions for scrutiny is to think what claims to knowledge can plausibly be drawn from different methods. Figure 1.1 illustrates in simple terms how there is a range of questions that surfaces through comparisons of qualitative and quantitative methods. Yet we think it will prove more helpful in the context of this book to look at differences *within* the general portfolio of qualitative methods.

Single cases or comparison.

Cause and meaning.

Context as against distance.

Homogeneity and heterogeneity.

Validity and the criteria of quality in social work research.

The relationship of researcher and researched.

Measurement.

Figure 1.1   Qualitative and quantitative methodology: A range of questions

We refer in a later chapter to the work of Bornat and Bytheway (2012) on archival materials. They helpfully distinguish 'recorded time' (time as part of the record of the course of life), 'formatted time' (time as present in datasets) and 'told time' (how time is represented in the development and telling of stories). They then compare two different qualitative methods and suggest how each lends itself to different potential knowledge claims.

EXAMPLE 1.3	Comparing Datasets in Terms of Temporality	
	LIFE HISTORY INTERVIEWS	DIARIES
RECORDED TIME	Retrospective. A focus back over the whole life, dating events and sequences	The 'here and now'. A focus on the events of successive days
FORMATTED TIME	Oral. A comparatively brief interaction between researcher and subject; including a sequential exchange of questions, answers and comments	Written. A sequence of dated entries produced over an extended period of time by a lone individual
TOLD TIME	Autobiographical. The interviewee's story of the life as lived and remembered	Biographical. Stories of unfolding, often collective experiences, told in the words of the diarist.

Source: Bornat and Bytheway (2012).

Analogous conclusions can be drawn from an earlier study of professional decision making, in which the authors set out the different qualities of interviewing and observation methods as part of a study of professional decision making when people are to be offered a place in a home for the elderly. Their interests were in aspects of the micro-processes of decision making, and to understand discretion and variations in such decisions (McKeganey et al., 1988).

As part of a comprehensive comparison, extracted in Example 1.4, they concluded that it was difficult to use observation to focus on individual decisions because decisions occur across several contexts. Interviews, by contrast, can cover every decision point. Interviewing was also judged stronger as a means of triangulating accounts by different professionals. However '[t]here may be a tendency for interviewers and interviewees to concentrate on only the formal components of the decision making process', whereas 'one of the benefits of observational work is precisely the capacity to focus attention upon the informal aspects of professionals' decision making' (ibid., p. 16). This formal/informal aspect was also reflected in their judgement that taken-for-granted dimensions of decisions may be harder for people to articulate in interviews, and better accessed via observation. Interviews may tend to recreate past decisions as if they were more rational than in fact they were. McKeganey and colleagues conclude that observational work can tap the more chaotic character of present decisions. Finally, they believe that professionals may use private decision categories that include moral or pejorative aspects – perhaps especially when the demand for a service outstrips the supply and they are obliged to ration. They concluded that interviews would be less likely to disclose these elements, and that observation would at least problematise the grounds of decision making.

EXAMPLE 1.4	Interviewing or Observation for Evaluating Professional Decision Making	
	INTERVIEWS	**OBSERVATION**
DATA LEVEL	Individuals	Processes
DECISION POINTS	Multiple	Few
TRIANGULATION OF ACCOUNTS	Strong	Less strong
COMPONENTS OF DECISIONS	Formal	Informal
ROUTINE DECISIONS	Less strong	Strong
NON-DECISIONS	Weak	Weak
RATIONALITY/NON-RATIONALITY OF DECISIONS	Overstate rationality	Strong on non-rationality
DISCLOSURE OF PRIVATE ACCOUNTS	Less strong	Adequate

Based on McKeganey et al. (1988).

However, Schwandt plausibly reasons that 'it is not readily apparent what "mixing" so-called paradigms or philosophies means or how that might be accomplished.' Mixing ethnomethodology's concern with the accomplishment of routines with symbolic interactionists' focus on the meaning of social life can go so far in that they share some concerns, but otherwise they are not compatible and employ 'different means to generate and analyse different kinds of data' (Schwandt, 2007: 165). We remain hesitant about the naïve pragmatic position that mixed methods – and especially those that bridge quantitative and qualitative strategies – will almost always yield optimum results. The position that is likely to prove most creative for social work research is that described by Greene and Caracelli as *dialectical*. This position accepts that philosophical differences are real and cannot be ignored or easily reconciled. We should work for a principled synthesis where feasible, but should not assume that a synthesis will be possible in any given instance. This represents,

a balanced, reciprocal relationship between the philosophy and methodology, between paradigms and practice. This … honours both the integrity of the paradigm construct and the legitimacy of contextual demands, and seeks a respectful, dialogical interaction between the two in guiding and shaping evaluation decisions in the field. (Greene and Caracelli, 1997: 12; c.f. Mertens and Hesse-Biber, 2013)

We avoid a partisan position on traditions and schools within qualitative social science. Nonetheless, we believe that social work researchers have been unduly selective in their awareness of developments in qualitative methodology. For example, in the next section we argue that qualitative social work research should be more strongly grounded in an understanding of and puzzling about issues of context. We also think that the concentration of qualitative research on the local, the small scale and the immediate has sometimes mistakenly been taken to justify an individualising approach to practice and research. This may follow from a misreading of what is entailed in a commitment to understanding matters from the actor's perspective. Wolcott, for instance, is cautious about saying he wants to understand things from the actor's perspective. 'It is system qualities I seek to describe and understand. To attempt to understand a system is not to claim to understand or be able to predict the actions of particular individuals within it, oneself included' (Wolcott, 1990: 146).

Qualitative *social work* research

We usually think of 'research' and 'practice' in precisely that order. Social workers and those with and for whom they work are regarded as the beneficiaries, often reluctant, of the outcomes of research. Researchers are taken to be the experts, while social workers are expected to dutifully 'apply' the results of expert inquiry to their practice. 'Findings' – data, practice prescriptions, evidence-based outcomes, assessment and prediction tools, generalisations and occasionally theories – are presented for implementation, often in the form of 'key lessons from research'. It is small wonder if practitioners quail at the very thought of the latest dose of expert knowledge. We explore the practice–research relationship fully in Chapter Fifteen.

We are persuaded that social work practice, human services and service users, and social work management, create and sustain rich and diverse agenda for the practice of qualitative research. These agenda commence from the problems and practices of social work rather than those of research methodology. In turn, the diverse, inter-related cluster of methodologies that makes up qualitative research challenges and recasts the conventional image of the relationship between knowledge, skills and values in social work. 'Knowing' and 'doing', research and practice, are not two wholly distinct areas that need mechanisms to connect them, but are to a significant degree part and parcel of one another.

Research in context

Qualitative research is largely bare of meaning when stripped from its context. At its most general, research occurs in time and place. More specifically, it frequently occurs in a context of social work *practice*, a point we develop in the next chapter. Yet practice is not homogenous. There are different organisational contexts *between* and *within* social work agencies.

Research also springs from and in large part is enacted within the *academy*. The university standing of qualitative research varies considerably between countries. It has been relatively dominant, for example, in parts of Europe and less so in much of the USA. It is not easy or even advisable to separate the context of the academy from that of the city. Chicago offers a good example of this. Chicago University was founded in 1890 as a Baptist institution by William Harper, its first president. He wanted the university to be marked by fundamental research, training and the improvement of society. The city of Chicago was central to much of this development. 'All of social life was here and being investigated by sociologists' (Plummer, 1997: 8). Plummer expresses it nicely as a place where 'a world of strangers and danger merges with a world of diversity and innovation. Here was the pathos of modernity' (Plummer, 1997: 7). The image of the city is writ large on the research of the time. This story has been told amply from sociology's orientation, but similar stories can be told for social work. An almost lost major project on Chicago housing was undertaken in the 1930s by Edith Abbott and associates (Abbott, 1936). In ironic counterpoint to Abbott's life-long teaching and advocacy of statistical strategies, her research accounts reveal a rich sense of ethnographic purpose, via graphic, novelistic descriptions of different neighbourhoods. In the final chapter, Example 16.4 exemplifies such realist writing.

Finally there are contexts of *politics* and also of *race*. Social work's links to mainstream political parties have been part of a submerged agenda in the history of social work. A social work colleague expressed the political context of British academic social work as follows:

> My take on this ... is that Labour Party membership is part of a pragmatic political engagement and I would see a connection here to social work research. In social work and in the critical social sciences as a whole I come across a lot of people who talk a radical talk and see themselves as very much on the left, but they aren't politically active – aren't involved in any local or national political organisation but channel their supposed radicalism solely into academic work ... I prefer the idea of mundane pragmatic political involvement to try and improve a few things in small ways. The same would go for social work research. I think the rhetoric of radicalism has its place but is usually less effective than getting your hands dirty – doing research commissioned by government for example, commissioned evaluations and so on. There's a common position here, I think, of pragmatic ameliorative politics.[4]

Contexts, however, are more – much more – than the collaborative endeavour of peers. One weakness of some interpretive sociology has been 'a failure to examine social norms in relation to the asymmetries of power and divisions of interest in society' (Giddens, 1993: 164). Giddens argues 'that the creation of frames of meaning occurs ... in terms of the differentials of power which actors are able to bring to bear ... *The reflexive elaboration of frames of meaning is characteristically*

---

[4]Personal communication.

imbalanced in relation to the possession of power ... What passes for social reality stands in immediate relation to the distribution of power' (Giddens, 1993: 120, emphasis in original). This underlines the central importance of both language and structure in grasping the significance of social work contexts.

Giddens summarises his argument as follows. Language is a *condition* of the generation of speech acts, and also the unintended *consequence* of speech and dialogue. Language is *changed* by speech and dialogue. He sees this as being at the heart of the process of what he calls 'structuration' and as reflecting the 'duality of structure' – 'as both condition and consequence of the production of interaction' (Giddens, 1993: 165). Hence 'structure must not be conceptualised as simply placing constraints upon human agency but as enabling' (ibid., p. 169), and structures are neither stable nor changing. 'Every act which contributes to the reproduction of structure is also an act of production, a novel enterprise' (ibid., p. 134). We explore in Chapter Nine how corresponding arguments apply to the importance of *written texts* in social work contexts. Texts can only be understood in context (Scheff, 1997: 4.4). As with settings and structures they are not fixed entities. Qualitative research and analysis can counter these tendencies by emphasising the spatial, temporal and practical contingencies associated with the texts. These contingencies entail the same interplay of intention and structure that we have already noted.

If the centrality of context pushes us uncompromisingly to explore intentions, structures, language, power and written texts, it also presents us with the problem of what we mean when we talk about 'cases'. The term 'case' is still part and parcel of the everyday language of social workers when talking about those who willingly or reluctantly use their services. Practitioner researchers also commonly use it if they describe their research as a 'case study'. In both instances an awareness of 'context' is vital. Suppose a social worker is asked to describe what makes a 'good client'. In the following extracts two social workers are identifying the grounds they draw on when supporting their belief that work had gone well in particular 'cases' (Shaw and Shaw, 2012).

'The client was positive and wanted to find other things to do instead of offending, so there was more of a rapport ... There were goals that were set by both of us ... he was the one who was coming up with them ... He was motivated to improve ... he was part of the working agreement ... he was the one who was keen to assess what was happening.'

'She was coping with the bereavement, trying to contemplate being a single parent ... She was able to talk about the kind of support she would have ... she was beginning to plan ... she was talking about her deceased husband in quite a healthy way. She was clearly projecting into the future rather than dwelling in the past. So really she was measuring herself in a way which I would have looked at as well.' (Shaw and Shaw, 2012: 328)

'Measuring herself in a way which I would have looked at as well' seems to be the key phrase. Here is someone who in effect approaches problem solving with the same set of assumptions as the professional – where partnership is possible, but perhaps on the social worker's terms.

We should not assume that practitioners will always view 'good clients' in this way. It is possible, for example, that good clients will be seen as those who clearly fit the 'gate-keeping' criteria for an agency as a clear-cut child protection case. They may also be 'good clients' in the sense of 'presenting' an interesting problem that matches the professional interests and agenda of the practitioner. In every instance the definition of a 'case' is context-dependent. Once again, the inference emerges. Cases are not fixed empirical entities of a general category – objects waiting to be found. It is more often true that they are waiting to be 'made' (Atkinson and Delamont, 1993).

It is precisely at this point that qualitative inquiry has something to offer to both practice and research. It is *contextualised* usefulness that social workers and managers need, and not 'decontextualised statistical power' (Braithwaite, quoted in Smith, 2005). This is because it is context that provides meaning rather than the 'universalised generalisations' that Riessman eschews. Smith concludes that context matters, and 'it makes little sense to try to understand a special project without reference to the local environment which sustains it (or fails to do so) (Smith 2005: 116).

In the next chapter we explore further questions that arise when we consider qualitative *social work* research.

Taking it further

Task one

Read the two pieces referenced below. Consider – either as a solo exercise or in small groups – the differences in the kind of questions they ask and the approach to the research. How well do they correspond to the characteristics of symbolic interactionist and ethnomethodological research as outlined in this chapter?

Hall, Tom (2001) 'Caught not taught: Ethnographic research at a young people's accommodation project', in I. Shaw and N. Gould (eds), *Qualitative Research in Social Work*. London: SAGE Publications. pp. 49–59.

Forsberg, Hannele and Vagli, Åse (2006) 'The social construction of emotions in child protection case-talk', *Qualitative Social Work*, 5(1): 9–31.

Task two

Turn to Chapter Sixteen and read Example 16.4 about Edith Abbott on Chicago tenements. If you can locate this long-ago book, find the chapter quoted from here and read it. Then find and read the article by Martin (2007). Megan Martin reports on findings from a research project that took place in

2006 on the border between two neighbourhoods on the east side of Detroit. The project addresses the stark racial, economic and physical divides between two adjacent communities. Alter Road serves as the real and rarely crossed border between the communities. Martin walked again and again across this boundary making notes as she did so.

Martin, Megan (2007) 'Crossing the line: Observations from East Detroit, Michigan USA', *Qualitative Social Work*, 6(4): 465–75.

How does the urban context for Abbott's and Martin's projects shed light on how we should think about 'context' when undertaking qualitative social work research? Can you find echoes of these questions in neighbourhoods and urban areas known first hand to you?

TWO
Researching the Social Work Field

We review what is known about four questions that shed light on qualitative research in social work:

What are the kinds of data that characterise social work practice and hence shape social work research?

How do the different domains and fields of social work similarly or variously shape the purposes and practice of qualitative research?

What challenges and opportunities are presented when one is researching on one's professional or academic home ground?

How far are key forms of thinking and practice in qualitative research and social work practice linked?

We have opened in the first chapter by scanning a broad landscape. On any landscapes there are outcrops and features that strike our eye from a distance. It is to a cluster of such 'outcrops' that we turn in this chapter. What are the kinds of data that characterise social work practice and hence shape social work research? How do the different domains and fields of social work similarly or variously shape the purposes and practice of qualitative research? What challenges and opportunities are presented when one is researching on one's professional or academic home ground? How far are key forms of thinking and practice in qualitative research and social work practice linked?

The act of posing these questions may seem to imply that social work research – qualitative or otherwise – is distinct from research in other fields and disciplines. Care is needed to make clear what is being claimed or denied in such an assertion. If we say social work research is distinctive we may mean any one or more of the following:

- Social work has distinctive values and (good) social work research will be imbued with social work values.
- Social work research will – or at least should – address the core concerns of social work practice. Therefore, social work research will always be, in some sense, 'practice research'.

- The methods of social work research should draw on and adapt the methods of social work practice, and therefore be characterised by distinctive methods.
- Social work addresses problems that are within the domain of professional competence of social work, and social work research should, and usually will, be focused on a range of research problems that are special to social work.

None of these is straightforward. They are all mixtures of normative and descriptive statements. They also all contain major premises – social work has distinctive values; social work has distinct professional competencies; social work research should address the core concerns of social work practice – that may be true but are not self-evident. Finally, they all, if strongly espoused, appear to exclude some forms of research that seem to us to possess perfectly sound claims to being (good) social work research. We are fearful whenever unequivocal voices are heard in support of any or all of these positions. Even when the term 'paradigm' is not used, these sorts of arguments have the marks of a naïve paradigm position. Hammersley is right to warn that paradigm talk on this level 'obscures both potential and actual diversity in orientation, and can lead us into making simplistic methodological decisions' (Hammersley, 1995: 3). To pick up his second point, it is simplistic when one hears the occasional argument that quantitative analysis is inherently 'positivist', and that qualitative methodology is somehow more reflective of social work values than quantitative. Social work and social work research will be the poorer if we over-emphasise the distinctives. It will make us disinclined to listen to the voices of colleagues in other disciplines and professions. On most occasions the right question to ask is not 'What makes social work research distinctive?', but 'What might make it distinctively *good*?' (Shaw, 2012).

At several moments in this and the following chapter we draw on a review of qualitative social work research, as a way of reining us in from being unduly speculative (Shaw and Ramatowski, 2013). The review is based on the articles in the first eleven volumes (2002–12) of the journal *Qualitative Social Work* – a journal committed to publishing work that falls solely within the purview of this book, and therefore the most representative and comprehensive deposit of qualitative social work research. The review of qualitative *methods* is covered in Chapter Three. Much of this chapter teases apart ways in which social work practice and qualitative research have different forms of kinship, but does so in the setting of our introductory observations about the misapprehensions and dangers of overstating the special qualities of social work.

What kinds of data characterise social work practice and hence shape social work research?

Vulnerable people

The remit of social work agencies varies much from one country to another. However, it is reasonable to generalise to the extent that social work is typically with those who are vulnerable in different ways. We asked on whom, in the first instance, was the focus of the research (see Table 2.1)?[1] This dimension is further grouped around actual or potential service user populations, people in their capacity as members of wider communities, and members of policy or professional communities. In this respect we doubt whether qualitative research engages with or is about people who are different from those who are the focus of and participants in more structured research forms.

The classification scheme is relatively new and hence there is little to go on by way of comparisons with other social work research. The range is diverse. One may reasonably wonder if it differs in spread from research by either practitioners or service users (Shaw, 2012b; Shaw, Lunt and Mitchell, Lunt and

Table 2.1   On whom is the primary research focus? (taken from Shaw and Ramatowski, 2013)

			Grouped categories	
		N	**N %**	
Actual or potential service user or carer groupings	1. Children, families, parents, foster carers	29	93 38.4	
	2. Young people (not offenders)	19		
	3. Young offenders/victims	3		
	4. Adult offenders/victims	3		
	5. Adults with housing, homelessness, education or employment difficulties	5		
	6. People with mental health problems	18		
	7. Older people	6		
	8. Adults/children with health/disability difficulties (including learning disabilities)	7		
	9. Adults/children who are drug/substance users	1		
	10. Equal focus on two or more different user and/or carer groups	2		
Citizen, user and community populations	11. People as members of communities	11	36 14.9	
	12. Service user, citizen or carer populations	4		
	13. Women/men	21		
Professional and policy communities	14. Social work practitioners/managers	30	64 26.4	
	15. Social work students/practice teachers/ university social work staff	14		
	16. Social work and/or other researchers	13		
	17. Policy, regulatory or inspection community	2		
	18. Members or students of other occupations	1		
	19. Jointly social work and other professional communities/agencies	4		

---

[1]The information in Tables 2.1 and 2.2 is drawn from Shaw and Ramatowski, 2013.

Shaw 2013). The only general shift – from an analysis of trends over the period not reported here – was that the proportion of articles focused on actual or potential service users grew from 32 percent to 42 percent, comparing the first five years with the second five years. This was at the expense of articles that were either methodological or theoretical in orientation (25 percent to 15 percent). We could not trace any difference in focus between authors from one part of the world or another.

Good practice in doing sensitive research

While not *all* of this research was directly *with* vulnerable people, the research problems, as set out in Table 2.2, show that the majority of the studies are concerned with people as the end beneficiaries. This makes questions about understanding what is meant by 'sensitive research' central to qualitative social work inquiry. In order to tease out and make these issues transparent, we draw on literature mainly from the year 2000 onwards. We do not believe that the ethical issues of sensitive research are different from the ethical issues of other research – but rather that they call for more explicit attention, a theme that we return to briefly in Chapter Six.[2]

Risks for participants

On questions of risks for participants, Mendis (2009) discusses the experience, from a feminist standpoint, of collecting data from mothers who have experienced childhood family violence. She refers to the practice that qualitative researchers ask participants to read their transcripts and comment on the content. However, in her project only three women agreed to read their transcripts. The others politely declined saying that they did not want to recall their bitter pasts again. She observes how this highlights the potential emotional risks to participants in research on sensitive topics and the risk that after reading their transcript, the women may experience emotional distress, of different kinds and levels. She concludes that the use of transcripts for authenticity/validation strategies in sensitive research needs careful consideration.

Not all researchers would agree with Mendis. Rabenhorst (2006) assessed the reactions of sexual assault survivors on three occasions following an experimental thought suppression task. She concluded that the majority of sexual assault survivors were not harmed in the short or long term by participation in a thought suppression paradigm introduced by the research team, in which the target was their own trauma. More generally, Corbin and Morse (2003) conclude from a review of the literature that, although there is evidence that

---

[2]Our search makes no claim to be exhaustive (e.g., we have not included studies of sensitive service delivery contexts, e.g., Brown and Wissow, 2009), but probably represents the range of ground covered in the literature.

qualitative interviews may cause some emotional distress, there is no indication that this distress is any greater than in everyday life or that it requires follow-up counselling. When research is conducted with sensitivity and guided by ethics, they conclude it becomes a process with benefits to both participants and researchers.

Langhinrichsen-Rohling and colleagues (2006) explored the impact of data collection methods on both findings and participants. They delineated distress related to answering personal survey questions about drug use, suicidal behaviour, and physical and sexual abuse. Rosenbaum and Langhinrichsen-Rohling (2006) recommend that the researcher should consider (1) what the impact of participation could be for the respondent, and (2) how the methods used could affect participation, disclosure rates and validity of the information provided. While ethical review processes have some control over whether and how such research is conducted, they advise that the researcher must bear most of the responsibility for keeping in mind these two considerations: validity of the data and protection of the respondents.

Methods for sensitive research

Some work has considered the implications of different methods for sensitive research. Jensen's conclusions (Jensen et al., 2005) point to the implications for methods used, which should allow for time so the participant can iterate and reiterate their experiences. Sensitive topics are not easily explored through the means of single, direct questions. There is a fair amount of prescription on what methods should and shouldn't be used in sensitive research, but on the whole limited consensus. One senses that researchers may tend to recommend those methods that they find themselves predisposed to use.

Orme, Ruckdeschel and Briar-Lawson (2010) summarise conclusions drawn from the development of methods for researching sensitive topics and giving voice to those within the situations. These include the use of ethnography to understand communication between professionals, the focus on the interrelationships between practitioners and between practitioners and service users in discourse analysis, and narrative research in organisational practice and research. Vignettes, focus groups, mobile methods, performative methods, telephone surveys, and automated telephonic methods have all been promoted (Colucci, 2007; Dinitto et al., 2008; Kitzinger, 1994; Rosenbaum et al., 2006; Ross et al., 2009; Wulff et al., 2010; Zeller, 1993).

Ross et al. (2009) discuss the possibilities that mobile research encounters offer for the exploration of sensitive topics, by providing contexts through which intimacies can be interwoven within narratives of the mundane ordinariness of the everyday. Dan Wulff and collaborators (2010) utilised stage performance as a means of increasing the extent to which sensitive information about racism was included. Kitzinger (1994) concluded that focus groups 'may be particularly effective when (they) draw together people who have previously been unable to share their experiences or who are physically isolated from one another, such as those caring for elderly relatives' (p. 169). Zeller's use of focus groups to learn about sexual decision making by young people suggests possible applications of the method to evaluating practice with sensitive problems (Zeller, 1993). Describing a comparison of methods for self-report data on sensitive topics, Rosenbaum et al. (2006) conclude that, while there was no difference in disclosure rates between methods, there were significantly higher participation rates for the automated telephonic methods. We discuss almost all these methods in Part II of the book.

Managing sensitive fieldwork

One approach to the management of sensitive fieldwork has been to develop protocols, either to aid the researcher in recognising people who may be at risk of adverse emotional reactions, or to provide guidance for the researcher when such situations arise (Draucker et al., 2009; Paterson et al., 1999). Less expert-driven approaches rely on addressing the power dimensions of the research relationship. Butler and Williamson (1996), interviewing children who had been in long-term care, made sure the children had control of the audio recorder during the interview, and could control the recording of any sensitive disclosures. A combination of these approaches is to develop guidance for the researcher based extensively on feedback from participants. Campbell et al. (2009) conducted an empirical study on 92 adult rape survivors' recommendations for interview practice. They asked survivors what interviewers should know about rape and how they should interact with participants. They conclude that interviewer training needs to emphasise diversity so that researchers are capable of working effectively with individuals with different life circumstances. The survivors also emphasised that interviewers need to show warmth and compassion and allow them to exercise choice and control during the interview process. Karnieli-Miller and colleagues (2009) start from similar assumptions.

We might reasonably conclude that all aspects of the research process are affected by the sensitivity of the topic or methods. Jaycox et al. (2006) take this wide-canvas view in their discussion of the challenges of evaluating school-based prevention and intervention programmes on sensitive topics. The research design (e.g., a repeated implementation–evaluation cycle), the recruitment of participant schools, recruitment of participants within schools, and the dissemination of findings all come under their spotlight. While not a qualitative study, their work helpfully illustrates 'the need for flexibility and cultural awareness during all stages of the process' (ibid., p. 320).

Some thought should be given to *researcher risks*. Mendis (2009) remarks that 'conducting sensitive research also posed emotional risks to me as the researcher' (p. 379). In an overview of the literature on researcher safety, Craig et al. (2000) distinguished four sources of risk to which the researcher may be exposed:

- Risk of physical threat or abuse.
- Risk of psychological trauma or consequences, as a result of actual or threatened violence, or the nature of what is disclosed during the interaction.

- Risk of being in a compromising situation, in which there might be accusations of improper behaviour.
- Increased exposure to the general risks of everyday life and social interaction: e.g., travel, infectious illness, accident.

It has generally been acknowledged that in social sciences there are more obvious risks to the researcher from qualitative methodologies. Bloor and colleagues (2007, 2010) were commissioned to assess such risks. Part of the risk stems from the blurring of the boundaries between the researcher and those participating in their study. While it would be naïve to suggest that researchers are unaware of boundaries (c.f. Dickson-Swift et al., 2006), this does not preclude the likelihood that research will have impacts upon them, and perhaps especially in sensitive research (Stacey, 1988). In a subsequent article drawing on the same data, Dickson-Swift and colleagues (2008) urge that researchers need to consider occupational health and safety issues when designing projects that deal with physical and emotional risks.

Bringing these issues together, the literature on sensitive research suggests four guiding considerations.

- Clear thought and planning is called for in relation to the nuances of different elements of 'sensitive' research. In particular, the distinction between the sensitivity *of* the research topic and the demands of being sensitive *to* something are different but equally important elements.
- We are concerned lest social work researchers get unduly drawn by the 'voguish' popularity[3] of a postmodern orientation that neglects continuing elements of privilege.
- While qualitative methods have particular advantage – and while there are no firm grounds to conclude that specialised methods are called for – research in this field calls for a variety of qualitative methods that will facilitate a range of method-linked knowledge claims, in ways that we referred to in the first chapter.
- Good qualitative research ought to reflect aspects of both good practice concepts (such as preparedness) and the methods and management of sensitive research.

Problem *foci* of qualitative social work research

Of the four ways distinctiveness sometimes is claimed for social work research, the most plausible one is that social work research should, and usually will, be focused on a range of research problems that are special to social work. This dimension has several significant features (Table 2.2). It includes a distinction that often is made in social work research between efforts to *understand* and attempts to *explain*, but we do not make any assumption that description is any more straightforward than explanation. Second, the dimension includes the recognition that social work research will on occasion carry an interventive

---

[3]A search on "postmodern*" on social work journal sites suggests the likely element of fashion in the employment of this term. Shaw (2010) has lamented this tendency in social work research.

purpose – hence ideas of 'strengthen', 'develop', 'promote' and 'respond to' recur in this scheme. Third, we have deliberately not split off the 'theoretical' from the 'applied'. 'Understand' and 'promote', and 'describe' and 'develop', are left side by side. We believe that the best qualitative social work research will, as with Merton's remark about sociology, 'manage to tread a path bordered on one side by the theoretical and on the other by the practical or applied.' (Merton, 1971: 793).

This evidence suggests a wide range of problem *foci*. We take this to be a positive sign. For example, there are no strong grounds to suggest that qualitative researchers invest most of their energies in a restricted number of problems, although there

Table 2.2   Primary problem focus of qualitative social work research, 2002–12 (from Shaw and Ramatowski, 2013)

What is the primary issue or problem focus of the research?	Total	%
1. Understand/explain issues related to risk, vulnerability, abuse, identity, coping, challenging behaviour, separation, attachment, loss, disability or trauma.	32	13.3
2. Understand/explain issues related to equality, oppression, diversity, poverty, employment, housing, education and social exclusion.	13	5.4
3. Understand/assess/strengthen user/carer/citizen/community involvement in social work; community organisation, partnership; empowerment.	5	2.1
4. Understand/promote the nature and quality of informal care, carer activity, volunteering, and their relationship to formal care.	6	2.5
5. Describe, understand, explain or develop good practice in relation to social work beliefs, values, cultural heritage, political positions, faith, spirituality or ethics.	6	2.5
6. Understand/develop/assess/evaluate social work practices, methods or interventions, including their recording/documentation.	23	9.6
7. Understand/evaluate/strengthen social work/social care services, including voluntary/independent sector.	12	5.0
8. Understand/explain practice or promote good practice in social work/social care organisations, programmes and/or management.	13	5.4
9. Understand/respond to issues of nationhood, race, ethnicity, racism.	3	1.3
10. Understand/respond to issues of gender, sexism, the role of women, the role of men.	10	4.2
11. Understand/respond to issues about the form and significance of the family	1	0.4
12. Demonstrate/assess the value of inter-disciplinary or inter-professional approaches to social work services.	4	1.7
13. Demonstrate/assess the value of comparative, cross-national, cross-cultural research; and of cultural distinctiveness/awareness.	9	3.8
14. Develop theorising.	16	6.7
15. Understand/appraise/develop the practice and quality of social work research (including user/carer involvement in research; uses of research, practitioner research, scientific practice, feminist research; anti-racist research methods).	77	32.1
16. Understand/promote learning and teaching about social work or related professions, and entry to career.	10	4.2
	240	

are some problems that may receive less research attention – ethnicity, the family, inter-professional activity and possibly issues around empowerment. Perhaps the most striking figure is that almost one in three of the articles seem to be addressed primarily to understanding, assessing and developing the practice of qualitative social work research. Another positive indicator is the evidence that matters of intervention and outcomes are far from neglected by qualitative social work researchers.

Best intervention – knowing what helps

The presence of research on intervention and outcomes raises an important question, because the default position in most social work literature is that if our aim is to improve intervention we must adopt controlled research designs such as randomised controlled trials. We explore the ways qualitative research can contribute to evaluative questions later in the book. However, we want to underline that concerns with difficult questions of causality are not out of place in qualitative social work research, and indeed are more likely to occur in social work than in much social science research, given the centrality of decisions about good practice in social work.

Traditional views of science treat 'explanation' as always a question about what *causes* something. This understanding stems from the empiricist philosopher, David Hume and later mediated through Emmanuel Kant. At the heart of the question lie different 'root metaphors' of what research is basically about. Kushner catches the different views about the core of research – for mainstream outcomes researchers and evaluators, he suggests, research is basically about *order*; for process researchers it is about *conversation* (Kushner, 1996). Hence his key test of what keeps evaluators awake at night. For outcomes researchers it is not managing to distil the evaluation into a single unified story; for process researchers it is having only one story to tell. Expressed more generally, any given research methodology that aims to contribute to causal understanding calls for a philosophical and methodological justification for doing so, but we should not assume there is a single mandatory justification for all forms of research.

One of the more influential developments has been the development of critical realism. Critical realism has developed through a number of British scholars including Roy Bhaskar, Margaret Archer, Andrew Sayer and, perhaps better known in the social work field, Ray Pawson. Qualitative social work researchers also have found relevance in realist positions (e.g., Longhofer and Floersch, 2012). Critical realists generally endorse the concept of cause in social science, in contrast to the positivist argument that causality is a metaphysical notion, and their general stance that all we can observe are associations between operationalised variables. For the critical realist there are two levels of reality – a surface, observable level and a level involving structures and mechanism (Brante, 2011). Hence, 'events themselves are not the ultimate focus of scientific analysis … Reality consists not only of what we can see but also of the underlying causal entities that are not always discernible' (House, 1991b: 4). The underlying reality produces actual events, of which we have empirical experiences and sense impressions. This is often described as a *generative* concept of causality.

> When we explain an outcome generatively we are not coming up with variables or correlates that associate with one another; rather we are trying to explain how the association itself comes about. The generative mechanisms thus actually *constitute* the outcome. (Pawson and Tilley, 1997: 408)

By way of comparison, House quotes Manicas and Secord saying that, 'For the standard view of science, the world is a determined concatenation of contingent events; for the realist, it is a contingent concatenation of real structures. And this difference is monumental' (House, 1991b: 5). Hence, instead of merely documenting the sequence and association of events, the realist seeks to *explain* events. While this view of cause does not necessarily require a qualitative methodology, it does clearly lend itself to such methods.

One should not over-draw the breach with some former ways of thinking. Much of this reasoning was anticipated, for example, by Lee Cronbach's arguments regarding causal models. Rejecting the idea of causation as events that can be predicted with a high degree of probability, Cronbach developed twin arguments. First, he argued that causes are contingent on local interactions of clusters of events. More than one cluster may be sufficient, but no one cluster is necessary. Second, he accepted that there are usually missing events or conditions that affect the outcome of a given programme, but about which we know little. He was the first theorist to produce a plausible explanation of contextual factors in evaluation. Hence he concludes that 'after the experimenter with his artificial constraint leaves the scene, the operating programme is sure to be adapted to local conditions' (Cronbach et al., 1980: 217). Repeated evaluations in different settings have value in identifying how contextual influences vary, but in the traditional sense 'a programme evaluation is so dependent on its context that replication is only a figure of speech' (ibid., p. 222).

This embeds conventional forms of outcomes research with inescapable limitations. The experimental intervention is neither necessary nor sufficient for a predicted effect to occur. An experiment cannot provide a critical test for the effectiveness of a programme. The traditional formulation 'is not the world of social programmes and, in general, is not the social world at all' (House, 1993: 135).

One strand of this argument is that, whether or not causality really exists, it certainly does exist in our everyday life and world, such that the world of ordinary language is full of causes and effects. In Example 1.2 in the previous chapter we reproduced an extract from a case discussion recorded by Pithouse and Atkinson, when discussing forms of talk. We invite you to return to an extended version of the same extract (Example 2.1), but here to illustrate the pervasive referencing of causes in social work talk.

EXAMPLE 2.1	Searching for Causes in Everyday Social Work Talk

This is part of a discussion about a 'case' between a social worker and her team leader. They are discussing a family where the daughter Jackie has got caught for shoplifting – not the first time. They are discussing how the family lulls social workers into a false sense of security 'and then they blow'.

Social Worker (SW): … She's got a lot of positives. She's a personable girl, pleasant, bright girl. One odd quality is an incredible neatness – her school work is absolutely immaculate. You can't tell the difference between one page and another. Every word the same.

Team Leader (TL): Sort of obsessional?

SW: Erm, well tidy. Very tidy people. I don't know what she's got. She's certainly got it up there for the application of graphics – she's a bright girl. Although she's a problem in school behaviour-wise, she's likely to blow up. She does reasonably well in examinations, she's got many positives, she's not a negative girl altogether.

TL: The criminal. It doesn't fit in with this part of Jackie does it?

SW: Well she's a well-known shoplifter – to the extent that a note comes to the house saying "Jackie, can you pinch me a pair of trousers, will pay five pounds for them". She's well known in her circle at school as being the top shoplifter.

TL: She's not far from becoming a labelled criminal?

SW: She er yes. But her criminality is in (*pause*) er strange really, it's almost a mania. It has a quality about it that is almost psychologically driven. I don't know if that's the proper use of the term 'psychology' but – you know – the drive is there, er because of an abnormal psychology, there's something there all right.

TL: Um how long has she been doing it?

SW: Got caught for doing this a year ago.

TL: But not much recently?

SW: She hasn't been *caught* so much! (*laughs*)

TL: Yes there's something *there* in the family.

SW: Um very much. Dad was an alcoholic ten years ago. Mother's diabetic. You see the strange thing about it all is she has three other sisters. Mary the eldest is (Educationally Subnormal). They've found a niche for her at (Special School), settled in quite well. The youngest had a school report which I didn't see but mother told me, and mother doesn't usually lie – she hides the truth but she doesn't actually lie – has A's in everything so she must be quite bright, and the third girl is quite bright. So you see there's lots of intelligence in the family which is quite a sort of solid working class family. Mum's background is better than what she's got, but the kids are immaculate, lovely kids really (*pause*) er father, father's a weedy little creature, the original weed.

TL: Natural father?...

Pithouse and Atkinson (1988)

More generally, everyday language is replete with evaluative impulses and perspectives. Easton explores this theme from forty years' experience of West African proverbs, or, as the Hausa word means, 'folded speech' (Easton, 2012: 519). However, he remarks on the danger of essentialising such cultural arti-facts and treating them as 'an infallible reservoir of … wisdom' (ibid., p. 520). Even granted the romantic assumptions about local culture, we may not always catch the meaning – as a Hausa proverb suggests, 'The outsider's eyes may be as wide open as dinner plates – he still does not see the real town'. And in a multi-cultural setting whose traditions count?

In helpful reviews of the use of qualitative methods for causal explanation, Maxwell (2004, 2012) takes a careful line that 'qualitative methods … can often directly investigate these causal processes, although their conclusions are subject to validity threats of their own' (Maxwell, 2004: 249). Process theory, as he labels it, proceeds 'based on a general interpretive framework, an under-standing based on the "fitting together" of pieces of evidence in a way that elucidates how a particular result occurred rather than the demonstration that a statistical relationship exists between particular variables' (ibid., p. 250). Hence, 'in qualitative interview studies the demonstration of causation rests heavily on the description of a visualizable sequence of events, each event flowing into the next.' This is 'not, however, an easy or straightforward task' (ibid., p. 250). He sees, following Popper, the 'ability to rule out plausible alter-native explanations or "rival hypotheses" rather than the use of any specific methods or designs … as the fundamental characteristic of scientific inquiry in general' (ibid., p. 250).

Maxwell's stress on visualisability is echoed more radically in Garfinkel's stress on the commonplace, local endogenous 'thisness' of daily life. Rather than assuming that the social order is *hidden* and must be rendered visible through the formal analysis of causal mechanisms, he insists that 'an order is *visible* in the mundane details of everyday interaction, if only we will look', though it is strange, elusive and, in Garfinkel's words, 'intractably hard to describe' (Packer, 2011: 193). More directly, the helpful emphasis on description as going hand in hand with causality is developed by Uprichard in her response to arguments by some sociologists that social scientists should abandon a focus on causality (Uprichard, 2013). 'The issue…is not whether or not to reject causality in favour of description, but rather what kind(s) of descriptions help to adequately explore causality and, conversely, what kind of causality helps us to make sense of the descriptions that emerge' (ibid., p. 379).

Causal explanations are also central to qualitative inquiry stemming from critical social theory. Habermas, for example, draws on elements of Karl Marx and the Frankfurt School when he argues that critical inquiry has an emancipa-tory purpose and needs to search for both understanding *and* causes 'because social systems and practices have an impact that operates outside members' awareness' (Packer, 2011: 313).

In summary:

- Causes are an important – probably inescapable – element of how we make sense of the everyday world.
- Qualitative methods can sometimes investigate causal processes.
- Critical realism, with its recognition of different levels of reality and the existence of underlying structures and mechanisms, provides a framework congenial to qualitative inquiry.
- All causal inferences are subject to threats to their validity.

Domains of social work and qualitative social work research

Social work readers of this book are likely to identify with one or other domain of social work – children and families, the community, mental health, young people, older people, and so on. We use the term 'domain' to refer to the broad practice contexts and also forms of service delivery within which social work research often takes place. This is intentionally a relatively context-loose frame of reference. The nature and boundaries of social work services is perhaps the area where there is the greatest degree of diversity between and even within countries. Take for example how the collaboration between Karen Staller and Tracie Mafile'o enables them to explore the domain of community from the very different national contexts of the USA and Tonga and New Zealand (Example 2.2; Staller and Mafile'o, 2010). They consider the different ways in which community is conceptualised in social work practice and research. This leads them to an overview of the historical unfolding of community-based research, including discussions of the settlement house movement, and developments in ethnographic practices, participatory action methods, feminist and standpoint theories, and indigenous/non-Western research, each as part of the evolving landscape of research methods as they relate to community domain. In Examples 2.2 and 2.3 we hear researchers talking about how they see the relationship between their domain of research and the methodological strategies that have developed. They talk mainly but not exclusively about qualitative work. These examples are not presented as 'this is how it should be done' but to illustrate how a practice domain and associated research problem foci shape how people think about and practise their research.

Example 2.2 provides an extended example that repays careful reading and rereading. The authors illustrate from their life experience in diverse cultures and societies, how the community as a research domain shapes how the location of the domain is pictured, the methods that they see as having a natural 'fit' to inquiry in and about community, the implications for the role of the researcher, and for the implied styles of research relationships.

| EXAMPLE 2.2 | The Community as a Research Domain |

'Not unlike social work practice, community can sit in a number of different locations in research design. For example it can provide the context. So the researcher might simply consider community as the environment in which inquiry would be occurring ... Second, it might be the actual object of study so a researcher may want to better understand the functioning of community itself. Third, community might be the object of intervention so researchers might be seeking to promote social justice through community change. Note that in each of these examples 'community' occupies a different spot in the study design. Community can be the unit of analysis, the location of the study, provide the sample, or be the object of intervention ...

Of course any number of different research methods might be employed in community-based or community-oriented research but there are some that are obvious candidates. For example, case studies which can use neighborhoods, networks, or institutions as objects of investigation; evaluation studies which look at the effectiveness of services or interventions; and action research or participatory research in which the methods employed may include organizing, educating, and promoting social justice or social reform ...

All types of community-based inquiry call into question the role of the researcher and his or her level of participation as well as the level of participation of the community. The researcher can be fully engaged as in some participatory methods or not at all as in some case-based methods. Similarly the community may be fully involved in the project or participate only minimally. Further in question is the ultimate goal of the project such as whether it is primarily descriptive, evaluative, or preventative, and whether it seeks to promote community change or not. Taken together this begins to illustrate the complicated landscape of community as a domain for social work research ...

Community-based social work research should be cooperative and collaborative, thus involving co-learning, co-doing, and should rest heavily on the participation of community members. It should promote community development, capacity building and social justice. Problem definitions cannot be imposed on the community but should be generated with and by community members. Social work community-based research should foster critical awareness while recognizing and building on community strengths.'

Staller and Mafile'o (2010: 366, 367, 375)

Example 2.3 depicts how very differently a research domain is framed. Starting by reflecting on the 'boundary restrictions' of research in this domain, Bywaters and Ungar go on to talk about the ways in which social work research is conditioned by methodological traditions, professional hierarches and developing social understandings of health and wellbeing.

| EXAMPLE 2.3 | Health as a Research Domain |

'[t]he terrain covered by social work research on health and well being internationally remains vast and disparate. For example, we can examine health through different lenses; focusing on individuals and families, communities and populations or institutions and social structures ...

One consequence of the limited volume of health related social work research overall ... and the even smaller amount of substantial research employing rigorous methods, is that there are few examples of the systematic reviews or meta-analyses. This approach to consolidating knowledge is a demanding task in disciplines in which RCTs are standard while methods for the systematic review of non-trial and qualitative research are less well developed ...

There is a strong case to be made for research that can document the processes of concern to social workers: the systemic concerns and processes of service utilization rather than the study of the aetiology of disorder...

Given that the focus of social work activity is often on groups of people who are marginalized in terms of mainstream services, including very elderly people, members of minority ethnic groups and gay, lesbian, bi and trans-sexual people, it is not surprising that awareness of the importance of inclusion has become a feature of health related social work research ... While social work research may have been weak in terms of large scale quantitative studies of effectiveness, in part this is because of social work's focus on access and inclusion. A strength of social work research is its willingness to engage with sensitive issues ...

There is a number of areas where it might be argued that social work is breaking new conceptual and methodological ground in health research ... Service user involvement in research has become vitally important to demonstrating construct validity in quantitative studies and authenticity (the validity of the representation of participant voices) in qualitative research ... A second trend is a shift in the research from illness to health ... [I]t is noteworthy that a good deal of the writing focusing on strengths, coping and resilience under stress is being developed by social workers ... A third, related, trend is the indigenization of health knowledge now in evidence in the social work literature. Studies of health, like that with Maori people in New Zealand ...'

Bywaters and Ungar (2010: 393, 395, 403)

Both examples illustrate how it is essential to reflect on the significance and influence of the domain as context for social work research. We should not break research into shards of fragmented sub-fields according to the domains of practice. Orme, Ruckdeschel and Briar-Lawson (2010), for example, trace commonalities in the dynamic changes and directions within the field. However, the illustrated contrast of community and health and wellbeing illustrate how values, methodological traditions and domain orthodoxies, government proximity or distance, and structures of services all steer – and in some cases are steered by – research agenda and strategies.

Inside and outside

What challenges and opportunities are presented when one is researching on one's professional or academic home ground? An unconsidered response, sometimes encountered in social work, is to claim – even unspokenly to assume – that being an 'insider' by its very nature will yield better research than being an 'outsider.' When talking to practitioner researchers in a study in Wales,

Several … negative characteristics were … mentioned about academic research, including limitations of understanding, experience, and 'grasp'. Helen viewed practitioner evaluation as more 'interactive' and more 'valid': "I am doing the job that I am researching. That's the difference – you are actually in the workplace doing the same thing." Sarah also expressed reservations about academic research: "But then I would say perhaps mainly somebody who does it as a job who has not been in the social work field for a while might forget how things work in the real world as well." Jane took this emphasis further and portrayed academic research as more removed from the grass roots: "With practitioner research you live and breathe it. You live and breathe it and you know it so much in depth." (Shaw and Faulkner, 2006: 58)

It is worth unpacking the kinds of arguments that might be involved in assertions of this kind. *First*, social work research ought to be *for* vulnerable or oppressed participants, and being an insider, is the only way one should do research that is for people rather than on or even with people. *Second*, being an insider enables one to know by virtue of closeness. Outsider researchers, for example, in universities or government departments, are distant and less able to see. The practitioners speaking in the quotation above seem to take this line of reasoning. This argument also sometimes has been used to say that qualitative methods are inherently more congenial and consistent with social work values than quantitative methodology. *Third*, a plea for insider research is sometimes introduced in the guise of an argument about the relationship between theory and practice. We find none of these positions persuasive, yet all of them pose important questions and we give space to them later in Chapters Fourteen and Fifteen.

In an earlier version of this book several of the contributors reflected on the relationship between *inquiry* and *professional practice*. Hall and – with careful detail – White recorded how they held both insider and outsider roles in relation to their research participants. Hall (2001) 'arrived' as an outsider for his ethnography of a young homeless project, but became in different ways a partial insider. White (2001) started as an insider for her research within her own social work team, yet found herself undergoing a fruitful, if potentially hazardous, process of de-familiarisation through which she became in some degree a marginal 'inside "out"' member. Scourfield (2001) focused on the research and practice relationship through his consideration of what it was like to interview expert professional social work interviewers.

| EXAMPLE 2.4 | The Ethnographer as Insider and Outsider |

A fish out of water?

…Thus, through the fieldwork experience, I became aware of the pervasive and unquestioned nature of the notion that children are 'made not born'. This does not mean that I am asserting that the discourse of child centredness is wrong. However, once one has become aware of it, one develops in response a critical control over one's thinking … For example, it became increasingly clear to me that, although formal knowledge (e.g., developmental milestones, attachment theory, immunization status, medical, forensic and psychological opinion) is palpably displayed in social workers' forms of talk and written records, many narratives have a transparently qualitative, evaluative and profoundly moral design. Indeed, rational-technical or evidential materials are often invoked to authorize *moral* judgements. So, a mother may be 'blamed' for being 'emotionally unavailable' to her infant and hence for failing to 'promote a healthy attachment'. In short, it became clear to me that theory and even apparently 'forensic' evidence could sometimes be invoked to provide *ex post facto* normative warrant for decisions taken on other grounds.

Once routinized forms of thought have been destabilized in this way, it becomes extraordinarily difficult to continue to think as usual. Towards the end of my fieldwork (and of my career as a team manager), I became increasingly conscious of a dialogue between myself-as-researcher and myself-as-social worker. As the research progressed, I became more and more self-conscious about this, which was a rather strange and desta-bilizing experience. However, rather than this being a bad thing, it opened up to question my taken-for-granted presuppositions. Practice is inevitably remoralized, and rendered more contestable and debatable as a result of the epistemological and ontological shift ... I have often been asked whether this destabilization was the catalyst for my departure from practice into an academic post. It may well have been, since the published results opened up that possibility. However, it was and is perfectly possible, if not always com-fortable, to continue to act, and also to 'see' oneself acting ... So, yes, defamiliarization can be hard work, but it is worth it ... because it offers the possibility of more realistic realism about professional judgement and hence of more robust ethical debate.

White (2001: 111–12)

Where should we stand on this debate? Its significance for qualitative methods with their claims of 'closeness' to the world cannot be sidestepped. While not offering a comprehensive template for thinking and action, we find it helpful to link the ques-tion to how the case for advocacy research sometimes has been developed. This field, especially through the contribution of some forms of feminist theorising and research, has often been referred to as based on a 'standpoint' epistemology. A help-ful perspective on standpoint positions can be achieved by revisiting in detail a classic paper on the sociology of knowledge by Robert Merton. Merton believed that as society becomes more polarised so do contending claims to truth. At its extreme, an active, reciprocal distrust between social groups finds parallel expres-sion in intellectual perspectives that are no longer located in the same universe of discourse. This leads to reciprocal ideological analyses and claims to 'group-based truth' (Merton, 1972: 11). Merton analyses the relative claims of this nature made by those who are epistemological *insiders* or *outsiders* to the group.

The Insider doctrine claims in its strong form that particular groups have monopolistic access to particular kinds of knowledge. In this form, the doctrine leads to the position that each group has a monopoly of knowledge about itself. In vernacular terms, 'you have to be one to understand one', because 'the Outsider has a structurally imposed incapacity to comprehend alien groups, statuses, cultures and societies' (ibid., p. 15).

Feminist standpoint epistemology exhibits some of the key characteristics of Merton's Insider doctrine. Put simply, in response to the patriarchal assumption that women are *less* able to understand, standpoint theorists argue that women are *more* able to understand. They argue this through two linked assertions – the double vision of the oppressed and the partial vision of the powerful. Women's experience is seen as a more complete[4] and less distorted kind of social experience. Objectivity is rejected for its alleged inherent masculinist bias. Hierarchy within the research relationship is rejected as not simply bad method but bad ethics and bad politics.

Merton develops several criticisms of strong Insider positions, but his key point for our purposes is that individuals do not have a single organising status but a complex status set. 'Aggregates of individuals … typically confront one another as Insiders and Outsiders' (ibid., p. 22). He enters several caveats that enable a reflective assessment of subsequent standpoint positions in social work. He stresses that he is in no way advocating divisions, nor is he predicting that collectivities cannot unite on single issues. Rather such unity will be difficult and probably not enduring.

Standpoint theory develops this position in an important respect. The 'double vision' of the oppressed is in fact an argument for being simultaneously an Insider and an Outsider. This is the idea that 'special perspectives and insights are available to that category of outsiders who have been systematically frustrated by the social system: the disinherited, deprived, disenfranchised, dominated and exploited' (ibid., p. 29). The Outsider is a stranger. Quoting from the early sociologist Georg Simmel, Merton concludes that the objectivity of the stranger 'does not simply involve passivity and detachment; it is a particular structure composed of distance and nearness, indifference and involvement' (ibid., p. 33).

Social work writers have often failed to distinguish strong and more muted versions of standpoint positions. The latter form of the doctrine claims that Insiders (*and* Outsiders) have *privileged* rather than *monopolistic* claims to knowledge. This is a position that avoids the erroneous assumption of some radical advocacy researchers, that social position wholly determines what understanding is possible. Group identities do significantly influence explanations, but the distinction between tendency and determinism is 'basic, not casual or niggling' (ibid., p. 27). Merton concludes that, having accepted that distinction, 'We no longer ask whether it is the Insider or the Outsider who has monopolistic or privileged access to the truth; instead we begin to consider their distinctive and interactive roles in the process of truth seeking' (ibid., p. 36). His conclusion has much to recommend it as a starting point for assessing the relative contributions of insider and outsider models of social work research.

---

[4]Trinder helpfully observes that feminist standpoint positions are ambivalent at this point, as to whether it is the privileged position of women in general or that of feminists (Trinder, 2000). Those who hold a classic Marxist acceptance of false consciousness will take the latter position. Trinder (2000) and Shaw (1999b) provide outlines and brief critiques of feminist standpoint theory in social work.

Qualitative research – qualitative practice?

How far are key forms of thinking and practice in qualitative research and social work practice linked? The dilemmas and puzzles that surface in everyday practice are variations of preoccupations shared with social researchers. Did my practice, in this instance, stem from an underlying and unified worldview, or was it a more or less appropriate and pragmatic case of opportunism in the face of human need? Is what seems to work in my practice unique to me, or can I generalise it to my immediate or even more distant colleagues? Is social work practice to be assessed by 'what works', or according to moral or political principles? Is my practice lacking integrity if I find myself implementing common sense versions of formal models of intervention? What matters more – the evidence-based outcomes of practice or the quality of service delivery? Are social workers agents of change or constrained by deterministic structures?

The terminology will sometimes differ, but researchers share corresponding puzzles. The following quandaries are almost the mirror image of the practice preoccupations in the previous paragraph. Should research methodology be founded on a paradigm or on pragmatic choices? Are research results locally, and only locally, relevant or can we safely generalise? What quality criteria should be used to assess research - moral authenticity or canons of validity? What is the relationship between common sense, everyday explanations and scientific theorising? Is quantitative research best for measuring service outcomes and qualitative research better for understanding social work process? If some research methods are strong on analysing constraining structures and others are strong on understanding action and intentions, does my methodological choice inevitably presume something about human nature? Indeed, as we saw in Chapter One, there are some social scientists that make a career out of such problems.

The idea that research is just like practice in its methodology is in many ways an enticing one, which in its naïve form promises more than it will yield. The dangers lie in drawing a too simple conclusion that the two either *are* or are *not* much the same – and in the risk of pushing normative positions about how professional practice (or research) ought to alter its ways. Two illustrations may help. At one extreme, Fortune has claimed that social work and research (in particular standard ethnographic studies) are fundamentally different (Fortune, 1994). She argues that the differences between ethnography and social work practice include:

1. 'Practice is action-focused, while qualitative methods, including ethnography, intend only to describe' (Fortune, 1994: 64).
2. The practitioner needs additional skills in deductive and inductive logic 'as well as a fine sense of timing about when to stop data gathering' (ibid., p. 65).
3. Ethnographers seek to generalise, whereas in social work practice 'there is no inherent need to communicate that reality to other persons or to generalize beyond the experience of that individual' (ibid., p. 65).

An almost opposite claim is Goldstein's belief in a natural affinity of ethnography and practice when he says 'the language of ethnography is the language of practice', and that 'both the qualitative researcher and the practitioner depend on similar talents' (Goldstein, 1994: 46, 48). McIvor advanced a more general argument of that kind. She pleads for practitioner evaluation in the British probation service from 'the twofold belief that practitioners should be encouraged to engage in the evaluation of their own practice and that they possess many of the skills which are necessary to undertake the evaluative task' (McIvor, 1995: 210). The skills she has in mind include problem solving, effective interviewing and planning, 'which can, with a little advice and support, be readily applied in assessing the effectiveness of their work' (ibid., p. 217).

Our own view is that these arguments about shared skills and purposes are unduly simple. A determined process of translation and 'colonisation' is needed if the potential for mutual dialogue is to be realised (Shaw, 2011b). A good example is developed by Lang, who explores the differences between the data gathering and data processing strategies of social work and qualitative methodology, and recommends the integration of the latter within social work practice, not only for knowledge building purposes, but also for 'action-deriving purposes' (Lang, 1994: 277). She compares the data processing of qualitative researchers and practitioners, and suggests that '[t]he practitioner "names" the data through reference to theory; the researcher "names" the data through a conceptualising process that derives from the features of the data' (ibid., p. 271).

She believes that several problems follow for social work because, '[t]he press to know what to do, what action to take, may close the avenue of knowledge development from practice for many practitioners' (ibid., p. 271). She invites an inductive, theory-building approach to practice, with the paradox that 'existing theory must have a more provisional status, a less central locus in our practice teaching, in order to open the possibility of theory-building' (ibid., p. 276). Social workers should pull action out of the features of the data rather than turn to existing theory as a first resort. Example 2.5 notes Scourfield's reflections on the symmetry of research and social work practice interviews (Scourfield, 2001).

EXAMPLE 2.5   **Research and Practice Interviews – Symmetry?**

Interviewing social workers for a research project mirrors social workers' interviewing of their clients. Social workers tend to rely very heavily on verbal exchange in an interview situation … In these verbal interactions, clients construct accounts for social workers as social workers do for researchers … The common base of interviewing can also lead to some confusion, however. University colleagues of mine have found that training social workers on qualitative research interviews is difficult because they assume they know all about interviewing. There are, in fact, some distinct differences between the two types of interview …

As well as the symmetry of interviewing interviewers, there is another respect in which my research process mirrors the social workers' practice. In this research project I am in the business of constructing knowledge about knowledge about people. In other words, the

> question of how I should understand the individual social worker in relation to occupational culture and professional knowledge mirrors the question of how social workers should understand individual clients in relation to their social circumstances. For both the researcher and the social worker there is tension between the individual and the social, between structure and agency …
>
> An awareness of this symmetry does not make the researcher's task easier, but could potentially make it more interesting.
>
> Scourfield (2001: 64, 65, 66f, 72)

A further example of how categories of action and thought interweave between research and practice can be found in how the notion of the 'case' has been to the fore for a century. In early social work and sociology, especially in the USA, the idea of the case provided a foundational framework for each field. In both there was an assumption that the case was not limited to or even primarily an individual category. There were differences of emphasis. For social work it was linked to the reform agenda, always stronger in social work than in sociology. For sociology, and for sociological social workers, it was central to efforts to understand the community. Continuing down to more recent years, Ruckdeschel began to develop comparable methods for qualitative case study that bridge sociology and social work. He follows Denzin's idea of 'behavioural specimens' as nearly complete descriptions of interactions between individuals within particular time frames (Denzin, 1989a), and also accepts that the case study's task is 'to give the poor a voice' (Ruckdeschel et al., 1994: 255).

Crossovers of these kinds challenge practitioners of both social work and sociology, creating the obligation, in Emily Dickinson's expression, to 'tell all the truth but tell it slant'.[5]

Social work is constituted by material, cultural and embodied fields and practices. In this respect, qualitative social work research differs from qualitative psychology, sociology, geography and so on. In saying it is 'constituted' we say more than 'it takes place in these fields and practices'. We have worked through the four questions that opened the chapter: What are the kinds of data that characterise social work practice and hence shape social work research? How do the different domains and fields of social work similarly or variously shape the purposes and practice of qualitative research? What challenges and opportunities are presented when one is researching on one's professional or academic home ground? How far are key forms of thinking and practice in qualitative research

---

[5]Her poem 'Tell All the Truth' opens:
Tell all the truth but tell it slant,
Success in circuit lies
Too bright for our infirm delight
The truth's superb surprise

and social work practice linked? The accounts presented when we deliberate on these questions are not separate descriptions of a reality but are themselves constitutive of that reality. As Packer expresses it, these 'social practices constitute *real* objects and subjects... embodied *know-how*' (Packer, 2011: 11). In the next chapter we turn more closely to qualitative methods.

Taking it further

This task is for practitioners and/or researchers. If you are engaged in social work practice or other professional practice that entails one to one verbal interaction, endeavour to secure the consent of a service user for this task.

Select an interview where you believe the occasion went well. Transcribe fully a key section or passage in the interview that you think demonstrates the main part of the interview. If you are a researcher select an interview transcript from a research project of your own, also taking a passage that you think demonstrates the main part of the interview.

Spend a minimum of an hour working with a fellow practitioner or researcher (both of whom must have read this chapter before undertaking the task), in which you separately and then together critically analyse the transcript in relation to two questions:

1. Were you seeking to ascertain causal understandings or explanations? What were they?
2. In what ways do you think the interview shared aspects of both practice and research interviews, and in what ways was it distinct?

THREE
Qualitative Methods in Social Work – a Review

After situating methods in a brief historical milieu, we set out what is known about present qualitative research patterns, practices and trends in social work. Within that context we ask how far we can trace emerging developments, and whether such trends should be seen as innovatory. In thinking about patterns, practices and trends we approach the question in two ways.

First, we present an empirical analysis of qualitative research methods in social work in the decade leading up to this book. We suggest a good-enough way of distinguishing one method from another – good enough for here and now.

Second, we set out and assess the formulation of a sequence of 'moments' in the history of qualitative research, as suggested and developed by Denzin and Lincoln, asking as we do so how far this applies to social work. We close the chapter by setting out working criteria for judging whether we are engaging in good qualitative research.

'Review' is a somewhat muddy noun and verb that may cloak as much as it discloses. Inspect, evaluate, critique, survey, reappraise, comment and recall are but some of the verbal forms that come to mind. One also may be reminded of a character in Margaret Atwood's novel *Robber Bride* of whom the narrator says 'He doesn't like being examined; it's too close to an evaluation, which is too close to a judgement. If there are judgements going around he wants to be making them himself.' Nonetheless, review we must, both here and, by way of prescription, in Chapter Four.

A historical moment – interviewing in sociology and social work

Clifford Shaw, author of the iconic Chicago study of *The Jack-Roller* (Shaw, 1966), commends the theoretical value of life-history data as a basis for causal 'hypotheses' (p. 19), and gives an account of his methodology as consisting of 'various techniques' designed to facilitate spontaneity and to 'follow the natural sequence of events in the life history of the delinquent' (ibid., p. 21), usually through a series of interviews 'which in some cases extend over a relatively long period of time' of some months apart (ibid., p. 21). They were recorded mostly by a 'stenographic record' to preserve the 'exact language of the interviewee' (ibid., p. 22).

Shaw is an intriguing figure. He came into sociology following an early career working in Chicago prisons. A naïve reading of Shaw's book leaves the reader with a provocative sense of having been inducted into a *mélange* of what we now know as 'sociology' and 'social work', but which to Shaw seemed a coherent stance. Ernest Burgess, the Chicago sociologist, was well aware of the tension but congruence of Shaw's stance. Speaking in 1927[1] he makes a pitch to a social work audience that is enticing, even at this distance.

> My proposal is actually quite simple and I think, entirely feasible and reasonable, in spite of the fact that I do not anticipate its immediate and general adoption. It is to enter into the case record statements made by all persons visited in nearly as humanly possible the language which they used. (Burgess, 1927: 192)

He immediately extends this with the complaint that he is

> strongly opposed to having the language of the father and the mother in the home, of the landlord, or the teacher, or of the employer, translated into the language of the social worker on the case. The translation invariably and inevitably distorts the point of view and the attitude of the person interviewed. Each informant has a right to have himself appear in the record in his own language. (Ibid., pp. 192–93)

Speaking a year later, he reiterates that the 'characters ... do not speak for themselves. They obtain a hearing only in the translation provided by the language of the social worker' (Burgess, 1928: 527). He sets the choice as one between a legalistic conception of the interview and a personal one.

> To enter the interview in the words of the person signifies a revolutionary change. It is a change from the interview conceived in legal terms to the interview as an opportunity to participate in the life history of the person, in his memories, in his hopes, in his attitudes, in his own plans, in his philosophy of life. (Ibid., p. 527)

This passing sketch immediately unsettles conventional views of how research methods develop. Burgess seems to have sensed he was knocking on

---

[1]'Speaking' is not an accident. Burgess gave frequent presentations at major social work conferences, and both his articles cited here originated for such occasions. The spoken voice remains transparent in the articles.

a stubbornly resistant door ('I do not anticipate its immediate and general adoption'), and he shifted the focus of his interest to the relationship between sociological and psychiatric methods (e.g., Burgess, 1930a).[2] Yet this social work/sociology connection, whereby sociology drew on the practice methods of social work and counselling, continued at least until the 1950s. Lee remarks, for example, of Carl Rogers, the non-directive therapist, 'that the work of Rogers had a significant influence on sociological practice with regard to interviewing …' He refers to ways in which Robert Merton and colleagues 'explicitly drew on Rogers' concept of non-direction in formulating their concept of the focused interview, which in turn underpinned the development of focus groups as a qualitative research method' (Lee, 2004: 876). Social work and sociology's failures to excavate this archaeology of their fields has ill served both.

Patterns, practices and trends

These historical contingencies surrounding qualitative research explain why we suggest a good-enough way of distinguishing one method from another – one that is good enough for here and now, rather than a categorisation that will survive for ever and a day. Table 3.1 gives the figures for the main research method

Table 3.1   Main fieldwork method

Fieldwork method	2002–6		2007–11		Total	
	N	%	N	%	N	%
Interview	31	41.3	47	44.8	78	43.3
Narrative	18	24.0	27	25.7	45	25.0
Group interviews	6	8.0	8	7.6	14	7.8
Observation/ethnography	6	8.0	12	11.4	18	10.0
Visual	2	2.7	1	1.0	3	2.0
Documents	7	9.3	9	8.6	16	8.9
Internet	2	2.7	0	0.0	2	1.3
Systematic review	1	1.3	1	1.0	2	1.3
Structured methods	2	2.7	0	0.0	2	1.3
Totals	75		105		180	

---

[2]He met with little reciprocal interest from across the campus in the Graduate School of Social Service Administration. The Dean, Edith Abbott, insisted in remarks directed at sociologists that she concedes were 'rather intimate and perhaps too frank' (Abbott, 1931: viii) that '[s]ocial workers must be so trained scientifically that they belong in the social science group. Their thinking should continuously be directed to the research interests in their own field and they must not, in this research, be directed by someone who comes from a more serenely academic atmosphere and therefore thinks himself more scientific than the person who really understands the problem that is to be studied' (p. 148).

used in articles in the journal *Qualitative Social Work,* divided in quinquenniel periods (Shaw and Ramatowski, 2013).

Several points appear to emerge from this table. First, and perhaps not surprisingly, verbal methods predominated. Over three quarters of primary methods (76 percent) were of this kind. However, a more nuanced and illustrative account from the texts of the articles would very likely reveal considerable variety of method within this range. The following summaries hint at the diversity within verbal methods:

1. Six women each giving two to three interviews plus a group interview.
2. 35 telephone interviews, plus 19 in depth phone interviews, and focus groups for a scoping study.
3. Mother and daughter triangulated interviews.
4. One selected interview (tape and transcript), student paper by interviewer, interview with interviewer – by email and then face to face.
5. 15 older women reflect via narratives on body image through their life course.
6. 18 social work students interviewed 18 experienced social workers; then returned to do validation interviews.

The data do not give any indication of the quality of the research. There is a tendency, for example, for a proportion of the articles to be founded on small sets of data and of only one kind. There were no apparent trends over time, although these are broad categories and shifts within them may not show up. A closer inspection of the instances of multiple methods suggests the diversity of choices in some articles (Figure 3.1)

Phone records, email records, minutes, meeting transcripts, interviews. 18 women.

Methods for young people with communication difficulties, e.g., non-verbal methods, symbols.

100 hours of observation and 22 interviews with members of theatre community project.

Eco-map; social network analysis; mapping; 'daily life story'.

Participant observation and field notes over 16 months; qualitative interviews (ten young people, each three times).

Videotaped observations [12], interviews [12], group interviews [4], case discussions [8], 'dialogue conferences' [2] and documents.

Figure 3.1   Examples of use of multiple qualitative methods

These are typically verbal methods in combination with ethnography, documents, visual methods, and a range of more specific fieldwork devices – a kind of combination that we consider in Chapter Seven.

Moments in qualitative social work inquiry?[3]

Denzin's much-cited scheme for periodising qualitative research approaches trends and developments rather differently. It is perhaps best understood as presenting qualitative research in a series of sequential discourses, marked in significant part by 'successive waves of epistemological theorizing' (Denzin and Lincoln, 2005: 3). Denzin speaks sometimes of qualitative research as a movement occurring in a 'complex historical field'. Qualitative research 'means different things in each of these moments', albeit a generic definition can be accepted. They define 'at least eight historical moments' as 'the *traditional* (1900–1950); the *modernist* or golden age (1950–1970); *blurred genres* (1970–1986); the *crisis of representation* (1986–1990); the *postmodern*, a period of new and experimental ethnographies (1990–1995); *postexperimental inquiry* (1995–2000); the *methodologically contested present* (2000–2004); and the *fractured future* … (2005–)' (ibid., p. 3, italics in original).

Their account is essentially a history of ideas through the lens of epistemology. '*Epistemology* is the word that has historically defined these standards' (Denzin and Lincoln, 2005: 14). For example, anthropology in the *traditional* period is marked by study of the Other as 'alien, foreign and strange'. They characterise this period as about the Lone Ethnographer. 'Returning home with his data, the Lone Ethnographer wrote up an objective account of the culture studied' (ibid., p. 15). They plausibly suggest that the text was organised around four beliefs and commitments:

> a commitment to objectivism, a complicity with imperialism, a belief in monumentalism (the ethnography would create a museumlike picture of the culture studied), and a belief in timelessness (what was studied would never change). The Other was an 'object' to be archived. (Ibid., p. 15)

They cast the Chicago period of sociology in similar terms referring to how 'They turned the deviant into a sociological version of a screen hero' (ibid., p. 16). This can be seen by rediscovering several of the classic studies of the period that, as with *The Jack-Roller*, read as much like social work as sociology. Frederick Thrasher's *The Gang* – a portrayal of over one thousand boy gangs in 1920s Chicago (Thrasher, 1927; c.f. Shaw, 2011a) – displays this tendency to romanticism. We find comments like '"Be blithe of heart for any adventure" might well be the slogan of the gang boy' (Thrasher, 1927: 119), and '"The night hath a thousand eyes", and they are all winking their invitations to boys to come out and play' (ibid., p. 121). On one page we find eight photos of faces of gang members, headed 'Full of Fun and Ready for Adventure', and includes 'A jovial adolescent' and 'bright, clean-cut little fellow' (ibid., p. 33). We suggest elsewhere in this book that

---

[3]In this part of the chapter we are heavily indebted to Nick Gould's extensive previous review of qualitative social work research in terms of an earlier account of historical moments (in Shaw and Gould, 2001: 33–38).

there have been continuing tendencies to romanticism in qualitative social work research.

The modernist and blurred genres moments are connected to the emergence of post-positivist arguments. In the *modernist* period many texts sought to formalise qualitative methods, dating back to the very first methods book in the late 1920s (Palmer, 1928). This was more marked in the USA than in most other countries, as university departments became established, with the concomitant demands for teaching materials. Uncertainty has been expressed about this academisation strand in social work and social science history, although this formalising tendency has proved a continuing strand, and can be seen in the work of writers like Patton (2002), Miles and Huberman (1994) and, in social work, in Padgett (2008).

In the *blurred genres* phase the humanities became central resources for critical, interpretive theory and qualitative research became more broadly conceived across different disciplines. The boundaries between the social sciences and the humanities had become blurred. 'A kind of methodological diaspora took place, a two-way exodus' (Denzin and Lincoln, 2005: 3). It is possible to detect later movements between disciplines. The more recent attention to time, place and space in qualitative research, for example, owes much to the influence of social geography.

Applied research was gaining in stature in this period, with qualitative research especially strong in the fields of education and medicine. The early and later writings of Geertz bracket this period. Denzin and Lincoln greatly overstate the shift when they say 'The essay as an art form was replacing the scientific article' (2005: 18), and indeed their own review is written entirely in the conventional scientific voice. At issue was 'the author's presence in the interpretive text' (ibid., p. 18). Stanley Witkin, in a more recent example, anticipated a talk on 'Living a Constructionist Life: A Personal Narrative' by saying 'My idea is to reflect on the ways in which adopting a social constructionist mindset has influenced the way I understand and "do" my life (including my work). My approach would be in the form of a narrative in which I highlight the salient encounters and events that formed the road on which I now seem to travel.'[4]

Denzin and Lincoln see an ever-faster pace of change. The *crisis of representation* 'articulated the consequences of Geertz's "blurred genres" interpretation' (2005: 18). New writing forms have emerged in this context. Without labouring each of the successive moments, they detect more recently the emergence of evidence or scientifically-based research, seeing it as a movement, and as in part 'a radicalized, masculinist backlash to the proliferation of qualitative inquiry methods' (Denzin and Lincoln, 2005: 9) with an emphasis on a single standard of scientific rigour.

It is at points like this that Denzin and Lincoln's analysis has failed to carry everyone. There has been sharp criticism, especially from within British and some European sociology. However, the value of their contribution is liable to

---

[4]From a lecture at the University of York, England, 2009.

be missed in the fog of war. Gould – a less abrasive qualitative social work researcher – nonetheless found it helpful to align social work trends cautiously to Denzin's earlier periodisation of five 'moments' (Shaw and Gould, 2001: Chapter Two). Gould's account should be read as it stands, but he associates the early work on case study to the traditional period, suggesting that Mary Richmond's work fits that category. He observed that Denzin's modernist 'golden age' was anything but golden in social work, but thin and 'dark'. Mayer and Timms' landmark study, *The Client Speaks*, was a product from the end of this period and fits into an emergence of post-positivist inquiry (Mayer and Timms, 1970). It was the first in a significant series of qualitative studies giving voice to the client (c.f. Sainsbury, 1975; Sainsbury et al., 1982).

The development of organisational ethnographic work associated in part with a period of blurred genres is reflected, albeit gently, in the social work projects of Hall and Rees in the late 1970s, each exploring agency entry and how clients are constituted through the referral and intake process (Hall, 1974; Rees, 1979). Satyamurti (1981) showed how social workers cope with working within irreconcilable ideological frames of reference. As Gould expresses it, 'theoretically located within a Marxist tradition of sociological studies of work but methodologically grounded in ethnography, Satyamurti attempted to elicit the internal and external worlds of social workers' (Shaw and Gould, 2001: 35). Organisational ethnography has continued to be one of the strengths of social work research. Floersch (2002) and White (2001) exemplify this from each side of the Atlantic.

Some aspects of grounded theory have been seen as evidence of the survival of the modernist moment, and it has continued to be a stimulus for social work research. However, Ruckdeschel expresses misgivings on this front. 'Grounded theory methods have sometimes been invoked as a kind of catch all, almost taken-for-granted method that does not require extensive description and discussion' (Ruckdeschel, 2013: 757). He underlines two major approaches to grounded theory.

> One is associated with constructivist approaches and the work of Charmaz ... The other comes out of a more objectivist (some would say positivist) tradition of Glaser and Strauss ... Another aspect of this debate is whether it is a broadly general methodology like thematic analysis ... or whether it is an approach with both qualitative and quantitative applications but with very specific methods and systematic procedures.

Overlapping influences of feminism and postmodernism are associated with the period Denzin calls the crisis of representation. The popularity, if occasionally rather superficially, of narrative research in social work is best represented in the work of Riessman, who has spanned social work, women's studies and sociology (Riessman, 2008; Riessman and Quinney, 2005). Strong forms of constructionist research have been prominent in the work of Witkin and those linked to the 'Global Partnership for Transformative Social Work' (Witkin and Saleebey, 2007). Increased focus has been devoted to writing forms and the voice of the author, and there are numerous instances of this influence in recent social work research.

From the close of the last century there has been a series of publishing embodiments of qualitative social work research that may signal greater visibility and perhaps a sense of identity. The Sherman and Reid edited collection (1994) remains, for its time, the conceptually best organised volume of edited work. Some of the finest writing has come from the pen of Catherine K. Riessman. Writing to audiences of social work, sociology and women's studies, she almost single-handedly fashioned an account of narrative methods that serves as well as any writing in the field (Riessman, 1993, 1994, 2008; Riessman and Quinney, 2005). Padgett's text on qualitative methods (Padgett, 2008) was one of the first authored texts in the field. Shaw and Gould (2001) is a part-authored, part-invited chapter book that gave more attention to social work contexts in addition to a range of exemplars of specific methods, but did not offer an overall text.

More recent work varies in purpose and interest. Carey's book in undertaking qualitative dissertation work is a quite excellent book of its kind (Carey, 2013). His text on qualitative research skills (Carey, 2012) is an introductory review of qualitative methods in social work research. Padgett's second edition (Padgett, 2008) provides a straightforward approach to working through methods in a traditional way. Her book takes the fairly direct form of a generic methods text, without extended attention to social work contexts. The successor volume to Sherman and Reid (Fortune et al., 2013) is more straightforward as an edited review of qualitative methods. Darlington and Scott (2002) combine discussion of key stages in the qualitative research process with extensive use of case studies from the field. Developing thinking is apparent in Longhofer and Floersch's association of qualitative social work methods with social work practice (Longhofer and Floersch, 2013). Transformative agendas in social work have sometimes been harnessed and reinforced by those who are primarily qualitative researchers (e.g., Witkin and Saleebey, 2007). One of the most significant developments has been the founding of the journal *Qualitative Social Work* in 2002, providing an international forum for innovative developments in forms and practices of qualitative social work inquiry. Witkin's tenure as editor of the journal *Social Work* in the opening years of the century also incentivised qualitative practitioners and researchers in the USA.

Returning to the sequential, overlapping moments understanding the history of qualitative research, criticisms are at one level straightforward. It is unduly USA-centred. Flick contrasts the USA and Germany when he concludes that 'in Germany we find increasing methodological consolidation complemented by a concentration on procedural questions in a growing research practice. In the United States, on the other hand, recent developments are characterized by a trend to question the apparent certainties provided by methods' (Flick, 2006: 19). The image of ever-increasing change, with new 'moments' every five years may well seem implausible through the gaze of future eyes.

But the more substantial reservations are in the main accepted by Denzin and Lincoln. Gould writes that '"moments" are not like geological seams which are mined to extinction, but overlap and are often mined simultaneously' (in Shaw and Gould, 2001: 34). Denzin and Lincoln express this more extensively. 'These historical moments are somewhat artificial; they are socially constructed, quasi-historical, and overlapping conventions ... each of the earlier historical moments is still operating in the present, either as a legacy or as a set of practices that researchers continue (to) follow or argue against' (Denzin and Lincoln, 2005: 2, 20). In a footnote they also say that 'any periodization hypothesis is always suspect, even one that rejects linear, stagelike models. It is never clear to what reality a stage refers, and what divides one stage from another is always debatable' (ibid., p. 27). Slightly less convincingly they say 'we are clearly not implying a progress narrative with our history. We are not saying that the cutting edge is located in the present' (ibid., p. 20). They refer to what they see as complex pressures both 'within and outside of the qualitative community that are working to erase the positive developments of the past 30 years' (ibid., p. 20) as a defence of their claim, but the reference to 'positive developments' does suggest they see an affirmative progression.

Yet we do find that the series of 'moments' offers a helpful sensitising framework for thinking about the development of qualitative research in social work. As Denzin and Lincoln rightly remark 'They permit a "performance" of developing ideas. They also facilitate an increasing sensitivity to and sophistication about the pitfalls and promises of ethnography and qualitative research' (2005: 2).

Innovations in qualitative social work research?

What might we mean when we ask if there is evidence of innovation in qualitative social work research, or to express the focus more precisely, innovation in research practices? Xenitidou and Gilbert (2009) define such innovation as referring to practices 'that have not yet filtered through to typical research methods courses or that impact on the research process in ways which are novel (inventions) or different to existing ones' (ibid., p. 6). They brought their own considered definition of research innovation to their review. Taking a different approach, Wiles et al. (2010) conducted a narrative review of qualitative research published between 2000 and 2009 in which authors made claims to methodological innovation. Their study found little evidence of paradigmatic developments within qualitative research methods, and conclude that the majority of the innovations involved the altering of existing methodological traditions. 'More significant innovation' involved 'transferring and adapting methods from other disciplines' (Wiles et al., 2009: 22).

In a review of innovation in social work research (Phillips and Shaw, 2011) qualitative developments figured more fully. They included discursive approaches, expressive and performing arts, mixed and multi methods, visual approaches, and observational and ethnographic approaches. A small sample can be sketched from a special issue of *The British Journal of Social Work* devoted to research innovation (Example 3.1).

EXAMPLE 3.1	Archives, Discourse, Space and Microworlds – Innovation in Qualitative Social Work Research

Adrienne Chambon, Marjorie Johnstone and Julia Winckler, in an article 'The material presence of early social work: The practice of the archive', work with a multiplicity of archival material (texts, images and objects) to viscerally examine the 'push and pulls' in child welfare. Using a mixed-methods approach and grounded in surprising theoretical choices, they expose the complex philosophical tenets that evidence social work as a cultural and political activity. Their paper bequeaths the value of innovative methods in examining the intricacies that constitute decision making in professional practice.

Chambon et al. (2011)

In an article on 'Understanding change in community mental health practices through critical discourse analysis', Michael Mancini offers a mixture of critical discourse analysis and critical participatory action research to show the potential for social work research to promote social justice in social work practice. He demonstrates the significance of collaborative research practices in which social workers, service users and service providers become co-researchers. As part of his research method, Mancini works with agency staff to form a language committee that ultimately leads to noteworthy changes.

Mancini (2011)

Sally Holland, Stephen Burgess, Andrew Grogan-Kaylor and Jorge Delva, writing about 'Understanding neighbourhoods, communities, and environments: New approaches to social work research', take us to projects in Chile, the USA and Wales. They describe a variety of spatially oriented research designs that allow for a more nuanced understanding of neighbourhoods and the everyday lives of people in these communities. Their article is an example of how innovative mixed methods have considerable transgressive potential in regards to traditional social work knowledge.

Holland et al. (2011)

Writing on 'Social work in the laboratory: Using microworlds for practice research', Sue White, Karen Broadhurst, Chris Hall, Sue Peckover, David Wastell and Andy Pithouse examine the decision-making processes and reasoning of social workers. Through new and previously untried designs, they produce a computer-based simulation that provides a unique view into 'practice culture'. Their subjects were active partners in a collaborative process of knowledge co-production.

Wastell et al. (2011)

A further field where qualitative methods have shifted in directions that would scarcely have been foreseen is in arts-based methods. It is not new to think of social work as art. Timms left us one of the most penetrating discussions of the question that long predates the recent interweaving of the humanities and the social sciences (Timms, 1968) and England devoted a whole book to the subject (England, 1986). Adrienne Chambon helpfully flags up an article by Norman

Denzin written expressly to a social work audience (Denzin, 2002) where he spoke of bringing social work closer to the arts via a 'poetics of social work'. She also celebrates the memory of Howard Goldstein who was 'the most adamant social work scholar' who 'repeatedly clamoured for an explicit convergence between social work, the humanities, and the arts' (Chambon, 2008: 592).

Creative and *arts-based methods* was the area where writers were most likely to claim that they were doing innovative research in a survey of journals in the first decade of the century (Wiles et al., 2010). In social work one of the main locations of arts-based approaches has been the journal *Qualitative Social Work*. Szto and colleagues (Szto et al., 2005) explore poetry and photography, Wulff and others (Wulff et al., 2010) use drama in relation to racism, and Phillips (2007a) draws on innovative writing forms to depict social work in a hospital, and on the visual arts to talk about social workers' experiences of loss and grief (Phillips, 2007b). Gallardo et al. (2009) draw on poetry and narrative to understand depression, and Poindexter (2002) likewise uses poetic forms of narrative when writing about HIV. Knowles and Cole (2008) have provided a comprehensive collection of work in this still developing area.

A different area where some claim to innovation seems plausible is in applications of a form of sociological social work through a 'methodological practice' that adapts, infuses, inhabits and translates qualitative research methods as a dimension of the different elements of social work – assessment, planning, intervention, review and outcomes (Riemann, 2005, 2011; Shaw, 2011b).

Qualitative writing

We noted earlier that the blurring of disciplinary fields was captured by Geertz and others as a question of *genres*. For example, we should note new writing forms. 'As a writer … you owe it to your readers to set yourself the most difficult challenge that you have some hope of being equal to.'[5] Staller (Example 3.2) illustrates how the way in which qualitative inquiry may be written is indeed a difficult challenge. We return more fully to the significance of *genres* when speaking of narrative and also of writing forms in later chapters.

EXAMPLE 3.2	**Writing and Talking About Writing**

Karen Staller is talking in 2012 about the experience of working with Joanne Terrell on the article that became Terrell, J. and Staller, K. (2003) 'Buckshot's Case: Social work and death penalty mitigation in Alabama', *Qualitative Social Work*, 2(1): 7–23.

(Continued)

---

[5]Jonathan Franzen 'The Path to Freedom', *Guardian* Review, 26 May 2012.

(Continued)

Karen is speaking by Skype link from Michigan to York in England. We have not edited her words because we want to use them as an instance of referring to a way of writing, but also as itself a way of talking. Hence we have not decontextualised the original format:

'The first of the four articles I want to talk about is entitled, "Buckshot's Case: Social Work and Death Penalty Mitigation in Alabama". It really started not with the written piece or even the project itself but rather with the *space* within an academic journal to put it. Here I am talking about a journal co-edited and founded by Ian Shaw and Roy Ruckdeschel, *Qualitative Social Work*, which has grown dramatically under their leadership since its birth about a decade ago. In this journal they created a space for what they called "New Voices". At roughly the same time I was working at the University of Alabama and had taken up running three miles every morning with a colleague at the University named Joanne Terrell who was also a practising social worker. During our early morning runs, I listened to her extraordinary stories about working on death penalties cases. In particular, about her role in testifying at mitigation hearings on behalf of men (mostly men) who had been convicted of felonies so serious that they were eligible for the death penalty. Her testimony was often the only thing standing between the sentence of Life in Prison Without the Possibility of Parole or execution. Her work seemed like the kind of story that should be told to a broader social work practitioner audience, in part, because so little is written about the role of social workers as expert witnesses in these kinds of cases.

Yet a traditional academic article made no sense to me because it was Joanne's first hand experiences and stories that made the material so compelling. It also didn't make sense to me to treat her like a research *subject*. So we ended up "co-constructing" a narrative about one of her cases, that of Buckshot.

When I say co-constructed it may be a misnomer. I wrote the entire article and did the literature review and embedded her case in some broader context. But I wrote it from her perspective using her voice. I also insisted that she be first author because the story, after all, belonged to her. The "new voices" space in the journal provided a forum for this kind of experimental writing and relationship between practice and scholarship. So in many ways the *opportunity* for this kind of writing happened because of the gift provided by a journal that was willing to house it and encourage it. In short, this manuscript came into being because there was a space for it to go.'

What is good qualitative social work research?

We are towards the end of the opening part of the book. These three chapters can be seen as a way of framing the doing of qualitative research. But before moving into that central section of the text, what count as criteria of good qualitative research? The question is not easy, and is one area where differences are likely to persist. Part of the problem with such statements is that they are always, to borrow Garfinkel's term, indexical. He took the position that 'the task of replacing all indexical expressions with objective expressions is an endless one' (Packer, 2011: 75) and that scientific language, as a form of context-free, non-indexical language, cannot replace ordinary language. What we think of as good is likely to be defined in terms of other criteria that in turn need defining.

Although this need not take us into a relativist version of the Möbius strip, it does mean that as soon as we begin to answer the question we soon find ourselves back at where we started. Asking about the criteria of good research is not quite the same as asking what counts as good research. We are likely to conclude that good research is intimately bound up with good social work. A secondary, but tricky, question is whether good *qualitative* research calls for a different answer from good *quantitative* research. If we resolve these questions, then who is to make the judgement? For various plausible reasons we are likely to feel uncomfortable if it is left to social workers to say whether something is good social work or not. By the same order, we should feel discomforted if we become drawn into assuming that it is only researchers – even *good* researchers – who are able to judge what counts as good research. A further secondary but not easily tractable question is what should count as expertise?

By way of getting into this topic we want to plead for seeking answers that fall at a middle level of generality. Vague as this sounds, we will try to show that this enables us to set out a way forward that permits a significant level of agreement across the social work and research community, but without dissolving into a naïvely pragmatic consensus (one of us has developed this position in some detail elsewhere – Shaw, 2010, 2012; Shaw and Norton, 2008). *At this level* we do not believe that good qualitative research calls for a different criteria from good quantitative research.

---

1. Achieves a thoroughgoing consistency with broader social work purposes.
2. Aims for methodological excellence in whatever it does.
3. Promotes social work inquiry marked by rigour, range, variety, depth and progression.
4. Sustains an active conversation with the social science community.
5. Gives serious attention to aspects of the research enterprise that are close to social work.
6. Aims to unsettle its preconceptions by taking seriously aspects of the research enterprise that seem on the face of it far from social work.

Shaw (2012)

Figure 3.2 Good social work research

While this is awash with indexical terms – what is methodological excellence, what is rigour, what counts as an 'active' conversation, and above all what are the broader purposes of social work – we are persuaded that taken as a whole these criteria support an image of and vision for social work research, qualitative and otherwise, and that they are recognisably different from other possible options. To take just two examples, it fronts up the value of identifying and exploring boundaries with other fields, and it insists on both 'inner-science' and 'outer-science' criteria – both methodological excellence and relevance to social work – rather than an either/or stance. At the back of this position lies a belief that social work research is a recognisable field with unresolved and perhaps best-left-unresolved tensions, diverse yet coherent, connected but critical.

Purposes of (qualitative) research

And yet the uncomfortable questions cannot be neatly disposed of. For example, how might qualitative research be thoroughly consistent with the purposes of social work? It will be so when it aims to:

- Generate or enhance theory and knowledge about social work and social care.
- Provide impartial evidence about and for decision making.
- Instrumentally improve practice and organisational learning.
- Highlight the quality of lived experience and advance practical wisdom.
- Promote justice, social change and social inclusion.

But how should these be held in conjunction with one another? Might emphasising the quality of lived experience lead to an indifference to justice and social change? Can qualitative researchers be committed to both impartiality and advocacy research? Our stance on criticality sustains how it is possible for a position to be advocated but not in partisan ways. For example, even *within* given stances – critical practice, evidence-based practice, etc. – there are diverse debates. We should resist ethnocentric tendencies through the cultivation of a critical (rather than polemical) and open stance. Social work qualitative researchers will often lead to non-conformity, and seek to challenge orthodoxies. Robert Merton's characterisation of the non-conformist deviant is a salutary caution at this point:

> There is no merit in escaping the error of taking heterodoxy to be inevitably false or ugly or sinister only to be caught up in the opposite error of thinking heterodoxy to be inevitably true or beautiful or altogether excellent. (Merton, 1971: 832)

Take for example the diversity within justice-based positions. There are older traditions worth acknowledging. Robert Dingwall discusses the moral discourse of interactionism and draws on Adam Smith for how the moral and the empirical plug together. He concludes 'If we have a mission for our discipline, it may be to show the timeless virtues of compromise and civility, of patient change and human decency, of a community bound by obligations rather than rights' (Dingwall, 1997c: 204). This example is taken from sociology and may have as few direct parallels in social work as it does in sociology. But the diversity of positions – UK Fabianism, differences on partisanship within Marxism, and the more conservative position of Dingwall – illustrate how general commitments can be part of a research community without requiring the same stance on the part of everyone.

Such tensions and positions are important to acknowledge. While qualitative researchers should not consent to them in a pluralist fashion, they ought where appropriate to accept that they are positions that can meaningfully be held and contested. To foster this position, qualitative researchers should develop critical, reflexive assessments of positions with which they themselves are associated.

Weighing one against another?

Having pleaded for a conjunction of tensioned research purposes, does this mean that all researchers in every project should take a similar position? We think not. Part of our response to these enduring questions is to enter a plea that social work research should be conceptualised in such a way that 'pure' and 'applied' research are not in conflict, and applied research is not seen in deficit terms as a methodologically lesser form of research. But this does not tell us whether some ways of expressing research purpose in social work ought to be given greater weight than others. We suggest that there are, in fact, three possible positions on this question, rather than just two.

Some research purposes carry greater weight than others. This may be argued from a belief that scientific knowledge always takes precedence over, for example, knowledge based on experience (hence rigour, accuracy and other 'inner-science' criteria, on this view, will always be more important than 'outer-science' criteria of relevance, impact, and the like). The same general stance may also be argued from, for example, a strong 'standpoint' position that the knowledge of the oppressed will always carry greater validity than that of the oppressor – though of course the direction indicators are given quite the reverse weighting, giving precedence to 'outer-science' purposes over 'inner-science' ones.

Second, *the weightiest research purpose in social work will always be contingent on local context* and the perspectives of the stakeholders, and cannot be 'assigned' in advance. This position is sometimes loosely referred to as a 'postmodern' position – 'loosely' because typically under-developed and perhaps assumed to be beyond countermanding. While we do not think this offers an adequate grounding, it has the merit of giving voice to a wider array of stakeholder interests, rather than requiring research purposes to be committed in advance either by the funders or the researchers.

A third position – and one with which we find ourselves in broad sympathy – is that *'inner' and 'outer' science criteria of quality are both indispensable,* and they should be brought to bear on any given research project or output. However, they should not be applied through a framework of 'criteriology' (Stake, 2004), but at a level of generality that does not require us to 'weight' dimensions against one another. On this premise, 'outer-science' norms or purposes (e.g., being useful or emancipatory) are neither more nor less intrinsically important than 'inner science' epistemic norms.

Quality judgements for a given research output are likely to be seen as stemming from several different criteria rather than from a single criterion. Hence, it seems reasonable to suggest that research quality should usually be assessed against a principle that good research will be 'good' on more than one dimension. For example, it will not be 'good' only because it has been useful, *or* rigorous, *or* emancipatory.

Who is the expert?

Who has the say-so in assessing whether qualitative research is good research? Does the researcher have any special priority in their appraisal of research? What about the policymaker, the practitioner, the manager, the service user or carer? Behind this is the question of how scientific knowledge relates to and compares with other forms of knowledge.

Anthropologists have suggested several reasons why we should treat common sense as a cultural system – 'a relatively organized body of thought, rather than just what anyone clothed and in his right mind knows' (Geertz, 1983: 75). If it *is* a cultural system and not mere matter-of-fact apprehension of reality, then 'there is an ingenerate order to it, capable of being empirically uncovered and conceptually formulated' (ibid., p. 92). Geertz undertakes this 'disaggregation of a half examined concept' (ibid., p. 93). He identifies properties of 'naturalness', 'practicalness', 'thinness', 'immethodicalness' and 'accessibleness' as those general attributes of common sense found everywhere, he suggests, as a cultural form.

Social work research cannot ignore the common sense ways in which practitioners endeavour to make evaluative sense of their practical activities. Common sense knowledge will often be tacit knowledge. Tacit knowledge can be defined as knowledge or abilities that can be passed between experts by personal contact but cannot be, or has not been, set out or passed on in formal statements, diagrams, verbal descriptions or instructions for action.

The question arises whether tacit, implicit understanding is in tension with more explicit, planned research. If it is no longer clear, as some claim, that scientists and technologists have special access to the truth, why should their advice be specially valued? In an influential, though controversial, discussion paper on studies of expertise and experience Collins and Evans (2002) aimed to reinstate the distinction between the scientific community and the 'laity', but without making that boundary coterminous with the boundary marking the possession or absence of expertise. They offer a provisional classification of expertise that has value for social work, and which they claim helps understand 'the *pockets of expertise* among the citizenry' and 'put citizens' expertise in proper perspective alongside scientists' expertise' (ibid., pp. 250, 251). They adopt the term 'experience-based experts' that almost exactly mirrors the term 'experts-by-experience' that is often adopted by service user researchers, but they caution that though the phrase 'experience-based experts' shows the importance of experience, '[e]xperience, however, cannot be the defining criterion of expertise. It may be necessary to have experience in order to have experience-based expertise, but it is not sufficient' (Collins and Evans, 2002: 252).

The scene has been set in these first three chapters. Not in final form, but rather like the artist working *en plein air* before attending to forms and figures in the studio. It is these forms and figures that take up the central core of this book in Chapters Four to Twelve.

Taking it further

The quotations in this task are taken in random order from a study in which social work researchers were talking about their own work, and explaining how and why they had assessed it in certain ways. This task is best undertaken in pairs or very small groups, all members of whom should have read this chapter.

- What kinds of criteria are people using when they speak about their work?
- How do they relate to the approach taken in this chapter?

> … you want to involve service users but the way that you have set it up and the methodology you intend to use and the design isn't going to work so you have to be pragmatic.

> … if I see it as something as a purely scientific function then I might rate this in a different kind of way from whether I take a much more applied kind of notion of the value of research in which case I might look at some of these other factors.

> I suppose … as measured against established benchmarks of quality it might be something that doesn't reach the sort of standards you would want, but because you're trying to push at the boundaries you accept a lower level of quality because you're able to open up to new areas of enquiry.

> I didn't include partly more descriptive writings … that doesn't in my mind have the same level as something which is more finely honed and possibly has more theoretical elements within it.

Speaking of epistemic considerations,

> they are preconditions, I think, otherwise you know, what are you talking about? How do you explain what you're doing? And you know, why does this mean anything other than any other sort of piece of work or people talking or … journalism?

Research should exhibit a

> creative spark … open up fields (that are) taboo and make people take notice of you.

> … what's much more important is that you have some central idea that informs the research which is not simply framed in terms of, you know, whatever the current orthodoxy is.

> I think there is a growing body of work and as a consequence of that I would say that the quality is better than (one) piece of research, an article or two, then onto the next topic.

One person mentioned research on joint work in child protection.

> It didn't try to oversimplify what was a very complex problem. I think sometimes … there's a tendency to, sort of, say well, yes, a very difficult thing to do,

but just go and talk about it … This paper didn't do that. It actually … demonstrated and understood the complexity of joint working in child protection and also said essentially there are no simple answers to this.

… because I think that has marked some new development in thinking which began in this paper which had an empirical basis … really thinking about the whole theoretical ideas behind classification.

If I haven't worked out how what I want to say about it relates to something that I would see as a sort of improvement in human well-being then I wouldn't write the article – full stop.

If it's methodologically poor research that has a large impact then I would judge it as not useful because it's actually influenced moves in the wrong direction, it's added to confusion and misunderstanding and bad policy rather than the reverse.

well I mean, … the fact that there has been all these hits on it (it) has be reckoned to be one of the most sort of influential articles, I suppose must say something.

What is the point of doing research that is stuck in a dusty journal on a library shelf and nobody ever sees it … and this has the potential to do a lot of other positive things.

I think we're beginning to make user involvement a kind of a test for quality and I think that is extremely poor methodology. I think what you have to do, just as with anything else, is justify user involvement as part of the methodology.

Shaw and Norton (2007)

PART II
Doing Qualitative Social Work Research

FOUR
Reviewing Research

Considerable changes have taken place in conventions for reviewing previous research and other literature. These changes relate to two linked factors: first, the almost universal favouring of various more or less systematic modes of review over more traditional 'narrative' reviews, and second, the huge increase in searching power available through developments in technology. In this chapter we describe and critically comment on these developments, making evident the ways in which social work research has been influenced. We note how the method of systematic mapping may provide a useful foundation for research reviews. We discuss the differences between aggregative and configurative reviews and much of the rest of the chapter is devoted to a discussion of different forms of review that adopt aggregative or configurative processes, or a combination of both. These include systematic review, meta-ethnography and narrative review. The chapter includes sections on searching for and storing research, appraising research for the purposes of review and a brief discussion about including policy and practice literature in reviews. The chapter concludes with a section on writing literature reviews.

Qualitative research projects in social work are usually interconnected with a number of other systems, including practice and policy. It is very unlikely that any qualitative project will be exploring completely uncharted territory and an important part of qualitative research is to *place* a project within previous and contemporary research and other literature. In the discipline of social work the policy, institutional and technical backdrop to reviewing the evidence base has changed exponentially over the last decade or so and continues to change at a rapid rate.

Social work, like other related disciplines in health and education, has moved towards a stronger favouring of more or less systematic forms of research reviewing and these are gradually replacing traditional, less systematic reviews of the literature. There is a wide range of terminology attached to the methods and approaches of literature reviewing and these are discussed in this chapter.

Increasingly sophisticated methods for scoping the literature are aided by the enormous increase in searching powers and the ability to stay abreast of current developments. University based scholars can search bespoke and sensitive databases to ensure that previous publications in the area come to light. Non-university based researchers and practitioners can use increasingly sensitive free databases such as Google Scholar or the social work specific database Social Care Online. Blogs, Zetoc[1] and email alerts help keep researchers abreast of new publications and they can modify notifications to specific interests. Gary Holden's New York University-based information gateway for social work updates constantly.[2] In the UK, the National Society for the Prevention of Cruelty to Children (NSPCC) sends a useful weekly update of research and policy developments. Increasingly all of these methods are becoming superseded by information about new publications becoming instantly available on Twitter. This increase in ways to access information has been accompanied by a surge in the amount of information that is available. Internationally, academics are under increased pressure to publish more frequently and in journals that are cited more frequently by others, i.e., that have a measured 'impact factor'. Journals are getting fatter, with more frequent issues and new journals launch frequently. The rise of open-source publishing is rapidly producing further changes in patterns of publishing and reviewing others' work.

The technological changes bring exciting possibilities in terms of keeping up with the literature in one's own area. They also increase expectations that reviewing can and should be more systematic than previously and require focus and discipline to avoid being overwhelmed. Almost all writers of reviews, whether senior academics, or undergraduates writing assignments, will struggle with balance in a review of the existing literature. Judgements have to be made about the balance of breadth and depth, efficiency and thoroughness. In our view the best reviews develop an argument through the written product, provide an authoritative synthesis and overview of previously published work in the area, highlight gaps and weaknesses and locate the current study within that field. As we discuss below, this does not mean that reviews can only be completed within a realist ontological framework that tests pre-existing theories. Reviews may also be exploratory, interpretive and cover a purposive selection of the literature, rather than a comprehensive one.

Reviews that are primarily designed to inform empirical research studies will be reported in 'Literature review' chapters of theses or dissertations or 'background' sections of books and articles. They will play a key role in informing the research questions and the research design. When the review is reported it places the empirical work within the wider body of research, showing why it is important, as well as any limitations.

---

[1]http://zetoc.mimas.ac.uk/

[2]http://ifp.nyu.edu/

Reviews that are an end product in themselves will answer a specific research question or set of questions, rather than simply provide an unbounded overview of a field. They are usually geared towards reviewing the evidence in a field for policy or practice, but may also be designed to provide a helpful summary of recent theoretical or methodological advances in one area of study. An example of this is Wiles and colleagues' (2010) narrative review of innovation in qualitative methods, in which they critically reviewed 57 papers published between 2000 and 2009, which claimed to have used innovative methods. Two examples in the field of social work include Turney and colleagues' (2012) extensive review of the evidence-base regarding assessments in child and family social work in the UK, and Fisher and colleagues' (2006) systematic review of older people's views of hospital discharge.

Whatever the purpose or length of a literature review, it should include most of the following. It should demonstrate that the author has a command of the topic at hand and is providing an authoritative overview of a topic for the reader of the thesis, report, article or book. It should collate, synthesise and summarise the available literature for the reader, rather than listing research and publications and expecting the reader to do the analysis. It is therefore usually presented thematically, although occasionally a chronological structure is helpful. It should evaluate the strengths and gaps in the coverage of the current literature and the validity and reliability of the research conducted in the area so far. It will usually summarise and evaluate the political, policy and theoretical debates surrounding the topic and demonstrate their connection to the research agenda. Finally it will usually draw conclusions about the research and policy implications arising from the findings of the review *or* justify the design and focus of the current or proposed research study.

Forms of review

Reviews have different forms according to their purpose and area of interest. Reviews might focus on effectiveness of interventions, key conceptual debates and policy developments in a field or the various methodologies that have been used to research a topic (Hart, 1998). **Rapid reviews** (we have heard them referred to as 'quick and dirty' reviews) might utilise some of the procedures of systematic reviews but streamline processes and take about half as long to complete as full systematic reviews. **Scoping reviews** quickly draw the main parameters of a topic and map key publications but are not usually aiming to appraise the quality of publications. Indeed they may form a precursor to a fuller, more systematic review (Booth et al., 2012). The Social Care Institute for Excellence (SCIE, 2010: 9) has developed **knowledge reviews** that combine a review of available research with a 'practice enquiry to explore stakeholder knowledge and practice not reported in the literature'.

Systematic maps are more extensive than scoping reviews. *Systematic mapping* is a process to map out and categorise the existing literature on a particular topic.

It was developed by the EPPI Centre[3] and has been adapted for social care research by the Social Care Institute for Excellence (SCIE, 2010). SCIE adopted this method as part of their reviewing work in response to the lack of results from traditional systematic reviews that concentrate on outcomes evidence. Frequently there were few suitable outcomes studies in the social care field under review, and, a source of frustration for this UK-based organisation, often no studies that had been conducted in the UK.

Systematic maps take a broad approach to develop a comprehensive 'map' of available literature. This will include, but not be confined to, empirical studies. While scoping reviews highlight 'headline' sources, a systematic map will attempt to cover the majority of available evidence in a field. It will describe the nature and coverage of literature in the field of study, identify gaps in knowledge and thus lead to the commissioning of more specific reviews and primary research, provide a searchable annotated, screened database of literature which, alongside the overview report, is openly accessible to practitioners, policymakers and service users (SCIE, 2010).

The first systematic map to be produced by SCIE was: Bates, S. and Coren, E. (2006) *The Extent and Impact of Parental Mental Health Problems on Families, and the Acceptability, Accessibility and Effectiveness of Interventions*, London: SCIE http://www.scie.org.uk/publications/map/map01.pdf

You can link to the database that lies behind this study, which is kept on the EPPI Centre site and contains 750 sources. http://eppi.ioe.ac.uk/webdatabases/ Intro.aspx?ID=9

There are very many labels for different types of review but they mainly fall along a continuum from aggregative to interpretive (Booth et al., 2012). Gough et al. (2012) provide a helpful typology of reviews that we find relatively unusual in its positive analysis of different review types. There is no attempt to fall into one 'camp' or another. Instead, the different purposes of reviews are clearly identified. These authors use similar but not identical terminology to Booth et al., and suggest two main review forms, with a helpful summary of their main features:

Aggregative reviews   are philosophically realist and aim to test theory. Review methods are set in advance and involve exhaustive searching. Studies with similar types of data are looked for so that results can be compared and sometimes combined. There will be clear quality appraisal of each study according to pre-determined criteria and the final product will have value in increased magnitude of findings through the bringing together of several smaller studies. Aggregative reviews will help draw conclusions about the effectiveness of interventions or diagnostic tools, cost-benefit analysis and measuring prevalence.

Configurative reviews   are more idealist philosophically and may aim to generate or explore theory. Review methods may be iterative, developing as the

---

[3]The EPPI Centre is the Evidence for Policy and Practice Information and Co-ordinating Centre (EPPI-Centre) and is part of the Social Science Research Unit at the Institute of Education, University of London. http://eppi.ioe.ac.uk/cms/

review progresses. Heterogeneous sources may be included and these types of review are likely to identify patterns in a wide range of studies and other writing. A sufficient number of sources to answer the research questions is aimed for, with searching ceasing once saturation has been achieved. Quality of method may be assessed in configurative reviews, but relevance and contribution of the study may be of equal importance. Configurative reviews aim to increase understanding of substantive or theoretical areas. More formal forms of configurative reviews may be labelled as meta-ethnographies, while other forms of configurative review such as those which trace the development of research in an area of interest may be labelled narrative review. Both these forms of review are discussed later in this chapter.

Adapted from Gough et al. (2012: 3–5)

While aggregative and configurative reviews may appear to fall easily within quantitative and qualitative traditions, Gough and his colleagues stress that it would be wrong to conflate these. The differences in types of review relate to the logics of the synthesis, not the types of research under review. Many reviews will include elements of aggregation and configuration or interpretation (Booth et al., 2012; Dixon-Woods et al., 2006, Gough et al., 2012).

Although these authors reviewed so far emphasise that review types are different because they serve different purposes, rather than being 'better' or 'worse' than each other, there has been a growing tendency in the social and health sciences to associate more systematic forms of literature review as 'good' and more narrative forms as 'bad'. Next in this chapter we examine three types of review – systematic, meta-ethnography and narrative – more closely, examining their strengths and limitations in the context of social work research.

Systematic reviews

Systematic reviews are the most resource intensive and clearly defined form of literature reviewing in the social and medical sciences. Their logic is aggregative, as described above. A review that is 'systematic' follows a protocol which makes its methods explicit and transparent. It should have clear research questions and a method for appraising the quality of studies and synthesising results. It should preferably be carried out by a team rather than a sole researcher. This maximises the chance of a knowledge/skills mix to include different research methods, practice knowledge and experience of using services. If the research under review is quantitative, it may be possible to analyse pooled results statistically in a method known as meta-analysis (MacDonald, 2003). The protocol should, in theory, allow for systematic reviews to be repeated in later years. Systematic review methods are dominated by the influence of the Cochrane collaboration, founded in 1992 and designed to synthesise and appraise the best evidence in medicine. The later Campbell Collaboration for educational and social interventions has similar goals and methods.

Although systematic reviews have strong origins in medical research, they are gradually becoming more common in social work research, albeit in modified forms. Examples include a review of interventions for learning disabled sex offenders (Ashman and Duggan, 2009), a review of the effectiveness of kinship care (Winokur et al., 2009) and a review of older people's views on discharge from hospital (Fisher et al., 2006). These three examples incorporate distinctly different baselines in terms of the designs of studies that were included in the reviews. The first only considered randomised controlled trials (RCTs) and found no published research at all to include in the review. The second included quasi-experimental studies and reviewed over 60 published studies. The last, as might be expected from the title, was a systematic review of qualitative research studies.

Systematic reviewing methods draw out some of the tensions in the social work research community, as Sharland (2012: 485) notes:

> The introduction of systematic reviews into fields such as education and social work has exposed a trail of epistemological and methodological fault lines within the research community and beyond.

Similarly, researchers at the EPPI-Centre write that systematic reviewing brings ideological and political challenges (EPPI-Centre, 2007). They suggest that ideological resistance comes from the myth that only randomised controlled trials are acceptable sources of evidence and that such reviews represent an instinct for centralised control of research production and use. They point to their user involvement strategies, their broad scope of research questions and the inclusion of non-experimental and qualitative evidence as examples to counteract this ideological resistance.

Certainly the use of a systematic approach using a clear protocol to review the literature in any given field brings advantages. If the evidence is available, a systematic review can provide clear evidence about the effectiveness of interventions in social work for policymakers, commissioners and practitioners. When interpreted broadly to be inclusive about research designs they simply provide a rigorous guide to the available literature in the field and need not be seen as a threat to qualitative and interpretive traditions.

Our general readiness to acknowledge a significant role for systematic reviews does not mean that we are blinkered about the problems associated with the trend towards the systematic review as the favoured form of literature review in social research. Most of these are associated with the forms of systematic review favoured in the medical field. The Cochrane model has been described by Dixon-Woods et al. (2006: 29) as the 'rationalist model of systematic review'. These authors, in an article commenting on their attempts to incorporate a wide range of evidence into a review of support for breast-feeding mothers, trace a more recent trend towards more pluralist models (c.f. EPPI-Centre, 2007). They note that most organisations that promote systematic reviews, including the Cochrane collaboration and the National Health Service in the UK, now allow for the inclusion of non-experimental data in some circumstances. Nonetheless, Dixon-Woods et al. (2006) note that the inclusion of qualitative research within a review that also considers quantitative, experimental evidence risks affording qualitative findings a much lower, complementary role if the primary research questions explore problems posed in quantitative form only.

Social work interventions are usually complex and multi-faceted. They are also usually tailored to individual needs, making it a challenge to investigate the effectiveness of interventions with conventional notions of rigour. The concentration on interventions that follow specific procedures, often targeting narrow aspects of behaviour or limited service user groups, can lead to analysis becoming rather divorced from the socio-political context of social work interventions. They can also favour the increasingly market-driven forces of manualised interventions. A further disadvantage of systematic reviewing is that it can be very resource intensive if conducted according to Campbell and Cochrane rules. Social work research is funded to a very low level compared to medical research (Marsh and Fisher, 2005). Most importantly for our purpose in this book, systematic reviews in the medical tradition tend to (but need not) disregard qualitative research. As discussed, these disadvantages are gradually being worked with through the increased use of broader research questions and better integration techniques for different forms of evidence, but it is clear why those working from a qualitative research tradition may remain critical of the increasing dominance of systematic reviewing and the methodological hierarchies that appear to be implied.

Meta-ethnography

Meta-ethnography is the most commonly practised form of formal qualitative synthesis (Campbell et al., in Booth et al., 2012). It is rather a misnomer in that it has come to include all forms of qualitative research, although the original proponents of the method were particularly interested in synthesising ethnographies of education (Noblit and Hare, 1988). It uses open coding of findings from a number of qualitative studies of the same field and constant comparison method of analysis to produce new integrated findings. Meta analysis *reinterprets* findings rather than reproducing them in an aggregative way (Doyle, 2003). It appears to be more strongly established in the fields of health and education than social work, but there are published examples of studies that have used this method of synthesis in substantive areas central to social work such as the experiences of unpaid carers of older people (Al-Janabi et al., 2008), parents' experiences of parenting programmes (Kane et al., 2007) and homeless women living with their children in shelters (Meadows-Oliver, 2003). Interestingly, all of these studies were conducted by researchers in health-related disciplines rather than social work or social care. Findings from meta-ethnographies are often structured as frameworks or guides for policymakers or providers and can even be used to produce measures (Al-Janabi et al., 2008).

Meta-ethnography and other related forms of qualitative synthesis may be an excellent form for bringing the best of qualitative research findings to the attention of policymakers and practitioners and producing new findings by analysing across studies. There are, however, drawbacks in the loss of the richness and complexity of individual papers and the lack of access to original data. Doyle (2003), however, notes that the use of extensive audit trails of decision making and analytic processes and the use, as much as possible, of the language of the original studies go some way to countering fears of dilution and opaqueness through secondary interpretation. Getting a balance between retaining the richness from the original studies and providing a new summary of findings through synthesis might be seen as parallel to dilemmas in qualitative analysis of finding a balance between member and research categories (see Chapter Eleven).

Narrative reviews

Narrative reviews are increasingly seen as the poor relation of systematic reviews, yet they remain a common type of review in many social work publications. Narrative reviews are not clearly defined and for some critics are distinguishable only in that they are *un*systematic (MacDonald, 2003). And, indeed, at their worst, they are entirely unsystematic and may create an aura of authority while missing important studies. Weak narrative reviews do not distinguish between different types of evidence. However, at their best they allow for a creative analysis of previous research, that is less bound by procedural conventions for processing information, and is also more ready to develop theorised reflections on the work of others. In doing so they are following a configurative logic of synthesis (Gough et al., 2012) as described earlier in this chapter.

Narrative reviews have the advantage over systematic reviews in being able to review broader, less clearly defined topics and being cheaper to produce, therefore making the approach more suitable for most students and unfunded researchers and practitioners. The disadvantages mentioned above can be significantly reduced if aspects of a systematic process are incorporated including, if appropriate, clear research questions, inclusion and exclusion criteria and some information about how results were analysed and synthesised (Collins and Fauser, 2004). This sort of information is particularly important for an assessed piece of work such as a dissertation or thesis that is solely literature based, or for research reports that consist solely of a literature review.

Narrative reviews have played an important part in social work academia, and journals such as the *Social Work Research, British Journal of Social Work* and *Child and Family Social Work* commission analytic reviews, critical commentaries or research reviews on topics that are seen as requiring contemporary appraisal and commentary. These journals require varying degrees of reporting of review methods. Such reviews can serve to highlight gaps in knowledge and may provide an impetus for the production of new research questions and research proposals.

They may review debates and policy development in addition to empirical research evidence, a topic we turn to next.

Reviewing the policy and practice context

Most of this chapter so far has related to reviewing published empirical studies, but most projects will require more than this in the reviewing that precedes a project. When planning a social work research project and starting to explore potential research questions and designs, we usually also need to review the current policy and practice context for the topic area and also explore relevant theory. For example, researchers considering designing research on permanency options for children in foster care will need to know about policy imperatives to increase stability and outcomes for children as well as understand debates about underlying theories which inform many interventions and policies such as attachment, resilience, systems theory and social capital. It can provide clarity to the reader if these are reviewed in separate sections of a report or thesis, although for some topics, separating out empirical findings, theory and policy will not work well, and a more thematic approach is required. An example of how one PhD student reviewed and wrote up the different sections of her literature review follows.

EXAMPLE 4.1 | **A PhD Literature Review**

Hayley Collicott's ongoing doctoral research explores informal child safeguarding activities, experiences and beliefs in one neighbourhood. She conducted ethnographic fieldwork over a one-year period in a modern city suburb in the UK. In reviewing relevant literature to inform her study she divided her review as follows:

1. Policy and political context: current regional and national social policies regarding child protection and safeguarding, and neighbourhood development were critically analysed. She also reviewed public discourses on public involvement in child safeguarding. For this part of the review she did not include empirical research findings, but instead searched government and third sector websites, read academics' analyses of safeguarding policies and searched media sources such as newspapers and news websites.
2. Theoretical background: here Hayley read widely round the subject to identify relevant theories including the nature of 'community', social capital and theories drawn from the sociology of childhood and the family. As her research progressed she found further theories to be relevant including the ethic of care.
3. Empirical research: in this section Hayley conducted a thorough search of major social science databases, relevant journals and 'grey' literature such as research reports from third sector organisations. She kept a record of her search terms and developed inclusion and exclusion criteria. In her reporting she took care to report factors such as sample sizes, settings and research design as well as thematically collating and synthesising

(Continued)

(Continued)

findings. Relevant research included designs based on ethnography, action research, randomised control studies and surveys and it was important to make clear the source of findings rather than simply stating 'Browne (2010) reports that...'.

These mini literature reviews enabled Hayley to first inform the development of relevant research questions and methods and second to 'place' her research theoretically and in terms of policy relevance. She was able to identify current gaps in our empirical knowledge in this field and demonstrate how her study contributed to or replicated previous research.

Searching

MacDonald and Popay (2010) suggest that as part of a literature reviewing protocol developed before a review begins, researchers should make clear decisions about the objectives of a review, criteria for considering studies (types of studies, types of participants, types of intervention and types of outcome measures), the search strategy and how the studies will be appraised once selected.

The field of searching has changed almost beyond recognition in the last two decades. Most searching is now done using electronic databases and search engines. This does require skills and knowledge of the field, however, to avoid either missing important references or becoming overwhelmed with references that are, at most, marginally relevant to your topic. In other words, there is a need to maintain a balance between sensitivity (avoiding missing relevant sources) and specificity (avoiding the inclusion of too many irrelevant sources) (EPPI-Centre, 2007).

In our experience, when students claim that they can find nothing directly relevant to their topic for their literature review, they are usually searching too narrowly. For example, a search to inform a research project about how to engage minority ethnic disabled children in assessments when there are concerns about sexual abuse might produce few results that cover all of those aspects but relevant evidence will include that on communicating with disabled children, discussing sexual abuse with children of all abilities, involving children of all abilities in assessments, evidence about child sexual abuse and children from BME communities, etc. Databases use systems of keywords and phrases and parameters can be put on searches according to criteria such as dates, type of publication and language. Some level of understanding of Boolean logic is needed, using operators such as asterisks and AND/OR. A brief training session in the library can save hours of frustrating, unstructured searching. Challenges in conducting electronic searches include the fact that, unless very precise terms can be identified, the vast majority of sources identified will be irrelevant. This is particularly a problem with the key words used in cataloguing qualitative research (Dixon-Woods et al., 2006) and poorly written abstracts (Sharland, 2012).

In addition to conducting electronic searches on databases (such as ASSIA and Web of Science) and search engines (such as Google Scholar), reviewers often check back catalogues of the most relevant journals. Many academics conducting systematic or in-depth reviews also contact established authors in the field to ask for recommendations of search terms and key studies and texts. Other sources of advice might be practitioners, policymakers and service users (EPPI-Centre, 2007). It should be noted that it is rare outside of clinical research for all sources to be found just by using electronic databases.

EXAMPLE 4.2 ─── **Literature Searching**

Greenhalgh and Peacock (2005) note that only 30 percent of their 495 sources in a systematic review were obtained through systematic searching according to their protocol. They describe their method of searching as follows:

'After extensive "browsing" in libraries and bookshops to get a feel for the overall research field, we used the following methods:

Protocol driven (search strategy defined at the outset of the study)

Hand search of 32 journals across 13 disciplinary fields

Electronic search of 15 databases by index terms, free text, and named author

"Snowballing" (emerging as the study unfolded)

Reference tracking: we scanned the reference lists of all full text papers and used judgement to decide whether to pursue these further

Citation tracking: using special citation tracking databases (Science Citation Index, Social Science Citation Index, and Arts and Humanities Citation Index), we forward tracked selected key papers published more than three years previously, thereby identifying articles in mainstream journals that had subsequently cited those papers

Personal knowledge (what we knew and who we knew)

Our existing knowledge and resources

Our personal contacts and academic networks

Serendipitous discovery (such as finding a relevant paper when looking for something else)'

Greenhalgh and Peacock (2005: 1064)

These authors note that reviews of complex interventions in health will always require this broad brush method of searching and this is true also in social work and social care. Fisher and colleagues' (2006: 14) review of older people's views of hospital discharge and de Boer and colleagues' (2007: 1034) review of patients' perspectives of dementia each found nearly half of their included studies using methods additional to systematically searching electronic databases.

We need to be aware of bias that can creep in at this stage of literature reviewing. Many of us in the Western world may restrict searches to English language only. We may not search enough sources, for example relying on only one or two discipline-based electronic databases, some of which exclude relevant social work journals, grey materials or books. There is also the problem of publication bias. Researchers and journals are more likely to publish the results of successful research, or successful interventions (MacDonald and Popay, 2010). Some journals are strongly orientated towards certain research designs. We may well make mistakes in the search terms and definitions we use. In social work, terminology differs greatly between nation states. For example, there are several terms for care and accommodation provided for children by relatives and friends (including kinship care and family and friends care). Elementary schools in the USA are called primary schools in the UK. There are numerous terms for intellectual impairments. Similarly, we can be too narrow in our disciplinary range. For social work topics we are likely to find relevant sources in databases based in the social sciences, social work, medicine, psychology and law. Specialist librarians and peers can help with countering some of these potential difficulties.

Recording

The researchers in the EPPI-Centre (2007) recommend the use of a search log, in which all strategies and results of searching are recorded. This is sometimes included as an appendix to reports and can bring transparency to the process, making it replicable a few years hence.

Whether conducting a full systematic review or a brief scoping review to get a sense of the field and start to formulate research questions, the use of electronic reference software from the very beginning helps with efficiency and organisation. Popular types are Endnote and Reference Manager, which being web-based replaced the earliest software that was uploaded through floppy-disk drives. These though may become increasingly replaced in popularity by Web 2.0 software, some of which can be sourced at no cost. Newer types of software, such as CiteUlike and Zotero have social networking features and work well with extracting information from pdfs, reflecting the changing working habits and expectations of students and researchers (Gilmour and Cobus-Kuo, 2011). They are also very easy to learn but may produce less accurate bibliographies than some of the paid-for earlier generation software (Gilmour and Cobus-Kuo, 2011). Using either Web 1.0 or 2.0 software, references can be imported directly from electronic sources such as journal pages without the need to re-type. Personal reading notes and reflections can be added, although, as Ridley (2008) suggests it is important to take care to distinguish between personal notes and those from the publisher or plagiarism could inadvertently ensue. Sources on such software are easily retrieved and reference lists are economically and accurately produced.

Appraising quantitative research

Although this is a book about qualitative research, in order to conduct a qualitative research project researchers need to be able to gain an understanding of the existing knowledge base in their field, including knowledge that has been developed through quantitative designs. In order to appraise quantitative research a more comprehensive knowledge of quantitative research designs is required than we can provide here. Martin Webber (2011) provides a very accessible summary for social workers. In Table 4.1 we summarise some of the main designs and the key questions that should be asked of studies that have utilised these designs. There are a number of appraisal protocols that have been designed to help structure appraisals of both qualitative and quantitative research. These can be used initially to help to decide whether or not to include a research study in the review. Secondly they can help rank research studies into quality grades from strong to weak. The gradings of the research

Table 4.1   A brief guide to appraising quantitative studies

Research design	Key appraisal questions
All	Is the study relevant to my research?
	Does the design suit the research aims?
	Are measures valid and reliable?
	Are data and statistical methods adequately described?
	Are the results statistically significant?
	How are null findings treated?
	Are ethical questions and conduct of study adequately discussed?
	How do the results relate to other studies?
	Additional design specific questions
Surveys	Who were the respondents, how were they recruited, was the sample size justified and what was the response rate? Can the results be generalised? How do they relate to previous studies?
Cohort studies	Was a control group required/used? Was the length of follow-up adequate and what was the impact of attrition of participants? What other factors might have influenced the outcomes?
Trials	Were participants randomly allocated and were investigators blinded to the allocation when assessing outcomes? What process factors might have influenced outcomes (e.g., variations to the intervention)? Were all allocated participants' results included, even if they did not take part in the intervention (this is known as 'intention to treat')?
Case-control studies	Is the control group appropriate? Have all confounding factors been identified?

(Crombie, 1996; Webber, 2011)

studies are often included in a systematic review report, but narrative commentary in a more interpretive review could also comment on the relative strength of studies.

Appraising qualitative research

It might be seen as debatable to transfer methods for appraising quantitative studies to qualitative studies and in the same way attempt to assess the strengths of studies in comparison to each other or according to a benchmark. It could be argued that using appraisal tools could bring an aura of objectivity to what would essentially be a subjective quality judgement. Nonetheless, it cannot be denied that qualitative research is an eclectic field and inevitably of varied quality, even when peer reviewed. It is possible to distinguish between the different kinds and qualities of research, without necessarily imposing a hierarchy in relation to qualitative designs, funding sources or sample sizes (Shaw and Norton, 2007). There have been numerous attempts to structure appraisals of qualitative research. There are at least 100 versions of checklists for qualitative appraisal available and:

> Few have distinguished between different study designs or theoretical approaches, thereby tending to treat qualitative research as a unified field. Many represent attempts by their developers to impose a dominant view of what 'good' qualitative research should be like, and point to territorializing tendencies in the qualitative community. (Dixon-Woods et al., 2006: 35)

Barbour (2001) cautions against the uncritical use of checklists to appraise the quality of qualitative research. They can be 'technical fixes' that could become divorced from broader understandings of epistemology and qualitative analysis. They can also serve to mask the reality that qualitative research remains a contested field. Dixon-Woods et al. (2006) set six experienced qualitative researchers to appraise twelve studies. They report that there was very little agreement on quality, relevance or even whether the methods in the papers could be classified as qualitative at all. Atkins et al. (2008) also report that their researchers had difficulty in determining whether a study had used qualitative methods or not. It is probably important therefore to retain some honesty about the subjectivity of appraisal methods, even where there is some attempt to introduce protocols, and the need to interrogate our own understandings of what qualitative research can and should be when undertaking a review.

Drawing on a number of guides to qualitative appraisal (Booth et al., 2012; Fisher et al., 2006; Webber, 2011), and our own experience (and at the risk of adding yet another checklist), the following headings seem to be the most useful when appraising empirical qualitative studies.

- Is the study relevant to my research questions?
- Are the research methods including data generation method(s), sample, ethical issues and analysis clearly reported?

- Did the design fit with the research aims?
- Are the data rich and is this evidenced through direct data extracts?
- Are the conclusions supported by the data and its analysis?
- Is there evidence that analysis has looked for and accommodated exceptional cases, anomalies and complexities in the data?

Asking such questions of existing research evidence can help make decisions about prioritisation and inclusion in the context of typically large numbers of possible sources. Some researchers attempt to grade qualitative projects and exclude studies that reach the lowest grade (see, for example, Attree's 2004 review about growing up in disadvantage) while others include all relevant studies but allow quality appraisal to emerge during synthesis (Atkins et al., 2008). There is no single agreed set of quality criteria (Dixon-Woods et al., 2006) but it is often helpful if the authors of a review explain the criteria used to appraise research and, if appropriate, display results in a table, or state that they excluded all those that did not meet the baseline criteria.

One of us (Ian Shaw) has produced tables for research students to help them methodically record their reading and appraisal of studies. He suggests that they develop two aids for this process:

- A form to record work on each single study. There will be a line for each study.
- A summary table bringing together all of the findings from the individual tables.

Headings for the tables will depend on the nature of the review.

Example of table recording work on each study

If the review is about the effectiveness of interventions in a particular field:

Example of table recording work on each study

Reference	Participants/ sample and setting	Intervention aims and method	Research method	Outcomes investigated	Summary of findings	Strengths and limitations

The summary table will summarise how many studies were looked at, what national settings they originate from (e.g., 5 from the USA, 2 from the UK, 3 from Canada, 2 from Norway, etc.), a typology of the types of interventions included (e.g., 2 group interventions, 1 individual intervention, 6 family interventions), the range of sample sizes, demographic features of participants, the range of research methods, how ethics were handled and so on. 'Strengths and limitations' should distinguish the author's own assessment and the reviewer's own assessment. The summary table can aid analysis and writing the literature review as a synthesised whole, as we discuss next.

Writing reviews

Reviews should provide something that brings added value and is more than a listing of relevant sources. The written product will be a synthesis that brings together a number of sources to form a new, single, coherent written account of the literature under review. We have already discussed different forms of synthesis as methods for conducting reviews. In this section we note that the process of synthesising is displayed through the writing of the review.

The work of synthesis involves placing individual studies or pieces of literature within the larger whole and finding and displaying where they fit (Booth et al., 2012). Standardised approaches to synthesis use data from individual study summary forms as described earlier in this chapter to populate a grid that provides a visual display, summarising overall findings. Qualitative free-text information can be included. Use of such grids allows quick summaries to be made such as the originating countries of studies, the prevalence of ethnographic methods across the included studies or how many include an explicit theoretical approach. The grids may be included in some types of publication but otherwise would be tools for synthesis rather than primarily for display purposes. Less procedural qualitative synthesis may not use such formal processes as display grids but, like all good qualitative analysis, will display a clearly analytic style that attempts to avoid over-inflating papers or results that appeal to the writer and does not sideline seemingly contradictory or less vivid literature.

Some of the weakest literature reviews we see tackle one research study per paragraph, describe each study but with little connection made between each one – in effect not synthesising at all. Others conflate empirical and non-empirical writings using phrases such as 'Shaw and Holland (2013) state that...' without explaining whether Shaw and Holland were simply expressing an opinion or reporting on a large scale research project. Excellent reviews on the other hand include paragraphs like the following example.

In Carol Smart's book *Personal Life* (2007), she reviews theoretical and empirical developments in the sociology of families and other intimate relationships in the first chapter. She authoritatively summarises and evaluates the key contributions of the last 60 years and develops an argument through an unfolding narrative.

> ... the issues which have formed a long-standing tension in the area of the sociology of family life; [are] namely the tension between broad, generalized, theoretical statements and small-scale, detailed empirical research ... it might be possible to say that broad theories of family life have been developed in relation to the trends in mainstream sociological theorizing, hence there have been functionalist theories ... Marxist theories (from Engels to some feminist work), feminist theories, and risk and individualisation theories ... (Smart, 2007: 7–8)

Conclusion

In this chapter we have noted that the changing world of information in contemporary society has a substantial potential impact on literature reviewing. A way forward in managing the complexity and volume of publications and other information sources is to adopt a form of procedure for reviewing that may be more or less systematic according to the review's purposes and the available resources, including time. As a minimum the review will work to clear research questions, although in configurative reviews the research questions may develop during the course of the review. It is usually helpful to have a strategy for searching and to record the progress of the search, including decisions made. Synthesis of included studies and publications can also be more or less systematised according to need. Such strategies should enable reviews to meet the need to be authoritative, trustworthy and informative and provide a guide to further action, whether that is empirical research, policy or practice.

Taking it further

The Parental Mental Health systematic map includes literature on the detection, extent and impact of parental mental health problems as well as interventions for families where a parent has a mental health problem. The map was published by SCIE in 2009.

1. Write a list of potential inclusion and exclusion criteria for studies that could have been included in this mapping exercise.
2. Write a list of potential databases and other sources to search on this topic.
3. Write a list of potential search terms to be used.

Now, compare your lists with those developed by the team, by accessing the report here: http://www.scie.org.uk/publications/map/map01.pdf and looking at the appendices. Don't be too surprised if your lists are much less comprehensive than those in the appendices. These were developed over a period of time by a team of researchers. However, the lists provide good examples of how to extend your reach in terms of searching for relevant literature on your topic.

FIVE
Qualitative Designs

This chapter serves as a foundation for the following chapters on research ethics, different forms of data generation and analysis. In this chapter we emphasise the importance of fitting design to the purpose of research: the design will follow from the aims and research questions. Although the main discussion of analysis occurs later in the book, emphasis is placed on planning the approach to analysis at the design stage and the integration of analysis throughout the process.

The chapter reviews a variety of design choices including action research, case study, longitudinal qualitative studies and secondary analysis of qualitative datasets. These are not the only design options in qualitative research but represent some of the important dimensions in qualitative designs: type of engagement with research participants, scale, time frame and data sources. We also discuss the use of several qualitative methods in one study and potential advantages, limitations and possible pitfalls in 'mixed method' designs where qualitative and quantitative methods are combined or used alongside each other.

This chapter focuses on planning for qualitative research. Subsequent chapters discuss the 'doing' of research in more detail but here we explore some of the early decisions that are made when planning research. This includes setting out the aims and research questions and making choices about methods of data collection and analysis. Research designs will also include plans for writing and dissemination. Research design in qualitative research is often an iterative process, with research questions and methods being reviewed and reworked during the research process. A flexible design can accommodate this iteration, while providing a coherent platform for beginning the research process.

Research designs in qualitative research have probably not been as readily categorised as in quantitative research and is necessarily less of a distinct *stage* than in quantitative designs. Quantitative research is necessarily much more structured and much quantitative research proceeds *via* a distinctive logic of explanatory inference that is seen to require a set of design decisions and a level of control that support that logic. Qualitative studies are often categorised by their methods rather than their design (visual methods, participant observation and so on), but in this chapter we emphasise that there are a number of design choices to be made that do not predetermine method, and we include here some of the most commonly used in qualitative research in social work: case studies, participatory and action research, qualitative longitudinal research, mixed methods and secondary analysis.

Pathways to qualitative social work research design

Qualitative research design may develop through a number of routes. A directly commissioned piece of research, such as a local social work project commissioning an evaluation of referrers' and service users' responses to their services will, of course, have more tightly drawn topic boundaries than those used by social work research students who often may choose any social work related topic and method that interests them for their research dissertation. Nonetheless, whatever the origins of the research, aims and subsequent research questions should evolve through a process of critical review of the literature, consultation with key informants (perhaps practitioners, service users, policymakers, carers) and reflexivity on the part of the researcher (see Chapter Eleven).

Figure 5.1 serves as a reminder that qualitative designs can be reviewed and reshaped as the research proceeds. Many qualitative analytic strategies call upon the researcher to revise sampling and questions as findings are analysed (see Chapter Eleven) and ideally data collection continues until theoretical saturation is reached, a point that can be estimated but not pinpointed before data collection begins. If the design is participatory, then aims, research questions, methods, analytic strategies and dissemination plans may be difficult to outline precisely prior to consultation with participants. This may mean that funding and ethics applications need to be done in a series of stages.

Table 5.1 starts to flesh out the elements of design listed in Figure 5.1 by introducing some of the initial questions associated with each aspect. The first column indicates where fuller discussion on each element may be found in this book and the third column introduces *some* of the potential choices and designs. A novice researcher may find it helpful to use the table as a checklist when writing a research proposal to ensure that he or she has considered all important aspects of design.

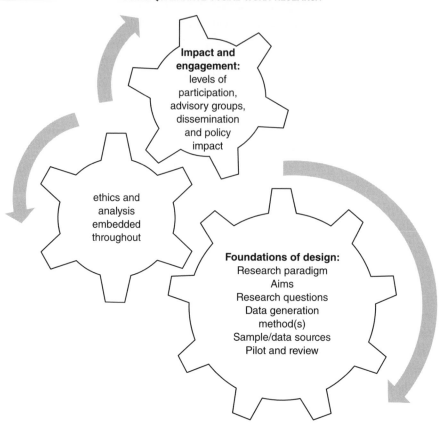

Figure 5.1   Research design process

Table 5.1   Elements of qualitative research design

Areas for consideration and where discussed in this book	Questions arising	Potential design choices and decisions
Paradigm – *discussed in Chapter One*	Is there an external social reality to be described (however imperfectly) by research? To what extent is all knowledge socially constructed? What would constitute 'evidence' in this research setting? Are transformative/social justice aims more important than methodological debates?	As discussed in Chapter One the philosophical and/or theoretical position within which we situate the research will affect all design decisions including how we view the status of our findings and the position of the researcher.
Aims – *discussed in this chapter*	What will this research study aim to find out? Is this an exploratory, evaluative, explanatory or comparative study? Will the study build or test theory? Will the research contribute to practice development?	The overall aims will affect fundamental decisions about cross-sectional, longitudinal, single/mixed method and comparative designs.

Areas for consideration and where discussed in this book	Questions arising	Potential design choices and decisions
	Are the research aims related to understanding participants' subjective understandings and experiences? Or are they related to how social worlds are organised and produced through interactions?	Data collection and analysis methods such as interviews, observation and analysis of recorded conversations allow us to explore different aspects of the social world. The aims will also affect decisions on participatory elements and use of advisory groups.
Research questions (RQs) *– discussed in this chapter*	What do literature reviews, early consultation with interested parties and cultural review (see Chapter Eleven) suggest are pertinent research questions? How do they relate to the overall aims of the research?	Research questions follow on from aims and will inform methods of data collection and analysis. They may be reviewed throughout a study.
Analysis *– discussed in Chapters Eleven to Twelve*	Will this study involve grounded theory, thematic, narrative or discourse analysis strategies? Will participants or other collaborators be involved in the analysis?	Different forms of analysis are likely to require different strategies for data generation and will affect sample size, transcribing protocols and, in some cases, mode of interview. Whatever the analytic approach, qualitative researchers will usually begin writing analytic memos alongside a research journal from the start of the project.
Sample *– discussed in this chapter*	Who or what will best help answer the research questions? How will I gain access to these people, settings or documents?	Sample size is often not fixed in advance with qualitative designs. Samples are likely to be purposive rather than probability-based.
Data generation methods *– discussed in Chapters Seven to Ten*	What method of data generation will best respond to the research questions? Will more than one method be required to answer the research questions and meet the aims? Temporal issues: will the study be cross-sectional (at one point in time), historical or prospective? Will several waves of data be generated, and at what points? How will methods be piloted?	Data generation methods are intimately related to research questions. They will be partly determined by resources. Ethnographies, participative designs and qualitative longitudinal designs are much more resource intensive than one-off interviews and focus groups. Secondary analysis of administrative records or previously collected data can be an efficient method of conducting research.
Ethics *– discussed in Chapter Six*	How will ethical approval be obtained? What ethical procedures can be put in place before the research begins? How will the research proceed ethically thereafter?	There is a need to determine which areas may need written protocols (e.g., child protection, researcher safety, anonymisation and data security).

(Continued)

Table 5.1   (Continued)

Areas for consideration and where discussed in this book	Questions arising	Potential design choices and decisions
		Research teams should agree how ethical challenges will be handled as research progresses. If there is ongoing contact with research participants or sites then consent needs to be approached as a process rather than an event.
Impact and engagement *– discussed in this chapter and in Chapters Fourteen to Sixteen*	Is the research likely to be of interest and use to social workers, policymakers, providers or service users? Is it desirable to include any of these groups in the research process?	Early engagement with relevant groups can aid the process from design to dissemination. A fully participative model may be used, or an informal or formal advisory group. Different platforms and forms of output may be appropriate.
Quality *– discussed in this chapter*	How will I ensure that my reported results are robustly drawn from my data? How will research audiences be reassured that my findings are credible?	Quality will be increased through a coherent research design, carefully executed and recorded data collection and thorough analysis. Credibility will be increased through transparent reporting of all research processes, including limitations.

Developing effective research aims and questions

Mason (2002: 18) suggests that all qualitative research should be constructed around an 'intellectual puzzle' and she suggests that a research puzzle might have one or more of the following elements, all of which tend to ask questions such as 'what, why and how'?

- How and why did *X* develop? (*X* might be a self-help movement, a policy, attitudes towards young people who commit offences)
- How does *X* work, or is constituted? (*X* might be relationships within a residential setting, decision making in a welfare benefits office)
- What can we learn by comparing *X* and *Y*? (e.g., the welfare systems of Sweden and France, or the experiences of young adults who were adopted and fostered).
- What influence does *X* have on *Y*? (e.g., what influence does an intervention have on behaviours and attitudes?)

The last question is usually answered by quantitative research but we argue in Chapter Twelve that qualitative research can – with circumspection – address issues of causality.

Research aims will state the overall objectives of the study. In social work research this may include the proposed impact on practice. **Research questions**

will be much more specific. In some studies there may be a hierarchy of research questions, with a small number of main research questions, but with each one broken down to smaller sub-questions.

EXAMPLE 5.1 | **The TLC Project: Social Workers Talking and Listening to Children**

Aims: This study will explore how social workers communicate with children in their everyday practice and how the social workers and children involved in these encounters experience and understand them.

Overarching research question: How do social workers communicate with children in a range of practice contexts and how do the social workers and children experience these encounters?

1. **What are social workers observed to do when they communicate with children in a range of settings (including children living at home and in foster or residential care) and with a range of aims (including child protection, assessing need and promoting wellbeing)?**

   - How do social workers create and seize opportunities to facilitate communication?
   - How do children respond to social workers in the observed encounters?
   - How do social workers manage communication in different contexts (e.g., in presence of parents/others, early encounters to established relationships, children of different ages from infants to adolescents, children living at home or in foster or residential care, in diverse cultural contexts, when communicating with different aims including child protection, assessing need and promoting wellbeing)?

2. **How do social workers experience and understand their communication with a child?**

   - What are social workers' reflections prior to and following a specific practice encounter and what do they identify as the strengths and weaknesses of the communication?
   - How do social workers manage the tension between the bureaucratic and therapeutic dimensions of their role when communicating with children, while maintaining a focus on the welfare of the child as paramount?
   - How do social workers conceptualise children, childhood and 'the family' and how does this impact on their practice?
   - What is the relationship between social workers' espoused theories of practice and their use of theories in practice?

3. **How do children experience and understand their communication with social workers?**

   - What are children's reflections prior to and following a specific practice encounter and what do they identify as strengths and weaknesses of the communication?
   - How do a small sub-sample of children experience their relationship with their social worker over a period of time?
   - Do children and practitioners identify similar or different indicators of successful communication?

(Continued)

(Continued)

4. **What factors best facilitate communication between social work practitioners and children?**

   - What is the impact of the practice environment (including national/local policies, practices, cultures)?
   - How does the purpose of the encounter shape the nature of the communication?
   - What is the impact of inter-personal factors on the communication process (including demographic features such as age and cultural background of child, experience and personal identity of worker, communication style, use of structured forms, tools and toys, level of concern, length of relationship)?

Research Questions 1 and 2 will be explored in phases 1 and 2 of the fieldwork. Question 3 will be explored in phase 2. Question 4 will inform an initial framework for analysis. The results will be used to produce practitioner training materials for dissemination in the final key stage of the project.

The TLC project: Social Workers Talking and Listening to Children is funded by the Economic and Social Research Council ES/K006134/1.

Punch (2000) notes that the process of development from overall research aim, to general research question, to specific research questions will develop inductively and deductively as these three layers are refined, but that however they are reached there should be a logical relationship between these layers and between aims, questions and methods. A critical review of research questions as they develop can review the potential for unquestioned assumptions into the research (Maxwell, 2005). For example, the question 'How do social care recipients cope with the stigma of receiving care?' assumes that this is a stigmatising process. A more openly enquiring question would be 'How do recipients of social care services experience care?'

Hypotheses are generally seen as incompatible with qualitative research. Nonetheless, some designs aim to develop theory and in grounded theory designs theoretical propositions will be developed from the data and then tested and refined through a process of further data collection. Importantly, whether grounded theory is used or not, in qualitative research the process of developing research questions to conducting fieldwork to analysing is rarely linear.

Sampling

Becker (1998) writes that, ideally, we want a 'full and complete description of everything that might be or is relevant to whatever we want to say with assurance about some social phenomenon … such a benchmark shows us what choices we make when we do, inevitably, leave things out' (p. 76).

There is little logic in attempting random or probability sampling with qualitative research studies. The people, settings or texts we choose to include in our studies will be chosen **purposively**, often because they constitute typical cases *or* extreme cases *or* a range of cases to achieve as much variation as possible. For example a study involving social workers' experiences of a new legislative framework may include a range of practitioners from newly qualified to highly experienced and in a variety of settings in order to gain maximum variability in potential responses to, and experiences of, the legislation. On the other hand it may prove more productive to only include practitioners experienced enough to have worked under the previous legislation so that they can reflect on the changes. Typicality can only be used as a sample criterion when there is a fair amount of knowledge about the potential sample already (Williams, 2003). It may well be easier to identify typical social work teams, for example, than refugees in a recent humanitarian crisis. The **critical** case may be used to test a proposition and if the proposition does not hold for that case then it is likely that it also will not hold for others (Flyvbjerg, 2006). For example, if it is assumed that low qualification levels is a factor in poor care of children in residential homes, then to study a home where most staff are better qualified than others may be more useful than choosing a home where staff have the same qualification levels as the average. If there is poor care in the home with staff members who are well qualified, then qualifications may not be the central problem. The **convenience** sample, much used by students in carrying out small-scale projects, is a weak form of sampling and can only be justified by a lack of resources to access a more purposive sample or where it is unlikely to make a difference which data source is accessed. **Snowball** sampling, where one participant recommends another may have more merit than a convenience sample, in that it draws on insiders' knowledge of the field and may lead to the inclusion of participants who could not have been accessed directly by the researcher.

In quantitative research power calculations can be undertaken to work out whether there are sufficient data to reach valid conclusions. In qualitative research the question of 'how many cases/participants/situations are enough?' is a much less precise question. Sample size will largely depend on the method. For example a narrative, biographical study can prove very effective with a very small number of participants with whom a number of interviews may have been collected. An ethnography will often take place in one setting, such as a social work team room or residential home, but will include many of the people and other sources such as documents that belong to the setting. A grounded theory approach will continue to collect data until theoretical saturation has taken place, and the composition of the sample may not be pre-defined but develop according to the developing theory. If the main method of analysis will be conversational or discourse analysis, then a very small sample may be required, but with particular care taken over the choice of setting and methods of data collection and transcription. In truth, many decisions about sample size are made on the basis of resources, purpose of the research (an undergraduate dissertation will be much smaller in scale than a PhD) and other rules of thumb. The general public and other consumers of research may be more impressed by a larger study (e.g., a study of 25 care homes rather than one, or 45 interviews rather than eight). This is not so much a concern of quality (more insight may be gained from a very detailed study of the workings of one care home than much briefer methods used with 25) but is about a sense of generalisability, of which we say more below.

Holstein and Gubrium (1995) dig deeper into notions of qualitative sampling, exploring the prospect of sampling meanings during an interview, rather than sampling at participant level. Hence the 'sampling frame' is meanings. 'The idea is not so much to capture a representative segment of the population as it is to continuously solicit and analyse representative horizons of meaning' (p. 74). If we take into account the ideas of respondents having 'narrative positioning, communicative context, and multivocality' then, '[e]ven though the formally designated respondent remains the same, the subject behind the respondent may change virtually from comment to comment' (ibid., p. 74). 'The possibility of positional shifts means that sampling can, and does, occur during the interview itself … When the interviewer explicitly encourages or seeks to clarify such shifts, he or she is, in effect, actively modifying the sample … The sampling process, then, is indigenous and never fully under the control of a sampling design' (ibid., pp. 75–76).

Case studies and generalisation

Case studies, Flyvbjerg (2006) controversially claims, are the only way in which we can truly come to understand human phenomena, because we learn and understand best through context-specific examples:

> As for predictive theory, universals and scientism, the study of human affairs is, thus, at an eternal beginning. In essence, we have only specific cases and context-dependent knowledge. (Flyvbjerg, 2006: 224)

While we find Flyvbjerg's position extreme, his general point about the value of knowledge gained from case study research is valuable – we understand and learn from specific cases and contexts.

What is a case? According to Stake (1995), writing in the field of education, it may be a child, a teacher, a classroom, an education programme or all of the schools in one country. It is less likely to be a teaching style, or the relationships between schools. 'The case is a specific, a complex, functioning thing' (Stake, 1995: 2). The case study will attempt to understand the richness and complexities of the case, whatever its size. In an example of a very small social work case study, Shea (2012) demonstrated the complexity of relationships in one child's network and hence the potential over-simplification of categories of relationship in permanency planning under the US Adoption and Safer Families Act, particularly in relation to foster carers. In contrast, a case might be the implementation of a new social care policy across a whole nation. A case study does not presuppose any particular method of data collection and it is common for more than one method to be used in case study research (Gilgun, 1994).

The nearness and subjectivity of the case study that is often the subject of criticism is, for Flyvbjerg, the main advantage of the approach:

> The most advanced form of understanding is achieved when researchers place themselves within the context being studied. Only in this way can researchers understand the viewpoints and the behavior, which characterises social actors. (Flyvbjerg, 2006: 236)

This bears comparison with those forms of social work research that have been described as practice-near (Ruch, 2013). Flyvbjerg (2006) asserts that rather than case study research tending to a verification bias (i.e., the researcher finds what she or he expects to find), the intensity of the approach is more likely to unearth new understandings and to uncover nuances and complexities that disrupt preconceived understandings. Eisenhardt (1989), too, suggests that the nearness of the researcher to the social world they are researching is more likely to complicate or refute any preconceptions and will 'unfreeze thinking' (p. 546).

The most common criticism of the single case study is that it is impossible to generalise from it. Flyvbjerg (2006) argues that a well-chosen single case site *can* lead to broader understandings, through the scientific process of falsification. For example, if there is a widely shared belief about a social phenomenon, then a single case study that finds a contraction or refutation of the belief can serve to disrupt that assumption and build new, perhaps more complex theories or propositions. Qualitative researchers can generate 'cross-contextual generalities' (Mason, 2002: 1) because of their method of 'connecting context with explanation.' Gilgun (1994: 372) refers to this form of generalisation as analytic and contrasts it with statistical or probabilistic generalisation. 'In analytic generalization findings extracted from a single case are tested for their fit with other cases and with patterns predicted by previous research and theory.'

Another potential form of generalisation from the case study is to use multiple case studies. Multiple case studies may have goals of comparability, generalisation or theory building. In general, multiple case studies have a replication logic (Yin, 2009) in that if a theory derived from one case is replicated in further cases, this is seen to strengthen the basis of the theory.

An example of a comparative study is Hopman et al.'s (2013) comparison of the implementation of a manualised intervention called EQUIP in juvenile detention centres in the States and the Netherlands. They observed the intervention, interviewed staff and analysed documents. They found clear differences in the hierarchy and emphasis of values in the two settings. Their results are perhaps not altogether surprising, but yield insights into the complexities of programme implementation in different cultural contexts. In their conclusion, the authors may be seen to be making *general* observations about the impact of values on styles of care, derived from their two comparative cases:

Taken together, this study has shown that youth care interventions are not merely a technical response to the conduct of children, but that different values regarding the aims of childrearing are expressed. Indirectly, these values may influence the development of children enrolled in youth care interventions and concurrently their perspective on life. (Hopman et al., 2013: 243)

Although, as can be seen, there are elements of generalisation that can be drawn from case study research, this is unlikely to be the most important goal of case study or any other qualitative research. As Stake (1995) notes, traditional quantitative designs generalise better. The goal of case study research is deep understanding and explanation of the particular: 'to thoroughly understand' (p. 9). As Geertz (1973) put it, 'The essential task of theory building ... is not to codify abstract regularities but to make thick description possible, not to generalise across cases, but to generalise within them' (p. 26).

Collaborative designs – from advisory groups to action and participatory research

The design stage may be enhanced by consulting or collaborating with interested parties. A fully *participative design* (see Chapter Fourteen) is likely to include participants, or representatives of the participating group (e.g., young people who are care experienced, people with learning disabilities, older people receiving social care) at the design stage as well as collaborating throughout the research process.

A slightly more 'hands off' approach is to use a *research advisory group*, or reference group. This is a commonly used approach in social work research and may include practitioners, policymakers, service recipients and other academics. Advice may be sought in face-to-face or virtual meetings and ideally groups will be involved at design stage, rather than simply presented with a *fait accompli* to comment on. Advisory groups can provide crucial advice on access, sampling, suitable methods and the policy and practice implications of findings. Sieber and Tolich (2013) suggest that two notorious studies from the early 1970s would have benefited from independent reference groups. Zimbardo's prison simulation, where students role played prison guards and prisoners and Milgram's study of participants' willingness to administer electric shocks to 'teach' learners who made mistakes both had 'quasi-reference groups' (Sieber and Tolich, 2013: 59) made up of colleagues and graduate students who, in the case of Milgram 'were more interested in his astonishing results than in the condition of the subjects'. They suggest that an independent reference group would have brought in more safeguards that would have stopped the experiments as soon as any harm to participants was suspected. In Zimbardo's case, Sieber and Tolich suggest that his dual role of principal investigator and prison superintendent prevented him from achieving the necessary distance from this form of fieldwork to make timely decisions about participant safety. Again, they suggest, an independent reference group would have helped.

In Example 5.2 a young people's advisory group contributed to important changes to a project when it was still at design stage.

| EXAMPLE 5.2 | The Impact of a Young People's Advisory Group on a Research Design |

The TLC project: Social Workers Talking and Listening to Children is a large qualitative project spanning the four UK nations (England, Scotland, Wales and Northern Ireland). The aims and research questions can be seen in Example 5.1. The design was developed slowly through a series of meetings between researchers from the four nations and some discussions with local social work teams about the focus and feasibility of various methods. When the project had begun to take shape, but before the funding application had been submitted, one of the team (Sally Holland) went to talk to an advisory group from a self-advocacy charity for young people who have lived in foster or residential care. The first stage of the project which proposed a researcher being embedded in a social work team and following social workers and observing them as they went about their work visiting families and communicating with children was fairly uncontroversial to the group. However, they did raise some objections to the proposed second stage, which was to video-record meetings between social workers and young people in foster or residential care and ask each participant to watch the video later and provide a commentary on successful and less successful communication in the meeting. The young advisers were worried that young people may find this exposing and uncomfortable. By the end of the meeting they had suggested several modifications to the design, all of which were taken up by the team. These included that young people could practise being videoed talking to someone else first, such as a friend, advocate or carer, they could control the 'on/off' switch on the video recorder, and for those who wished to take part, they may choose to be audio-recorded instead.

The team built in funding in the research bid to support further consultations with the group throughout the project and the team is convinced that the success of the application partly hinged on the consultations with practitioners and young people.

The TLC project: Social Workers Talking and Listening to Children is funded by the Economic and Social Research Council ES/K006134/1.

Action research can be seen as part of the spectrum of participative models in that it explicitly rejects a traditional distance between researchers and research subjects and between research and action (Gredig and Marsh, 2010). The approach tends towards the local and often aims to understand and act within one organisational setting rather than seek to make any wider claims (Marshall and Rossman, 2011). Action research explicitly seeks to promote *change* through cycles of research, reflection and action and may be seen as a particularly apt model for social work research which often has aims related to better understanding of social work practices and policies and improved experiences and services for service users. Writing about one action research project, Curran (2010: 821) suggests that there is 'a heritage of resistance and creativity in social work that can be built on to transform relations of vulnerability.'

Bradbury and Reason (2003: 156) provide a useful definition of action research when writing about its application in social work:

Action research is grounded in lived experience, developed in partnership, addresses significant problems, works with (rather than simply studies) people, develops new ways of seeing/interpreting the world (i.e., theory), and leaves infrastructure in its wake.

There is not just one 'action research' design and designs labelled as action research may be practically 'inseparable' from constructivist forms of qualitative inquiry, particularly those based on critical theories (Bradbury and Reason, 2003: 157). Participative Action Research (see Chapter Fourteen) has been particularly developed within a tradition of working with socially excluded groups but action research more broadly has been implemented with practitioners, policymakers and elite groups in the business world (Bradbury and Reason, 2003).

Two interesting examples of potential applications of action research in social work come from Sung-Chan and Yeung-Tsang (2008) who describe an action research project on a Master's programme for potential social work educators in China and Curran (2010) who carried out an action research project with social workers with disabled children in the UK. Sung-Chan and Yeung-Tsang note the challenges of integrating mainly Western social work theories and practices of reflection and critical inquiry with local norms and values in the emerging, and rapidly expanding field of social work education in China. They implemented a process of mapping the strengths and limitations of the existing practice approaches, collaboratively constructing a new practice framework and, alongside the graduate students, experimenting with this framework on concrete social problems, reflecting on its experimentation and refining the framework.

Curran (2010) worked within elements of a Foucauldian theoretical framework and held monthly meetings for eighteen months with five social workers. They deconstructed dominant discourses about listening to disabled children and set up a cycle of exploration, action and evaluation. The author herself evaluates the project as largely, although not wholly, a success:

> This action research project as a whole might initially be celebrated as a progression from medical/welfare discourses to more social discourses. Increasingly, the social workers authored themselves as creative and develop community-based forms of practice. 'Listening' was no longer marginalised as a matter of specialist communication technique ... (but it is) important to note that the discourse dynamics found in the problematisation (stage of the project) continued to be apparent in each stage and the project can not simply be read as a process of progress. (Curran, 2010: 816–17)

Qualitative longitudinal research

As with case study designs and action research designs, qualitative longitudinal research designs do not presuppose any particular data generation methods. In design terms it can imply a continuous study that takes place over a long period but is more often associated with longitudinal cohort research – returning to the same site or participants several times over a long period of time (Holland et al., 2006). It may be distinguished from life history approaches (see Chapter Eight) in that it is prospective rather than retrospective and follows people's lives over 'real time' (McLeod and Thomson, 2009). Many qualitative longitudinal research studies have involved different teams of researchers revisiting the subjects or communities of earlier studies, highlighting the need for careful recording of methods of data collection and analysis if some form of replicability is a goal.

In a scoping review Janet Holland and her colleagues consulted widely within the academic community and drew up a list of the sorts of substantive issues that may be investigated using qualitative longitudinal research methods. All of the resulting list could be relevant to social work so it is worth repeating it here:

- Study of the family and the life course, including: formation and dissolution of relationships; the negotiation of home/work responsibilities over time; the impact of key life events such as marriage, birth, parenting, divorce, redundancy, retirement, frailty, death of intimates, etc.
- Identity construction: any area of research concerned with identity construction and formation, change and process. This includes the identities of individuals but also communities, organisations, institutions, geographical locations and nations.
- The study of specific processes, such as: ageing; the onset of disability; the onset of chronic illness/addiction/problematic behaviours; social mobility.
- The careers of key groups about which little is known and/or who are difficult to define: young people at risk of offending; people who will progress into anti-social behaviour; problem gamblers.
- Organisational and community change, including: clinical action research; evaluation of community-based policy; tracing of changes in social efficacy within communities, institutions etc.
- Trends, including: changes in values and attitudes over time among key groups; changes in behaviour over time; the impact of cultural shifts and specific events on values and behaviour (Holland et al., 2006: 20).

A range of data collection methods can be used, including interviews, observation and diary-keeping and units of analysis can include individuals, groups, communities, organisations and time periods.

EXAMPLE 5.3 ⊢ **The Timescapes Projects**

This suite of projects was funded by the Economic and Social Research Council in the UK between 2007 and 2012. Its website explains its focus and aims:

> The broad aim was to scale up and promote Qualitative Longitudinal (QL) research, create an archive of data for preservation and sharing, and to demonstrate and encourage re-use of the resource. The Timescapes projects explored how personal and family relationships develop and change over time. Our researchers focused on relationships with significant others: parents, grandparents, siblings, children, partners, friends and lovers. We investigated how these relationships affected people's well-being and life chances, and considered the implications for the long term resourcing of families.

> Studies included following up first-time mothers who had taken part in interviews a few years previously. Research with older people aged over 75 explored their identities and relationships through interviews over an eighteen-month period while other family members kept diaries and took photographs.

> http://www.timescapes.leeds.ac.uk/about/

Mixing methods

Many studies use more than one form of data collection. In this section we discuss two types of mixing methods: using more than one form of qualitative data collection and using both qualitative and quantitative methods. There are a number of ways in which mixing methods might be viewed as enhancing studies. Some might try to 'triangulate' findings by assessing whether similar results are obtained from different approaches, as we explore in Chapter Eleven. A different aim is to attempt to enhance or extend findings by exploring different areas of a phenomenon using different methods. These two forms of mixing are simultaneous. A third approach is to carry out sequential mixing, where one research approach lays the foundations for the next (Morse, 1991).

Many qualitative research designs include more than one qualitative method and examples of such designs are included at several points in Chapters Seven to Ten. Common combinations in social work research include documentary analysis of case files alongside observation of social work practices and semi-structured interviews with practitioners and, where possible, service users. In using different qualitative methods, researchers have been able to explore how social work is accomplished differently in different spaces, such as in official records and in conversations with colleagues and supervisors (see, for example, Pithouse, 1998). Gabb (2009: 37) in her in-depth study of family relationships used mixed qualitative methods (including biographical–narrative interviews, emotion mapping, photographs and group interviews) to 'generate multidimensional material' and produce a more dynamic if messier account than one method might have generated.

Combining more than one qualitative method in one study is seen as enhancing and extending the study. The same argument might be made for including qualitative and quantitative methods in one study but this has proven more controversial as we describe next. It is not a new phenomenon (Johnson et al., 2007). Many early community studies used mixed methods such as surveys and life history interviews. However, debates about mixing have grown more heated in the last few decades and 'remain highly contested', with the most difficult area to resolve being the issue of whether methodological approaches based on fundamentally different philosophical understandings can ever be combined in one study (Greene et al., 2010). Flick notes that some qualitative researchers only mention quantitative research to show how it differs from qualitative research and 'there are still quite a number of quantitative researchers who ignore or reject the existence of qualitative methods' (Flick, 2007: 7). However, Flick also notes that for others, 'the practice of research is characterised by a more or less pragmatic eclecticism in using a variety of qualitative and quantitative methods according to what the research question needs in order to be answered' (ibid., p. 7).

In a widely cited article, Johnson et al. (2007) attempt to define mixed methods research, which they describe as the third major approach after qualitative and quantitative research. They surveyed 31 practitioners of mixed methods to ask for their definitions of mixed methods and tabulate their responses in the article. Most define it as combining quantitative and qualitative research, but some include within paradigm mixing such as using more than one form of qualitative research. Johnson and colleagues bring together the various definitions to produce the following, rather neutral definition:

> Mixed methods research is the type of research in which a researcher or team of researchers combines elements of qualitative and quantitative research approaches (e.g., use of qualitative and quantitative viewpoints, data collection, analysis, inference techniques) for the broad purposes of breadth and depth of understanding and corroboration … A mixed methods study would involve mixing within a single study; a mixed method programme would involve mixing within a programme of research and the mixing might occur across a closely related set of studies. (Johnson et al., 2007: 123)

Some of the original statements from the 31 researchers are somewhat punchier. One, Donna Mertens, advocates the use of mixed methods in transformative research that aims to further social justice. She suggests that including historical and contextual factors in a study can aid understanding of power relations. A few raise the difficulty of ignoring fundamental issues of paradigm mixing, related to epistemology (the nature of knowledge) and ontology (the nature of reality). Stephen Miller is quoted as stating that:

> (Mixed method research) must adhere to some form of 'minimal realist' ontology, where either social reality is 'One' but can be accessed by different methods separately or working in conjunction, or social reality is multiple in nature and can ONLY be accessed through mixed methods. Present day attempts to couch mixed methods within some broad notion of pragmatism are not satisfactory. (Miller, in Johnson et al., 1997: 120)

Margarete Sandelowski's definition meanwhile raises the issue that qualitative research does not simply fall under one paradigm (as is implied indeed in most of the Johnson et al. article) and that, for example, some qualitative research is approached under a largely positivist epistemology. She thus raises the question, 'So, if a researcher is doing grounded theory (positivist style) and an experiment (positivist influence), are any methods actually being mixed?' (Sandelowski, in Johnson et al., 1997:121).

A further criticism of mixed methods research is the tendency for quantitative methods to be the primary driver for studies, with qualitative methods being used to provide interesting vignettes to illustrate conclusions already drawn through qualitative research, or to help develop more relevant and successful quantitative measures (Hesse-Biber, 2010). Greene et al. (2010) provide two interesting examples of studies which appear to regard qualitative and quantitative methods as equally important means to answer the research aims. One study by Peter Sommerfeld of adults returning to society after a period of incarceration in prison or psychiatric hospital *measured* selected psychic functioning over a one-year period using quantitative 'real time monitoring' on hand-held devices. Regular reflecting interviews about the quantitative measures with participants revealed their understandings of why the measures showed critical phases of instability after release. A second study, led by Wendy Haight, explored the experiences of professionals, parents and children in families with methamphetamine-involved parents in rural Illinois. They aimed to measure the impact on children's development and develop suitable family interventions within an understanding of their complex socio-cultural contexts. Such studies, the authors argue, 'illustrate the power of mixed methods inquiry to meaningfully engage with the rich and full complexity of human action and interaction at both micro and macro levels' (Greene et al., 2010: 330).

Debates about mixing methods are excellent examples of the interconnectedness of the different elements of research design. Deciding how to collect data is intimately connected with the philosophical assumptions of the research design. Political considerations, such as a desire for research to be transformative, might override ontological debates. For some, mixing methods addresses issues of validity, through triangulation, with each method compensating for limitations in the other.

Secondary analysis

A final research design option to be considered in this chapter is secondary analysis of qualitative data. This includes data collected for another purpose such as government policy documents, inquiry reports, case records, court reports, newspaper articles, websites, internet chatrooms and tweets. Methods for exploring these are discussed in Chapter Nine. Here, we briefly consider a separate data source: archived qualitative data from previous studies.

Conducting further analysis of qualitative data has a number of advantages. Firstly it might be seen as ethical to reuse data, some of which has involved a great deal of participants' time and effort, but which may have only been partially analysed within the resources and timescale of the original project. Another ethical advantage is that it reduces the need to conduct primary data collection with potentially vulnerable populations, such as bereaved relatives or those receiving end-of-life care (Long-Sutehall et al., 2010). An economic imperative is that it serves to maximise the use of previously funded research and it may be possible to answer new research questions without the expense of collecting new data. Finally, secondary analysis is an excellent way for unfunded students to gain research skills and carry out valuable studies when they may lack finances, time and research access to be able to carry out primary research.

Secondary data analysis should have clear aims and research questions in the same way as a study involving primary data collection would have. Re-using data is not a straightforward or objective process. 'The original researcher's identity permeates the archive – in notes, selection of materials and so forth … the secondary analyst is not simply a miner of the archive, but brings to the analysis their research histories, emotional investments and vulnerabilities, co-producing meaning and re-contextualizing the research study' (McLeod and Thomson, 2009: 137). A reflexive awareness is needed of the relationships between the original researcher and the participants (as far as is discernible) and the secondary researcher and the data. We return to these issues in Chapter Twelve.

A particularly good source of qualitative data for secondary analysis is a data archive. An advantage of using data from an established data archive is that consent and anonymisation issues will usually have been checked by the archive keeper.

Table 5.2 Qualitative data archives

The UK Data Archive: http://www.data-archive.ac.uk)

The Council of European Social Science Data Archives: http://www.nsd.uib.no/cessda/home.html

The Inter-University consortium for political and social research: http://www.icpsr.umich.edu

The Mass Observation archive: http://www.massobs.org.uk/index.htm

The Timescapes archive: http://www.timescapes.leeds.ac.uk/archive/

Considerations of quality

Approaches to understanding quality in qualitative research differ according to the theoretical framework of the researcher. Largely realistic approaches will seek to establish reliability and validity using processes that have some comparison to quantitative methods. This can include using a range of methods, increased sample sizes and a constant awareness of conditions that may affect participants' responses (Franklin et al., 2010). Researchers working within a more interpretivist approach are, however, much less likely to be concerned about 'fraudulent data' or that '[l]ying and malingering may also come into play in some qualitative studies' (Frankin et al., 2010: 362) because their interest is in accounts, narratives and discourses rather than an objective truth.

For those attempting to improve the scientific credibility of their qualitative study, strategies for increasing internal validity can include aiming for prolonged engagement in the field, thus exploring emerging findings through further data collection. Having more than one researcher conducting coding and analysis can also be seen to strengthen validity. This might be viewed in a slightly mechanistic way – if more than one person comes to the same conclusions, independently, then they are more likely to be correct. Rather than simply seeing techniques such as double blind coding (with two or more researchers coding the same piece of data and checking they have comparable results) as increasing *accuracy*, we would suggest that a more important result is to increase reflexivity. Finding that your co-researcher has understood the data differently, and exploring that together, can be equally illuminating in uncovering assumptions and extending understanding. Another tactic used by some qualitative researchers is to attempt some form of 'respondent validation' (Bloor, 1978; and see the 'Taking it further' exercise in Chapter Ten), where analysis is presented to some or all research participants for comment. This can be very useful in a number of ways. Ethically, it can be rewarding for participants to know what has happened to the data they were involved in generating and to have an opportunity to comment on whether their views or actions have been portrayed fairly as they understand it. If research is being viewed within a largely positivist paradigm, then this technique can be seen as improving accuracy of the analysis. If research is being approached in a more interpretivist paradigm, and as a dialogic co-production between researcher and researched, then this stage can be viewed as a further stage in the cycle of data generation and analysis, rather than an attempt to make research more accurate or true.

Whatever the theoretical assumptions of the researcher, most would wish to conduct research that is credible to a range of audiences. Several authors have outlined some of the minimum requirements in the *reporting* of a qualitative research study to increase readers' ability to appraise the validity of the findings. Huberman and Miles (1994) and Altheide and Johnson (1994), although holding very different positions on validity, produced checklists suggesting elements that should be included in a research report in order that an informed reader may be able to draw conclusions about the relative strengths of the findings. These are listed below, with our own additions.

Table 5.3   Enabling appraisals of quality through qualitative research reporting

---

Funding and potential conflicts of interest

Sampling decisions made, both within and across cases

Access, approach and self-presentation

Instrumentation and data collection operations

Database summary: size, how produced

Software used, if any

Overview of analytic strategies followed

Inclusion of key data displays supporting main conclusions

Field relationships

Decisions on narrative style

Reflections on limitations of the research

Ethical approval and ethical decisions made and actions taken

---

It is worth mentioning two other writers who have slightly different views on quality in qualitative research. Blackstone (2001, in Shaw, 2010: 260) moves beyond issues of transparency and accuracy to suggest that research validity may be assessed under the following hierarchical dimensions, firmly headed up by relevance.

Relevance

Timeliness   Accessibility

Accuracy   Intepretability   Coherence

And Mason (2002) reminds us that critical, reflexive practice on the part of the researcher is the most important element for ensuring that qualitative research is of the highest quality. We should consider our own claims until we are confident that our conclusions are supported by careful, systematic data analysis.

Conclusion

In this chapter we have aimed to set a foundation for the next chapters about the 'doing' of research. These chapters cover research ethics, then the main data generation methods of enabling people to tell stories and share their perspectives through interviews, writing and visual methods, observing and exploring written documents. The data generation chapters are followed by analysis chapters, but, as we have emphasised in this chapter, anticipations of analysis should be part of the design from the outset. Research designs may be flexible and evolving in qualitative research, but even a design that is developing during fieldwork needs careful forethought.

Taking it further

A local self-advocacy group for adults with learning disabilities has approached your university department to ask for help in putting together a research proposal in response to a government call for social care research bids. The grants are expected to be about enough to employ a researcher full-time for a year and pay for some fieldwork costs. The group would like to research employment prospects for young adults with learning disabilities in the local community and particularly wish to explore the experiences of employed and unemployed young adults. The group would also like to lead the research with assistance from the university researchers.

Consider the following questions:

What could be a potential research aim, and what research questions might arise from that aim?

What are the strengths of the case for including group members in the research? What barriers or limitations might be present?

What might be the potential sources of data and how might you collect or generate data?

What would be the ethical implications of this emerging research design?

What would be your position as a researcher and what knowledge, experience, assumptions and values would you bring to this research area?

What else would you need to know before embarking on a research design?

Finally, how would you characterise your emergent research design? (e.g., 'a longitudinal, participative study using mixed qualitative methods', ' a narrative study using mobile methods within an emancipation framework', 'an action research study using peer interviews led by a self-advocacy group with support from xxx university', 'a cross-sectional, phenomenological study using semi-structured interviews and participant observation.')

SIX
Ethics in Qualitative Research

In this chapter we emphasise the ethical conduct of qualitative research as a preoccupation that precedes and succeeds institutional ethical approval processes. We pay particular attention to the micro-ethical issues of everyday research practice. After a general introduction about ethical principles and the relationship between ethical social work research and practice, we list key qualitative methods and the main ethical issues associated with each one. The chapter continues with a consideration of the central issues of beneficence and harm, researcher safety, consent, anonymity and confidentiality and the special case of internet research. The chapter concludes with an example of how research ethics can be relational, reciprocal and responsive in the field.

Ethics in qualitative social research has, over the years, provoked strong responses from many writers. Criticisms of the rise in regulation of research by formal groups known variously as institutional review boards and research ethics committees centre on concerns that a medical model of regulation has been inappropriately applied to the social sciences: 'the template of medical research and the stirring of moral panic seem to work against the benefits of qualitative methods' (van den Hoonaard, 2002: 176). Hammersley (2000b) asks whether methodology has become inappropriately 'ethicised' such that broader methodological questions get absorbed in a reductionist way into ethics. More broadly, Adler and Adler – in an essay that is perhaps too obviously cross in tone – ask whether the American Sociological Association has 'totally capitulated' to demands of institutional review boards, and sociologists have become 'the "stoolies" of law enforcement' (2002: 39). They fear a danger as a consequence that some areas of qualitative research will become off-limits, for example, studies of illegal activity or powerless groups, studying publicly accountable individuals or elites, and investigative/covert research.

In contrast, Sieber and Tolich (2013: 185), while concurring on the issue of medical ethics being sometimes applied over-clumsily to qualitative research, illustrate the need for institutional regulation with a series of examples of what they regard as unethical, under-regulated research. These include Venkatesh's book based on ethnographic research, *Gang-leader for a Day*, and some examples of autoethnography: 'Ethically, autoethnography without IRB (Institutional Review Board) oversight has been a failure' (p. 185). Our position is similar in that we perceive benefits in anticipating and planning for ethical issues through a process of institutional review, while recognising that ethical research conduct is an ongoing process from the early development stages to dissemination and beyond.

Ethics in research are concerned with protecting the interests and safety of participants and others who are, or could be, affected by the research (Hugman, 2010). These principles have been disaggregated in different ways. The most familiar approach to the field includes ensuring *informed consent* by participants and, if necessary, those who have responsibility for them. Other measures include protecting the *privacy* and *anonymity* of participants, and promoting honesty in terms of *avoiding deception* of participants or of the users of research through the dishonest use of data. *Confidentiality*, except when a vulnerable person is thought to be in danger of experiencing significant harm, is regarded as a core principle. In addition to protecting the interests of participants there is also a need to be aware of protecting the interests of researchers, institutions and funders. For example, there is an ethical imperative to spend research funds as they are intended and to avoid damage to the reputations of the researcher's institution and funder (ESRC, 2010). The researcher's safety, both physical and mental is also an important consideration.

A UK example of an ethics framework may prove a helpful point of reference at this point (Box 6.1).

Box 6.1   The Six Key Principles from the ESRC Framework for Research Ethics

1. Research should be designed, reviewed and undertaken to ensure integrity, quality and transparency.
2. Research staff and participants must normally be informed fully about the purpose, methods and intended possible uses of the research, what their participation in the research entails and what risks, if any, are involved.
3. The confidentiality of information supplied by research participants and the anonymity of respondents must be respected.
4. Research participants must take part voluntarily, free from any coercion.
5. Harm to research participants must be avoided in all instances.
6. The independence of research must be clear, and any conflicts of interest or partiality must be explicit.

Adapted from ESRC (2010: 3)

Qualitative research projects usually involve more intense and sustained interaction with research participants than quantitative designs, with the associated hazard that the 'friendly-façade' can risk becoming a 'pseudo-intimacy' (Shaw, 2008: 404). Data generation tools are less fixed than those used in quantitative designs and the research focus and design may evolve during the course of a project, thus making it almost impossible to fully anticipate all ethical issues that may arise. Qualitative research in social work can, therefore, bring specific challenges in the field of ethics, but we would argue that these are not intrinsically different from those in quantitative research, and neither more nor less weighty. We also distance ourselves from the claim sometimes made that qualitative research is somehow more ethical than quantitative research. No research strategies are especially privileged. To borrow a phrase from Ernest House, qualitative researchers do not live in a state of methodological grace (House, 1991a: 245). In this chapter we explore some of the specific ethical issues associated with qualitative research in social work.

Ethics in qualitative social work research

Ethics of practice and research

Butler's proposed code of ethics for social work research clearly links research and practice/professional ethics, and brings the implicit assumption that research and practice ethics are comparable. This stance is exemplified particularly in the second clause that states that social work research should aim to 'seek to empower service users, promote their welfare, and improve their access to economic and social capital on equal terms with other citizens' (Butler, 2002: 245). From his premise that social work research and practice occupy the same territory in terms of subjects, fields of interests and audiences, he concludes this means that the ethics of social work research should be 'compatible if not coterminous' with the ethics of the profession more generally. Professional codes can thus be inspected for how they provide a framework for considering the ethical conduct of research, including issues such as respect for the individual, protecting the vulnerable, preserving confidentiality and whistleblowing if abusive or illegal practice is observed. The USA's National Association of Social Workers' code is a case in point, as are the American Evaluation Association's 'Guiding Principles', which cover practice both disciplinary and professional in its nature.[1] The NASW social work practice code, for example, includes:

> Social workers engaged in evaluation or research should obtain voluntary and written informed consent from participants, when appropriate, without any implied or actual deprivation or penalty for refusal to participate; without undue

---

[1]http://www.socialworkers.org/pubs/code/code.asp http://www.eval.org/publications/guiding principles.asp

inducement to participate; and with due regard for participants' wellbeing, privacy, and dignity. Informed consent should include information about the nature, extent, and duration of the participation requested and disclosure of the risks and benefits of participation in the research.

In a considered reflection on this area, Ungar and Nicholl argue that there are similar goals for qualitative research and human services, i.e., 'to enhance the discursive power of silenced voices' (Ungar and Nicholl, 2002: 137). In ethics terms they argue we need supportive environments in which to nurture this discourse, while 'respecting the diversity of knowledge claims from marginalized groups' (ibid., p. 137). Describing themselves as 'affirmative postmodernists' (ibid., p. 148), they believe that the qualitative researcher and the social work practitioner both seek reflexivity (the researcher through choice of methods and the practitioner through choice of practice) and that 'qualitative research is an integral part of an anti-oppressive practice' (ibid., p. 151).

   This does not mean that the presence of a professional value base and code of conduct means that ethical decisions are therefore straightforward with an obvious 'right' way through difficulties. Social work, and hence social work research, is essentially a moral and political endeavour (Butler, 2002; Taylor and White, 2001) and there are many potential competing claims. Butler (2002) claims that in setting out an informal ethical framework for social work research he is not proposing an unshakeable code, but a platform from which to act and build, even while inviting criticism and debate.

Sensitive research

Much social work involves the exploration of sensitive topics. Responsive to, fragile, tactful, easily offended, difficult – all are possible synonyms for 'sensitive' (*Oxford Thesaurus*, 2005). We can readily recognise that research may be sensitive for *participants* or for the *researcher*; it may be ethically sensitive, or socially controversial. The very expression, 'doing sensitive research' conveys through its studied ambiguity that it is impossible to disentangle ideas of being sensitive *to* something (e.g., responsive, gender sensitive, and tactful) from the sensitivity *of* something (e.g., controversial or difficult). Social work research participants who tend to be stigmatised or marginalised in society pose issues about being sensitive *to*, while research topics such as child abuse and neglect, suicide, experiences of the care system and adoption, mental illness, domestic abuse and abuse of vulnerable adults are often sensitive in the second sense. There is surprisingly little literature that reflects on – rather than assumes – what counts as a sensitive topic for research. Even researchers wishing to say that power relations should be shifted in sensitive research (e.g., Campbell et al., 2009; Karnieli-Miller et al., 2009) tend to bring prior assumptions about which subjects will prove sensitive.

   For such research to be ethical it should, when directly involving vulnerable participants, have utility (for example, be likely to inform policy or practice), be carried out by competent individuals, use appropriate methods for data collection and ensure that support is in place for participants for whom taking part may have inadvertently caused distress. Researchers too may need support when collecting or analysing data on such topics. The challenging question becomes *how* researchers can involve participants in dialogues about sensitive matters in ethically sound ways. It may be so that the more personally relevant and sensitive a research topic is, the more challenging it is for the researcher to elicit the participant's experiences, feelings and thoughts, and thus the need to address ethical issues comes to the fore. General ethical obligations are made more demanding if one accepts the argument that the researcher cannot sidestep an obligation to contribute to the wider good (Bogolub, 2010).

Ethics and research methods

Table 6.1 highlights some of the ethical issues that may arise with specific forms of data collection. Some ethical issues are fairly generic across research designs – such as the need to ensure informed consent and handle data securely, but some methods do give rise to specific issues. The individual data generation methods are discussed in Chapters Seven to Ten, but we have summarised them here. In Chapter Fourteen we include a section on ethical issues associated with participatory approaches.

Table 6.1 Data generation methods and specific associated ethical concerns

Data generation method	Specific ethical issues arising
Individual interviews	– Participant may be distressed during or after the interview
	– Unexpected presence of others
	– Researcher safety
	– Breaching confidentiality/whistleblowing if harm reported
	Field example: Swain et al. (1998) 'Public research, private concerns: Ethical issues in the use of open-ended interviews with people who have learning difficulties', *Disability & Society*, 13(1): 21–36.
Group interviews	– Impossible to guarantee that all participants will maintain confidentiality
	– Over-disclosure of personal information that is later regretted
	– Group members may use abusive or discriminatory language or behaviour to other participants.
	– Need to consider cultural appropriateness including language issues and potential need for single sex groups.
	Field example: Culley, L., Hudson, N. and Rapport, F. (2007) 'Using focus groups with minority ethnic communities: Researching infertility in British South Asian communities', *Qualitative Health Research*, 17(1): 102–112.

(Continued)

Table 6.1   (Continued)

Data generation method	Specific ethical issues arising
Participant observation and ethnography	- Covert/overt presence of researcher
	- Gaining and maintaining informed consent
	- Anonymising sites and individuals
	- Breaching confidentiality/whistleblowing if harm observed
	- Reporting/ignoring criminal activity
	- Researcher safety
	Field example: Higgs et al. (2006) 'Engagement, reciprocity and advocacy: Ethical harm reduction practice in research with injecting drug users', *Drug and Alcohol Review*, 25(5): 419–423.
Documents	- Gaining consent – who owns the information?
	- Anonymising records and safe data handling
	Field example: Hayes, D. and Devaney, J. (2004) 'Accessing social work case files for research purposes: Some issues and problems', *Qualitative Social Work*, 3(3): 313–333.
Visual materials	- Gaining consent – especially if participants are using cameras independently (unwitting inclusion of non-participants)
	- Data storage – how long should images of people be kept? (especially children)
	- Dissemination – when can identifying images be shown?
	- Copyright and ownership of materials
	Field example: Castleden, H., Garvin, T. and Huu-ay-aht First Nation (2008) 'Modifying photovoice for community-based participatory Indigenous research', *Social Science and Medicine*, 66(6): 1393–1405.
Internet-based research	- Gaining informed consent (e.g., from children who may be accessing the internet independently of their parents or guardians)
	- Covert/overt research (e.g., taking part in discussion boards as a researcher)
	Field example: Willis, P. (2012) 'Talking sexuality online: Technical, methodological and ethical considerations of online research with sexual minority youth', *Qualitative Social Work*, 11(2): 141–155.

The ethical issues highlighted above are now considered thematically in sections on beneficence and risk to participants and researchers, consent, confidentiality and anonymity, data handling and dissemination.

Beneficence and harm to research participants

Most social work research will involve service users directly, or indirectly through records. Almost by definition, most service users can be classified as vulnerable in some way and at the very least will lack in power in comparison to researchers and institutions. Some will face multiple vulnerabilities in terms of having the capacity to freely choose whether to take part in research, including living with one or more of the following: being resident in a secure environment, being involved with social services on an involuntary capacity, living with intellectual impairments, mental illness or degenerative illnesses, being young, having illegal or uncertain residency in the nation state, being dependent on drugs or alcohol or having sensory impairments.

Institutional boards that review ethics applications, funders, research supervisors, gatekeepers and participants themselves will wish to know how the researcher will minimise potential harm to those who take part in a study. For example they could be excluded – or believe they are at risk of exclusion – from a service because the service was being offered on condition that recipients take part in a research project. They might make the researcher aware that they were breaking the law or harming someone else and the researcher may feel ethically compelled to act on this knowledge. Harm could be experienced by a group, for example, members of a marginalised population that felt they were misrepresented in a research study, or where culturally inappropriate methods were deployed (Castleden et al., 2008). They could experience harm to their reputation or feelings if confidentiality was breached. For example, following a focus group, a member of the group might share with others something personal they learned about another in the group. Physical harm could result from someone already being in a situation of violence, perhaps domestic abuse or gang-related, and being thought by another to have given away information to a researcher (Ellsberg and Heise, 2002). Finally, participants may experience harm because the research method had caused them to revisit or explore difficult emotions and experiences. This last potential harm is particularly pertinent to qualitative research in social work.

In social work, researchers often use methods that promote the in-depth exploration of experiences and feelings. Swain et al. (1998) argue that in some cases the beneficial effects of obtaining rich data that illuminate understanding for a wider audience may be outweighed by the potential for harm to an individual. They note that skilled interviewers, using techniques such as limited self-disclosure to make connections with the participant, may in fact encourage more disclosure by the participant than they might otherwise have made.

Despite these risks, it can be argued that taking part in research can be beneficial for participants, as well as the more common motivation of benefit to the wider community of service recipients. It is common for participants who have had difficult or even abusive experiences to express a motivation for taking part in research in the hope that it will help others by educating service providers or the public at large (Scott, 1998; Swain et al., 1998). As Scott (1998: 4.4) writes about the expectations of her interviewees who were survivors of ritual abuse,

> Knowing that the media, legal and psychiatric systems largely characterised them as unreliable witnesses to their own experiences, they were hopeful that 'being researched' could transform their experiential knowledge into legitimate academic discourse.

Individual benefits include effects such as satisfaction in knowing that one's experiences are valued and of interest and even the possibility of building new self-insights in the co-construction of knowledge alongside the interviewer (Holstein and Gubrium, 1995). Nonetheless, Murphy and Dingwall (2001) caution against assumptions such as that increased self-knowledge is beneficial (it could lead to dissatisfaction with one's living arrangements, for example) or that emotions reported immediately after an interview will be stable or long lasting. These authors remind us to avoid simplistic assumptions about either harm or beneficence from qualitative research.

Researcher safety

Bloor et al. (2007) conducted an inquiry into researcher safety in qualitative research, comprising a literature review, submissions by researchers on a website, focus groups with researchers and a discussion of interim findings at an academic research methods conference. The authors highlight the predominance of emotional risks over physical risks in the literature and in the researcher postings on their website (although there are instances of injury or even, rarely, death) and the gendered risks of harassment associated with women researchers in predominantly or solely male environments. Researchers' accounts about unease concerning their physical safety are more common than accounts of actual harm.

Even researchers who are experienced practitioners may find aspects of fieldwork distressing. In our experience, some research methods, such as life-history interviews and diary-keeping, may provide more in-depth information than is commonly provided in a social work encounter. It is relatively uncommon for practitioners, other than therapists, to encourage service recipients to talk relatively uninterrupted for an hour or more. Therefore, even researchers who are also experienced practitioners may find the extended and in-depth accounts in qualitative research distressing. It may be upsetting, too, to immerse oneself in reading secondary data. Fincham et al. (2008) have written about the distress caused by reading coroner's records about suicide cases and Moran-Ellis (1997: 181) has written about her 'pain by proxy' when hearing about pain suffered by abused children discussed in interviews with practitioners.

EXAMPLE 6.1 — **Emotional Risk**

Sara Scott describes her journey through her doctoral research which involved life history interviews with survivors of ritual abuse. The research was conducted in a period in the UK when scepticism about the existence of such abuse had reached a peak and Scott and her interviewees were engaging with this disbelief at a number of levels. Some interviewees were reluctant to discuss certain aspects, perhaps due to a fear of disbelief, and Scott's own emotional response was made more complex by her personal experience as carer of a teenage survivor of such abuse.

'Each interview was a personal encounter that I relived in slow replay in the course of transcription. As a counsellor and carer I had worked with such traumatic material before, but the sheer quantity of stories in the research process created a high level of stress. I had dreams about dying, and dreams in which I learned that none of my interviewees had told me the truth. Staying in an unfamiliar house after one interview I walked in my sleep for the first time in my life, and during the weeks of transcription I endured stomach cramps and nausea on a regular basis ... My research diary during this period records my own struggles with disbelief which ranged from wanting not to believe: "Who would want to believe this stuff? Have it in their consciousness? What does this knowledge do to you?" (Research diary 3/7/96) to anxiety about the truth status of ritual abuse accounts: "What if they're right I keep thinking, the False Memory lot, the Moral Panic lot ... it's all an elaborate fantasy ..."' (Research diary 28/8/96)

Perhaps surprisingly, Scott continues,

Odd though it may sound, it was questions of epistemological grounding rather than of infant sacrifices that kept me awake at night.

She was concerned about the relationship between seeking 'real' knowledge about the highly contested phenomenon of ritual abuse and understanding her interviewees' accounts as narrative productions. She found some epistemological relief in Hammersley's (1992) 'subtle realism' approach but does not describe how she found relief from her nightmares and physical symptoms of stress.

Scott, S. (1998) 'Here be dragons: researching the unbelievable, hearing the unthinkable. A feminist sociologist in uncharted territory', *Sociological Research Online*, 3(3) http:// www.socresonline.org.uk/3/3/1.html

Scott, S. (2001) *The Politics and Experience of Ritual Abuse: Beyond Disbelief*. Buckingham: Open University Press.

Researcher safety can be planned for in a number of proactive ways. Physical risks can be lowered through the avoidance of lone working if risks are thought to be high. Most fieldworkers will need to have a clear system of ensuring that someone on their team knows where they are conducting fieldwork and is informed when they have returned safely. Supervisors and colleagues can ensure that fieldworkers feel confident to not enter or leave a situation if they perceive risks. Most workplaces, including universities, will have lone worker policies that can be followed. As ever with ethical conduct there is a need to balance sensible anticipation of risk against a level of risk aversion that may prevent some research taking place. One of us has experience of having to explain to research ethics committees why research interviews *should* take place in service recipients' homes or a place of their choosing, rather than providers' offices, even if the latter might appear less risky.

Emotional risks might be lowered by ensuring space for debriefs after data collection, transcription or analysis. Lone workers who report that they are physically safe after a fieldwork episode might also be given the opportunity to discuss how they are feeling. In some studies, it is predictable that researchers will be encountering difficult emotional territory, such as Corden and colleagues' study with bereaved parents (2005). They set up a model of group psychotherapy to support the research team.

Informed and ongoing consent

In any research, except the rare occasions where covert research is justifiable, researchers are required to ensure that participants' consent to become involved in research, or for their personal data to be included (from files, for example), is freely given. They need to understand what the implications are if they take part in the research and should suffer no adverse affects (such as being excluded from services) if they refuse to take part. Involving advisers such as service user and carer groups in the design of information for participants is a good way of getting the tone and level right.

House (1980) set out rules for negotiating a fair evaluation agreement in which *all* participants should meet the demanding conditions that they:

- Not be coerced.
- Be able to argue their position.
- Accept the terms under which the agreement is reached.
- Negotiate. This is not simply 'a coincidence among individual choices'. (p. 165)
- Not pay excessive attention to one's own interests.
- Adopt an agreement that affects all equally.
- Select a policy for evaluation that is in the interests of the group to which it applies.
- Have equal and full information on relevant facts.
- Avoid undue risk to participants arising from incompetent and arbitrary evaluations.

House defended this reformist position in response to critics who suggested he was biased to the disadvantaged, saying 'It seems to me that making certain the interests of the disadvantaged are represented and seriously considered is not being biased, though it is certainly more egalitarian than most current practice' (House, 1991a: 241–2).

Some claim that ethical regulators' over-cautious approach to consent stifles less conventional forms. In a written style unusual for a peer-reviewed academic journal, Rambo (2007) outlines her struggle to gain her institution's ethical approval for her to publish a peer-reviewed and accepted article which constituted an auto-ethnographic account of her own childhood sexual abuse and her intimate relationship with a male student.

> Ultimately, the key determinations ... turned on the interpretations of a nine-person committee trying to enact their identities as academics, located inside a system of evaluative discourse, that does not match the contingencies of autoethnography, nor ethnography in general. (Rambo, 2007: 365)

Rambo, as signalled in the opening page of this chapter, is not the only qualitative researcher to have claimed that Institutional Review Boards do not understand the tenets of qualitative research and therefore put unreasonable barriers in its way. Boden et al. (2009), for example, claim that committees are part of a shift in power from the researcher to new centralised, ethical bureaucracies. Nonetheless, despite the negative responses from boards that some qualitative researchers undoubtedly have experienced, we would argue ethical review enables, indeed compels, research teams to engage in anticipatory reflections on the type of moral and ethical 'important moments' (Guillemin and Gillam, 2004) that may occur in the field, including consideration of how competing rights and responsibilities claims may be worked through.

However, consent does not just involve a once and for all negotiation and in qualitative projects it will often be necessary to negotiate consent on an ongoing basis, particularly when there is more than one fieldwork encounter (Guillemin and Gillam, 2004). Participant observation and participatory and longitudinal designs particularly demand ongoing consent (see Chapter Fourteen for further discussion of ethics and participatory approaches). The case example that follows incorporated all three of those elements in its design, as well as including further potential ethical issues of group working with vulnerable young people and the use of visual methods.

EXAMPLE 6.2 — **Consent and 'Becoming Participant'**

Emma Renold and colleagues conducted a participatory, multimedia longitudinal research project with young people living in foster, kinship and residential care, called Extraordinary Lives. The project was funded to explore methodological issues and one of the key research questions concerned the ethics of longitudinal, participative research. Young people were invited to take part in a project to explore their everyday experiences and identities and were encouraged to choose their own individual research questions. Nine young people chose to pursue individual biographical projects using methods such as diary-keeping, collage-making, photography, video, mobile interviews and group conversations. The group met fortnightly for a year and young people also generated data independently between meetings and in individual research meetings with members of the research team.

In their paper about how consent was actively negotiated throughout the project, Renold and colleagues began by highlighting the 'ethico-political' (2008: 431) tensions at play in researching with this group of young people. On the one hand, there was a political impetus to bring forward a different understanding of these young people's everyday lives that avoided framing them in terms of social problems. On the other hand, there was a risk of scrutinising yet again a group that was already subject to much official 'gaze'. The research team hoped to counter the latter point through the research design that attempted to enable the young people to seize some control of the research design.

As with any project involving looked after children, gaining initial access and consent was a complex process (Munro et al., 2005). Ironically, after weeks of preparation of carefully constructed information leaflets and a DVD, young people and their carers were largely uninterested in consent *materials* prior to the research beginning. Although formal consent procedures were completed prior to fieldwork commencing, the research team considered

(Continued)

(Continued)

that active consent was negotiated incrementally as questions arose through the *doing* of the research. In this small, longitudinal project, young people individually developed their own consent procedures. One research participant edited and deleted sections of her video diaries before showing them to the research team. Another would record a research conversation, then listen to it back and make a decision about whether it could be used in the research or not. One boy, having shown doubts throughout the project about whether he was willing for data about him to be used in the research or not, eventually made a judgement that the researchers could write about his forms of participation in the project, but not about his life experiences.

Neither the young participants, *nor the researchers*, knew fully what consent involved at the start of the project. The participatory design meant that the research methods were fluid and the implications of participation not fully predictable. The young people were thus constantly in a state of 'becoming participant', with no absolute end to the consent process. The paper concludes with a listing of some of the techniques and practices used by the research team in this project to ensure that consent was actively worked with throughout the project:

    Rendering participation visible throughout – embedding 'ethical talk' in everyday fieldwork relations

    Always in-negotiation – recognising that participation is a travelling concept and demands a blurring of the hierarchical binary of consent as give (active) and take (passive)

    Responsive and directive – considering the constraints and possibilities of the ways in which 'ethical talk/behaviour' is directly sought or responded to 'in the moment'

    Developing personalised ethical protocols – working out and working with individualised cultures of participation and communication

    Beyond linearity – resisting the singularity of informed consent as one-off or renewed practice towards the ebb and flow of participation – non-participation

    Reflexive mapping of ethical 'speed bumps' – cyclical and reflexive ethics-in-practice before, during and beyond the fieldwork period.

Renold, E., Holland, S., Ross, N.J. and Hillman, A. (2008) 'Becoming participant: problematising "informed consent" in participatory research with young people in care', *Qualitative Social Work*, 7(4): 427–447.

The Extraordinary Lives case study, as others have found (Swain et al., 1998) illustrates some key problems with informed consent. Firstly, how can someone with no experience of academic research, its products and methods realistically be helped to understand the full implications of their participation without taking them through a very lengthy, detailed and possibly quite boring process? As was seen in the case study above, despite the researchers' best efforts, the young people were generally uninterested in the formal consent process, at least at the start of the project. Equally, with open-ended qualitative projects, particularly those designed to be partly shaped by the participants, neither the researcher nor the participant can fully anticipate the implications of consenting to take part.

> We might like to secure consent that is informed, but we know we can't always inform because we don't always know. We would like to protect personal privacy and guarantee confidentiality, but we know we cannot always fulfil such guarantees. We would like to be candid, but sometimes candour is inappropriate. We do not like to think of ourselves as using others as a means to our own professional ends, but if we embark upon a research study that we conceptualise, direct and write, we virtually assure that we will use others for our purposes. (Eisner, 1991: 225–6)

Consent needs to be negotiated throughout the process of research, as the nature of the research becomes clearer to participant and researcher. It will not be formal and written at every stage but at the very least, for one-off research encounters, would include a reiteration at the end of the interview or observation about what is going to happen to the data and the participant's rights to withdraw some or all of the data pertaining to them. In longitudinal research studies participants may need to be reminded that they are engaged in research and may be shown some examples of research products, such as PowerPoint presentations, research reports or papers to show how their data are being used. Davies and Kelly (1976) provide an early example of the difficulties of negotiating informed consent over a period of time. They embarked on ethnographic research in a radical youth project in Manchester in northern England. The nature of the project meant that there was a high turnover of young people using the project and newcomers did not necessarily realise that the researcher, who took part in activities in the manner of a worker, was observing and analysing the relationships and cultures in the organisation. The first report was shared with staff and young people. A group of young people were furious about how they had been described and their objections led to the data generation method changing to interviews. Although this study was conducted before formal ethical regulation forced overt consideration of such issues in the research process, the authors demonstrate a high degree of sensitivity and reflexivity on issues of consent and research relationships over time.

Some participants may not be able to give informed consent due to their young age, learning disability, dementia or mental ill-health. The age of consent for research is related to, but not necessarily the same as, the legal definition of childhood in many jurisdictions, and in the USA age limits are set at State rather than Federal level (US Department of Health and Human Services, 2012). In the UK, children may give consent in their own right at any age if they are considered to have sufficient understanding of the implications of consent (Heath et al., 2007). Although competence is not age-based, most research ethics committees will require parental consent for children under the age of 16. It is important to note that when parental consent is required by an institution or research ethics committee, children who are competent should also be asked, independently, to give active consent (Shaw et al., 2011). For children who are not regarded as having sufficient capacity to give consent in their own right, a parent or other person with parental responsibility will be asked to consent on their behalf. It is then generally assumed that the researcher will seek assent from the child by, for example, explaining who they are and checking that the child is comfortable with them observing or asking questions and withdrawing if the child expresses dissatisfaction with their presence either verbally or non-verbally. As Cocks (2006: 258) suggests, when discussing assent and research with disabled children,

> Seeking assent requires the researcher to remain constantly vigilant to the responses of the child at all times. It is not something gained at the beginning of the research, then put aside. It requires time and constant effort on the part of researchers, who need to attune themselves to the child's unique communication in order to know when to remove themselves.

EXAMPLE 6.3 — **Assent**

Nick Pike, in doctoral work that involved ethnographic observation of a residential special school for young people with complex and profound learning disabilities, explains how he down-graded his expectations of active assent from the largely non-verbal teenagers, to one where he continued his observations as long as the young people were not showing distress at his presence. Here are some extracts from field notes:

> As far as the young people are concerned, it is not clear to me that any of them are really aware of my presence. Three (Sandy, Amarjeet and Ryan) have come up close to me, and two (Sandy and Amarjeet) have briefly touched me, but there was no sense of any attempt to communicate with me. I got a couple of good hard slaps from Amadi during a period of disturbed behaviour, but I had no sensation that this was targeted and personal; I was merely an object in the way.

> ... Amadi spent a lot of time 'exploring' me this morning. ... Frequently, he would look carefully at my face (but without making proper eye contact). On a number of occasions, he picked up my right hand and held it to his nose, sniffing gently. Sometimes he would stroke my hand and others press one of my fingers between his thumb and forefinger. I responded by gently stroking his head, rubbing his hand and patting his shoulder. At one point, he came and stood with his head against my armpit before moving away ...

> At one point, three members of staff were engaged holding one young man back from getting at the screen and I found myself on my own with Bryn. He reached for my left hand and intertwined his hands around mine, as I had seen him do with other staff. After a while, he removed his hand and began to explore my watch (which I removed), my glasses (ditto) and my 'visitor' badge. Whilst it would be hard to say that he was making any kind of a relationship with me, I felt that he had noticed me and was happy to be sitting with me.

Pike (2012: 84–85)

The participants in Pike's study cannot give active informed consent and their inclusion in a study is ethically complicated. Legally, the inclusion of people who lack capacity in research should give added value to the potential outcomes (Department for Constitutional Affairs, 2007). In other words, if the same information could be found out by only including carers, family or professionals then it should not include the people who lack capacity. Clearly an ethnographic study, such as Pike's (2012) study of care relations in a residential school, would lose much of its value if it did not include observations of relationships with the recipients of care. Alternative approaches such as interviews with the staff and examination of records would have produced very different data.

Informed consent is predicated on the basis that the participant not only has competence to consent but also that they are able to express their own agency in the social context (Heath et al., 2007). In some settings, participants' agency will be curtailed such as in schools and secure settings. In schools, data generation tasks are sometimes set up as a classroom activity and children and young people as 'schooled subjects' are very likely to conform and complete the task, whether it be completing a survey, taking part in a discussion or writing a story (Denscombe and Aubrook, 1992). Research ethics committees will want to know how realistic it is for young people to opt out of research and how any opting out will be organised. In secure settings such as prisons and locked psychiatric wards, participants are potentially even more vulnerable to actual or perceived coercion and again it will be important for researchers to consider in advance how they will ensure that consent to take part in research is freely given. Nonetheless, despite the potential concerns, a study by Edens and Epstein (2011) of over 600 inmates of prisons and psychiatric correctional facilities in Texas and Florida found a surprisingly low level of reported coercive influences on their ability to give informed consent to participate in research, while beneficial effects, such as improved self-reported mood levels, have been reported elsewhere (Rivlin et al., 2012).

These ethics issues arising from particular cultures suggest the need to consider ethics in non-western cultures. We have gained understanding of this from working with doctoral students. For example, there are cultures where a strong social hierarchy means people will feel some expectation or perhaps social pressure to answer in accord with what their 'superiors' may have said elsewhere in the project, or may say were they to read the research report. There are also issues of societies where reciprocity means ethics work on an informal and sometimes quid pro quo basis. Mulder and her colleagues (2000) were a culturally diverse team who conducted research with rural women in Bolivia. They noted that in this setting collective consent appeared to be more appropriate than individual consent, the seeking of which was reported as implying indifference as to whether some took part or not. Similarly the outlining of potential risks had the potential of implying that the researcher was willing such evils to happen. These authors resist any simple dichotomising of participants in developing countries as vulnerable and marginalised and researchers as powerful and suggest the need for self-reflection of cultural and ethnic locations by researchers in all contexts. They comment that:

Informed consent cannot be reduced to the subject's individual will. Custom, tradition, social and cultural obligations, prestige, access to material and symbolic resources, and past experiences can all powerfully affect personal and collective decisions. (Mulder et al., 2000: 106)

Confidentiality and anonymity

Questions of confidentiality and anonymisation are typically treated in fairly conventional ways in qualitative research in social work. For example, participants will be assured that their data will be kept confidential, if within certain limits. One such limit is that if a researcher becomes aware that a vulnerable person (child or adult) is at risk of significant harm, then confidentiality will be breached and protection for that person sought. A further limit might be if the participant discloses knowledge of a serious crime, particularly violent crime, or an act of terrorism. In terms of child or adult protection, either the researcher's institution, or the institution in which they are researching, will have procedures to follow if harm is suspected. These issues are not, of course, always clear-cut and many researchers will feel the need to discuss their concerns first with a supervisor or manager before acting formally.

Confidentiality is generally managed through the anonymisation of data. This is achieved by not only changing all names and addresses, but also other potentially identifying information as very specific life circumstances. Sometimes it will be necessary to exclude a particularly interesting or pertinent case or quotation from a publication because it is simply too identifiable. The use of case studies within publications, commonly used to illustrate arguments, can also be identifiable. In single settings, as are commonly used in qualitative research, it may be necessary to remind participants that absolute anonymisation may be impossible (Murphy and Dingwall, 2001). The case study from Susan Eisenhandler's work illustrates how issues of this kind may not be as straightforward as textbook prescriptions sometimes suggest.

EXAMPLE 6.4	**Anonymity in a Study of Older People and Minority Faiths**

Susan Eisenhandler (2008) has written about her research with older people in four non-Western faith groups in the state of Connecticut. The qualitative design involved interviews with small numbers of participants in each of the groups in urban areas of the state, and the work followed previous studies of the role of religion in later life by the same research team. Following exploratory interviews with religious leaders the study was abandoned because the authors realised that socio-spatial aspects of the communities meant that the type of rich description likely in the study outputs would mean that insiders might be able to identify individuals. Heightened tensions between communities following a highly publicised incident in another state might lead to risk or discomfort for participants. The author writes that the rich

> potential of qualitative methods, which she calls 'the rose' for this topic were accompanied by the 'thorn' of the difficulty of protecting privacy in a study with a very small sample.
>
> Eisenhandler, S.A. (2008) 'The rose and the thorn: Some ethical dilemmas in a qualitative study of older adults', *Journal of Religion, Spirituality & Aging*, 20(1–2): 63–76.

Although anonymisation has become a routine part of social research ethics, Tilley and Woodthorpe (2011) make the case for a re-examination of this norm for twenty-first century research. They note that participants or funders of research may wish for some identification of place or even individual participants. They argue that an insistence on anonymisation can undermine participants' autonomy, particularly in more participatory forms of research. They also note that increased dissemination on the internet can make identification easier and that anonymisation should not be seen as synonymous with maintaining confidentiality.

Such contemporary debates about anonymisation are sharply focused in the increased tendency to archive research data for secondary analysis by approved researchers (see Chapter Five). Ideally, participants will be informed of this possibility when considering whether to take part in the research. Anonymity of the dataset, except where participants have fully consented to being identified, becomes more vital than ever and concerns about this can lead to resistance from researchers to the concept of archiving or sharing datasets. However, Van den Eynden et al. (2011) argue that, as long as anonymisation is thorough, archiving meets the spirit and the letter of ethical codes due to provisions that allow particularly sensitive data to be excluded from datasets.

Ethics in digital research

Digital research is an important area because its rapid growth and change means that researchers and institutions need to come to grips with changing ethical issues as new technologies, and use of those by the general public, emerge. While there are ethical continuities with more conventional research, research about or using the internet throws up additional challenges relating to all of the ethical areas considered so far in this chapter. For example, direct quotes from a digital source may be instantly traced back to their original site, whether blog, chatroom or Twitter account, even if anonymised in a research paper or thesis. There are special difficulties surrounding the ethics of consent. There are four key questions. First, can we treat all information taken from the internet as public information? We think probably not, although this is far from agreed. Waruszynski (2002) and Kitchen (2002) give contrary answers. Second, are we free to exploit fully the results to which we have unfettered access? How does informed consent relate, for example, to material taken from chatrooms, or from listservs? Are there special issues of group consent? How can these be dealt with, assuming it is a real problem? Third, when it comes to interpretation and dissemination, who owns the story? We are not convinced that the same standards ought to apply to, for example, the material on a moderated discussion list or newsgroups and, say, a breast cancer survivors' list. Fourth, research of this kind increasingly uses technologies to do the research that in other contexts may be criticised as intrusive.

We recommend the thoughtful guidelines published by the Association of Internet Researchers Ethics Committee (Markham and Buchanan, 2012). They note the three main areas of consideration in internet-based research: defining whether research involves 'human subjects' (a usual threshold for ethical review), the contested nature of private/public digital spaces and, particularly in large 'anonymised' datasets, the digital connection between data and individuals. 'Although we as researchers might like straightforward answers to questions such as "Will capturing a person's Tweets cause them harm?" or "Is a blog a public or private space?" and we as authors of this document might like to supply answers, the uniqueness and almost endless range of specific situations defy attempts to universalize experience or define in advance what might constitute harmful research practice' (Markham and Buchanan, 2012: 7). This international group recommends a case-based approach rather than attempting to produce guidelines that may be applicable in all or most situations. They have produced a useful series of questions that those conducting research on the internet will need to consider before, during and after fieldwork, particularly within the field of social media.

Ethical research practice as reciprocal, relational and responsive

Ethics are not simply something we *apply to* research participants. In most research, particularly qualitative research, ethics are worked through as the project progresses with, through and sometimes *by* participants and gatekeepers (Renold et al., 2008). Despite any careful advance planning and processes, the micro-processes of ethics-in-action are worked out in practice. Relational aspects of this kind are shot through with issues of power differentials of the kind we have mentioned earlier. In the following case study, on-the-spot ethical decisions made by and with research participants in a study of parental substance misuse are illustrated.

| EXAMPLE 6.5 | **Research with Parents who Misuse Substances** |

In an evaluative study of an intervention for children for whom there are serious child protection concerns and who live with parents who misuse substances, the researcher, Annie Williams, conducted qualitative semi-structured interviews at home with parents, at an average of 6 years after they were referred to the intervention. The interviews centred on the impact of substance misuse on family life and of various attempts by helping agencies to intervene. Annie made very careful efforts to follow the procedures agreed with a university research ethics committee for ensuring confidentiality, informed consent and the safety of children, vulnerable adults and the researcher herself. Such regulatory, anticipatory aspects of research ethics can be associated with an ethic of justice (Held, 2006). Nonetheless, many ethical issues arose during the research, some of them difficult to anticipate, which for the team illustrated the potential association between ethics-in-the-field and some of the features of an ethic of care: attentiveness, trust and responsiveness (Held, 2006).

Attentiveness: the researcher needed to watch for clues about informed consent. For example, an agreement to participate but pretending not to hear the doorbell may be a passive refusal of consent. Similarly, attentiveness to signs of distress or a desire to change tack, led the researcher to suggest pausing or ending the interview.

Trust: as interviews progressed and participants relaxed some became prepared to give more difficult information (e.g., that the baby was in foster care and not 'out'). Others gained the confidence to ask certain information to be withdrawn from the study, or to ask to be referred for help.

Responsiveness: on-the-spot ethical decisions were made by participants as well as by the researcher. For example, more than one participant who had said it was fine for their teenagers to listen to the interview realised that the material was potentially distressing and asked the teenager to leave. Some appeared to take care of the researcher by following up an upsetting disclosure with a humorous addition to lighten the emotional atmosphere.

Overall, the experience of conducting this project emphasised to the team the *relational* aspects of ethical encounters (Tronto, 1994) and that rather than a set of procedures applied *to* participants *by* researchers, they are reciprocally developed in the field.

Holland, S., Williams, A. and Forrester, D. (2013) 'Navigating ethical moments when researching substance misuse with parents and their children', *Qualitative Research*. First published online 24 January 2013.

This case study cautions us against treating research ethics as a cut and dried set of practices, by prompting attention to the interweaving of ethics and morality – that 'welfare professionals have to be personal exponents of the values they presume to trade in professionally' (Clark, 2006: 76). Clark may be talking about social work practice, but his conclusion will stand for research.

Taking it further

If you have access to the following article please read it in full before answering the questions: Carol Rambo (2007) 'Handing IRB an unloaded gun', *Qualitative Inquiry*, 13(3): 353–367. In short, the author writes about how her attempts to publish an autoethnographic account of her relationship with a student in a peer reviewed journal was refused by her university Institutional Review Board on ethical grounds including harm to herself, harm to the student and harm to the institution. She writes:

No one on campus outside of the Police and Judicial Affairs knew the identity of 'Eric'. All records of the incident are sealed in an envelope in the Judicial

Affairs Office at the University of Memphis. The events represented in the manuscript occurred almost a decade ago. These facts, coupled with the reality that the chances of Eric picking up a copy of Deviant Behavior and recognising himself as the fictionalised character in the manuscript were remote, serve as evidence that the IRB's joint, collective, action regarding my manuscript was 'overkill'. As a result of their performance, I have been silenced. 'Eric', who was not offered a choice to speak, was silenced also. (Rambo, 2007: 365)

Do you think that autoethnography should be subject to ethical regulation in the same way as more conventional research with 'human subjects'?

Should other people who appear in autoethnographic accounts give their informed consent, even if anonymised?

What general ethical issues does this unusual case bring to the fore?

SEVEN
Asking Questions

This chapter introduces, compares and where appropriate contrasts question-asking forms of inquiry. As a form of inquiry, the interview involves:

- Eliciting and making meaning
- Accessing subjective meanings
- An understanding of the relationship between qualitative interviews and social work interviews
- Variations in interactional forms

Most of the main options when considering differences and distinctions in qualitative interviewing can be understood in terms of:

1. Variations in the structure of and participants in the interview.
2. Opportunities for various participant-led interview forms.
3. Adjuncts and complements to the interview.

We spend much of the chapter developing accounts and examples of these three issues.

In the following central part of the book we address elements of the 'doing' of qualitative social work research around the following four themes: questions, stories, location, and (mainly written) traces and deposits. We have taken these slightly general ways of expressing fieldwork methods intentionally. It matters that we step away from discrete choices of method to set them in a wider context. Qualitative research is not a single homogenous strategy, but a distinctive orientation that includes overlapping but very distinct fieldwork methods each of which is associated with different knowledge claims. By setting methods in these broader frameworks it suggests the fruitfulness of thinking of different qualitative methods as working together. This is not the same as riding the popular 'hobby horse' of calling for mixed methods as a default research approach, on the grounds that different methods always work in a cumulative, congruent manner to build knowledge. Our intention is to offer accounts of how methods work together in a more tensioned, question-raising way to enrich and widen understanding, rather than in a simple additive fashion.

There are, of course, other ways to cut the cake of qualitative fieldwork. Flick, for example (2006), distinguishes verbal methods (interviews, narratives, focus groups, etc.) from 'multi-focus data' (observation, documents, visual data, the internet, and so forth). Asking questions (this chapter) and telling stories (the following chapter) are linked, but we find it helpful to retain the distinction, partly because of the wealth of experience and literature on each theme.

Dingwall was lamenting a perceived trend in qualitative sociology when he complained that

> The dominant kind of qualitative study appears to be one in which the investigator carries out a bunch of semi-structured interviews which are then taped and transcribed. The results are thrown into a qualitative data management package and a few themes dragged out in a way that seems rather like what we used to call 'data dredging.' (Dingwall, 1997: 52)

The clearly implied criticism is well taken perhaps especially in applied fields where qualitative methods are borrowed and sometimes bowdlerised in instrumental fashion. Countering such tendencies, this chapter introduces, compares and where appropriate contrasts question-asking forms of inquiry. We address dimensions of varying structure; styles of talk; divergent researcher/participant relationships; and individual/group forms of inquiry. We consider social work writing on the similarities and differences between professional interviewing practice and research. We call attention to recent forms of asking questions, for example through visual methods, such as film and photography, and online forms of research. Finally, we will spend some time considering a few of the important and intriguing ranges of challenges and issues that qualitative interviewing in social work poses. While it is not possible to be exhaustive within a single chapter, we have aimed to be representative of the field, and thus provide a foundation with clear indications of the necessary superstructure for good research. We hope to destabilise the apparent assumption among social worker researchers and practitioners that they know how to interview and therefore can easily conduct research interviews.

Qualitative interviews have been given various designations:

- collaborative
- in-depth
- focused
- guided
- semi-structured
- open-ended
- dialogical

Rather than being interchangeable, these terms allude to important different issues. When we call an interview collaborative, dialogical or guided, we are drawing attention to the nature of the exchange relationship between researcher and participant. If we call an interview semi-structured or open-ended we are indicating the extent to which the categories of meaning are pre-shaped by the inquirer's own thinking. In-depth and focused refer to the relative importance of breadth and depth of understanding. These last two terms probably import other associations. 'Focused' is no doubt a reference back to the work of Patricia Kendall and Robert Merton some sixty years ago (Merton and Kendall, 1946) – a link that we consider briefly later in the chapter – whereas 'in-depth' may be a reference back to a period in the development of research where the association between research and therapy was closer than it is today. We have considered the importance of such connections in Chapter Three.

These are important concerns because they show how some of the central deliberations and developments in research methods have been carried out through proxy debates about the relative merits of different approaches to interviewing. Perhaps the single most influential trigger for these debates was Cicourel's germinal text on *Method and Measurement in Sociology* (Cicourel, 1964). Partly as a consequence, interviews increasingly have been seen as close to everyday interaction. Therefore there has, at least until recently (c.f. Hammersley and Gomm, 1997), been less concern with 'bias' or even with specialist skills. This view sees interview talk and emerging data as the product of local, collaborative interaction. To fully understand this we need to make a distinction between interview data as a *resource* (a source of data about the world) and interview data as a *topic* – e.g., as a social construction. A second major development in shaping how we view interviews has been decades of feminist work on unmasking and challenging the power imbalance between researchers and participants. Both of these developments figure through this chapter.

Forming the interview

These important influences make it difficult to generalise about qualitative interviews. Furthermore, much of what applies to interviewing is also true of other forms of qualitative research practice. In addition, a fascinating characteristic of the qualitative methods field is how debates about specific methods stand as proxies for discussions and sometimes arguments about the nature of qualitative work. Nowhere is this truer than for interviewing. As a consequence there is a huge literature, and major works can and have been devoted to this sole topic (e.g., Gubrium and Holstein, 2002). Nonetheless, it is possible to say *something* about the form and forming of interviews. 'Form' in this context as about what 'kind' or 'mode' of activity; 'forming' as the acts of both recognising and giving something a 'look' or 'shape'. We have several things to ask and say about the kind and shaping of qualitative interviews, although most of these observations recur elsewhere in the book:

1. Interviews involve both *eliciting* and *making* meaning of participants' lives and experience.
2. Qualitative interviews face the challenge of claiming to have access to peoples' subjective meanings.

3. When qualitative interviewing is undertaken for and in *social work* the professional and disciplinary orientation brings characteristic emphases to the various foci of inquiry.
4. Qualitative interviewing is not a homogenous or uniform enterprise, but includes varying interactional forms.
5. Given that different qualitative methods support different knowledge claims, it is important to be clear about the limits of the qualitative interview.

Eliciting and making meaning

We choose to interview when we want to 'gather contrasting and complementary talk in some theme or issue' (Rapley, 2004: 18). However, 'because the researcher is the instrument in semistructured or unstructured qualitative interviews, unique researcher attributes have the potential to influence the collection of empirical materials' (Pezalla et al., 2012: 166). This realisation that the researcher is an active respondent in the research process, and that 'ways in which the "how" of a given interview shapes the "what" that is produced' (ibid., p. 167) has placed ideas of interviewer reflexivity at the centre of fieldwork practice. Flick expresses the point clearly:

> Unlike quantitative research, qualitative methods take the researcher's communication as an explicit part of knowledge instead of deeming it an intervening variable. The subjectivity of the researcher *and* of those being studied becomes part of the research process. Researchers' reflections on their actions and observations in the field, their impressions, irritations, feelings and so on, become data in their own right .... (Flick, 2006: 16)

Qualitative interviews have often been compared to conversations. Is this helpful? In some ways yes, because it points to these issues of reflexivity and, as Pezalla and her colleagues illustrate, to the nature of what is happening in the interview. Appropriately understood and allowing for the variety of kinds of conversation, it cautions against a one-size-fits-all model for interviewing. But in other ways the comparison can be misleading. Despite the many instances where this is not so, we normally think of a conversation as one between equals. Qualitative interviews are often carried through *as if* the relationship is one of symmetrical equality, perhaps induced by the researcher as a means of gaining rapport and encouraging disclosure. But Packer (2011: 48–9) observes that, unlike for example a meeting of friends on the street:

- It is scheduled, not spontaneous.
- It often takes place between strangers.
- It is not between equals, and there is an asymmetry of power.
- An interview is conducted for a third party – for an audience.
- There is much in the literature about the stance the interviewer should take, most of which distinguishes it from everyday conversation.
- It is not about the here and now but typically about the past, or about something abstract.
- It aims to gather a certain kind of data that can thence be interpreted.

While we think this makes too much of things (how many conversations between friends, for example, carry a partly hidden agenda?), an undue comparison with conversations is paradoxical in the light of the importance often placed on representing the qualitative interviewer as a neutral facilitator, who seeks to facilitate without directing, by asking non-directive questions that are selectively followed up, while allowing the person interviewed to talk at length, in order to elicit detailed and comprehensive accounts. 'Such work is concerned to minimize the interviewer's presence, so that they become *neutral* (but interested) *observers*' (Rapley, 2004: 20).

Yet we should be clear just what is being said at this point – not so much that the interviewer *is* neutral, but that they are 'doing neutrality' as a means of eliciting the meanings participants give to their lives and experience. The interviewer, to quote Rapley again, writing about a particular researcher, 'is engaged in "neutral*istic*" conduct *but* he is not "being neutral" in any conventional sense' (ibid., p. 21).

Interviews do not only elicit some personal, tacit or hidden meaning. They also participate in making new meanings. Denzin, in talking of epiphanies in qualitative research (Denzin, 1989a: 71), includes episodes whose meanings are given in the reliving of the experience. Neander and Skott's work is a cogent and insightful example. Basing their analysis on eleven joint interviews with parents and identified 'important persons', they offer an incisive and upbeat account of families that have struggled with their relationships to their children, and who have identified people who have had a positive influence on the child. In their qualitative interviews with these 'important persons', who were from a range of professional backgrounds, new understandings emerge – mutually on the part of both parent and professional – which they express as new narratives of emerging trust, which overcome obstacles, replace old negative narratives. They conclude that utmost care should be taken to safeguard and nourish these unpredictable 'important meetings' where 'ordinary magic' may happen (Neander and Skott, 2006).

At this point the qualitative interviewer may find herself on the borders between fieldwork and analysis. One form this may take is when the researcher intentionally plans her fieldwork so that interviewing and analysis alternate (Wiseman, 1974). We return to this in the chapter on analysis. But in a more general way this borderline territory stems from 'how an interviewee crafts a way of *saying* to invite a way of *seeing*' (Packer, 2011: 9).

Accessing subjective meanings and the limits of the interview

This brings us briefly to our second and fifth points in this section. How is what is *said* related to what is *experienced*, to what is hidden inside, and what are the limits of qualitative interviews? Qualitative researchers always need to be circumspect when drawing conclusions about participants' experience. We have just noticed how interviewers sometimes encourage the participant to create meanings. If that is the case, does this mean that – rather than discovering subjective meanings – interviews form what we call subjectivity, as an effect of the interview? There are some ways in which qualitative interviews can mitigate the limitations of simply tapping people's perceptions. For example, it is often advantageous to press participants to offer recent and grounded instances. This is illustrated in the following chapter when we talk about life stories, where there are many issues related to retelling stories from the past and the sort of stories people want to tell about themselves. To similar effect we give space later in this chapter to helpful developments in interviewing that offer what we call adjuncts and complements to the standard form of semi-structured interview. In some cases (e.g., by using vignettes and other simulations, participant provided visual images, or ethnographic interview contexts) these prompt the participant to consider instances that may depart from their generalised perceptions of life. An illustration of this approach can be seen in a study in which social workers and probation officers were asked to give detailed accounts of particular cases, as a means of getting beyond generalised perceptions of practice (Shaw, 2012: Chapter 17). Yet there are limits to what can be learned from an interview, and 'a time comes when we want to consider not just what people *say* but what they *do*' (Packer, 2011: 122).

Qualitative interviews and social work interviews

Are qualitative interviews in some way congenial to the aims and practices of social work? There are two very different questions at issue here. First, should qualitative interviews regularly be employed because they are strong as a means of understanding problems central to social work? Second, are the skills and processes of qualitative interviews similar in important ways to social work interviews?

Our answer to the first question is 'Yes – sometimes'. An interesting argument for using qualitative methods as a means of understanding micro-processes has been suggested by McLeod in a thoughtful assessment of the potential of qualitative methods for understanding outcomes of counselling. He suggests that qualitative interviews are more likely to elicit critical perspectives than questionnaires arising from the 'demand characteristics' of extended interviews. 'In terms of producing new knowledge that contributes to debates over evidence-based therapy, it would appear that qualitative evaluation is better able to explore the limits of therapeutic ineffectiveness' (McLeod, 2001: 178). Combined with their potential for eliciting positive relations between intervention and outcome, he concludes that 'Qualitative interviews appear to be, at present, the most sensitive method for evaluating the harmful effects of therapy and also for recording its greatest individual successes' (ibid., p. 179; c.f. Patton, 2002: 472–3).

On the second question, the potential of qualitative interviews is both an attraction and a trap for social workers. We say this because of the seductive but in large part illusory assumption that social workers know how to interview service users and therefore will be at ease with research interviewing. Most social workers would probably believe that if they are skilled in any method then it is in the interviewing process. Social workers are indeed among the most skilled of interviewers. As early as 1928 social workers were producing work that the sociologist Ray Lee describes as 'the early development of a – to modern eyes – quite sophisticated understanding of interview practice by social workers in the United States' (Lee, 2008: 291; c.f. Queen, 1928 and Young, 1929).

However, we suspect that the range of interviewing styles in social work looks very different from the range of research interviewing methods. Hence social workers may be tempted to make ill-founded assumptions regarding the scope of their research interviewing skills. The selection of variants of interviewing represented in this chapter, while not exhaustive, is sufficient to show that while social workers are often skilled interviewers, they engage in a limited range of kinds of interviews. We have introduced the more general form of this question in Chapter Two and we explore it further in Chapter Fifteen, but for the moment it may be worth reflecting on the words of a practitioner researcher –

> I think it's been harder for me to be a researcher in terms of talking to children, I thought it wouldn't be difficult but actually when I was listening to, thinking of one of the transcripts – Oh my goodness! I have really gone right over the … I'm not this neutral encouraging person, I'm much more acting as a practitioner. (Shaw and Lunt, 2012)

It is quite possible that, because researchers routinely have access to recordings of their interviews, they are in a privileged position regarding reflecting and improving on their interviewing skills, in comparison with practitioners who more rarely get to review recordings of their practice interviews.

Variations in interactional forms

We noted above how interviewers 'do neutrality' as a means of eliciting participants' meanings. We also remarked that when we call an interview collaborative, dialogical or guided, we are drawing attention to the nature of the exchange relationship between researcher and participant. But being 'neutral' and collaborating sound like rather different positions. The reason for this tension lies in the ideal that a good interview will be based on a constructive rapport between interviewer and participant. Much ink has been spilled on this topic.

Example 7.1 accentuates the sharpness of the issues at stake. We suggest reading this through twice and reflecting on it before moving to the subsequent text. The extract is from an interview with someone the researcher knew as a friend and is about illegal drug use. We join the interview about one hour in (the lower case is how it appears in the source, Rapley, 2004: 23–4).

	EXAMPLE 7.1		Confessional Interviewing	

adam	there's so much information all I've all I've done is told you the a – z really
tim	yeah [yeah
adam	[there's loads of places along the way
tim	yeah, yeah [yeah yeah
adam	[and you need to think of some questions about what I've said
tim	yeah (1.0) i don't know I mean (1.0) i mean for me i mean this is yeah this is very yeah this is my confession for me um I am that alcoholic but but from my own point of view you know
adam	mm
tim	I I I got to that point where no you know i could you know when you were saying about um I'm not functioning any more as a human being
adam	mm
tim	I'd really to to the point when I wasn't a human being any more that I could recognise [in any
adam	[yeah
tim	way shape or form and I and that was purely my you know addictive personality. I don't know whether that exists you know me being um (0.6) just a monster
adam	yeah
	…
tim	yeah yeah yeah basically it got to the point where erm for me it got to like I mean [the end of the line
adam	[was that all drugs
tim	all drugs, yeah [other than alcohol and tobacco]
adam	[you never taken anything] ever since
tim	nah nah nah but that was literally to save my sanity [you know
adam	[yeah
	(continues)

Rapley (2004)

Whether extreme confessional forms are advisable is a matter of case-by-case judgement, but Rapley's text yields a stark example of how very different interactional modes may co-exist under the umbrella of qualitative interviewing. For example, discussions about rapport sometimes focus on how much self-disclosure should take place on the part of the interviewer. We suspect that if you were unfamiliar with this text you would have been at best confused as to who was the interviewer or may have assumed that Adam was interviewing Tim. The reverse is in fact the case.

A helpful way to think about this issue is through the commonly stated but often unexplained idea that in qualitative research the researcher *is* the instrument rather than 'using' an instrument such as a measurement scale, questionnaire, etc. We think the term has limited value if it is meant as a distinguishing mark of qualitative inquiry, primarily because researchers in all methods, face-to-face or more distant, qualitative or quantitative, are 'instrumental' in the sense intended here. But the idea is important and lies behind some of the important choices open to the researcher that we outline in the following section.

Most of the main options when considering differences and distinctions in qualitative interviewing can be understood in terms of:

1. Variations in the structure of and participants in the interview.
2. Opportunities for various participant-led interview forms.
3. Adjuncts and complements to the interview.

We do not wish to labour the distinctions. Adjuncts, as we will see, sometimes involve greater participant influence, and variations in structure often entail complementary activities linked to the interview. But these general traits help disentangle the many threads of interview work. Under the rubric of varying structures and participants we include *joint interviews*, where there are two participants; *group interviews* and *focus groups*; and *key informant* and *elite interviews*. We also draw attention to the use of *simulations*, whether through vignettes or through more extended quasi-role play. Under the second broad distinction – participant-led interviews – we introduce some lesser-known options including the *self-interview, systematic self-observation*; and the *running commentary* method. When we turn to the growth of add-ons and accessories, the choices increase almost by the year. We touch on *photo-elicitation, walking* interviews, *email* interviews and *journals*.

Structure and participants
Joint interviews

Earlier in the chapter we commended Neander and Skott's account of families that have struggled with their relationships to their children, and who have identified people who have had a positive influence on the child (Neander and Skott, 2006). Their work is interesting for a further reason, in that it offers a relatively rare instance of interviewing two people together.

Their subsequent article follows this with an exploration of the reflections of parents and professionals on their shared experiences of therapeutic intervention (Neander and Skott, 2008). Their cogent and insightful analysis focuses on experiences that had been found helpful, the strength of the paper lying in the shared and mutual reflections by the participants – on the parents' initial fears, their steps to make sense of the situation, and the altering of inner images following their striving towards mutual responsiveness. In Example 7.3, a mother is speaking about the expert role of the therapist, and relates how she felt about her contact with therapist Lillian. While we do not hear the voice of the research interviewer, she is present and facilitated this three-way occasion by undertaking the joint interview (Neander and Skott, 2008: 302. The mother's words are in italics, and the square brackets indicate overlapping speech).

| EXAMPLE 7.2 | Joint Interviews – Parents and Professionals |

One looks at those who work in a place like that,
one sees them as experts.
[Yes.
[In some way . . .
You could easily concoct anything and I would feel calm . . . (laughter).
One takes your word for the truth, kind of. But we still had a dialogue . . .
Yes.
It was me who really found the way, but you helped me to find it.
Yes.
So that . . .Yes.
Yes, I think it's a bit like that, that one should help people to work things out for them-
selves. That everything feels OK . . .
Yes, because you never came up to me and said, 'This is how it is'.
No.
That's not how it was. Instead you asked or said 'Ya, what do you think?'
Yes.
So then I could, yes . . .

The authors comment how the parents acted as both informants and co-researchers, through a research approach that they call an investigative partnership (Neander and Skott, 2008: 293). The relevant point is that the joint interview method made this possible. Morris reflects on her joint inter-views with couples in the context of cancer in terms that resonate with Neander and Skott's work:

> What makes joint interviewing different from individual interviewing is the interaction between participants, who usually have a preexisting relationship … Joint interviewing provides the opportunity for combining something of the intimacy of individual interviewing with the public performance of a focus group. In particular, it places emphasis on the relational possibilities of a pair's situation, asking them to represent themselves not just as individuals but also as concurrent participants in a relationship. (Morris, 2001: 558)

Because of this 'the joint interview technique allows glimpses of "sharedness" under construction' (ibid., p. 559). There were also instances where pairs filled in gaps in the narrative. The styles taken by participants will vary, sometimes offering monologues, perhaps in turn, and other times engaging in dialogues that develop and reinforce or perhaps 'edit' emerging accounts. A therapist in Neander and Skott's study demonstrates this in her remarks about her relationship with the mother to the effect that 'Because I think somehow that we share something that means we can kind of recognize each other. We are verbal and talk a lot, we find it easy to express ourselves in words and we're close to our own feelings. Because I'm like that too. [. . .] We match each other' (Neander and Skott, 2008: 302).

Group interviews and focus groups

More familiar are group interviews and focus groups (Barbour, 2007; Bloor et al., 2001; Gibbs, 1997; Stewart et al., 2007). The origins of focus groups are not straightforward. The usual link back to Merton and Kendall's early paper on focused interviews is probably 'more intellectual than historical' (Merton, 1987: 560). Focus groups have three particular advantages. First, the group interaction is itself the data – 'the interaction is the method' (Jarrett, 1993: 198). Kitzinger says that the method 'enables the researcher to examine people's different per-spectives as they operate within a social network and to explore how accounts are constructed, expressed, censored, opposed and changed through social inter-action' (1994: 159). Second, focus groups are a form of participatory evaluation. They are valuable when there is a power differential between participants and decision makers, and hence have considerable potential for application within social work. Finally, they introduce a valuable approach to learning the extent of consensus on a particular issue. 'The co-participants act as co-researchers taking the research into new and often unexpected directions and engaging with each other in ways which are both complementary ... and argumentative' (Kitzinger, 1994: 166).

A variant of focus groups is illustrated by Bond's account of a day's pro-gramme for three ten-year-old short-term foster girls, in which their views were sought about a family centre. A group discussion format was set up. Dressing up, food, paint, cooking, poster preparation, photography and a presentation were used in an innovative attempt to learn user views from children. It was a care-fully planned initiative, and exemplifies a potential for focus group work which falls well within the resources for small qualitative projects in most residential and day care settings (Bond, 1990–1991).

Butler and Williamson also undertook group interviews with children. In understanding the purpose of humour they describe how some children display 'serious listening inside a funny shell' (Butler and Williamson, 1994: 46). Kitzinger concludes that focus groups 'may be particularly effective when (they) draw together people who have previously been unable to share their experi-ences or who are physically isolated from one another, such as those caring for elderly relatives' (1994: 169). Zeller's use of focus groups to learn about sexual decision making by young people suggests possible applications of the method to evaluating practice with sensitive problems (Zeller, 1993).

Despite the promise of this method, focus groups should be used within their limitations, and there are situations where focus groups probably should not be used. They should not be used if the intention is to improve partici-pants' communication or group skills. It has until recently been advised that focus groups should not be utilised when the main purpose is to secure imme-diate action. Notwithstanding Kamberelis and Dimitriadis' (2005) radical widening of focus group uses that we discuss in a later chapter, this still holds as a general principle. If information, understanding or explanation are not central to the group's agenda, then other methods of research should be used.

There are other practical constraints on focus group work. As with joint inter-views, if personal views cannot readily be expressed in such a context, or if breaches of confidentiality are likely to be a problem, then the method should not be used. When group members know each other particularly well then focus groups are also ill-advised.

Simulations

The focus group is at some levels a contrived setting for conducting research, but it remains naturalistic insofar as members are drawn from the research popula-tion and often interviewed within or close to their communities. Vignettes are one of the most familiar forms of simulation and lie some way in between the *most* and the *least* structured approaches to data collection. There has been growing and helpful literature on their use within interview research (Barter and Renold, 1999, 2000; Jenkins et al., 2010; Wilson and White, 1998). They have frequently been used in focus groups, although they have an earlier history. In an early article Finch focused on their use in survey research, and described them as 'short stories about hypothetical characters in specified circumstances, to whose situation the interviewee is invited to respond' (Finch, 1987: 105). She discusses their application in the context of research on beliefs and norms, the empirical study of which pose 'some of the most difficult methodological ques-tions for sociology' (ibid., p. 105).

EXAMPLE 7.3 — **Vignettes in Policy Research**

A study was carried out on the introduction of the UK government's Integrated Children's System (ICS). The ICS is a government-led initiative and part of a wider package of develop-ments for children's services, designed to introduce e-government and promote effective services for children and families in England and Wales.

A series of focus groups convened with local professionals who were tasked with steer-ing the implementation. Here are three examples

A *At Newtown local authority the implementation group were highly organised, but the implementation of ICS has been fraught with difficulties. Problems have included numer-ous software issues, providing practitioners with access to PCs and motivating staff about the new system.*
Prompts:

- Does anything in this story resonate with your experience of the implementation of ICS?
- What problems have you encountered? Have you been able to get around them?
- What aspects of the way your department works here have facilitated the implemen-tation of ICS?
- What aspects of the way your department works here have not facilitated the imple-mentation of ICS?

B Sarah, an experienced practitioner who qualified in the 1980s, was worried about using ICS. She had successfully completed an evening class called 'Computers for the Terrified', but was concerned about whether she could cope with the ICS software. But following a department-wide training and induction programme, her fears proved unfounded, and the system did not pose her too many problems.
Prompts:

- How do your experiences compare with those of the character in this story?
- Has there been anything particularly helpful about the way ICS has been introduced?

C At Newtown Social Services Department there was some confusion amongst the ICS implementation group about who should input data. Some team members felt a goal of ICS was to reduce the amount of time devoted to administration. Others saw ICS as an aid to practitioners to support and encourage good practice.
Prompts:

- Have you imagined ICS as a data management or practice tool?
- Who inputs data into ICS here – administrators or practitioners?
- Who has ICS helped the most in terms of performing their role?

(Shaw et al., 2009, carry some general conclusions from this study)

An interesting social work development of the vignette is given by Eskelinen and Caswell. They describe 'the use of the video vignette method in a specific context, i.e., in studying case-talk and case evaluation in social worker teams working with unemployed people within the field of active labour market policy' (Eskelinen and Caswell, 2006: 490). 'The vignette represented a kind of standardized case that permitted comparison between the teams' and could be 'characterized as a modified authentic whole case file on a videotape. One example showed a conversation between an unemployed 34-year-old woman and a female social worker in a municipal social service department' (ibid., pp. 490, 491). As with some other interview methods 'the indeterminate relationship between beliefs and actions, i.e., the missing link between "talk" and "action", remains the main methodological challenge' (ibid., p. 490).

Taking contrivance further, there are research situations in which participants can be simulated or role played in order to explore the impact of particular variables, such as gender or ethnicity, on a situation. Simulations have the potential to provide 'a unique and innovative tool that has not yet been widely applied' (Turner and Zimmerman, 1994: 335). Since Turner and Zimmerman wrote these words the picture has changed somewhat. Simulation introduces an element of structure into research that, in that respect, is borrowing from quantitative methods. So far, examples tend to arise from housing, legal or employment research, typically where researchers want to examine the influence on selection or allocation decisions of varying the demographic characteristics of applicants (e.g., Wasoff and Dobash, 1992). However, using actors or others to simulate service users also has the potential for researching how individual social work practitioners exercise judgement and discretion in interview situations, or comparing between different professions how they respond in an interview situation to a simulated client presenting the same 'story'. Thus, one particular limitation of naturalistic qualitative research – that events cannot be replicated in order to control independent variables – is managed by simulating people or events. This illustrates a significant but too rarely exploited methodological point about 'mixed methods'. What is being 'mixed' in this case is not two different methods, but the *methods* of qualitative research with the design *logic* of structured and measurement oriented approaches to inquiry by introducing a proxy 'control' element.

There are obstacles to research based on simulated interviews, for instance that they are resource intensive, need extensive preparation such as life scripts and rehearsal of the simulated participants, and may raise ethical objections where covert measures are thought necessary (for instance researching discriminatory responses by professionals). Nevertheless, it has relatively unexplored potential as a research method.

Key informants and elites

A simple internet search on each of these terms shows up their huge currency. This is as much a hazard as a resource, and in both cases the terms are severely under-theorised. This has led to a situation where 'scholars have shaped their definitions to match their respondents' (Harvey, 2011: 432f). The two terms have some overlap but are not coterminous. We take a limited definition of a key informant as a member of the policy, practice, service participant or research communities, who has special expertise. Unlike elite interviews (c.f. Odedahl and Shaw, 2002), key informants are not necessarily people who have power, but those whose judgement, through their expertise, carries authority. Because of these qualities they may be invited as research participants precisely because they are not representative, in probability terms, of the social or professional group to which they belong.

In consequence of this, they are as likely to be chosen to comment on the research data as to contribute directly to it. For example, key informants may be interviewed at a relatively early stage when interpreting the literature, should they have made an important contribution to work under review; or a policy, practice or service participant expert may be interviewed towards the end of a project when seeking to formulate recommendations. There is an association of ideas in this second use with approaches such as deliberative and appreciative evaluation, and we pick this up when we discuss the contribution of qualitative inquiry to understanding and acting on outcomes of professional work in Chapter Thirteen.

There is an important issue in this context of what counts as expertise – an issue we discussed in Chapter Three. Following from the moderate standpoint position we take in this book, we believe that service users, along with members of other research-related social groups, have a distinctive but not exclusive inter-pretive grasp of their field and experience.

There is a further distinction between elite interviewees and key informants, in that the former are interviewed precisely because they are believed to stand in a relational position to others, although they may not see themselves in this light. For example, long ago Weiss spoke with officials in the mental health field regarding decision making and their use of research (Weiss, 1980, 1988). In the event, decisions were perceived to be fragmented both vertically and horizon-tally within organisations, and to be the result of a series of gradual and amor-phous steps. Therefore, 'a salient reason why they do not report the use of research for specific decisions is that many of them *do not believe that they make decisions*' (Weiss, 1980: 398). This suggests one reason why precise definition of elites is not easy and 'it is problematic to segregate people into simplistic dual-isms of "elites" and "non-elites"' (Harvey, 2011: 439), partly because elite status is highly context-specific.

An example of elite interviews is provided by Shaw and Norton (2007) who interviewed senior academics who were asked to talk about an example of their research chosen by them as 'good research'. Harvey stresses that researchers of elites 'must show they have done their homework' (2011: 434), and in the Shaw and Norton case careful reading in advance of sometimes extensive research publications was essential.

Participant-led interviewing

Social work research literature is replete with the advocacy of user-led, partici-patory and empowerment forms of research. We develop a more general argu-ment about these important claims later in the book. For the present our focus is on interview methods that offer lesser-known options. These include the *self-interview, systematic self-observation*, and the *running commentary* method. To our best knowledge none of these has been developed in the qualitative social work literature, although some significant developments and advances have appeared in journal pages, especially in *Qualitative Social Work* and *Qualitative Inquiry.*

Self-interview

One of the more valuable resources in UK qualitative research is the 'Realities Toolkit' series from the University of Manchester.[1] Our debt is apparent at sev-eral points in this section of the book. Allet and her colleagues explain the method as follows (Allet et al., 2011). Participants use an audio recorder to 'record themselves responding to a particular topic and to related media, objects

---

[1]http://www.socialsciences.manchester.ac.uk/morgancentre/realities/index.html

and/or spaces' (ibid., p. 1). They develop a rationale in terms of it providing 'a space away from the usual imperatives of a face-to-face interview' (ibid., p. 1). They argue that its 'main strengths lie in enhancing informants' reflections on remembering practices and in capturing remembering as it is performed in everyday life' such that 'the self-interview records memory in process' and 'in ways that are relatively unimpeded by the researcher' (ibid., pp. 2, 4). It is used along with a guidance sheet, 'to explain what they need to do and what to focus on. This can provide a structure that helps people organize what they want to say. It can also be revisited to remind them of areas they have forgotten to mention or consider' (ibid., p. 6). The researcher guidance distinguishes this from more usual diary methods.

Their application of the method was in the context of the association of music and photographs in remembering, so they encouraged participants to move around the house commenting on photos and music as they did so. So as they look at their photographs and listen to music the process 'creates a space in which they can reflect on their memories and cross-temporal associations as they happen, *in situ*' (ibid., p. 3).

The method illustrates a creative cross-fertilisation of interview methods with ethnography, for example through mobile methods of fieldwork – an area that has been particularly creative and fruitful in the last decade. But our focus for the moment is on how self-interviewing can be seen as part of a 'family' of more participant-led interview forms. It can also be related to the oft-noted difficulty of qualitative (and indeed structured) interviews when inviting memory recall. We introduce another partial method solution to memory below (systematic self-observation) and have already referred to the value of focusing on specific instances in research interviews. Finally, and incidentally, the authors suggest it is 'particularly helpful for researchers wanting to gather data on mundane or habitual acts and their significance', whether they use media, objects, or spaces (public or private) (Allet et al., 2011: 6).

Systematic self-observation

Self-interviewing of the kind described above utilises visual methods and self-direction as complements to interviewing. The method described here elides interviews with observation methods in a form of structured ethnography (Rodriguez and Ryave, 2002). As a qualitative research tool they see systematic self-observation (SSO) as training informants 'to observe and record a selected feature of their everyday experience', so that participants 'go about their lives while alertly observing' the matter of interest (ibid., p. 2). The focus is on understanding the ordinary, in particular the covert, the elusive and the personal. In an effort to overcome the 'numbness to the details of everyday life' (ibid., p. 4) respondents are asked to observe 'a single, focused phenomenon that is natural to the culture, is readily noticeable, is intermittent ... is bounded ... and is of short duration' (ibid., p. 5) and also to focus on the subjective.

The recording involves writing a narrative about the situation, the participants, what occurred, the words spoken and thoughts/feelings experienced at the time (i.e., not retrospectively), and doing it as soon as possible after the event. When observing they are instructed in no way to act differently than usual, to never produce instances nor to judge the propriety of the action – 'do not judge it, do not slow down, do not speed up, do not change it, do not question it – just observe it' (ibid., p. 17). They refer to a key skill as gaining a 'new mindfulness' about everyday life. In their own studies they have used the method to research telling lies, telling secrets in everyday life, withholding compliments and the role of envy in making social comparisons – mundane everyday matters that are not far from the concerns of social workers. The method is linked to a subsequent interview that proceeds in some ways akin to meaning elicitation in methods such as photo-elicitation.

Compared with structured single system designs, discussed a little in Chapter Thirteen and widely advocated especially in the USA as an evaluative device, systematic self-observation may well be a preferred method in two respects:

1. It will allow a more contextualised and richer understanding of the nature of an issue or problem in a participant's life.
2. Single system approaches are committed to behavioural approaches that typically proceed by counting and measuring the incidence and prevalence of incidents and problems. SSO is, as we have noted 'more appropriate for the study of hidden or elusive domains, like the motives, memories, thought processes, withheld actions, thoughts and/or emotions that accompany overt behaviours' (Rodriguez and Ryave, 2002: 11).

In deciding and formulating the topic with research participants it will be necessary to avoid abstract language. Rodriguez and Ryave also advise against over-specifying the topic or providing definitions, because this 'deviates from the goal of problematizing the ordinary' (ibid., p. 13). In advising participants on how to be 'mindfully attentive', the key skill involves how to observe. In tune with what is noted above, in no way should they act any differently than usual, and they should never 'produce' instances. While this research approach calls for a relatively high level of motivation and engagement on the part of the interviewee, it offers quite innovative opportunities where those conditions are in place. Examples of how this can be applied within a social work practice research context have been suggested by one of us (Shaw, 2011b: 100–2, 107–9).

The running commentary

The little-known running commentary method, developed in the 1990s by a British sociologist is a further example of an interview-related method that also could be viewed as linked to participant-led methods (Witkin, 1994). The method requires informants to imaginatively relive events and to run a commentary on them in the present tense as though they are happening now. The aim is to make visible the skilful negotiations, perceptual strategies and understandings of subjects together with their occasioning contexts. He describes his development of the approach.

> For the most part I have used this method in researching 'work' processes and work cultures in organizations of different types. Quite simply, the method consists in getting subjects to re-live, that is, to 'simulate', imaginatively, certain encounters or events that have actually occurred in their work and to run a commentary on these events, using only the present tense, as though they are happening now. (Witkin, 1994: 265)

He is making the point that asking questions and giving answers happens in a context that is generally absent in a conventional research interview, although feminist accounts of interviewing have countered this assumption. He laments the 'profoundly disempowering' aspect of such research encounters. 'The would-be informants lose the right to "voice" their understandings and to "name" their world... Voicings and namings are profoundly constitutive of the very meanings and understandings which the researcher is aiming to discover or to disclose' (ibid., p. 266).

He found that interviews gave richer data when people were asked to ground their 'theorizing' in actual instances. This led him to look for what he calls a process of 'person-centred reflection' that would give 'present-ness' – to elicit 'a monologue with certain characteristics'. While the method as such is relatively simple it is 'subtle and delicate and to obtain good results with it requires a degree of sensitivity and skill on the part of the interviewer' (ibid., p. 270). An important distinction has to be made 'between accounts which are constituted as historical accounts, as interpretations of past events and which are constructed in terms of their relations to concerns and interests in the present, and accounts which purport in some way to recover the *presentness* of past events, to provide an insight into ... the ongoing thoughts and feelings and understandings through which choices at the time were made' (ibid., p. 268). A short extract from a longer example by Witkin (p. 273) follows:

> I leave the train. I think to myself – there's such a crowd here. My first thought is to look for the exit and I make my way towards it... I see the sign for access to the top. I climb the stairs. I look around to get my bearings, although it's an environment that is quite familiar to me. Several years ago I took this exit from the Metro quite often. I see the clothes shop 'Vicky', then I move towards the turnstiles. I glance at the window. I remember that the last time I came it was to a conference on Sexology here at the University of Quebec and, on the way out, I stopped at the little clothes shop. There were some winter hats, reduced in price. I bought one, a little hat in blue angora wool with a little flower on the side which I found fun.

Needless to say, 'the relationship of the imaginative reconstruction to the original historical events is, of course, a problematical one. There can be no certainty that the description given is an accurate one in the sense of being true to what actually happened' (ibid., p. 271). But the primary purpose of the method is not to discover facts but is a way of eliciting, with an immediacy, participants' thoughts, judgements and feelings. The experience will often be found enjoyable but also anxiety provoking, and it is important to convey that this is not about trying to discover people's secrets, and they should not talk about anything they do not wish to talk about. Also, assuming that the approach is used more than once, it should start with less complex and less difficult to talk about instances. This will also help avoid any tendency to speak defensively or in a mode of self-justification. Participants may need to be supported to preserve 'a sense of involvement in the process and ... not feel, as some subjects do, that an act of theft has occurred' or that unwitting disclosure has taken place (ibid., p. 281).

Adjuncts and complements

Self-interviewing and systematic self-observation as described above are participant-shaped methods that also include complementary methods. In this part of the chapter we take further the association of visual methods, place, technology and writing with qualitative interviews.

Visual and material methods

Daily experience is made of a multiplicity of dimensions, which include the visual and the sensory, and which are worthy of investigation but cannot always be easily expressed in words... The inclusion of non-linguistic dimensions in research, which rely on other expressive possibilities, may allow us to access and represent different levels of experience. (Bagnoli, 2009: 547)

Bagnoli applied a variety of drawing methods – self-portraits, relational maps and timelines – to 'enhance participants' reflexivity' (p. 549). In each case they were used in conjunction with interviews as a way of eliciting meaning. Bagnoli reflects how 'a creative task may encourage thinking in nonstandard ways, avoiding the clichés and ready-made answers which could be easily replied.' But she cautions that 'even visual data may be *clichéd* and produced in a standardized way' (Bagnoli, 2009: 566).

An extension of visual methods is the use of three-dimensional objects in interviews. One of us (Holland) has termed these 'material methods' in training sessions, grouping together the use of objects such as puppets, clay and toys in interviews. These are commonly used in therapeutic settings and their use in facilitating communication is familiar territory to practitioners (c.f. Bond, 1990–1991 above). Researchers with children commonly use objects in interviews (see Karen Winter's [2011] use of 'reality boxes' with young children) but there is no reason why objects should not be used in interviews with adults.

EXAMPLE 7.4	Button Eco-map

In her doctoral research Suzanne Spooner, an experienced social worker, was researching the impact of taking part in volunteering on the lives of young people who are looked after by the state or are care leavers. To facilitate conversation during the longitudinal, qualitative project Suzanne invited her 20 participants to use what she terms 'third objects' during semi-structured interviews. These include a wide range of antique and modern buttons that they can use to create a pictorial representation of their support systems and cards to prompt the retelling of their volunteering journey. Young people embraced these methods with enthusiasm and they were successful in enabling in-depth discussions, despite low levels of formal education among some of the participants. Suzanne was affectionately termed 'the button lady' by her doctoral colleagues and participants.

Walking interviews

Ronander, a cultural geographer, researches and writes to contribute to 'wider methodological concerns with how spatial practices are embodied and practiced through a reflection on walking not only as an object of study, but as a method of research' (Ronander, 2010: 3). She carried her work out through an ethnographic approach described as 'talking whilst walking'.

> This is done within the context of my ongoing doctoral research into group walking practices and subjective well-being. The paper is organized around a consideration of how walking together with participants enables insights into the social dynamics of group walking and the importance of social relations for the 'restorative experience'. (Ibid., p. 3)

The method of 'walking while talking' has also been applied to research with young children at home, as in Stevenson and Adey's reflections on walking-whilst-talking with young children at home (Stevenson and Adey, 2010). A recurring *motif* of the use of this research method is the realisation that it allows for the creation of meaning, and the ability to connect time and place. Inwood and Martin apply this idea through what they call roving focus groups (Inwood and Martin, 2010). Stevenson and Adey relate thinking about place to children whose geographical mobility is limited, as part of a study of young children's learning with toys and technology at home, and in a research setting that has obvious context links with social work practice. Ross et al. (2009) carried out mobile interviews in cars and on foot with children in foster and kinship care in a longitudinal participatory research project. Place was particularly pertinent for these participants because of their relatively mobile histories dislocating their connections to kinship networks and communities. Child-directed tours of neighbourhoods were complemented by routine car journeys, transporting the participants to and from home. In this project some young people opted to record the conversations in these regular car journeys. Like Laurier et al. (2008) these researchers noted how the car setting framed interactions within a closed off but publicly visible environment, gazing forward and not at each other, some-how enables what might otherwise be intense or difficult conversations to take place. 'It was evident that talk of interest to our substantive research themes was set within the more everyday car talk of routes and directions, the mundane talk of driving and "passengering"', as the following extract demonstrates.

Rosie: The other day my sister

Sally: Yeah

Rosie: Are you going straight up?

Sally: I have gone this way now, yeah.

Rosie: Yeah, my sister, has seen him, my dad up –

Sally: Oh 'cause it's funny because we were just talking about him last time and you were saying that you hadn't seen him for years.

Rosie: I know! I haven't, but my sister has seen him, but I don't want to see him. No way will I!

Sally: No. And how did your sister feel about it?

Rosie: Well it's not her dad is it? We're

Sally: Oh I see.

Rosie: We're like half sisters

Sally: I know you are.

Rosie: But we think we're like, we're proper sisters… Yeah, but we got like, – Go straight up here if you want. I know the way.

This extract, like many of the conversations Rosie and Sally shared as they travelled back and forth together, was interspersed with intimate talk about places passed and associations with events that took place there involving Rosie and her family' (Ross et al., 2009: 610–11).

Mobile interviews are an example of how 'place' has influenced different methods – 'We developed the method … as a way of understanding senses of place and neighbourhood attachment, and the extent to which social networks are contextualized and reproduced spatially' (Clark and Emmel, 2010: 1). Their data comprised an audio recording of the walking interview and sometimes a photographic record produced by the participant. Following an explanation of the rationale and what was expected from the event, participants chose where the walk began and ended and the route followed. Among their practical tips are:

> A good quality small microphone (such as a lapel microphone) with wind guard is essential, but even with this equipment researchers should be prepared to accept that not all discussion will be recorded because of traffic noise, wind, the voices of passers-by and other sounds.

> At the end of each interview it is important that the researcher records the route taken, for example on a street map. (Clark and Emmel, 2010: 4)

They offer seven reasons why walking interviews may be chosen over 'room based' ones, and we reproduce the list here in full:

1. The method can afford participants a greater degree of control over the research process, deciding where to take the researcher, for example.
2. The participant gets to show rather than describe the environments that the researcher is interested in, or which make up the spaces that are significant to the participant.
3. Placing events, stories and experiences in their spatial context can help participants to articulate their thoughts.
4. The participants' narratives told in their lived environment can add detail to the researcher's understanding and insight.
5. The environment and locations walked through can be used in an elicitation process to prompt more discussion or encourage further questioning that may not occur in room-based settings.
6. The method can provide opportunities for the serendipitous and the unanticipated. Walking interviews can throw up issues of contradiction.
7. The method can be adapted to fit in with a participant's everyday life, while also revealing some of their everyday practices. (Clark and Emmel, 2010: 2)

Email interviews and social media

It has become fairly commonplace for researchers to mail schedules to people who prefer to complete them at their leisure. People with mental health difficulties or those whose first language differs from that in which the research is conducted may prefer to deal with interview schedules as and when they are able.

Our focus here is somewhat different, referring to an interview mode more akin to qualitative interviews, in which questions singly or in small sequences are mailed to the participant, before the questions proceed. On the face of it this method may seem very much the same as a semi-structured interview, and with the advantage of facilitating access to those who may not otherwise be accessible. However, there are important differences. In brief:

1. The email interview produces a written rather than an oral account.
2. The pace is slower.
3. 'Physical remoteness makes the situation very difficult to read' (Bampton and Cowton, 2002/2008: para 11).
4. The emotional 'bandwidth' of an email interview is more restricted, notwithstanding the availability of relatively simple emoticons.

Bampton and Cowton neatly capture how the email interview 'entails two types of displacement, relating to two fundamental dimensions of human experience. In relation to time, the interactions between interviewer and interviewee are likely to be asynchronous, with pauses of varying lengths between bursts of communication or "episodes"; while in terms of space, the relationship takes place "at a distance" through the medium of electronic, screen-based text' (ibid., para 6).

Regarding it as a written rather than oral account, Gibson concludes that 'potentially, it would be more fruitful to compare email interviews to methodological approaches such as diary methods, mass observation directives, or other research methods that generate written accounts' (Gibson, 2010: 2), finding that her data had more in common with diaries than face to face interviews. Bampton and Cowton suggest rather differently that the email interview should observe the conventions of email writing, which may be that answers should be fairly brief. This question of the balance and weight of questions and answers relates to the issue of the pace of the interview. It will be important to allow each interview to develop at the pace of the informer – some may answer by return while others may take a week or more. While this allows the interviewer time to reflect on each answer and give a carefully nuanced following question, 'a balance has to be struck between putting too much into any one episode, which might lead to stalling, and having too many episodes, which might lead to interview "fatigue"' (Bampton and Cowton, 2002/2008: para 13). They go on to say that 'it is probably less easy to sense when an e-interviewee is wanting to finish, without their being explicit' (ibid., para 14), and see this as 'part of a general problem with the e-interview, namely the lack of tacit signs, which results from the physical separation of interviewer and interviewee' (ibid., para 16). A further consequence of physical distance is that it will not be clear to the researcher what resources the respondent has drawn on when crafting an answer to a question. Indeed, Gibson found that if she compared her email interviews with her face-to-face interviews 'the email interviews did tend to produce less spontaneous and more carefully crafted data' (Gibson, 2010: 3).

Wide developments in social media do of course extend how we think about interviewing. In an interesting example, Hedin and colleagues (2012) conducted non-standardised, low-structured, focused interviews with twelve persons including three adolescents, their foster parents and three biological parents. The focus was on everyday interactions including rules, routines, feelings, influence, trust, support, conflicts, etc., sometimes compared to their previous experiences. With the adolescents an additional method was text messages via mobile phone ('beepers'), used to investigate their here-and-now situation – what they were actually doing at specific times. The adolescents received text messages around six times a day, for six days, and each time answered the same four questions: Where are you, with whom, what are you doing, how does it feel?' (ibid., p. 618). Adolescents also drew a network map of significant others to clarify the strength and quality of these relationships, for instance within the foster family and birth family.

Journals

The crafting of written responses, albeit in an interview structure, connects with our final adjunct to qualitative interviews – the use of participant prepared written logs or journals. We mention this only in passing, and with a single example, because it belongs more properly to Chapter 9.

There are, however, forms of life story practice that provide useful complementary elements of interview research. Thomson and Holland give an account of their 'creation of memory books as a method to be used alongside interviews in a longitudinal qualitative study of young people's transitions to adulthood' (Thomson and Holland, 2005: 201), in an attempt to place young people at the core of the construction of their own identity. 'We were particularly interested in methods that had been employed in child therapy in which young people were encouraged to compile memory boxes in order to create a resource for the maintenance of a coherent sense of self in the face of parental bereavement, adoption and fostering' (ibid., p. 203). Memory books become an instance of a story told, retold and retold back once more. Thomson and Holland explain how the response to their work was interesting but varied. Researchers will almost certainly initially struggle to find ways of engaging with the material in memory books. They are both a document of the self and also a means of inventing the self, or in the words of Thomson and Holland, a distinction 'between their function as sources of documentation, resources for elaboration, and critical tools for the understanding of identity' (ibid., p. 201).

Culture for example

We have focused extensively on the nature, variety and respective value of different interview forms. There is much more that could be said. Issues of gender, the meaning of silence in interviews, interviewing vulnerable groups or children, interviewing on sensitive topics, and so on. Some of these are touched on elsewhere in the book. Rather than skate over the surface of this range of issues, we close the chapter with an example of interviewing that helpfully obliges us to examine our assumptions that we know how to interview. Sahar Al-Makhamreh is talking about her ethnographic doctoral research in a Jordanian hospital (Example 7.5).

| EXAMPLE 7.5 | Interviews Across Cultures |

My identity as a Jordanian woman influenced my role. During the fieldwork I practised the same strategies as those used by Jordanian female social workers. These were informal strategies of resistance in order to deal with the gendered hegemony of the medical hospital setting. I interacted and constructed my behaviour according to Jordanian social perceptions and understandings of gender. For example, in negotiating access with practitioners and potential respondents I used informal strategies by utilising the informal but respectful nomenclature 'mother of x' or 'father of x' rather than their first names or formal names. I used fictive kinship terms in order to build up and gain trust so that I would address clients, nurses, social workers or doctors as 'sister' or 'brother' in conversation. This device is widely used in Arab society and is a way to frame interaction with a man in a non-sexual way and to indicate solidarity with a woman. It is widely used in cross gender interactions.

With male patients for example, I kept my distance – not getting close to them, touching or looking at them directly in the eye. Also, with elderly people I would use fictive kinship terms addressing them as 'father' or 'mother' or 'grandfather' or 'grandmother' to indicate respect. Sometimes I might recite a poem to show appreciation and understanding of their status. This was very helpful in gaining their acceptance as an insider in order to conduct the interviews in their households after being discharged. Furthermore, I was very careful about my dress code covering my arms and legs at all times.

Despite being a Christian, I used a range of well-known vernacular phrases concerning Allah, such as 'Allah kareem' (God is generous) and Destiny ('Naseeb or Kader') in my conversation. There are a range of formulaic greetings and ways of wishing people comfort and relief that have a formal response and are vital in communicating. These phrases open and close conversations or are used when listening to a narrative such as 'Ma shaa Allah' (What God wants), 'bism Allah' (In God's name) or 'al Hamdi lullah' (Thanks be to God).

Al-Makhamreh and Lewando-Hundt (2008: 17–18)

We offer this example without exposition because, for one of us, it showed how, after a career of research, centrally important aspects of research interviewing had not been fully understood. If we think we have 'got it' when it comes to qualitative interviewing then we probably have not.

Taking it further

Select one of the three themes that have been dealt with in a major part of this chapter:

1. Variations in the structure of and participants in the interview.
2. Opportunities for various participant-led interview forms.
3. Adjuncts and complements to the interview.

Take one example from your selected theme (e.g., Clark and Emmel on mobile interviews; Witkin's running commentary method as a participant-led interview method; or Neander and Skott's work using joint interviews).

Locate and read the original source. Create a memo to yourself identifying how your reading poses questions about your research interviewing.

EIGHT
Telling Stories

In this chapter we explore the role of stories in qualitative social work research. Concentrating mainly on narrative research as a whole, we also mention and acknowledge the role of a range of different methods and approaches under the narratives umbrella, including life story and oral history interviews and the exploration of biographies through arts-based methods. After a general discussion of narratives in social work research, we explore narratives in four ways: as sources of substantive knowledge about individual and group experiences, as being functional in creating and reproducing group identities and memories, as being produced in relationship to others and in having form as well as content. In the second half of the chapter we discuss methods and approaches for exploring and generating narratives, ending the chapter with an example of a narrative-based project that involved social work practice and research alongside each other. The 'Taking it further' exercise invites readers to read an interview extract as a narrative account.

Introduction and definitions

Narratives are produced and performed in accordance with socially shared conventions; they are embedded in social encounters; they are part and parcel of everyday work; they are amongst the ways in which social organizations and institutions are constituted; they are productive of individual and collective identities; they are constituent features of rituals and ceremonies; they express authority and expertise; they display rhetorical and other aesthetic skills. (Atkinson and Delamont, 2006: xxi)

This chapter is about researching narratives and related approaches. As Atkinson and Delamont note in the extract above, narratives play a central and everyday role in social life. Perhaps because of this, there is possibly a tendency to overuse the label 'narrative' in qualitative research (Chase, 2005; Riessman and Quinney, 2005). When we research people's narratives we are interested in both the content of their account and in the form, context and process of the making of the account. Some research studies will emphasise one of these aspects more than the others and there is indeed a wide range of research that is labelled as 'narrative'. There are many overlapping definitions and fields of narrative research but there is some agreement that narrative research explores people's written, spoken or more rarely visual accounts. These are often first-hand biographic accounts, which may explore a whole life, themes or periods of a life, or individual incidents or episodes. In social research the narrative will usually be used to illuminate or deepen understanding of a social context. Narratives may be produced as part of a research process or be naturally occurring. In this chapter we mainly use the all-encompassing term 'narrative approaches' to include a fairly wide range of related approaches such as life history, oral history, life story, biographical, autoethnography and memory-work. These are certainly not all the same; they emerge from different disciplinary traditions and have different aims and methods. However, in this chapter we particularly concentrate on their common element – attention to narratives – while from time to time referring to one or more of these different approaches.

Narratives in social and historical research have been common for at least a century. Biographical approaches in the form of life history interviewing were common in the Chicago sociological school in the 1920s and 1930s, as in the famous *Polish Peasant* research of Thomas and Znaniecki, and by anthropologists (Atkinson and Delamont, 2006; Chase, 2005). Oral histories were collected throughout the twentieth century to capture the memories of those who had survived major events such as slavery or the Holocaust, or who were elders in communities; or traditions thought to be dying out, such as First Nation communities in North America (Chase, 2005). Squire et al. (2008) note that narrative research in the social sciences since World War II comes from a range of very different traditions, theoretical developments and disciplines. These include, firstly, a humanist post-war development in psychology and social science research promoting life histories, biographies and case studies as counter to empirical positivism and, secondly, a series of critical theories including psychoanalytic, post-structuralist and postmodern approaches. These critical theories focus our interest on the structure of the story, a de-stabilised subject and the power relations within which narratives become possible, or silenced. Both traditions of humanist and poststructuralist narrative research 'are brought together by their shared tendency to treat narratives as modes of resistance to existing structures of power' (Squire et al., 2008: 4). It can be seen therefore that narrative approaches touch on issues of social theory, politics, history, culture and identity. They also raise important methodological issues relating to realism, subjectivities, co-production and the research product.

This chapter explores the many different ways in which narratives are understood and the purposes they serve. Methods for generating or collecting narratives in social work settings are discussed, with many examples from different national and practice contexts. The final part of the chapter explores the use of narratives in research and practice and provides a case example of a research project that had both research and practice aims. Narrative *analysis* is discussed in Chapter Twelve.

Narratives in social work research

There is little consistency in social work research on the use of the term 'narrative' (Hall and White, 2005) and Riessman and Quinney (2005), in a review of narrative methods in social work research, found limited use of methods that fitted their definition of narrative research, although many claimed to use narrative methods. There is, indeed, a risk that any form of open-ended qualitative data will be labelled 'narrative' (Chase, 2005), but for Riessman, drawing here on Mishler, narrative research features:

1. Reliance on detailed transcripts
2. Focus on language and contexts of production
3. Some attention to the structural features of discourse
4. Acknowledgement of the dialogic nature of narrative
5. A comparative approach that interprets differences and similarities among participants' stories (where appropriate)

Adapted from Riessman and Quinney (2005: 398)

Chase (2005: 651) sees narrative research as a specific form of qualitative inquiry that can draw on a number of disciplines and a number of methods of generating data but 'all revolving around an interest in biographical particulars as narrated by the one who lives them'. Narratives are not just about the individual, nor the structure of the account, but provide a way to explore the interplay between the individual and society (Squire et al., 2008). Some researchers will focus more on the substantive content of the narrative, and others on the form of story telling and its context, such as the impact of the audience.

Despite the difficulties in definition, Hall and White (2005) make a series of powerful arguments about the useful part that narrative approaches might play in furthering our understanding of social work practices. They argue that narrative methods contribute to understanding of social work in terms of promoting individual reflection, examining particular decisions and judgements and asking questions about institutional and occupational practices and norms:

Discourse and narrative methods create opportunities for making sense of an action and 'learning from experience'. Broadly, they offer a method for developing understanding of the conversational worlds of professional practice, and can play a valuable role in professional training and supervision, by providing practitioners with the tools with which to practise reflexively. (This kind) of interpretive social science ... lends itself to the examination of professional judgements, decision making and use of knowledge claims with individual cases. (It) offers a way of interrogating the institutional practices and specialist knowledges of particular domains and how they are put to work in everyday practice. (Hall and White, 2005: 388)

Since Riessman and Quinney's (2005) rather pessimistic review of the overuse of narrative methods across a wide range of social work journals, a more recent review of articles in the social work journal, *Qualitative Social Work*, (Shaw et al., 2013) found that one quarter of papers used narrative methods as the main fieldwork method, suggesting a recent surge of interest in the approach and perhaps later adoption by social work authors of a more general 'narrative turn' in the social sciences in the last few decades (Atkinson and Delamont, 2006). In this chapter we include several examples of narrative methods being used in social work research.

Understanding narratives

There are many overlapping ways in which narratives may be understood in research and this section of the chapter explores some of these under the following four headings:

    Narratives as substantive knowledge

    Narrative functions

    Producing narratives

    Narratives as a research product

    Narrative forms

Narratives as substantive knowledge – 'walking in the shoes' of others

An important, perhaps the most central, aspect of narrative research is the substantive content. Cortazzi (2001) lists reasons for exploring ethnographic data as narrative and the first three of these are related to understanding others' experiences. Firstly, direct accounts from others allow us to share the meaning of the experience for the narrator and wider contexts. They provide a fairly quick and direct route into the story-teller's ways of explaining their social context and wider social structures. Secondly, such methods directly allow people's voices to be reported: 'life as they know it' (ibid., p. 386). Thirdly, these methods are particularly effective for relaying human qualities such as love, conflict, struggles, angst, enthusiasm and so on. Narratives can be particularly useful as a means 'to make sense of the ambiguity of human lives' (Savin-Baden and Major, 2013: 228).

Much narrative research is undertaken in order to provide access to people's direct experiences of a social phenomenon. Narrators may belong to a particular social category, such as being chronically ill, or have lived through or taken part in a social movement, such as civil rights campaigning. Brought together, a number of narratives can begin to tell a collective story (Elliott, 2005). Messerschmidt's (2000) life history research with teenage convicted sex offenders in the United States is a powerful example of how narrative forms of data collection can provide direct access to the accounts of rarely heard narrators – in this case a stigmatised, marginalised group. In a paper from 2000, Messerschmidt uses two extended case studies to relay powerful and sometimes shocking accounts of these young men's psycho-social circumstances prior to and during their serious sexual offending, mainly against younger children. The author writes 'I have attempted to walk in the shoes of these boys' (ibid., p. 287). This research, although based on individual stories, raises wider societal issues of the understanding and performance of masculinity, bodily practices and sexuality in home and school settings. Other examples of narrative research with rarely heard narrators include Yoshihama's (2002) research with Japanese women who have lived with domestic abuse. Although narratives of domestic abuse are (sadly) fairly familiar in western social work research, such narratives were less familiar in Japan when the research was undertaken. Mayes and Llewellyn's (2012: 121) analysis of the 'daily life narratives' of mothers with intellectual disabilities in Australia, who had had children removed on an involuntary basis, similarly brings to the fore the direct experiences of people who often are the subject of formal written reports, such as case records and court reports, but whose lengthy and complex accounts of their experiences are often absent.

In the 1980s, a group of West German feminist socialist scholars and activists used narrative methods to explore issues of gender and the body. Frigga Haug and others used methods they labelled 'memory-work' to explore women's written and photographic memories and analysed these through group processes (McLeod and Thomson, 2009). Such endeavours from this period attempted to bring to the fore previously unheard voices in what has been labelled by Atkinson and Delamont (2006: xxv) as a 'recuperative or redemptive view of oral history and narrative inquiry'.

This type of research has been criticised for unproblematically implying that we can directly access people's experiences in an unmediated fashion and that such research also risks individualising social phenomena that are rooted in social and economic inequalities and structures. Nonetheless, as McLeod and Thomson (2009) note, Haug was reportedly dismayed that memory-work appeared to be interpreted by some as an opportunity for personal confession only, rather than a process to locate memories in wider structural inequalities.

> At its best, memory-work insists that we interrogate what and why we remember and forget. And although it invariably begins with the personal, most approaches to memory-work ultimately seek to comment on wider social, cultural and historical processes. (McLeod and Thomson, 2009: 30)

Many authors, such as Hubbard (2000) claim that narrative approaches are ideal means to explore the interplay of agency and structure. In the case of Hubbard's research on youth transitions, life history interviews helped explain why some young people do not follow the trajectory most common to their class and gender background. Riessman (2001: 75) links this to social work research more specifically:

> Attention to the social in a 'personal' narrative can embolden social work research, and unite research and practice around the values of social justice and equality … The approach attends to contexts (local, cultural, and historical) in the interpretation of personal narratives.

Narrative functions

Most contemporary understandings of the functions of narratives in society and in research include the notion that narratives not only provide a window into group and individual identities, they also produce and reproduce them. In other words, the act of narrating can be an important part of how identities become understood. New members of groups can learn how to be a member of a group by listening to and eventually producing their own narratives. In social work this can apply in a wide variety of settings such as self-help groups, social worker-service recipient interactions and occupational and team cultures. Research using narrative methods can help us to critically investigate such institutional and group processes (Hall and White, 2005), as Dingwall's classic study illustrates in Example 8.1. Hall (1998: 35) notes that 'One way of approaching social work accounts is to investigate the extent to which it performs community, how is it heard as social work? How are relations established between a particular account and concepts and conventions available in and recognisable as social work?'

EXAMPLE 8.1	Narratives Producing and Reproducing Group Identities

Robert Dingwall (1977a) in a study of trainee health visitors in Britain in the early 1970s shows how their occupational identity is worked out and taught to newcomers through stories, including 'atrocity stories' about relationships with other professionals. Students need to learn and reproduce the group culture 'to achieve recognition as competent members of the group' (Dingwall, 1977a: 402) and that part of developing a recognisable identity for a profession 'involves asserting claims to a certain relationship with other occupations' (ibid., p. 408).

These accounts do not need to be lengthy to tell their story. Here is a complete story from a group discussion among students:

Rosemary: 'The health visitor was worried quite early on, but the GP pooh-poohed it until after the developmental assessment.' (Ibid., p. 399)

In this story, Dingwall claims, Rosemary is not merely making a complaint about the GP, but showing how the GP was wrong and the health visitor was right through the use of the vivid word 'pooh-poohed'. And the health visitor is thus 'the active character who triumphs over the incompetence or foolishness of others'.

Dingwall suggests that there is often little to distinguish health visitors' role from social workers, except that they have more medical knowledge and a more preventative role than social workers. An oral culture had developed among the health visitors that Dingwall studied that presented social workers in a generally negative light, to the extent that short cuts can be taken in the accounts about them.

'One of the health visitors comes in. She says she's been down at the Social Work Department. This provoked a burst of laughter from the other health visitor in the office.' (Ibid., p. 401)

Dingwall suggests that such stories may become self-fulfilling, blocking positive relation-ships and information-sharing between professional groups who have learned to mistrust each other. This insight is as relevant and important today as it was nearly half a century ago when this research fieldwork was undertaken.

Dingwall, R. (1977) '"Atrocity stories" and professional relationships' in *Sociology of Work and Occupations*, 4(4): 371–396. Reprinted in Atkinson, P. and Delamont, S. (eds) (2006) *Narrative Methods, Volume 1: Sage Benchmarks in Social Research Methods*. London: SAGE, pp. 391–411.

Narratives usually recall something that has happened in the near or distant past. Narrative can be understood as retrospective meaning making (Chase, 2005). It is a way of ordering and making connections between events, therefore forming much more than a chronology. The narrator consciously comments and provides their analysis of the importance of the events and the connections between them. The researcher, therefore, will be investigating the meaning that events hold for the nar-rator, as much as the content of the events themselves. The meanings held by the narrator will not be stable. The act of story telling in itself will shape and shift understandings (Gubrium and Holstein, 1998). Cortazzi (2001) notes that there-fore the story will be subject to multiple interpretations in that it will be subject to the interpretation the narrator makes at the time of the event, then further inter-pretation affected by memory, by subsequent re-tellings and the current audience. Stories will be compressed and usually not told chronologically in order to make them easier to tell and to listen to. A further layer of interpretation is that carried out by the researcher, as is discussed below.

In addition to retrospective meaning-making and the development of indi-vidual and group identities, narratives will serve many other, often overlapping, functions (Cortazzi, 2001). For a patient or service user it may be to aid diagno-sis or an assessment of need, or for a professional to a supervisor or colleague they may justify action, inaction or resource distribution. Narratives may be told to elaborate on, or clarify, a point in a discussion, they may make an argument stronger, for example in court, or to train or teach others.

Producing narratives

Almost all discussions of narratives explore the notion that narratives are pro-duced in relation to other people (Chase, 2005; Cortazzi, 2001; Hollway and Jefferson, 2000; Riessman and Quinney, 2005). In common with other qualita-tive interviews, but perhaps even more so due to their often intense nature, they are *co-productions* with an audience, whether present or absent. Narrators can manage their listener's response in context, by using phrases such as 'speaking to you as another woman', and 'don't get me wrong' (Gubrium and Holstein, 1998: 170), and the listener's questions can in turn influence the direction of the narrative.

Although some narrative methods attempt to minimise the impact of the researcher in narrative interviews, most will incorporate the understanding of the relatedness of narratives into analytic strategies. Gubrium and Holstein (1998: 181) elaborate on this point, noting that it is not simply the fact that there is an audience, but *who* the interviewer or listener is plays an important role in this co-construction of narratives.

> We must also be sensitive to issues of narrative collaboration. Listeners are not simply narrative depositories or passive receptors. Neither are they discursively homogeneous. They collaborate in both the whats and hows of narrative practice, invoking cultural meanings and expectations and supplying biographical particulars of their own, all in relation to the local auspices of narration. (Gubrium and Holstein, 1998)

Example 8.2 shows how particular listener–narrator dyads produce particular forms of narrative. In this case, women in substance misuse treatment programmes develop and mimic narrative forms – 'scripts' – in their therapy dialogues. These scripts can get reproduced in research interviews.

EXAMPLE 8.2 | **Narratives as Co-Production**

In Summerson Carr's (2011) study of a drug treatment programme in a North American city for homeless women, she conducted oral history interviews alongside ethnographic observations. When meeting 'Nikki' for a third and final oral history interview in a restaurant she was struck by how physically changed Nikki seemed since their last meeting. In this interview conducted after her treatment had been terminated, Nikki relayed to Carr that she had resumed use of cocaine. Despite this she seemed eager to continue to take part in the interviews: 'I sensed that Nikki enjoyed these recorded events, a chance to do what she did most brilliantly: talk' (Carr, 2011: 17). Carr briefly recapped on the previous two interviews and reminded where they had left off. The previous interview had taken a highly confessional form, 'laden with clinical explanations, and replete with the kind of religious sentiment characteristic of mainstream, American addiction treatment' (ibid., p. 18). It had ended with a story about a romantic relationship with a recovering alcoholic who had encouraged her to seek treatment.

I: So that's where we left off [in our last interview].

N: (long pause ... laughter). Oh my. (laughter)

I: What ... What?

N: I told you that (laughter)

I: Yeah (giggle) ... Don't you remember?

N: You knew that didn't happen, right? (laughter) Please tell me.

I: What?

N: Oh, poor ole' Summerson (sigh). Girl, don't you know, I flipped a script on you?! (Carr, 2011: 18)

Carr suggests that clients of the programme use such 'script flipping' to meet the therapeutic expectation that one uses language to demonstrate recovery, especially through making references to inner thoughts and feelings. This is a conventional expectation as well, which plays into any number of social interactions – including the research interview. The difference this time was that no longer in treatment, Nikki now had nothing to prove and nothing to lose. She therefore owned up to her previous script-flipping. And 'at that moment I understood that my charge as an ethnographer was to account for the complexity of speech events, however much I, myself, was implicated or involved in them' (ibid., p. 21).

Such methodological experiences gave Carr insights into 'the possibilities and limitations of language as a means of detecting or denoting inner states' (ibid., p. 19). 'After all script-flippers demanded that their analysts – whether anthropologist or therapist – consider their narratives as effectual, context-sensitive social actions with histories and futures of their own, rather than transparent reports on the content of their psyches' (ibid., p. 18). Script-flipping ultimately gave Carr insight into the expertise of the clients of the service in interpreting and manoeuvring the linguistic conditions of any situation.

Carr, E. Summerson (2011) *Scripting Addiction: The Politics of Therapeutic Talk and American Sobriety*. Princeton, NJ: Princetown University Press.

As Elliott (2005: 127) writes: 'narrative identities should not be understood as free fictions'. They are produced using recognisable forms using cultural resources available to the narrator and the audience. That audience will be located in a historical and cultural context and may also be within an institutional or group setting.

The complex relationship between experience, identities and the telling of narratives is explored in some depth by Hollway and Jefferson (2000). They use psychoanalytic theory to explore some of the processes of biographic interviewing. They note that, in post-structural theories, it is increasingly proposed that there is no 'real' unitary identity of the self. These authors find it rather bleak, however, to *finish* with the idea that we are all de-centred, fragmented, multiple identities. They suggest that by drawing on psychoanalytic theory we can find 'a coherent, agentic "I"' (Hollway and Jefferson, 2000: 168) in people's narratives. Hollway and Jefferson do nonetheless acknowledge postmodern insights on the discursive production of subjectivities to note that the biographical self is mediated by a number of factors:

1. The authors, drawing on psychoanalytic theory, assume that we are all anxious, defended subjects. We **produce accounts of ourselves** that draw on our motivation to not fully understand or know certain aspects of ourselves. In other words, accounts are produced rather than simply known.
2. Narrations will **draw on conventions** – as will researchers. We are looking for meaning, links, explanations, unifying theories and concepts. This does not fit with the psychoanalytic approach that aims to acknowledge contradictions and lack of reason.
3. Narratives are **co-produced** in the interview and the interviewer is often in a different and more powerful position.

The sorts of questions asked in the biographical interview, both those prepared in advance and those arising out of the research interaction, are replete with meanings which cue the other's responses in ways that are profoundly influential and yet not subject to much conscious control. (Hollway and Jefferson, 2000: 170)

Therefore 'the biographical "I", as with the psychoanalytic subject, is a dynamic, intersubjective product of the relationship' (ibid., p. 171). In other words, the interview does not simply take information from the participant, which is then analysed by the researcher, but instead there is a more complex process of developing the narrative within the interview.

Narratives as research product

It has been seen that narratives are co-produced in interviews with researchers. A further iteration of the narrative then usually takes place. In traditional, non-participative research designs, there is a period of analysis conducted by the researcher following data collection and in the absence of the research participants. The researcher then will usually reinterpret, compress, select, re-order and reinterpret the significance of the participant's narrative account before it is presented to a research audience (Cortazzi, 2001).

The respondent's account of past experiences and the researcher's theoretical framework are interwoven to create the final story. In this respect, the final account of a respondent's story is not strictly their story, but an interpretation of their life history by the researcher. (Hubbard, 2000: 11.1)

The researcher's presence in interpreting and representing the data may be done at different levels. The researcher's voice may be the authoritative interpretative voice, providing analysis around narrators' extracts. An alternative version is an interactive voice, where the researcher's reflections on their interactions with the narrator, that is the researcher's story, are given a role in the research product (Chase, 2005). In Hall's (1997) book on social work narratives in children's social work, he uses the technique of including imaginary dialogues between himself, social workers portrayed in the book and other walk-on characters, including Foucault, to discuss the debates and dilemmas involved in presenting social work documents and interviews as narratives. Here is a short extract from the first of these:

Social worker: This talk about it all being 'narrative', you mean it's just a story, a fabrication. I know you are not saying I tell lies, but that what I say is just a load of jargon and professional claptrap, as a judge said to me once.

Author: No, no, I am not trying to rubbish your reports; on the contrary, I marvel at the 'artful practices' you display in making links between people and their circumstances.

Social Worker: Thanks, I think I can take that as a compliment. But I have a more serious complaint. I don't think you are taking this subject seriously enough; I mean this dialogue. Don't you realise that children are suffering out there. ...?

Author: ... Perhaps we can meet again in Chapter Three. Though that last question will come up again; it does worry me. (Hall, 1997:18)

A further approach for the researcher is to minimise their influence on the participant's narrative, only providing a 'supportive voice' (Chase, 2005: 665), and simply including introductory commentary. Even where there is an attempt to provide only a 'supportive voice', however, most narratives will have been subject to some re-ordering and editing. Even Marjorie Shostak's (1981) well-known anthropological book comprising a vivid first-hand account of over 300 pages from a !Kung woman, *Nisa*, living in the Kalahari desert, was subject to some reformulation:

> The chronological sequence in which the narrative is presented does not necessarily reflect the order in which the stories appear in the (30 hours of) interviews. In a number of places, a memory presented as continuous is taken from more than one account of the same incident ... apart from these changes, the narrative is faithful to the interviews. (Shostak, 1981: 43)

Narrative forms

Many narrative researchers are as interested in the narrative form as they are in the content. Narratives are analysed as stories, with a structure, form and purpose. Key authors, such as Labov (1972) pioneered methods of analysing transcripts of talk in a wide range of settings to explore how past events are narrated in the form of stories. Narratives may be understood as texts with structures including elements such as abstract, orientation, evaluation, resolution and coda. Stories require that a complication is set up and resolved (Hall, 1997). Subsequent authors have criticised Labov's lesser attention to the partial and constructed nature of accounts, the decontextualised nature of the analysis and a gendered emphasis that appeared to sideline women's often more interactional style of narrating (Patterson, 2008). Nonetheless, Labov and other researchers who have paid attention to narrative forms and structures have been strongly influential in the field of narrative research.

In social work research, this aspect of narrative investigation has many applications. Christopher Hall (1997) shows how social workers use narrative forms to make their written and oral cases more persuasive. He demonstrates how accounts are structured as stories, but also how they require a listener or reader to render them as narrative accounts. White et al. (2009) analyse the ways in which a new child assessment form in English children's services departments disrupts established narrative forms of 'case-telling' by practitioners. They draw on Gubrium et al. (1989) to demonstrate the 'descriptive tyranny' of forms. Although many practitioners felt frustrated in their inability to give a full picture of a child's circumstances on the forms, the authors show how short narratives are still produced in the open text boxes: 'They are using it to manage accountabilities and accomplish disposals in locally artful ways' (Gubrium et al., 1989: 1212). One example is of including reported speech to reinforce a case that parents have the best interests of their child to the fore and that help should be forthcoming. The social worker notes that 'K is much loved by her parents … She gets lots of affection and support'. The parents are directly quoted: 'We need support now, before it is too late – as promised by the previous Head' (ibid., p. 1208). The reported speech in this context implies a degree of complaint and places the parents as active participants – and potentially troublesome if resources are not forthcoming.

Phillida Salmon explored the narratives not of professionals, but of someone more likely to be a recipient of the helping professions. She interviewed a man called Percy, who has schizophrenia, every week for a year. Salmon shows how Percy's accounts do not meet usual narrative norms. He doesn't provide temporal ordering, a sense of subjectivity (with motives and feelings) nor any moral stance or evaluative element. She quotes one story: 'I was a Post Office clerk. So I jumped off Westminster Bridge and I went for a ride in a police launch' (Salmon and Riessman, 2008: 79). With this work she is able to show how people living with schizophrenia may become socially excluded as 'an outcome of their inability to present their lives as socially intelligible projects' (ibid., p. 79).

Methods for generating narratives

Many of the methods used for generating or exploring narratives for research are discussed in other chapters of this book. For example, arts-based methods (see Chapter Twelve), using media such as film, photography, poetry and drama are likely to engender personal and group narratives. Diaries (Chapter Nine), whether research-prompted or written for other, more personal purposes, can be seen as narrative accounts, unless the researcher has imposed a particular structure that discourages narratives. Not all narratives will be elicited by the researcher and in social work professional narratives in supervision, team meetings and more informally in team rooms are naturally occurring sources (see Pithouse, 1998; White, 1998). In Chapter Nine we discuss social work records which can contain rich narrative accounts of individuals and families and can also be read as a narrative of professional identities and justification of decision making. As seen in the example from Sue White and colleagues (2009) earlier in this chapter, many modern electronic recording formats challenge practitioners' wishes to provide a narrative account, but some are able to use forms artfully to include them. It may be, however, that in modern social work environments verbal narratives will be more fruitful sources of narrative data than the lengthy case records of the past and, indeed, White and colleagues found this to be the case.

Narrative interviews

There is no single method for a narrative interview and a full discussion of the various forms would take an entire book (see, for example, Andrews et al., 2008). What follows, therefore, is necessarily brief and selective. As noted in the introduction to this chapter, some interviews aim to enable a person to tell their entire life story, while others will be exploring a particular period of life (for example becoming a new parent, experiences of a war or life since developing a chronic illness). While there are a range of different traditions of research broadly labelled as narrative, most authors on the topic seem to place much importance on the style, format and wording of questions. The idea of the narrative interview is to provide a different form from the semi-structured Q&A method (Jovchelovitch and Bauer, 2000).

Questions should:

- Use everyday language rather than sociological language. Questions which replicate research questions simply invite interviewees to shape their narratives according to the researcher's analytic frame.
- Use the interviewee's vocabulary to ask further questions.
- Avoid asking 'why' questions (yet see Williams' exemplar below)
- Try not to interrupt stories in full flow. In doing so you give a message that you are trying to train the interviewee to give the 'right' answers.

Elliott (2005); Hollway and Jefferson (2000); Jovchelovitch and Bauer (2000)

Some researchers have developed specific methods to research narratives. For example, Jovchelovitch and Bauer (2000) provide a fairly detailed and regulated idea of narrative interviewing – the 'rules of engagement' (p. 61). Their instructions include that the interviewer's influence should be minimal, acting as someone who knows very little about the subject. The tape-recorded interview should consist almost entirely of an uninterrupted account, with follow-up questions mainly limited to the period after recording finishes and to aid analysis rather than act as primary data. This form became popular in Germany in the 1980s but may be criticised in that there is always an audience effect, despite such attempts to minimise it. The participant will still be trying to anticipate what the interviewer might want to hear, for example. The rules in this prescribed format do not necessarily aid everyone to talk. One of the authors, Bauer, relates that in one study using this method the shortest narrative was only one minute long.

In contrast, Gubrium and Holstein (1998: 176) suggest the interviewer should use the relationship to enable longer narratives to emerge:

After all, one needs conversational 'space' if one is to tell an extended story; teller and listener must work together to create the conversational environment in which a story might emerge. Indeed, listeners are often active co-participants in both the elicitation and production of stories, working with the machinery of ordinary conversation to shape storytelling.

Questions may span more than one interview, where the researcher reviews and analyses between interviews, helping to build rapport and depth (Hollway and Jefferson, 2000). In a series of studies exploring issues of gender and class, Valerie Walkerdine (Walkerdine et al., 2002) has used a narrative method of three psychosocial interviews to build a relationship between interviewer and research participant where issues of affect may be safely explored. For example, in a study of young men in a deindustrialised ex-steel town in Wales, three interviews were carried out with young men and supplemented with two interviews with their mothers and fathers (Jimenez and Walkerdine, 2011). The researchers found shame among the young men and some scapegoating by the rest of their community for their inability to find work seen as gender appropriate.

| **EXAMPLE 8.3** | **A Simple Narrative Question** |

A classic of thematic narrative research is the medical sociologist Gareth Williams' (1984) research on the genesis of chronic illness. He asked a simple question – 'Why do you think you got arthritis?' Despite the advice of many narrative researchers not to ask 'why' questions, in his case this led to narratives that addressed the genesis – we may say 'causes' – of their arthritis, and in ways that were very different from the medical mainline account of hereditary predispositions. He might have asked 'how did you get arthritis?' with perhaps different sorts of answers. The question as asked prompted *narrative reconstructions of their biographies.*

Bill – narrative reconstruction as political criticism:

'I didn't associate it with anything to do with the works at the time, but I think it was chemically induced. I worked with a lot of chemicals, acetone and what have you. We washed our hands in it, we had cuts, and we absorbed it. Now, I tell you this because it seems to be related. The men that I worked with who are all much older than me – there was a crew of sixteen and two survived, myself and the gaffer that was then – and they all complained of the same thing, you know, their hands started to puff up. It seems very odd.'

Gill – narrative reconstruction as social psychological:

'Well, if you live in your own body for a long time, you're a fool if you don't take note of what is happening to it. I think that you can make naive diagnoses which are quite wrong. But I think that at the back of your head, certainly at the back of my head, I have feelings that this is so and that is so, and I'm quite certain that it was stress that precipitated this. Not simply the stress of events that happened but the stress perhaps of suppressing myself while I was a mother and wife; not "women's libby" but there comes a time in your life when you think, you know, "where have I got to? There's nothing left of me".'

Betty – narrative construction [note, not reconstruction] as theodicy:

'I've got the wonderful thing of having the Lord in my life. I've got such richness, shall I say, such meaning. I've found the meaning of life, that's the way I look at it.

> My meaning is that I've found the joy in this life, and therefore for me to go through anything, it doesn't matter really, in one way, because I reckon that they are testing times . . . You see. He never says that you won't have these things. He doesn't promise us that we won't have them. He doesn't say that. But He comes with us through these things and helps us to bear them and that's the most marvellous thing of all.'

Mixed methods for exploring narratives

A number of methods can be used together in a research design that is primarily aiming to explore narrative. An example of this is Jacqui Gabb's (2008) intensive, narrative-based research with families. She was exploring family members' experiences of intimacy and emotions and as well as biographical narrative interviews about their life-long experiences of intimacy in family life, she used a range of additional qualitative methods to enable family members to participate. This included 'emotion maps' of the house, drawing with children and use of diaries.

Elliott (2005) advocates for the use of mixed qualitative and quantitative methods for narrative research. Narratives pay attention to temporal elements and the individual in society. Individual events' meanings are related to a larger whole (in the life course or in that social context). Therefore, Elliott (2005) argues, some aspects of narrative research can be answered using quantitative methods, especially from cohort studies, and ideally designs will include both quantitative and qualitative data.

Narratives in research and practice

In social work practice, narrative approaches are often used consciously to enable service recipients to find new ways of understanding their situation and to imagine alternative, more hopeful, narratives for their life trajectories (Parton and O'Byrne, 2000). Practitioners who attend to narratives can move beyond 'seeking the views' of an individual and start to understand the complex and dynamic ways in which they understand themselves, their position in their social world and how they wish these to be understood by the listener (Holland et al., 2008).

In social work, attention to narratives can help us to hear untold or marginal stories and challenge dominant ones. For example, a dominant narrative that a family is problematic can be transformed when some of the family's success stories are told and listened to (Cedersund, 1999). Cedersund, in her analysis of conversations between social workers and service users in Sweden, shows how some social workers can either cut off or allow clients to describe their personal circumstances and how they have reached the situation they now find themselves in. The struggle to tell narratives and to have them listened to highlights the power and influence of talk. 'Research is thus needed on who has the right to say what, and in what situations various people are believed' (ibid., p. 83). In some circumstances researchers do not simply analyse social work practice but may blur the boundaries between practice and research. In Example 8.4, the authors created biographical accounts, in the form of life story books with adults with profound learning disabilities, that could contribute to more individualised care and in doing so were able to analyse how biographical accounts are reproduced in practice.

EXAMPLE 8.4

Biographical Approaches in Research and Practice: Life Story Books for Adults with Profound Learning Disabilities

Middleton and Hewitt describe a research project that explored how carers worked with, produced and attended to the biographies of people with profound learning disabilities who were unable to do this biographical work themselves, as they moved from hospital to community based care settings. The researchers created life story books for each individual by interviewing people who know/knew them, adding photographs and looking at written records. They therefore collected biographical data using several data sources, carrying out work that was both research and practice.

There were clear research aims. The authors were exploring how carers work with issues of identity, how life story books contribute to identity-work and its visibility in care settings and continuities and discontinuities in remembering across transitions in care settings.

But it was also practice. They were interested in how a biographical focus, as enabled through the making of life story books, can lead to more sensitive and individualised care plans. They explore the evidence for this through detailed analysis of the biographical talk of carers and by producing the life story books in the setting.

The interplay between research and practice is powerfully demonstrated, using the example of 'Lance', an adult with profound learning disabilities. Through these methods, carers and family are enabled to talk in a nuanced way about Lance's agency, participation, potential future participation, memories and preferences in a level of detail unlikely to be part of an institutional care plan. Issues of interdependency, participation and agency come across strongly and provide an alternative biographical account about an individual with high levels of care need.

Middleton, D. and Hewitt, H. (2000) 'Biography and identity: Life story work in transitions of care for people with profound learning difficulties', in P. Chamberlayne, J. Bornat and T. Wengraf (eds), *The Turn to Biographical Methods in Social Science*. London: Routledge, pp. 261–275.

Conclusion

In this chapter we have resisted the notion that data 'speak for themselves', nor that it is possible to unproblematically report participants' 'voices'. All talk and writing is produced in a social context and for an audience, often in interaction with others such as an interviewer. Stories are central to human interactions and play an important role in social work practice. By paying attention to the form and context, as well as the content, of research data we can uncover insights that are invaluable to furthering our understanding of social work.

Taking it further

The following extract is from the first of a series of three life history interviews carried out with a young woman who spent much of her later childhood in foster and residential care. She is now employed, married and a mother and is reflecting back on her life experiences. She was one of 16 young adults interviewed for a study conducted with care experienced young people (Holland and Crowley, 2013).

Read the extract. Although this is only a small proportion of the overall interview, consider it as a narrative. How has Grace (pseudonym) structured the account of her early days in foster care as a story? What role does she give herself and the other protagonists in the account? What is the interviewer's role? What does Grace want the interviewer to understand about this period of her life? Contrast Grace's narrative with the short narrative from Percy, a person living with schizophrenia, earlier in this chapter.

Grace:	...they came out, took us down the family centre and they couldn't get my baby sister off me until gone six o'clock, you know, they had found foster placements, but they tricked me, they said, you know – you're upsetting the baby now, put her on the floor and let her play with some toys and as I done that a social worker came in and grabbed her, pulled me back and just took her and like and ... When I first got taken to my foster placement ...
Interviewer:	So, you were put into different foster placements?
Grace:	Yeh – we were all split up and none of us were together. They put me in (*place*), a lovely woman, named (*name*), she already had her own daughter – I'm still in contact with her now, I was only there for a month, you know, it was just – it was (*date*) we got taken into care, I went straight to the foster placement in the evening. One of the children, one of the foster children, was due to go to Brownies, so it was literally in the door with the social worker and out the door with the foster mother, back around the corner! You know, everything was just such a rush and like it was all up in the air and I was so confused. But B, like she was lovely, she was sort of like – I'd never known, like, what a normal family, like sort of, upbringing was and I never knew how a normal family like, sort of, acted. It just sort of like – as soon as I went there, although I was uptight and I'd just had my brothers and sisters taken away from me, my mother – I didn't give two shits about anyway. It was just my younger brothers and sister because I was like ... One of the reasons they said they took us into care was because I was playing the mothering role in the home – because I was looking after them and stuff. Well she was really sort of – like soft and like calming like and she

was really like happy and bubbly and stuff as well. Like when I first went there she knew like I was feeling really uncomfortable and she sat down and like she tried to explain to me the reasons from the information she was given – but it weren't enough like, you know there weren't an explanation kind of thing there. And it kept me confused then for quite a while afterwards. And then, because the other foster child which was around the same age as me – (*name*) – she kicked up a fuss saying 'oh you said you weren't going to take in any more kids before Christmas', kind of thing, so (*foster carer*) had to let me go then. So she had to ask the social worker to move me and then I got moved onto a placement in (*place*), and she was lovely as well, though she'd had wear and tear from runaway teenagers and stuff like you know but … For the first – I was there for about a year and a half, it was my longest placement and it was really good like at first. She got me back into school, because I had stopped when I was at (*previous carer's*) and I just refused to go, and there was still like the effect – (*previous carer*) – still affected my next placement because she sent me on like with sacks and sacks full of presents for Christmas. She bought me loads of new clothes which I'd never had before, all my clothes had come from either the nearly new shop or the family centre which are obviously old and smelt like granny's! Or like, they came from car boot sales sort of stuff. All of a sudden like I had these nice new dresses and it was like 'oh wow I've got a nice tight-fitting little black dress I can go out in' and you know, it sort of like, I started feeling like a bit normal because I was sort of looking like a bit more normal, and I started using some hair gels, because my hair's like afro – it's like a black person's hair, it's like really frizzy, and like my foster mother introduced me to hair gel and hair spray and I thought that was amazing.

(both laugh)

Interviewer: So, you got looked after a bit?

Grace: Yeh, yeh, and I sort of like was shown the ropes like of how to brush my hair properly, how to do a plait and … how to wear a bra, that was the highlight of my life!

(both laugh)

NINE
Traces and Deposits in Texts and Documents

In this chapter we note and offer explanations for a return of critical and empirical interest in research based on traces and deposits, mainly but not only written. We take up much of the first half of the chapter in addressing the challenges and opportunities of such research. The examples given are deliberately of a very diverse kind.

We take the social work case record and social work archives as two fields that enable us to explore and contextualise the general themes.

While in much of the chapter we point to ways in which diverse forms of text and document pose comparable challenges, in the closing part of the chapter we distinguish and discuss personal and practice texts.

'If I were … asked to give just one piece of advice to the novice researcher, it would be as follows: look at the documentation, not merely for its content but more at how it is produced, how it functions in episodes of daily interaction, and how, exactly, it circulates' (Prior, 2004: 388).

We noted in an early chapter that research involving documents, personal records or archival data were present in just under one in ten research papers in the main social work journal publishing qualitative research. We will critically assimilate the special opportunities and relevance of such research in this chapter. Discussion of the opportunities and challenges of such research is often missing or thinly dealt with in the social work methodology literature.

We are indebted to the elements of the idea for this chapter title to Webb and colleagues' (1966) early discussion of 'erosion and accretion' in their enticing book *Unobtrusive Measures*. We are not convinced that a distinction can be applied across the board between qualitative and quantitative approaches to the subject, largely because texts, records and documents are better viewed as extraordinarily diverse *sources* of data rather than a method of data collection. The chapter title also reflects that developments in the field of organisational documents, personal texts, secondary analysis and archived materials blur – helpfully we believe – older distinctions within and between different qualitative methods.

A helpful way of distinguishing such data sources is that 'their existence is independent of the researcher's actions' (Padgett, 2008: 125). This is not a watertight distinction, in that some of what we talked about in the previous chapter also draws on materials that are not directly elicited by the researcher. Also, when researchers refer to texts of the kind covered in the following pages, they usually have in mind written rather than oral sources. We will have cause to press apart this distinction later in the chapter.

Padgett suggests that documents as sources of data have fallen out of favour (ibid., p. 125). We are not so sure. It certainly was the case historically that, 'in industrialized countries, the importance of administrative records as a source of data for research analysis declined, as specially designed research studies were created to replace or to complement records-based data' (Hakim, 2000: 46). It is more than half a century ago that Benney and Hughes remarked that sociology had become the science of the interview, in part because interviews had 'become the favored tool of a large army of sociologists' (1956: 137).

But we believe the situation is changing. While early social work and social science research was more likely to draw on records than on interviews, several factors have contributed to a significant shift. Computer access to, and digitisation of, records has opened up significant new potential for such research. Think, for example, of the relative difficulty of extracting and anonymising data from traditional paper-based case files and electronic files, and the risks in the former of a further layer of administrative glossing. This should not be overstated, as access to the bulging files in social work agencies' record cabinets that continue to accumulate swathes of paper records would show. The broader development of the internet has greatly increased the deposits of chatrooms, blogs, and social media accounts. Social work research shares with other disciplines an increasing influence from the humanities. Library studies have helped foster an interest in the archive, as well as leading the way in extensive programmes of digitisation. Growing interest in historical social science research, and crossovers with cultural anthropology and social geography have helped highlight the potential of material forms of data. In conjunction with these developments there have been helpful assessments that place such research in a wider framework of ideas and methodology (e.g., Prior, 2003; Scott, 1990).

The possible applications of these sources have also widened. Restricting herself to administrative records Hakim suggests and illustrates how they 'can provide the basis for longitudinal studies, quasi-experimental designs, historical research, area-based studies, cross-national comparisons, studies of organizations and the policy process, as well as being especially useful for research on minority groups and rare events' (Hakim, 2000: 48).

Making use and making sense of texts and documents

The general approach of earlier writing about research methods of this nature was to set out procedures that optimised the possibility of gaining, in the words of the title of Webb et al.'s opening chapter, 'approximations to knowledge', usually through a process of internal analysis of the document and external sources that may question or provide confirmatory instances of the document. 'Approximations', in part, because 'absolute, isolated measurement is meaningless. In all useful measurement an implicit comparison exists when an explicit one is not visible. "Absolute" measurement is a convenient fiction' (Webb et al., 1966: 5f).

This tradition is perhaps still the dominant one in mainstream research. Example 9.1 illustrates a careful application of the 'best approximation to knowledge' approach to documents – and one of neglected value to social workers in the mental health field.

| **EXAMPLE 9.1** | **Archival Research on Service Utilisation** |

A cluster of researchers applied documentary research methods to yield comparative historical understandings of welfare service data.

A. Healy and colleagues undertook a careful analysis and discussion of morbidity and mortality data in North Wales and compared service utilisation in 1896 and 1996 (Healy et al., 2005). Among their conclusions, they point to how the major increase in the number of forensic psychiatrists in the thirty years prior to their study census date 'parallels an increase in the number of patients now locked up in secure facilities'. Hence 'it might be naïve to think we could have expected that a massive increase in the number of psychiatrists would ever lead to anything other than the treatment of more patients than ever before' (Healy et al., 2005: 40). Yet they exercise appropriate scepticism when underlining that they make no claims to the existence of or trends in relation to real illness entities. 'In one sense studies like this ... are as likely to indicate what social bodies ... can live with, as they are to reveal what has afflicted them' (ibid., p. 40).

B. A different project from this group of researchers yielded a further persuasive analysis of historical records. Hirst and Michael (2003) exemplify how it is possible to bring research questions to documentary data, to afford a 'prehistory of community care' (p. 145) through an analysis of 'Lunacy Returns'. In so doing they afford an illustration of how records are for an audience in that 'From the standpoint of the local administration, the object was to meet statutory requirements without stimulating further demands or intervention from the central authorities' (ibid., p. 149). Thus the mentally ill might be hidden among the records of those with learning disabilities in a process of 'bureaucratic concealment.'

One of the frequently observed issues in research using any kind of document, although especially organisational 'running records', is that of incompleteness – or as Webb et al. expressed it, the twin problems of selective deposit and selective survival. Take the first problem. We noted Hayes and Devaney's (2004) illuminating study of ethics issues in two research studies utilising children's case records in Chapter Six. They encountered 'difficulties for the researcher associated with their length and legibility … their use of language, incompleteness … and the fact that they contain contradictory information' (ibid., p. 319). On the question of incompleteness Hayes, in his study, 'examined 289 case files and noted that basic information such as the age of adults, employment status, housing status and ethnicity is rarely recorded'. Similarly, Devaney found in his own research 'almost no reference in the assessments of over 200 children on the impact of social deprivation on the family situation' (ibid., p. 319). Scourfield and colleagues in a study of a sample of 100 suicide case files from a coroner's office discovered that 'missing data' of a kind that as researchers they would have wished to explore included ethnicity, social class and sexual orientation (Scourfield et al., 2012).

Such incompleteness may have telling implications for both participant and researcher. Dorothy Atkinson refers to an oral history project with people with learning disabilities in which she worked with people for over two years. She powerfully remarks that they are 'people whose lives are "missing" because of their institutional histories and because their personal case notes (often the only documentary record of their lives) are fragmented, lost or even destroyed' (Atkinson, 2005: 429). Her research drew her into 'gaining access to the documented past, in all its formality and starkness, and working with people to make sense of records couched in the language of the past', and comments 'In my experience, it means facing the raw truth about separation and rejection with the person who wants to find out what really happened to him or her in childhood' (ibid., p. 431). The brief extract from Karen Staller's (forthcoming) work in Example 9.2 captures and illustrates the partial yet 'raw truth' that resides in some formal records.

EXAMPLE 9.2 — **Heroic Stories in Trace Materials**

In 1942 … John Chester Munn[1], a young man who had received services provided by the Children's Aid Society (CAS) of New York City, penned a letter to his guardian and social worker, Miss Helen Baxter about his experience in the US Navy during WWII. The letter resides in his social work case file. A partial passage of the war-time correspondence reads:

> I've changed a great deal since the beginning of this fracas. Honestly, I developed a wider vision of seeking the true facts in the reality of life. If the people only knew the truth. I've undergone many stirring and harrowing experiences which will remain in my memoirs until the end of my days. (Oct 8, 1942)

It may be true, that social work case records are like desiccated botanical specimens or pickled Mexican Sierras however, none of this helps explain why I would be moved to tears reading John's social work case record. Nor why I am still haunted by its content. Nor why I feel like John and his social worker, Miss Baxter, have become real characters in my life; although I never met either one. Nor why I have felt a paralyzing need to tell John's life story 'truthfully' and 'correctly', in spite of the fact that reconstructing a life can never be fully done from the trace evidence of its existence.

Karen Staller

We wrote 'missing data' in inverted commas earlier in this section because, as Hayes and Devaney readily concede, what is 'incomplete' or 'inaccurate' for the researcher may have been appropriate for the author. They nicely quote from Spratt on the consequences of the inevitable compression of the case record, when he says that in the social worker's memory rests 'the certain edge to the teacher's voice and tone, the anxiety, the unrecorded asides' while the researcher 'is limited to the coded meanings of the written word' (Hayes and Devaney, 2004: 320). This reference to the contextual 'mood music' is indeed often intangible in documentary research. Schwab is talking about a different strategy and setting, but his remarks transfer well in this connection when he says 'It is local context that matters – the curriculum will be brought to bear not in some archetypal classroom but in a particular locus in time and space with smells, shadows, seats and conditions outside its walls which may have much to do with what is achieved inside' (Schwab, 1969: 12).

Trusting texts

Texts have been assessed against four criteria (Scott, 1990). Are they authentic? In other words, is a text genuine as to its authorship and origin? Second, are they credible? Credibility includes the two aspects of accuracy and sincerity. Third, is the evidence typical of its kind? This is the test of representativeness. Finally, what does the text mean? Is the meaning clear and comprehensible?

Authenticity is not always a problem for social work researchers in that often they are not working with historical texts but with the original document. Some years ago it was thought that the growth in the use of information technology would increasingly remove some of the threats of copy error. However, the present and pending proliferation of diverse forms of technology in social work has rendered the authenticity (and authorship) of some texts less obvious (Hill and Shaw, 2011). The test of *credibility* is a more difficult one to satisfy. The accuracy and 'sincerity' of records both come under threat. The test of sincerity is whether the author believed what they recorded. Scott suggests that the best filter of sincerity is to ask what material interest the author had in the audience reaction to the record. For example, reports to courts may often function as 'sad tales' which emphasise determinist, and hence by inference relatively 'excusable' interpretations of behaviour. This brings us immediately up against the character of records as socially produced texts.

Credibility defined as *accuracy* is often put at risk in social work by the fact that case records are typically not eye witness accounts. The main partial exceptions to this are some records of residential settings, and some group work and family therapy work. The point needs more carefully stating. Practice texts are usually not eye witness accounts of *behaviour*, although they may more often be direct witnesses of *attitudes* and perhaps *beliefs*. However, even in these cases, written practice texts often suffer credibility threats arising from the lapse of time between practice and 'writing up' that practice. We should not conclude from this that written accounts will always be superior to spoken, oral texts. For example, Sainsbury long ago discovered that client memories of some aspects of social work practice were fuller and more accurate than practitioner records of the same event (Sainsbury, 1975). It is possible that in a subculture where writing is not the customary means of preserving evidence and memories, oral accounts may be more accurate. A reading of the work on oral history would illumine and enrich social work research in this regard (Roberts, 2002).

The selectivity that threatens the credibility of a text also risks jeopardising its *representativeness*. For example, records of inquiries to an agency intake/reception team are likely to be selective and therefore not representative of all the inquiries that are made. But selectivity is not only about selective *deposit*, but also about selective *survival* and *decay* – 'the gnawing criticism of the mice' as Marx famously expressed it.[1] The routine use of digital records poses questions of this kind that are as yet unresolved. A different problem of representativeness arises from the widely varying extent to which access to texts is possible (Example 9.3). If texts vary in availability the texts we can use will vary in representativeness. For example, personal texts created by service users, practitioners or managers especially for research purposes will almost certainly be unrepresentative of unsolicited personal texts, although it would be unwise to exaggerate the importance of this criticism given the nature of all personal texts as storied lives.

EXAMPLE 9.3   Social Work Texts

Access	Personal	Practice
Closed	Service user diaries	Some agency case records
	Personal correspondence	Housing records
Restricted	Family stories	Some agency case records
	Carer life stories written for a social worker	Service contracts
		Some equal opportunities data
	Photo collections and family artifacts	
		Reports to other agencies
	Online discussion boards	
Archive	Family tree archive websites	Voluntary society archive
	Photographic record sites	Performance indicator reports
		Commissioned community profiles
		Project funding bids
Public	Published accounts by former or current service users	Annual agency reports
		Public inquiries
		School or hospital 'league tables'
		Small area Census reports

---

[1]In the Preface to his *Critique of Political Economy*, speaking of an unpublished joint manuscript with Engels.

On the question of the *meaning* of such sources, Cicourel expressed the issue half a century ago as clearly as anyone when he reflected on the fact that 'Any researcher who has worked with official records has experienced the problems of making sense of often abstract and highly condensed and incomplete records of complex events' (Cicourel, 1964: 146). This is partly because 'organizations develop various ways of communicating official and unofficial material which is not recorded but nevertheless treated as basic information when writing and reading actual records' (ibid., p. 146f). Therefore there are both public and private meanings in documents, and 'the public and private character of the meaning structures communicated can vary with the ways in which the materials are assembled, the projected audience envisioned by the writer, the various audiences who might be exposed to the materials under consideration, the language used, and the cultural and subcultural definitions employed' (ibid., p. 147). Similar points can be made about social work case records and other clinical records.

> The clinical folder is elliptical and vague, resting on a vast body of taken-for-granted assumptions, and its therapeutic meaning can only be grasped by participants who understand the situation in which it was produced. The record is constructed so as to allow medical staff to reconstruct the therapy and so legitimate their actions. (Scott, 1990: 124)

In interpreting such materials 'the researcher generally has no access to the setting in which they were produced' and 'it is difficult to separate re-construction or re-creation from imputations and innovations supplied by the researcher's own perspective' (Scott, 1990: 143). Yet the importance of 'unstated meaning structures' is central for understanding both organisational and personal documents such as diaries, newspapers, interviews, official records and novels.

With Kitsuse, Cicourel wrote a modestly titled but classic paper on the uses of official statistics that elaborates on this process by which meaning structures are embedded in documents and subsequently influence their wider meaning and use (Kitsuse and Cicourel, 1963). In the field of deviancy research they take delinquency statistics as significant less for what they tell us about actual rates of deviant behaviour but more for what they illuminate about 'rate-producing' behaviour. In contributing to the then emerging ideas of labelling theory, they conclude that on this view of the world, 'the focus of inquiry shifts from the forms of behaviour … to the "societal reactions" which define various forms of behavior as deviant' (Kitsuse and Cicourel, 1963: 135). This has clear implications for how research problems are identified, and for showing that how we see documents is not a technical matter but central to the theorising and methodology of research. For example, we will start to do research that asks how different forms of behaviour come to be seen as deviant by various groups or organisations in society, 'and how [they are] classified, recorded and treated by persons in the society' (ibid., p. 139).

Prior makes the point tellingly in the quotation that heads this chapter, in a context where he argues that the written word has been subordinated philosophically to the spoken word in the West. He is interested in the written document not as resource receptacle/content but as 'topic'. He is interested in how documents are *produced* and how they are *used* – as he puts it, 'the significance of inscription in organizational settings' (Prior, 2004: 376). Hakim, if less radically, refers to the same distinction of content and meaning when she writes 'Administrative records are also used in their own right, rather than *faute de mieux*, for research on the policy process itself and in evaluation research. In this case, records and documents ... are part of the reality being studied' (Hakim, 2000: 49).

In a contribution to an insufficiently well-regarded book on the relation of method and context, Gale Miller, through a study of residential social and nursing care, focuses on 'how institutional texts are inextricably linked to the social contexts in which they are produced.' By context he means 'interpretive domains ... which structure, but do not determine, how institutional texts are assembled and interpreted' (Miller, 1997: 77). Drawing on Dorothy Smith's idea of 'textually mediated social organization', he points up the problem that texts become crystallised 'when we treat them as authoritative representations of stable, objective realities'. 'The words, numbers and images "freeze" the ongoing events of life.' The consequence of such freezing is that we 'gloss over the various contingencies and other contextual factors associated with the texts' production and use in institutional settings' (Miller, 1997: 78). Although organisational contexts do not determine the meanings assigned to everyday life by members of the setting, 'the settings might be described as "encouraging", "privileging" or "preferring" some interpretations over others' (ibid., p. 79).

Take for example children's services in many western countries where standardised, online forms for assessment have been developed with pre-set categories of meaning and interpretation. An example of this process can be seen in the growth over the first decade of the century of electronic assessment and intervention records for children and families. The UK's Integrated Children's System (ICS) yields such an instance (Shaw and Clayden, 2009; Shaw et al., 2009). The ICS reflects late modern developments towards evidence-based practice and the congruent development of standardised, manualised tools for use in direct practice (Nygren et al., 2006; c.f. Parton, 2008).

The practice model lying just below the surface of the ICS is one where the sequence of assessment, planning, intervention and review represents a *linear model* that is outcome-focused and structured. This may be true more generally of social work record forms: 'Forms demand description framed in terms of unidimensional, typically unilinear, timing. The chronological demand assumes that events reported ... are points of time in the client's experience' (Gubrium et al., 1989: 198).

Shaw and Clayden elaborate ways in which the ICS actively shaped practice, brought issues into focus, rendered social work visible and distanced the service user. Taking just the first point, they observed five areas where practitioners and managers believed they saw evidence, sometimes deleterious but not always so, of shaping and 'configuring the user'.

1. The recording formats served to partialise practice in ways that made it difficult to see the whole story.
2. The ICS had an implicit weighting of what practitioners should consider as 'important' or 'serious' evidence and what counted as less 'serious' or substantial.
3. The ICS unhelpfully 'fixed' the character of social work evidence, by unwittingly making the future-time development of analysis and associated plans less likely.
4. ICS 'pre-coded' some aspects of practice and left others 'open-ended'.
5. ICS shifted the language forms of social work.

Associated concerns were raised by Thomas and Holland (2010) where they give examples of copying and pasting of texts describing children and their needs *between different cases* and also where different social workers within a team were the 'authors' of the assessments. Yet the meanings afforded such institutional texts are not fixed, but sometimes contested, such that it is possible for institutional actors 'to construct and justify meanings that might be called "dis-preferred"' (Miller, 1997: 80). This process is briefly illustrated in Example 9.4 – here people are talking about changes to the standardised forms that took place during a pilot period.

EXAMPLE 9.4 | **Voices from the Integrated Children's System**

I've noticed ... with several changes over a number of years ... that people who are producing good records of the work they do are doing it despite the framework within which they're asked to do it. (Key informant 1)

We're actually now looking at the content of the documentation in the way that we didn't for the first 12 months because we tried to ... keep the integrity of the exemplars because it was a pilot and ... it didn't seem sensible to us to ... fiddle about with them before we tried them. So now ... we've tried them ... we're looking at ways in which we can refine them without taking stuff out but just to make them ... helpful to practitioners... rather than things ... that are seen as ... a hindrance.

(Key informant 2)

Which forms should be used? – The need for interim measures to ensure that the social work practice is not at risk. It was agreed that this is the most serious issue. Currently there is confusion and a lack of consistency on which forms should be used.

(Implementation Committee minute)

Examples of this kind illustrate how 'the meanings of institutional texts are always potentially unstable' (Miller, 1997: 83). Qualitative research that blends organisational documents with interviews and ethnographic elements, as in the examples of Miller and Shaw et al. (2009), illustrates a contribution to policy debate. There are two ways in which this is valuable. First, 'to provide public officials and other citizens with new understandings of the information found in institutional texts' and second, 'by countering the orientations to texts that objectify and justify relations of ruling … (and) demystifying institutional authority' (Miller, 1997: 90, 91).

How are social work records regarded by the various stakeholders? Practitioners are likely to see them as service records, which document the 'contractual' relationship between social worker and client, about the relationship between them, about whether obligations have been met. Managers/administrators may see it as 'an *actuarial* record' (Scott, 1990: 124), and part of a system of supervision, and will want it to ensure an adequate database for accountability statistics. This is not to stereotype practitioners as professionally caring and managers as actuarial bean-counters, but records which may be regarded as 'poor' by administrators begin to 'make sense' when seen as the ingredients for a potential service contract. A knowledge of how records are constructed in social work can enable the practitioner as well as the researcher to deal (albeit critically) with records as resources of information. The credibility and meaning of records can then be more adequately assessed. In addition, service users may see them as inaccurate and unfair judgements of their lives. In as yet unpublished research one of us (Holland) records a care-leaver not wanting to see records of their early life because they fear it will cast unfair judgements on their parents (having seen through experience how partial records can be), and other participants wanting to see the records to help them reach an understanding of their lives and identities (so expecting a form of truth and resolution).

Scott draws together the distinctions into research practice advice when he concludes that 'we must recognise three aspects of the meaning of a text – three "moments" in the movement of the text from author to audience' (1990: 134). We must distinguish the meaning the author *intended* to produce and the *received* content, or the meaning constructed by the audience. In doing so we should not assume that there is just one intended or received meaning. Texts typically have multiple meanings. But there is also a third meaning of the text, as constructed by readers who were not members of the original intended audience. For example, as we have implied above, a social worker may intend a community care contract to be a means of empowering service users. A line manager may see the same document as a more or less adequate protection of agency accountability. A subsequent reader may interpret it as reinforcing or challenging conventional gender roles. Texts may have meanings beyond their intentions. But as soon as a third party reads a text to interpret its meaning s/he becomes part of its audience.

This is a theme that we have had occasion to return to several times in this book. Take, for just one example, how the *motifs* of narrative research resonate with documents, particularly personal documents. When we hear the service user we need to distinguish the teller's story, the telling of the story, the life experience of people in the story, our experience of the story, and the wider audience of people who read our text or account. In consequence, the researcher operates 'in a forest of events and stories pointing inward and outward, and backward and forward' (Clandinin and Connelly, 1994: 418). As Clandinin and

Connelly later went on to express it, narrative practitioners are 'walking in the midst of stories' in the two senses of being 'somewhere along the dimensions of time, place, the personal and the social' and also 'as in the middle of a nested set of stories – ours and theirs' (Clandinin and Connelly, 2000: 63). Roberts remarks to similar effect in his excellent book on biographical research that 'In studying the lives of others we are also researching and constructing ourselves … The "mere" recounting of a life itself may well alter the life perspectives of the researcher and the researched' (Roberts, 2002: 50, 23).

Case records – again

The neglect of case records, and the limited ways of conceptualising their potential for research and practice was captured long ago by the Chicago sociologist Ernest Burgess and the Boston proto-constructionist social work writer, Ada Sheffield. An exam question for his sociology students set by Burgess in June 1929 reads

> What seems to you to be the values and limitations of the first person method of case recording for purposes (a) of social treatment of cases; (b) of sociological research? (University of Chicago, Special Collections. Burgess Papers. Box 184. Folder 7)

Burgess was not posing this merely as an opportunity for intellectual exercise. The interesting and little known observations of Burgess we gave in Chapter 3 bear repeating, because his specific proposal is enticing, even at this distance.

> My proposal is actually quite simple and I think, entirely feasible and reasonable, in spite of the fact that I do not anticipate its immediate and general adoption. It is to enter into the case record statements made by all persons visited in nearly as humanly possible, the language which they used. (Burgess, 1927: 192)

He immediately glosses this with the complaint that he is

> strongly opposed to having the language of the father and the mother in the home, of the landlord, or the teacher, or of the employer, translated into the language of the social worker on the case. The translation invariably and inevitably distorts the point of view and the attitude of the person interviewed. Each informant has a right to have himself appear in the record in his own language. (Burgess, 1927: 192–93)

In an article in the following year he shows how this matters as an indicator of respect for persons.

> Existing case records seldom, or never, picture people in the language of Octavia Hill, with their 'passions, hopes, and history' or their 'temptations', or 'the little scheme they have made of their lives, or would make if they had encouragement.' The characters in case records do not move, and act, and have

their being as persons. They are depersonalized, they become Robots, or mere cases undifferentiated except by the recurring problems they present. (Burgess, 1928: 526–7)

When Burgess complained of the 'atomic view of the individual' he was in fact talking by way of contrast with Ada Sheffield, a Boston-based social worker, of whom he said 'with her theoretic statement I find myself in complete agreement' (Burgess, 1928: 525). We remarked in Chapter One that her 1922 book on *Case-study Possibilities* stands as a forgotten classic – forgotten in part because it was vilified in an unfortunate *ad hominem* fashion by Virginia Robinson, an early *doyen* of the psychodynamic school (Robinson, 1930). We saw how she anticipated a constructionist stance when she said of the case worker that 'selection of facts amounts to an implicit interpretation of them' (Sheffield, 1922: 48) and that 'Not only do two students perceive different facts, they actually in a measure make different facts to be perceived' (ibid., p. 49). She inferred a criterion of evidential rigour in that 'the social student … should exercise caution in condensing the original record of these items in the case histories.' 'Compression is in itself a process of interpretation', and by doing so 'a student is imposing his own diagnosis upon them in a way that is not open to review by other students' (ibid., p. 49).

Archives and history

The glance at an almost lost aspect of Chicago sociology and at the collectively suppressed memory of Ada Sheffield brings us back to one of the sub-plots of this book that surfaced in our earlier reflections on the history and development of qualitative social work research and methods. Walter Lorenz has suggested that it is as if we are 'too embarrassed to look seriously at our history, afraid of the disorder we might find, too eager to distance ourselves from the pre-professional beginnings' and are, in consequence, homeless and 'disembedded' (Lorenz, 2007: 599). Lorenz's conclusion has point for research as much as for practice, for sociology as well as social work. 'All social work practices are deeply embedded in historical and cultural habits from which we cannot detach ourselves at will'. He aptly infers from this that we should be practising history 'in the dual sense of positioning ourselves in a historical context and of giving our interventions a historical dimension' (Lorenz, 2007: 601).

Archives of social science interest have come to the fore, partly from developments in technology and also in librarianship. But in considering deposits of material created without the presence of the researcher, we have in mind more than organisational and administrative records. They also include life history, biography, journals and diaries. For example, there is an unknown autobiography in the University of Chicago Special Collections, by Stuart Queen. He occupied a significant place on the borders of what later became the more distinct fields of social work and sociology. Taking his autobiography as a basis for documentary research illustrates the crossover between written and oral forms that we touch on below. This paragraph occurs on the fourth page of his opening chapter called 'Personal Experiences in the Field'. He is referring to events that took place in the USA around 1909.

| **EXAMPLE 9.5** | **Stuart Queen – Becoming a Sociologist** |

'It was decided I should go to the University of Nebraska in Lincoln. Quite by accident this proved to be a turning point in my life.

The important event was not playing in a very good band, which kept alive my earlier interest in music as a vocation. It certainly was not working 35 hours a week as a waiter in a restaurant. It was the course in beginning Sociology with George E. Howard. Someone had said I ought to take a course in Sociology. I asked, "What is that?" My advisor did not clarify the matter, but I decided to take a chance. The text was Deeley and Ward, A Textbook of Sociology, a rather dull summary of Ward's Dynamic Sociology and Pure Sociology. This might easily have driven me away from Sociology, but Professor Howard was a brilliant lecturer and immediately aroused my interest. He not only interpreted Ward, but he told us about other sociologists, mostly American, what they were doing, where they were teaching, and how he rated them. He said one day that by all odds the best place to study Sociology in the world was at the University of Chicago. So in the course of one semester I made up my mind to be a sociologist and to attend the University of Chicago, if this could possibly be arranged.'

We anticipate and indeed rather hope you will find this extract puzzling. This is a narrative about Queen's life, and is interesting for what it tells us about the processes through which a life is constructed. But it is also a narrative about sociology – sociology as his life. For the moment, we can focus on the time dimensions of the extract. Interest in time has been important in shaping social science theorising and research (owing initially to Barbara Adam's earlier work, Adam, 1990; c.f. Adam, 2004), but in ways that more applied qualitative research has not always recognised. Bornat and Bytheway (2012) helpfully distinguish:

1. Recorded time – time as part of the record of the course of life.
2. Formatted time – time as present in datasets, and how the medium figures in the construction of accounts over time.
3. Told time – how time is represented in the development and telling of stories.

Linking these categories to examples we have dealt with in this chapter, *recorded* time is seen in case records and also in diaries, and *formatted* time in the studies by Healy et al. (2005) and Hirst and Michael (2003). Queen's autobiography is an example of *told* time. Formatted time also comes under scrutiny in assessments of government reports. In the UK, Butler and Drakeford have explored archival material in their work on the Maria Colwell inquiry (Butler and Drakeford, 2011), and the same field has been explored in relation to the death in London of Victoria Climbié which became a template for collective self-appraisal within and beyond the UK shores.

More generally, Mark Smith (2010) offers sharply critical conclusions as he questions the way accounts of historical abuse of children in residential care 'intertwine to construct a master narrative of endemic abuse and systemic cover-up in care settings' (p. 304). He argues that existing accounts 'give no convincing insight into the nature or scale of abuse in care settings'. His qualitative argument is that this stems from naïve realism, and leads to victim narratives being privileged.

While he believes that 'many of the stories of abuse are told for no reason other than that they are true', he draws on a report in Scotland to conclude that victim accounts in such sources 'are invariably fragments of lives, shorn of context, denied interpretation and manipulated for particular (political and ideological) ends' (Smith, 2010: 313). He argues the case for a strong constructionist approach to historical material in documents, in which they are 'subject to rigorous hermeneutic and reflexive interrogation and interpretation by those with a grounded understanding of practice in this area' (ibid., p. 317).

In recent years 'newer archives have been established with the express purpose of providing textual and visual data for reuse by social researchers' (Crow and Edwards, 2012: 259). This development blurs the boundaries between secondary analysis and use of documents. There are 'emergent methodological issues for social scientists working with various forms of archived textual and visual data from a variety of perspectives' (ibid., p. 259). Developments in technology facilitate remote access, as well as greatly increasing the searchability of the materials. Crow and Edwards also suggest the play of the impulse stemming from 'the sense of loss relating to materials no longer available, which for one reason or another have been lost to posterity' (ibid., p. 259f).

Chambon and colleagues' recent work illustrates the welcome development of a more nuanced and diversified understanding of material archives (Chambon et al., 2011). They acknowledge the familiar problem of incompleteness and say that '[d]ue to the fragmentary nature of statements found in the archive, multiple, at times contradictory paths of elaboration are made possible' (ibid., p. 626). However, they believe there is potential for relatively rich depictions. In describing their concentrated focus on a series of annual reports, the photographs of children within the reports, and an internal archive for a children's group, they emphasise 'we anchor these documents in the materiality of the archive. Through our inter-disciplinary collaboration between social work and visual studies, we approach each source as a complex multifaceted object whose many features offer windows into the practices and values that sustained the development of the organization' (ibid., p. 626).

They explore how 'the material traces of the archive bring embodied actions and practices to the foreground' and how '[b]oth the said and the unsaid tell us something about the rules of society'. They ground this by exploring 'the agency's own practice of producing archival material' (ibid., p. 627), in ways akin to Prior's focus on how documents are produced. For example, talking of the photos of children over the years in the agency's annual reports they reflect on the images 'as both mirroring and creating discourse ...' (ibid., p. 632). Drawing on others' work they elaborate that 'an image ought to be refracted through several lenses: (i) how it describes an event (which is largely due to the photograph's own indexical properties); (ii) through its iconic properties – how the image interprets that event (the photographer's technical and aesthetic framing); and (iii) as a key image that contributes to collective interpretations through exemplification' (ibid., p. 632).

While our focus is on the researcher, it is also true that there are issues for the archivist and the social researcher who may be archiving data. Indeed, Chambon and colleagues make the process of agency archiving a central part of their own research. There is a problem over what to archive given the explosion of possible material. Digitisation does not solve the problem. In addition, 'The more material that is collected and placed in an archive, the more possibilities are likely to emerge for research participants to be identifiable' (Crow and Edwards, 2012: 260). This risk may well increase as more linkages between datasets develop.

Personal and practice texts

Through this chapter we have sometimes distinguished personal and organisational texts, and sometimes spoken of them as sharing and raising common concerns. But distinctions do of course matter, not only *between* each general category but also *within* them. In distinguishing different personal texts we follow closely the outline in Clandinin and Connelly's review of personal experience methods (Clandinin and Connelly, 1994). They distinguish between annals and chronicles. *Annals* can be envisaged as a 'line' which schematises an individual's life divided into moments or segments by events, places, years or significant memories. This allows a sense of the whole, including highs and lows, and the rhythms they construct around their life cycle. *Chronicles* are an elaboration of a single point in the annals. Both together are 'a way to scaffold their oral histories' (Clandinin and Connelly, 1994: 420), and re-collect their experiences. They are also a way to begin to hear a person's family stories. These family stories about family members and events are handed down across generations. Through them people learn self-identity, both internally and in the relation of the family to the world. It is the atypicality and on occasion impoverishment of family stories that mark many people with whom practitioners work. Photographs, correspondence, trinkets and other artifacts mark times, events and persons, around which stories are constructed and reconstructed, often by women to children.

Journals provide a way of giving accounts of experience. Clandinin and Connelly (1994) quote a delightful analogy to the effect that journal entries were to one woman like children's tiny sweets which are so small that separately they are not worth eating, but which together provide a pattern of enjoyment.[2]

---

[2]Known as 'Hundreds and Thousands'. For an interesting UK children's agency website that picks up the same phrase, see http://www.hundredsandthousands.org.uk/. Accessed January 2014.

Children and adolescents sometimes keep journals of their thoughts, activities and stories. Most of these remain private, and it is usually only the accident of history that brings to public view the childhood writings of an Anne Frank or the Brontë children. Childhood memories of those who come within the sphere of influence of social workers are more often emotions recollected in the relative tranquillity of older years. But it is likely that some children and young people keep journals as attempts to make sense of their experiences – 'capturing fragments of experience in attempts to sort themselves out' (Clandinin and Connelly, 1994: 421). Adults recording their experiences as a child raise special difficulties for the hearer. Who is speaking? 'Is it the adult interpreting the childhood experience, in which case it is the adult speaking? Or is it the adult expressing the child's story as the child would have told the experience, in which case it is the child speaking?' (ibid., p. 424). The answer may not be only one or the other.

The texts of personal experience disclose the scene and plot, the dimensions of place and time. Plot, meaning and interpretation are far from straightforward. Today's meanings may become items in tomorrow's chronicle of events, as the participants change their understandings. There are ethical considerations that need careful guarding. 'Personal experience methods are relationship methods' (Clandinin and Connelly, 1994: 425), and the research agreement will need making explicit. Ethical issues are raised by the fact that as we encourage people to tell their stories, we become characters in those stories, and thus change those stories. This can be positive, and be one way of helping someone to get 'unstuck' in their work on a problem, but it also carries risks and re-emphasises that research must be done with care and not as 'a raid on mislaid identities'.[3]

Researchers often perforce hear the voices of those outside the mainstream of society, and hence 'need to uncover stories from the past so that we can preserve more than a bureaucratic account of a person's life' (Janesick, 2010: 15). Social worker researchers walk in the midst of stories associated with the lives of others, e.g., domestic abuse, offending careers, disability, children's accounts, for example, of abuse, community work, adoption, fostering and life transitions. A central value of life stories and documents lies in the access they afford to ordinary, ambiguous and personal meanings, and depend as much as anything on an awareness of the presence of stories almost everywhere.

Personal texts are a mix of the oral and the written, the material and that which has no physical substance. The relationship between the two is often complex, as we illustrated earlier in the chapter when talking about public and private meanings in documents. In a later paper, Cicourel explored the distinction through a different lens. He noted how 'modern society epitomizes the production of objective knowledge. Enormous resources are devoted to the reproduction of abstract and detailed knowledge in public and private sectors of nation-states. The reproductive knowledge process occupies a central role in the way modern societies achieve stability and change' (Cicourel, 1985: 170).

---

[3]Dannie Abse's phrase, from his poem *Return to Cardiff*.

Constructed or schematised knowledge of this kind is said to be governed by context free inference rules, sometimes called 'declarative' and often 'objective' (ibid., p. 162).

In contrast to this, a central feature of folk models is their use of a taken-for-granted knowledge base or 'personal', 'commonsense' or 'procedural' construction by individual actors. The hallmark of procedural or common sense knowledge is that comprehension is contingent on their embeddedness in, and sensitivity to, the settings in which their elements emerge and are used in daily life.

Cicourel continues to find the procedural/declarative distinction of some use 'while recognizing that all human social interaction, including reading and writing, presupposes both of these broad categories' (p. 172). For example, 'the physician converts the often idiomatic and sometimes ambiguous language and personal beliefs or folk theories of the patient into statements with the appearance of unambiguous declarative knowledge and a systematic notation system' (ibid., p. 173).

The argument and illustration show how all that is said in this chapter about traces and deposits – by and large written and material – must not be read independently of what we say in the chapters either side of this one. An important theme running through this central part of the book is that the difference between one method and another should not be overstated. For example, the links between text, documents and narrative have been to the fore more than once in this chapter. Yet there remains a distinct craft when working with traces and deposits, well represented by Hakim's suggestion by way of metaphor that whereas in primary research the architect is the apt metaphor, in record-based studies the builder is the better metaphor – that one starts with the materials rather than planning for them.

Taking it further

We acknowledge that research of the kind discussed above continues to be on the margins of much social work research.

In the light of this, it would pay dividends to return to a recent research study in which you have played a significant role – anything from a large scale team project to a graduate dissertation or thesis – and critically consider how it might have been conceived and conducted differently in the light of this chapter.

TEN
Living in Place, Space and Time

This chapter explores methods for understanding social work contexts. The main approach discussed is ethnography and the chapter includes examples of ethnographies of social work practice from several different national contexts. The role of the researcher and ethical issues are given particular attention. In this chapter we also discuss how qualitative methods may be used to explore a range of dimensions of social life, particularly space, time and the senses such as sounds and smells.

This chapter focuses on research methods that allow us to explore an understanding of the places of cultures (social and occupational), space and time. The methods discussed here might be used to further understand the contexts of the lives of service recipients, with studies of communities of place and communities of people. They can also help us to understand the occupational cultures and working practices of social work in different settings such as offices, home visits, street work, hospitals, day centres and shelters.

Much of the chapter is devoted to a discussion of ethnography, a methodological approach that is rooted in the discipline of social anthropology. Ethnography in the social sciences, in its many guises, shares with anthropology 'a commitment to the first-hand experience and exploration of a particular social or cultural setting on the basis of (although not exclusively by) participant observation' (Atkinson et al., 2001: 4). Anthropology might be seen as a discipline that seeks greater understanding of cultures and societies, and some distance from 'applied' disciplines such as social work. Indeed, Edmund Leach, a former President of the Royal Anthropological Institute stated in 1974 that,

> The whole field of social welfare and social administration . . . lies right outside the professional competence of social anthropologists, and the Institute will soon find itself in grave difficulties if it attempts to dabble in 'practical problems' which lie within this domain. (Leach, E., 1974, quoted in Davies and Kelly, 1976: 229)

Despite this perception of social work's applied perspective putting it beyond anthropology, there is a wealth of ethnographic scholarship in social work settings. In this chapter we draw on international examples of ethnographies in social work over several decades. We also discuss and provide interesting examples of social work research that has used other developments within ethnographic traditions to pursue research questions about culture and context, particularly those related to place, space and time.

Culture

Culture is a difficult word in our context. For almost everyone outside the social sciences the term goes *with* 'art' and, for those familiar with C.P. Snow's famous 'two cultures' lament from the 1950s, *apart from* 'science' – a fierce debate that goes back in the UK at least as far as Matthew Arnold and Thomas Huxley in the 1880s. But there is no easy social science definition of culture. In an oft-quoted remark, Clifford Geertz said 'Believing, with Max Weber, that man is an animal suspended in webs of significance he himself has spun, I take culture to be those webs' (Geertz, 1973: 5). This helps, among other things, in the perspective we bring to doing ethnography. 'From one point of view, that of the textbook, doing ethnography is establishing rapport, selecting informants, transcribing texts, taking genealogies, mapping fields, keeping a diary, and so on. But it is not these things ... that define the enterprise. What defines it is the kind of intellectual effort it is: an elaborate venture in "thick description"' (ibid., p. 6). When we wonder if culture is people's beliefs or material objects, Geertz chides us that 'Once human behavior is seen as ... symbolic action ... the question as to whether culture is patterned conduct or a frame of mind, or even the two somehow mixed together, loses sense' (ibid., p. 10). What matters is the import, the use, the practical aspects of what is and what happens.

This does not offer a final answer. It is, to borrow the quotable Geertz once more, an 'interminable, because unterminable' debate (ibid., p. 10). For example, we still have the difficult problem of how one bridges individual experience and the world – 'things-in-themselves' and 'things-as-they appear' (Packer, 2011: 165).

Defining ethnography – the hurly-burly of the everyday

White (1999) used an ethnographic study of a social services department in the mid-1990s as a means to understanding the social work *habitus* (Bourdieu, 1977). While acknowledging that there are many readings of the concept, she uses *habitus* to encompass the notion of embodied expertise: 'a set of presumptions held by social workers as an occupational group, an embodiment of ways of doing and being based on ways of having done and been before' (White, 1999: 88). Through observations and recordings of naturally occurring team-room talk, she is able to demonstrate how information is given meaning through ordering and prioritising information and decisions about where to begin narrative accounts of social work cases. She argues that this attention to the 'rich detail of the everyday' (ibid., p. 98) provides a different under-standing of the social work occupation than that produced by analysts of policies or of (extraordinary) scandals, which tend to depict front-line prac-titioners as simply the recipients of guidance and directives. 'In failing to examine the hurly-burly of institutional discourse, they have tended to edit out the productive and reproductive capacity of agents' (ibid., p. 98). Pithouse (1998:7), too, argues that general analyses and critiques of social work as a profession fail in this regard: 'Theories of social work as a liberal bulwark of human rights or the disguised interest of class dominion, fail to capture the subtle and often contrary world of daily practice'. Ethnography thus provides access to the rich detail of the everyday. Its approach helps us to move down from the level of policy analysis, but up from the individual account or experience captured by the interview to an understanding of the 'repeated and the shared' (Juhila and Pösö, 1999: 279).

Ethnography often takes place in a specific site, such as a neighbourhood, social work team room or day care centre. Sites are not necessarily geograph-ical places however. Hannigan and Allen (2013) for example, focused on six recipients of mental health services and explored the unfolding of their 'car-ing trajectories' over a period of five months. By focusing on the recipients, rather than the service providers, they were able, through observations, inter-views and documents, to identify both the 'usual suspects and invisible work-ers' providing care and support for the study participants. The researchers identified vital members of individuals' support networks who were not known to one other, despite the emphasis on inter-disciplinary and 'joined up' working.

Most ethnography involves naturalistic observations of people and activities that are present before the researcher arrives (Hammersley and Atkinson, 2007), but Trigger et al. (2012) note a lessening of this emphasis. They give examples of research that co-produces knowledge alongside participants, for example by delib-erately bringing people together in a *para-site* (Deeb and Marcus, 2011). Renold et al.'s (2008) ethnography of a participatory project with care-experienced chil-dren set up by the researchers might be seen as a social work example of a 'para-site' in an ethnographic project.

This emphasis on the co-production of knowledge is a more explicit acknowl-edgement of a phenomenon that is common to all ethnographies – they are not an objective set of observations that coolly reveal the social order of an observed site. Instead, the data (in the form of field notes) and the analysis are produced by the researcher, in interaction with the site and its inhabitants. The next section therefore discusses the role of the researcher.

'Doing' ethnography

Access

Access for fieldwork is at its most pertinent in the early days of a research study, but access can continue as an issue for negotiation and re-negotiation throughout a project (Hammersley and Atkinson, 2007). Agreeing access with a senior figure in a workplace or community is often a first step, but it must be followed by further access negotiations at ground level. There are numerous accounts of successes and setbacks in negotiating access to ethnographic fieldwork. Scourfield and Coffey (2006) write about the remark made by a senior social services figure when Scourfield approached a local authority in the UK about a proposed ethnography about men and child protection work. The gatekeeper made a comment about the potential for a researcher to be a child sex offender seeking access for criminal reasons. The authors note that, while the remark rather shook the researcher, it proved productive for beginning to theorise about the topic and clearly marked the start of the data collection.

The access encounter with the social service manager that we have described presented opportunities to reflect upon the positioning of male clients within child protection work and the discourses of risk and masculinity, as well as upon more practical fieldwork and field-role realities (Scourfield and Coffey, 2006: 38).

Unlike Scourfield, D'Cruz (2004) was already an employee of the Australian social services department in which she sought access for an ethnographic study of two community-based social work offices. However, as a research officer in head office she was still regarded by some gatekeepers and informants as a 'spy' (ibid., p. 29), despite her attempts to demonstrate her distance from her organisational role by carrying out the research in her own, unpaid time. Although she successfully gained access, and completed her doctoral studies, she had to carefully negotiate her position as insider–outsider throughout the project. D'Cruz's difficulties were associated with the concerns of those being observed that their work is being evaluated, and that they will be found lacking. Example 10.1 provides a description of such concerns in another setting. By way of contrast, Floersch (2002: 12) found that his previous employment in a mental health centre in Kansas meant that 'I was a familiar face. I had earned the respect of clients and staff; and mutual respect produced a curiosity about my research. For these reasons I was easily absorbed into the life at CSS.'

EXAMPLE 10.1 ┤ **Accessing the Field**

It can take some confidence to allow researchers to observe everyday practices, as Tadd and her colleagues (2012) found when attempting to access care homes for older people for participant observation and interviews. Only care homes that had received ratings of two or more 'stars' from inspectors (on a scale of 0–3) allowed access. Once access to eight care

(Continued)

(Continued)

homes had been agreed, acceptance by staff was relatively straightforward in all but one of the homes. Researcher field notes (Tadd et al., 2012: 69) record the initial encounters:

> I sense a real reluctance, almost hostility towards my presence here – I think it will be tough to be accepted here. I meet the team leader on the middle floor, a nurse in her late 50's, possibly 60's. She asks a lot of questions and seems very annoyed that I'm here observing them – feels it's a waste of money and the money should be spent on providing more staff. The manager tries to reassure her that perhaps my observation will give them some ammunition to help them try to get more staff and that I can feed back that need to the powers that be. She tries to explain that I'm on their side and not 'spying' on them. I'm not sure how much she is reassured. The manager tells me that some staff have already complained to her that they don't have time to be inter-viewed and she has told them that it's not compulsory – she thinks I might have a better chance interviewing the night staff as they are not so rushed.
>
> (Fieldnotes, Care home 8, Evening)

This extract highlights the intrusion that might be felt by those being observed; intrusion in the form of taking up time, the researcher as an intruder who may extract information and report to others and the unnecessary intrusion of research when the money could be spent on welcome initiatives such as more staff.

Many ethnographic studies come to rely on key informants or informal 'spon-sorship' (Hammersley and Atkinson, 2007: 47). A classic example is 'Doc' who enabled access for Whyte (1955) to the mainly Italian-immigrant community of 'Cornerville'. In a more recent study of community safeguarding in Wales (Holland, 2012), key roles were played by a community worker and a local resident 'Karen'. Karen happened to attend an early, exploratory meeting with a mothers' group. She became an enthusiastic supporter of the research and enabled access to residents' accounts from a socio-economically deprived area, which the research team had initially been informed would not be amenable to researchers, by championing the research with friends and acquaintances. Both of these examples, from contrasting locations and generations, were attempts to understand aspects of the social worlds of members of stigmatised communities and both highlight the iterative nature of ethnographic research, a topic discussed next.

Developing a focus

An important aspect of ethnographic research is its evolving and often contingent nature (Hammersley and Atkinson, 2007). 'The unpredictability of social life sup-ports the value of maintaining open-ended approaches to the data gathering that do not rest on preordained or methodologically foreshadowed analytical purposes'

(Trigger et al., 2012: 516). There is a need to be spontaneous in the field, as opportunities arise and some doorways close. Research questions are likely to develop as understanding increases. Some methods for data generation, that appeared to be just right in the research proposal, may turn out to be less useful in the field. Tom Hall (2004a), who spent a year with young homeless people in a hostel in England, initially tape-recorded unstructured conversations with young people. He records, however, that fieldnotes emerged as more productive in understanding and recording his observations and he abandoned his recordings, with the slight stilting effect they had on conversations, and the subsequent transcribing. Others may change the focus of investigation rather than the research methods. Burke (2007), in an ethnographic study of social work services in an Alaskan rural Yup'ik village found that there were few formal interactions with social services clients to observe and she broadened her focus to include attention to informal helping. McMahon (1998) began his fieldwork with the intention of investigating child welfare practices with Native American children and their families in Illinois. His subsequent work does, indeed, have interesting and important things to say about Native American experiences of child welfare, but it also became a more general problematisation of the nature of child protection work. Carr's (2011) ethnography of an addiction treatment day centre for homeless women in a North American city, took on a sharper focus on linguistic practices after an insight-provoking encounter with a client (see case example in Chapter Eight of this book).

This unplanned nature of the work, coupled with its resource intensity, can make it difficult to convince funders and ethical review boards to back the research (Atkinson, 2009; Murphy and Dingwall, 2001). These types of bodies often require great specificity regarding aspects such as sample sizes and data generation methods, both of which can discourage the necessary opportunism of ethnography. It is probably therefore unsurprising that many ethnographic accounts of social work and social welfare practices have emerged from doctoral projects (e.g., D'Cruz, 2004; Hall, 2004a; Pithouse, 1998; Scourfield, 2003; White, 1998) where the most expensive resource – labour – is provided at little cost by the student.

Fieldnotes

Fieldnotes are usually the main data generation method in an ethnographic study, and we talk more about them later in the book when we discuss qualitative writing. In the past they have been treated as rather private and are rarely shared in full, making it difficult for novice researchers to be clear how to produce them (Hammersley and Atkinson, 2007). Some accounts of ethnography provide little detail on the production of the notes, but others explain how and when they produced them. Hall (2004a: 12) writes:

> Fieldnotes are hard work. I spent several hours of almost every day in Southerton writing in my notebooks, anxious to get everything down but sometimes fed up with the time it took to do so. I seldom took detailed notes in company because

it proved impractical to do so. I couldn't keep up with events and conversations if I was simultaneously recording these with paper and pen … but I did keep a small notebook with me at all times in which I made (surreptitious) scribbled notes and jottings whenever the opportunity presented. These served as a valuable *aide-mémoire* when, last thing at night or first thing in the morning, I sat down in my room to write.

Hammersley and Atkinson (2007) suggest that fieldnotes should be highly detailed ('if in doubt write it down', p. 144) and meticulously kept every day. They recommend jottings in the field, followed by expansion and development as soon as possible thereafter. They suggest that speech should be recorded with verbatim extracts and events written about with concrete description. D'Cruz (2004: 38) appears to have followed this highly disciplined style in her participant observations in an Australian child protection team:

> The participant observation was recorded in separate field diaries for each site. Each diary entry on numbered pages included the date, participants' first names or initials (later anonymised), their organisational positions/roles in the recorded events, and a detailed description of the context of the event.

Hammersley and Atkinson (2007) recommend that analytic notes, memos and fieldwork journals should be developed in a similar disciplined manner but in a form that is distinguishable from fieldnotes. This does not mean, of course, that fieldnotes are objective recordings of facts. They have been described as 'messy, fragmented and complex creations of ourselves and the other selves in the field' (Coffey, 1999: 122). Emerson et al. (2001) claim that only in the last couple of decades has proper attention been given to fieldnotes as written texts. Attention has been paid to strategies used by fieldworkers to produce authoritative and authentic fieldnotes. Emerson et al. (2001: 353) note the following features of fieldnotes. They are generally:

- *Contemporaneous*, in that they are written during or soon after the events observed.
- A form of *representation* because they necessarily transform events, people, places and interactions to written accounts.
- *Selective* in what the researcher chooses to record and not record, and in how observations are framed. They can never be a complete record.
- *Descriptive* accounts, with personal reflections on these. Nonetheless, the very act of producing accounts will begin interpretation and analysis.
- Part of a larger *corpus*. Fieldnotes accumulate gradually to become a larger dataset, although there is almost never an intention that all will be incorporated into a final text, or even that all will be relevant for the analysis.

This connects with the idea of 'thick description', mentioned earlier in this chapter. 'Thick' description is not about the amount of material or detail but 'how ethnographers "inscribe" the events they have witnessed and turn them into "accounts"' (Packer, 2011: 19) – how they interpret.

Beyond these generalities, there will be many different styles and uses of fieldnotes. Van Maanen (1988) categorised these as realist tales, in which the researcher is largely absent; confessional tales where the ethnographer and their responses to the observations are more central; and impressionist tales that provide striking accounts of events using a more self-consciously literary style. All such styles maintain the ethnographer in a position of power in terms of representational style, inclusion, exclusions and framing. More recently researchers have experimented with a range of other forms to more directly represent participants' perspectives, as discussed in Chapter Thirteen on social justice and Chapter Sixteen on the writing of qualitative research.

Whatever form they take, most ethnographic fieldnotes may be seen as 'writing the self' (Coffey, 1999) as well as writing about others, due to the role that ethnographers play in fieldwork. Fieldwork roles, from 'outsider' to the ultimate insider role, autoethnography, are discussed next.

Interactions

'Where participant observation is involved, the researcher must find some role in the field being studied, and this will usually have to be done at least through implicit, and probably also through explicit, negotiation with people in that field' (Hammersley and Atkinson, 2007: 4).

Whyte (1955) was a complete outsider to the Italian 'corner boys' of 1930s urban America and the following extract shows how this was reinforced in his encounters.

> At first I concentrated upon fitting into Cornerville, but a little later I had to face the question of how far I was to immerse myself in the life of the district. I bumped into that problem one evening as I was walking down the street with the Nortons. Trying to enter into the spirit of the small talk, I cut loose with a string of obscenities and profanity. The walk came to a momentary halt as they all stopped to look at me in surprise. Doc shook his head and said: 'Bill, you're not supposed to talk like that. That doesn't sound like you'. (Whyte, 1955: 304)

Whyte did find himself becoming more like the young men during the fieldwork and he goes on to explain that when he was most deeply immersed in his fieldwork he found it difficult to engage in academic discussions in the university. However, the later controversy Whyte found himself in, regarding the accuracy of his portrayal of the community and the identification of 'Doc' in a third edition of the book, demonstrates the complexity and potential long-term consequences of misunderstandings over research roles and relationships (Boelen, 1992; Whyte, 1992). Perhaps Geertz was right when he concluded that to imagine ourselves 'something more than an interested (in both senses of that word) sojourner … has been our most powerful source of bad faith' (1973: 20).

We explore issues of interested engagement further in Chapter Fourteen.

Levels of engagement need to be navigated carefully in fieldwork, and may change during the course of the research. Sometimes participation in the work being studied is an important part of the research design. White's (2001) study of child protection fieldwork took place while she maintained her employment as a team manager in the setting under observation. De Montigny's (1995) ethnographic observations of social work practice in a Canadian team were based on his own practice and those of his colleagues, although how he managed this dual role is not known as there is no conventional description of his research design in his book. Kulkarni and colleagues (2008) worked as volunteers helping to resettle evacuees from New Orleans following Hurricane Katrina, while conducting ethnographic fieldwork that aimed to understand evacuees' experiences and needs. More commonly, fieldworkers' participation is as researcher rather than an employee or volunteer and methodological notes report sitting in team rooms and following participants around as they go about their daily life or work (for example, Pithouse, 1998; Ferguson, 2011).

Pithouse (1998: 185) explains how he immersed himself in the life of the social work office during twelve months of fieldwork and how he became less of an outsider over time.

> During the initial weeks I was seen as something of an 'outsider'. As time progressed I came to be seen more as a 'local'. I took messages, made beverages and generally tried to be of practical help if the occasion arose ... Over the many months of observation I sat at a spare desk near the two teams and frequently took part in the *ad hoc* talk and easy banter of office membership.

In contrast, in a study of probation practices in Finland, Juhila and Pösö (1999: 280), although social work academics, found their position as outsiders in the probation office to be productive. When observing encounters between probation officers and clients the officers felt the need to provide explanations. This gave them access to 'shared institutional and cultural accounts'.

Many ethnographies of social work are based mainly in the team-room and other institutional premises. Some, however, like McMahon (1998) and Ferguson (2011) followed practitioners into the unpredictable territory of home visits. For McMahon this led to some tricky moments.

> I stood apprehensively in the hallway of a house while two policemen and a worker took an African American child from her parents. I wrote in my notebook, 'Amid the crying, weeping, cursing, and screaming, I stood in the hallway, conscious of my intrusion, not wanting to go in or leave, but uncomfortably aware that I would be seen as a cause of the commotion'. (McMahon, 1998: 114)

Despite the discomfort of feeling intrusive in tricky moments, in most ethnographies of social work teams, including McMahon's, the reader gains a sense that the practitioners used the good listener stance of the researcher to offload and reflect on their work. Scourfield (2003) reports that practitioners ruminated about personal and professional thresholds regarding child neglect. In Ferguson's

(2011) project the workers appear to have used the car journey back from home visits to reflect on the home visit the researcher had just observed.

The self

Whether a participant or non-participant observer, role and status (as insider or outsider) can be used productively to aid understanding of a social context, with the aid of reflective notes, supervision and discussions with participants. Kulkarni et al. (2008), aware of racial and class aspects of the Hurricane Katrina disaster, note the ethnicity and gender of the members of their research team. They tried to 'monitor racial and cultural biases' (ibid., p. 405) by keeping self-reflexive field notes and debriefing with colleagues of African American and New Orleans backgrounds. These authors are exploring difference, while others who regard themselves as insiders may be 'fighting familiarity'. White (2001: 107) reflects on the challenges and analytic insights brought about by the process of 'defamiliarisation' when conducting fieldwork in her own social work workplace. 'However, it was and is perfectly possible, if not always comfortable, to continue to act, and also to 'see' oneself acting' (ibid., p. 112). Emerson et al. (2001) note that recording emotions and personal responses to observed events in fieldnotes can help with identifying biases on the part of the researcher, logging changing relationships and attitudes and may prove useful in providing analytical leads. McMahon, an Australian male, ends his ethnographic monograph with the following reflections:

> Thick description allows the reader to understand the interpretation of child welfare work. What I have told and interpreted was what I saw and understood. Another person, an American, a woman, a minority person, a Native American would see differently and tell the story differently. Just as my own biography framed the question so it has framed the interpretation. (McMahon, 1998: 118)

There are many ways in which personal, reflexive accounts of ethnographies have been incorporated into more 'scientific' ethnographic texts. These have ranged from the common use of methodological appendices (e.g., Hall, 2004a; Pithouse, 1998; Whyte, 1955), through texts which include ethnographic dialogues and encounters in the main analysis, to autoethnographies (Reed-Danahay, 2001). It is in the last of these genres that the self moves centre-stage as a subject of analysis (Coffey, 1999).

There is some scepticism about the value of many forms of autobiographical ethnographic writing. 'The published corpus of autobiographical work tends to reinforce our long-held view that social worlds of "others" are almost invariably more interesting and more illuminating than the authors' own reflections' (Hammersley and Atkinson, 2007: 205). Delamont (2007: 2) argues that it is intellectually lazy, erring as it does towards the experiential and away from the analytical; its spread is 'pernicious'. Yet Witkin (2000b) argues that it is puzzling that social work academia should have embraced so readily the straight-jacket of formal academic writing. In the case of writing in the United States he notes that most social work students are taught to write formally in the style of the American Psychological Association. This presents a false aura of scientific objectivity and can, he suggests, marginalise or exclude those who may wish to write about their experiences in alternative forms, including users of social work services and practitioners. Autoethnography is a process by which the author puts their personal experience in a social and cultural context, often challenging established forms of knowledge on the topic (Witkin, 2000b). Some of the most successful examples have focused on experiences of living with chronic sickness, impairment or mental illness (Coffey, 1999; Witkin, 2000b). Berger (2001) has written what she labels 'narrative autoethnographies' about her own relationship with religion when researching a religious community, as well as her relationship with her deaf sister and her experiences of her father's mental illness. She argues that 'The stories I write about my fieldwork put me in conversation with myself as well as with those I am researching' (ibid., p. 507) and that this form of writing helps readers engage with the analysis, as well as enhancing her own analytic understanding of her own experiences and those of others.

Ethics and ethnography – over-research, covert research and disclosure

'As an old joke tells it, the "definition of a Navajo household is one Indian home with eight anthropologists living in it"' (Sukarieh and Tannock, 2013: 497). Societies of interest because of their social and economic marginalisation or the distinctive nature of their First Nation or other minority cultures have long risked being subject to too many researchers seeking to understand them (Clark, 2008) and, as Sukarieh and Tannock note, this can be particularly acute when a community has experienced an extreme situation such as war, has shown distinct organising skills or resistance or, simply, is conveniently accessible from a university department. Quoting residents from a heavily researched Palestinian community, they note that research questions tend to be posed from outside and that residents feel particularly resentful about the same problems being highlighted over several years but with no tangible improvements for the community.

'Why don't people write about the talents in the camps?' asks Khalil, 'If they keep talking about the problems, the west will say, "They can't fix the problems of the camps … how will they handle a country if they return?" I think they harm the cause, they do not help us' (Sukarieh and Tannock, 2013: 506).

A direct contrast to participants' perceptions of over-exposure to researchers is the issue of covert research. Covert research has long been controversial because of ethical concerns about participants' rights to autonomy, but it is increasingly recognised that the distinction between overt and covert research is not clearly dichotomised (Spicker, 2011). In observational studies in particular, it is often not practical to inform all present in a complex social setting that a researcher is present (Murphy and Dingwall, 2001). Equally, the degree of openness about the exact research aims is sometimes regarded as a matter of judgement, as much for the sometimes obscure and theoretical nature of some social science projects as to any intention to deceive. Some researchers have made decisions not to disclose aspects of their private lives, such as sexuality or religion, because they feel that these identities may be marginalised or mistrusted in the community they are studying (Hammersley and Atkinson, 2007).

In the context of these shades of openness and covertness, fully covert research is relatively rare. We are not aware of any covert studies of formal social work practice, but covert, or semi-covert research has been carried out in related fields such as drug-dealing and sex-working (Hammersley and Atkinson, 2007). Ward (2008) describes her participant observation of illicit drug selling as semi-covert, in that she made many of her participants aware that she was a researcher, but that many appeared to forget over time and she did not frequently, nor explicitly remind them. She justifies the lack of informed consent partly because those she was observing were mainly educated, successful students and professionals.

Covert research is usually justified as a way to research in places that would be difficult to research, such as groups that are secretive due to criminal behaviour (e.g., Pearson, 2009, on football hooligans) or who are suspicious of outsiders because they are marginalised in some way (e.g., Humphreys, 1975 on men who have impersonal sex with men in public places). In researching covertly, the assumption is that the researcher will come closer to 'participants'. However Hall (2004b), in an essay reviewing several books by journalists who had worked covertly in low paid jobs, makes the opposite argument. By keeping their purpose covert, these journalists have 'little or no room for what is otherwise one of the strengths of ethnographic research: openly acknowledged difference and the (then mutual) attempt to work across this' (ibid., p. 626). Hall, here, is arguing against covert research for reasons of research quality, rather than ethics. Spicker (2011: 127) quite reasonably argues that 'At root, the tests that need to be applied to covert research are the same as the tests that apply to other forms of research – whether there is a potential for harm, whether people's rights are infringed, whether the research is intrusive and what safeguards are needed.'

Further ethical issues that are perhaps particularly pertinent to ethnographic research are issues of over-disclosure and potential later feelings of shame or exposure (Boelen, 1992). The ethnographer's relational work will often lead to a relaxed relationship between researchers and participants and is likely to lead to different aspects of personal lives being revealed than in, for example, a one-off semi-structured interview or focus group. The usual concentration on a single site will lead to participants being able to identify themselves, and often colleagues or neighbours, however well protected the site is from the general readership through anonymisation (Murphy and Dingwall, 2001). In writing ethnography, the researcher may need to decide to omit rich data to protect individuals. The ethical regulation of ethnographic research has been heavily criticised (Atkinson, 2009; Dingwall, 2008) as a clumsy and time-consuming effort to impose regulations arising from individualist medical research that often misunderstand the nature of observation. Nonetheless, as we argued in Chapter Six, the most helpful mode of ethical regulation will enable researchers to anticipate and plan for predictable issues (such as anonymisation and whether research is to be fully overt) while equipping them to respond ethically to the many unpredictable issues that inevitably arise in the field.

Exploring different dimensions of social work contexts – space, time, sounds, smells and vision

Space

Although ethnographies centred around participant observation are often concerned with spatial aspects of social work, such as neighbourhood work and community organising, there are other qualitative means to explore places and this section briefly discusses some of these. Qualitative methods are particularly apt within the context of the 'spatial turn' in social sciences in recent decades (Crang and Thrift, 2000). Places are understood as relational and complex, with even seemingly quantifiable aspects such as geographic boundaries subject to local and individual dynamic social constructions (Massey, 1991).

Geographic Information Systems (GIS) are increasingly used in social science research beyond geography and qualitative uses of such systems (QGIS) are becoming more commonplace (Verd and Porcel, 2012). Verd and Porcel describe how QGIS data can be incorporated into qualitative data analysis software (CAQDAS) and note that the latest versions of commonly used programmes all enable geocoding. These authors, in a study of urban regeneration in Barcelona, added georeferences to qualitative data generated from interviews, urban planning documents, press releases, photographs and memos. This allowed the generation of maps in which quotations and visual images could be located in specific geographical points, aiding both analysis and graphic display of the findings.

Digital geographic data can also be generated during data collection. Mobile interviews have already been discussed in Chapter Seven. An extension of the 'walking and talking' involved in most mobile interviews is to map the routes taken using Global Positioning System (GPS) devices. These small tracking devices are increasingly found on mobile phones, but small separate GPS devices that can fit in a pocket are also available. Smith (2011) used GPS when he carried out participant observation with an urban welfare outreach team in a city centre. Because he 'tagged along' with the workers' usual street patrols, the subsequent maps ('digital breadcrumb trails', Smith, 2011: 2) provided more insight into *routine* spatial practices than walking interviews generated for the interviewer (see Example 10.2).

| **EXAMPLE 10.2** | **Spatial Methods in a Neighbourhood Study** |

In a neighbourhood study of children's safeguarding in Wales, Sally Holland and colleagues explored residents' everyday experiences and perceptions of children's safety and risk, and their interactions with voluntary sector and statutory service providers. Two neighbourhoods were selected that had contrasting socio-demographic features *and* rather different spatial features. For example, the first neighbourhood had open gardens with low walls and shared play spaces. The second had much more individualised play spaces for children. In the following excerpt, the researchers explain how different aspects of the neighbourhood were explored through mobile interviews, interviews of residents in clusters of neighbouring houses, historic documentary data and participant observation of life in the neighbourhoods.

> Particularly *spatial* approaches are embedded in the design. Four examples of how specific qualitative methods can aid our spatial understanding are as follows. Firstly, we have conducted mobile walking and driving interviews with parents, children and community workers. Some of these have included the generation of GPS tracks of the interview routes. Secondly, we have conducted qualitative interviews with residents within micro-localities – clusters of neighbouring houses – about their interactions with their environment and neighbours. This generates data not about 'this *kind of* place' but '*this* place' and starts to build a rich picture of the interactions of perceptions and relationships involved in children's wellbeing at neighbourhood level. Thirdly, we have collected historic data about the places we are researching, through council meeting minutes, newspaper reports and old maps, to understand how the intersection of children's welfare and place has evolved and changed over time. Interviews with older residents and activists have also aided this understanding. Fourthly, participant observation by researchers in the community centre, in neighbourhood meetings and walking about neighbourhoods provide rich descriptions in field notes of neighbourhood life across seasons and at different times of day and evening. (Holland et al., 2011: 695–696)

Social networks are a further means for exploring spatial aspects of individuals' and groups' contexts. Although often associated with quantitative research, qualitative explorations of social networks may be carried out alone or in tandem with qualitative measures (Edwards, 2010). Social networks have long been of interest to social workers and community organisers. A routine part of many social workers' practice is to draw up 'ecomaps' and 'genograms' with their clients in an attempt to visually represent and understand social contexts (Holland et al., 2011). Qualitative social network methods have the advantage of being able to explore the dynamic and contested nature of networks, in a way that quantitative mapping cannot always capture (Edwards, 2010). Methods for data generation can include visual mapping and mobile interviews (Emmel and Clark, 2009).

Time

It is virtually impossible to investigate social actors in their context, without considering temporal elements (Adam, 1995; Hammersley and Atkinson, 2007). A focus on time can lead to insights that might otherwise be lost. For example, a study of community safety that observed street activities only during weekday daytime would, of course, miss the different patterns of activity at nights, weekends and as seasons change. A focus on time in social work might focus on the 'artful' ways in which practitioners manage time restrictions on their practices (Broadhurst et al., 2010), a consideration of how developmental time periods are considered in relation to perceived risk to children (White, 1998) or an analysis of how changes in parenting skills and attitudes are measured and constructed in in-depth assessments of parenting (Holland, 2011). A temporal focus might also include an historical element, with an awareness of themes that echo, or evolve, across generations. Kulkarni et al. (2008) note the cultural context for many African-Americans of histories of dislocation, including the forced transportation of slaves and the Great Migration of the twentieth century when African-Americans moved from the south to northern and mid-western urban areas to work in factories. They quote one elderly evacuee as speaking of his experiences as being 'in the hull of a slave ship' (ibid., p. 420).

| EXAMPLE 10.3 | 'Speed-Practices' |

Karen Broadhurst and her colleagues conducted a multi-site ethnographic study of 15 'duty and assessment' teams across five local authorities in England and Wales. Much of their analysis considers temporal elements of these frenetically busy work places, powerfully reinforcing the researchers' critique of flawed information technologies and misdirected performance management targets in contemporary social work.

The authors highlight the strategies used by practitioners to attempt to cope with a non-stop rate of referrals of child concern, such as logging incomplete assessments as complete, while 'holding' them for 'review'. Other strategies included passing as many referrals as possible onto other organisations and developing policies of minimal or non-responses to some categories of referral such as first notifications of domestic violence or referrals relating to older children. The rich descriptions afforded by the ethnographic approach give insights into the exhausting pace of the work.

'The IT systems maintained the pace of work, typically by providing digital reminders of deadlines and timescales. In one site, we found an e-tracking device in the form of traffic lights, which informed workers about how much time was left before the specific episode was deemed out of timescale. In another site, "higher management" were planning to print out weekly graphs of levels of attainment in meeting targets, alongside tables exposing individual failures. Whilst local contingencies of practice shaped the actual conditions of pace, across our sites, we found much reference to key points in the working day; the start of the day was significant, bringing new work, whereas, by 3 p.m., anxieties were mounting as the close of business drew nearer and the day's tasks were not yet complete'.

Broadhurst et al., (2010: 360)

Sounds and silences

Some attention has been paid to the role of sound in qualitative research (Hall et al., 2008). These authors argue that sounds are an integral part of the everyday, yet we work hard to keep out extraneous noises from the primary qualitative research tool, the interview. Sounds are particularly important, they note, in understanding places and these are brought together in the 'soundscape'. Drawing on Schafer's work from the 1970s, Hall and colleagues explain that the soundscape enables researchers and audiences to pay attention to the 'sonic landscape' and 'presents an opportunity to think with sound about concepts of space and the everyday' (Hall et al., 2008: 1030).

Soundscapes have been used in participatory research projects to generate data with participants that reflect their cultures and localities. They are 'aural collages' (Lashua, 2006: 393) that incorporate recorded speech or music with 'found' sounds such as street noises. Brett Lashua (2006) acted as a researcher, teacher, artist and collaborator with small groups of 14–20-year-old marginalised young people, mainly Aboriginal, in inner-city Canada. He describes how he worked with the young people's existing relationship with music and popular culture to help them produce soundscapes that expressed narratives of their identities and everyday experiences; street sounds, such as traffic and underground train announcements and layered with beats and raps composed by the young people as they walk through the city with the researcher.

> Soundscape 1: We're walking slowly and recording city sounds along 101st Street, in the center of downtown, on our way to Churchill subway station when 'Shannon' raps: "I'm walking down one-oh-one, freestyling, going buck wild," then stumbling to find some rhyming phrases, he adds "I'm kinda thinking dumb, but that's okay 'cause I'm in the middle of the inner-city slum! What are we gonna do? We're going to, like, roll to the beat of an invisible drum." Traffic, footsteps, subway trains, speech, city rhythms: These are our 'invisible' drums. We scribble down keywords about things around us, scratching with a pencil in a notebook: "Businessmen with cell phones look at us funny" and then "buses rumble". Shannon reads nearly every sign and checks out every car, incorporating the words and images into his rhyming rap as we amble along: "I'm a 6'3" treaty Cree in the goatee, pants saggin' and draggin', looking like the rear end of a 1978 Ford station wagon."

There is much potential for social work researchers to use soundscapes with service recipients to understand everyday lived experiences and identities and disrupt normative assumptions about marginalised groups in our societies.

By way of contrast, qualitative research can also investigate silences. This can include the fine-grained analysis associated with conversation analysis, where silences and pauses are attended to alongside utterances, turn taking and interruptions (see Hall et al., 2006, for how this approach has been taken in social work settings). In organisational settings, studies of silence and voice can investigate motivations for employees to raise concerns, whistle-blow, express an opinion or remain silent. 'Silence can be caused by fear, by the desire to avoid conveying bad news or unwelcome ideas, and also by normative and social pressures that exist in groups' (Morrison and Milliken, 2003: 1353).

Smells

Harry Ferguson (2011) uses data from historical child protection records and his own fieldwork in which he followed child protection social workers on home visits, to discuss what he terms 'intimate child protection practice' (ibid., p. 16). Ferguson explores multiple dimensions of practice in his analysis, including mobilities and touch but a particularly original contribution of his work is the attention to smell.

> Where, I want to ask, has the smell of practice gone today? There have been changes over the past 100 years, but at a deep, even primitive level, the smell and bodily experience involved in visiting homes and trying to gain access to children is still there. What has disappeared is our ability to acknowledge it, evoke it and understand it. Our understandings of child protection have been deodorised. (Ibid., p. 17)

Ferguson argues that revolting smells are one of the reasons that practitioners avoid physical contact with children and the physical environment of the home, but that this distaste is present only in informal talk and gestures. Similarly, Floersch (2002) uncovered the impact of sensory aspects of consumer–case manager interactions through the informal remarks between team members about the discomfort of sharing car journeys with very obese or odorous consumers of mental health services, and by participating in those car journeys himself. It is only by using the particular method of accompanying social workers as they conduct out-of-office practices in the home and car that Ferguson and Floersch are able to pay full attention to multisensory aspects of practice, including smell.

Vision

Mason and Davies (2009) point out that, rather illogically, sensory methods are sometimes written about concerning touch, sound and smell as if separate from visual methods, despite vision being quite clearly one of the senses. They see no merit in investigating any sensory aspects, including the visual, as if they can be untangled from each other. Using examples from their family resemblances study, they also note that sensory dimensions are entwined, too, with other sociological categories, such as class, culture and gender. Visual methods are excellent ways of exploring places and contexts, using photographs, drawings, maps and videos. They are also excellent methods for involving participants and therefore we reserve a fuller discussion of visual methods for Chapter Fourteen.

Conclusion

This chapter has explored methods for developing a greater understanding of contexts for social work practices. This has included participant observation and methods for exploring space, time, sounds and smells. It is to be hoped that the research examples have demonstrated that different forms of understanding are to be found using such methods than data generation using interviews and documents alone. Participant observation in particular can produce rich descriptions and analyses of social work cultures. We wish to argue that ethnographic and related methods have much potential for transforming practices and policies. Bloor (1997) suggests that the very act of seeing detailed description and analyses of occupational practices provides practitioners with the potential to compare and reflect on their own work. One of us (Holland) had the experience, as a newly enrolled doctoral student, of reading an earlier edition of Pithouse's (1998) ethnography of child protection practices. Having just left a very similar setting she found it quite revelatory, as it revealed practices that were on the one hand very familiar, but on the other hand had been given new meaning through Pithouse's analysis of the social organisation of the workplace. Such moments may be as much a spur to practise changes as long lists of recommendations. Broadhurst and colleagues' (2010) descriptions of more contemporary practices had a profound impact on public and policy awareness of how ICT systems are shaping and dominating children's services in England (Munro, 2011). Such studies are time-consuming, expensive and, as has been seen in this chapter, at times ethically challenging. Nonetheless, we have made clear that we believe that ethnographic studies are invaluable to social work.

Taking it further

Relationships, ethics and authority

In this section we mention three pieces of ethnographic research, all carried out in the earliest stages of the researcher's career, where the process of feeding back findings to participants caused the researcher to reflect on the meaning of the researcher–participant relationship or, in the case of Whyte, caused later controversy. In reading these accounts from the 1930s, 1970s and early twenty-first century, consider the following:

1. What are the merits and barriers to sharing your analysis and writing with participants in ethnographic studies? Does the ethical terrain shift when researching with a socially marginalised group compared to, for example, professionals in the workplace?
2. Should participants be in a position to veto the publication of findings they disagree with?

In a robust response to Boelen's (1992) critique of the ethics and veracity of his analysis and writing about his ethnography of Italian immigrant male society in an American city in the 1930s, Whyte (1992) expresses astonishment at her suggestion that he should have had his participants approve his book before publication. While quoting instances of participants' favourable responses to the book *after* publication, he states that 'this is an ethical procedure invented by Boelen. I know of nowhere in the literature where such a principle has been stated, nor can I recall anthropological or community studies where such community feedback has been attempted' (ibid., p. 58).

Fifteen years later, and seventy years after Whyte's fieldwork, Burke (2007: 188) provides a detailed discussion of her attempts to meaningfully gain permission from the Alaskan community in which she had conducted ethnographic fieldwork on social work relationships. We recommend the whole article, but here are some extracts:

> When the analysis was complete I presented the findings to the village community and to the tribal Human Research committee for their approval or dissent. A formal letter of approval from the tribal committee, written only after the village Traditional Council approved the document, is appended to the dissertation. Mostly positive in tone, it specifies some reservations about the descriptive findings. The tribal committee continues to approve (or not) all dissemination from the project. The committee has approved the publication of this paper.

So far, so good. But Burke goes on to describe how difficult this became when her dissertation defence date approached, the tribal committee delayed its approval until further conditions had been met, and she was required to graduate in order to take up a new post. She found a solution to this with the university, who kept the dissertation pending until the letter came in but she adds, 'I am chagrined by the superficiality of my commitment to including community voices. So long as it was easy, or merely inconvenient, I could take the moral high ground. When my own well-being was threatened my instinct was to prioritise my own needs.'

In a paper published between Whyte's and Burke's studies, Bloor (1978) reflects on his attempts to feed back the results of his analysis from his observational study of Ear, Nose and Throat specialists to the doctors he had observed. Much of this was a success, with many endorsing his analysis of their individual diagnostic practices. However, Bloor felt that there were two main problems. One was how to 'frame and present one's analysis in such a form and in such a setting that one can be confident that one's respondents will fully understand it, react to it in a critical spirit and honestly and coherently tell one how it strikes them?' (Bloor, 1978: 550). The second, related issue was that they were only marginally interested 'with a feeling that it displayed a certain peculiar charm perhaps' (ibid., p. 551). Bloor concludes that if respondents are largely uninterested in research they may uncritically evaluate the results. If they are very interested, they may expect the results to conform to their own accounts of their worlds, an equally problematic relationship for the researcher.

ELEVEN
Anticipating Analysis and Making Sense of Qualitative Data

Analysis is shaped by how we approach research as a whole. We review grounded theory and critical interpretivism as contrasting illustrations of this point. We nonetheless emphasise that there are anchoring shared *motifs* in qualitative analysis. We explore ideas of discourse (briefly) and reflexivity (more fully) as examples of such motifs.

In the second part of the chapter we discuss the steps through which we anticipate and prepare for qualitative analysis, underlining the interweaving of fieldwork and analysis. Fieldnotes, field diaries, memoing, transcription and coding are reviewed, and in each case treating them as methodological rather than simply technical decisions. We conclude with an overview of the challenges and opportunities afforded by computer assisted qualitative analysis.

Pauline Young studied Sociology at Chicago almost a century ago. She was supervised by Robert Park. She later wrote, in ways that well reward revisiting, about social work (e.g., Young, 1935). In subsequent years she wrote a memorandum on 'Dr Robert Park as a Teacher', referring to his advice on her draft research analysis for her subsequent book *Pilgrims of Russian Town*.

'To this day I have kept the original manuscript with Dr. Park's blue-penciled annotations, as sort of sacred heritage. Several of his notes read as follows:

> 'Think more about your data;
>
> view them from various aspects …
>
> let the classification of the data turn around in your head …
>
> sleep on your plan and ideas …
>
> you need to get better perspective.'

Seeing she was struggling and 'Sensing I was ready to give up, Park spoke more tenderly – but not less challengingly – than ever before: "Of course, you know that if I did not see promise in your material I would not bother about you. You are almost grasping what I am trying to tell you these data need." He suggested a different perspective and "I was off on a new street"' (Robert Ezra Park, University of Chicago, Special Collections).

Delving into the archives held at the University of Chicago one is gripped by the sense of exhilaration that engaged those who researched and wrote. 'Think more about your data; view them from various aspects ... let the classification of the data turn around in your head ... sleep on your plan and ideas ... you need to get better perspective' stand well today as advice for those who set about making analytic sense of their data.

Approaches to qualitative analysis

Within qualitative research there is a multiplicity of analytic strategies. Some are fairly specific and associated with particular strategies such as conversation analysis. But more generally, how we tackle analysis of fieldwork data is shaped by how we approach research in general. This is sometimes a point about the ethics and values we bring to research. For example, if we are committed to the importance of research as a means of challenging conventional forms of social relationships within research, we may engage in participatory analysis, of the kind we discussed in Chapter Nine. Holland and colleagues explored data from a participatory research project with young people in the care of a UK local authority (Holland et al., 2010). They express their thinking as follows:

> Young people who are looked after are often subject to fixed categorization and an official 'gaze' at intimate aspects of their lives, with categories such as 'self care' and 'identity' discussed at events such as review meetings and care proceedings. Ethically, we did not want to intensify this scrutiny by predetermining the areas of their lives that the young people should explore during the project. A partici-pative approach therefore was part of an ethical framework ... (Ibid., p. 364)

Their summary of their methodology and analysis can be read in Example 11.1.

EXAMPLE 11.1 ⊣ **Participatory Analysis with Young People**

'We wished to explore the ethical and analytical issues raised and challenged by enabling young participants to choose and define their own means of representation. To this end, the researchers undertook an ethnographic study of this participatory research project, keeping full fieldnotes and taping research meetings, in order to research the participatory method, as well as the substantive findings. Analysis was carried out initially on an indi-vidual basis, paying close attention to the social and cultural context in which data are produced (e.g., participant-generated video-diaries through to researcher–participant 'talk'). Themes relating to each young person's everyday life were generated and shared and then developed with the young person. Data were then coded according to these themes and cross-'case' analysis was carried out with the use of AtlasTi (qualitative analysis software) to further develop the substantive and theoretical themes that emerged from the individual analyses ... Our intention was to gain a complex understanding of how these young people's subjectivities are articulated, developed and enacted in their everyday lives, and to further develop an understanding of the ethics and power relations embedded in the workings of participative, longitudinal research.'

Holland et al., 2010: 365

This example is helpful in another respect in that it foreshadows several of the issues addressed in this and other chapters. Field notes, allowing for analysing the research method, the development of codes and themes (what Robert Park probably had in mind when he counselled 'let the classification of the data turn around in your head'), the utilisation of computer assisted qualitative data analysis packages, the unfolding phases of analysis, theorising and generalising are all alluded to.

In addition to value positions, approaches to research are often related to our explicit or tacit epistemological standpoints. We illustrated in Chapter Three that the range of possible positions is considerable. To capture something of this diversity we spend the next few pages unpacking two analytic frameworks that in many ways stand at opposite poles from one another. These are grounded theory and what may be referred to as critical or poststructural interpretivism.

Grounded theory

'The grounded theory perspective is the most widely used qualitative interpretive framework in the social sciences today' (Denzin, 1994: 508). It is equally in the foreground of qualitative social work research, especially in the USA (c.f. Gilgun, 2013), albeit perhaps more honoured in the breach than in the observance (Ruckdeschel, 2013). In an article offering a settled summary of the central aspects of grounded theory, Corbin and Strauss remark how researchers may 'end up claiming to have used a grounded theory approach when they have used only some of its procedures or have used them incorrectly' (Corbin and Strauss, 1990: 6). While there are differences of emphasis within the grounded research tradition, this article yields a helpful sketch of the general principles and 'canons' of the approach. The example is helpful also in that, although in important respects it represents a particular and distinctive type of qualitative analysis, several of its prescriptions are adopted by qualitative researchers more generally.

Corbin and Strauss take the general position that 'the usual canons of "good science" should be retained, but require *redefinition*' (ibid., p. 4), and in that context they set out the canons and procedures (Example 11.2).

EXAMPLE 11.2 — **Canons of Grounded Theory**

1. Data collection and analysis are interrelated processes.
2. Concepts are basic units of analysis.
3. Categories must be developed and related.
4. Analysis makes use of constant comparisons, for similarities and differences.
5. Patterns and variations must be accounted for.
6. Process must be built into the theory, noting shifts and changes and conditions thereof.
7. Writing theoretical memos.
8. Hypotheses about relationships among categories should be developed and verified as much as possible during the research process.
9. Broader structural conditions must be analysed however microscopic the research.

Based on Corbin and Strauss (1990)

Their opening principle influences all that follow. In grounded theory 'analysis is necessary from the start because it is used to direct the next interview and observations' (Corbin and Strauss, 1990: 4). They echo this later when they say 'if one does not alternately collect and analyse data, there will be gaps in the theory, because analysis does direct what one focuses upon during the interviews and observations' (ibid., p. 13). A strength of this position, and indeed a central sense in which the approach is 'grounded', is that 'Every concept brought into the study or discovered in the research process is at first considered provisional. Each concept earns its way into the theory by *repeatedly* being present in interviews, documents, and observations in one form or another – or by being significantly absent' (ibid., p. 7).

A further characteristic feature of grounded theory is the stress on analysis of *concepts*. 'A theorist works with conceptualizations of data, not the actual data *per se*' (ibid., p. 7). A central distinction in grounded theory is that between concepts and categories. The rationale is that concepts become grouped into categories, and in turn those categories are the cornerstones of a developing theory. A category must be actively developed 'in terms of its properties and dimensions of the phenomenon it represents, conditions which give rise to it, the action/interaction by which it is expressed, and the consequences it produces' (ibid., p. 7f).

The fronting up of concepts relates to the familiar grounded theory notion of theoretical sampling – in other words sampling concepts not people. This illustrates the deductive aspects of grounded theory. The presumption in favour of theoretical sampling is mirrored in how ideas of representativeness are viewed. Representativeness is seen as indeed canonical, but it is 'representativeness of concepts, not of persons' (ibid., p. 9). Gilgun, a leading social work advocate of grounded theory, refers to a change of position from her earlier writing, in saying 'The primary reason I prefer the term *deduction* is my belief that induction is not possible as an initial step in the doing of research' (Gilgun, 2013: 122). By way of illustration, were someone to study social workers' work she would go to where social workers work, but rather than sampling social workers she would sample incidents, events and happenings that denote the work that the social workers do, the conditions that facilitate, interrupt or prevent their work, the action/interaction by which it is expressed, and the consequences that result.

From a grounded theory perspective 'coding is the fundamental analytic process used by the researcher' (Corbin and Strauss, 1990: 12). Coding is viewed roughly as operating at three levels of analysis, captured in the terms open, axial and selective coding. These are understood in relation to the distinction between concepts and categories, the latter of which in turn are divided into core categories, categories and sub-categories.

In *open* coding actions, events and interactions are coded. They are then compared, hypotheses are generated and these also compared. This entails a mix of deductive and inductive thinking. Open coding is pursued through questioning and through constant comparison, as a way of 'fracturing the data' (Corbin and Strauss, 1990: 13). They make no mention of what may be called 'member categories' – those words, phrases and interpretations that are offered by participants. This absence seems to follow from the strong emphasis on abstraction and researcher language in grounded theory. As Denzin aptly remarks, in grounded theory there is 'a textual style that frequently subordinates lived experience and its interpretations to the grounded theorist's reading of the situation' (Denzin, 1994: 508). Consistent with this, it is noteworthy that, whatever occasional protestations to the contrary, grounded theorists place very little weight on the notion that we cannot split data and interpretation apart.

A further central idea is that the generation of provisional concepts gives the researcher questions to guide the return to the field. It can perhaps be argued that this interweaving of fieldwork and analysis at every stage is the single most important feature of grounded theory.

In *axial* coding categories are related to their sub-categories. Those relationships are then tested against the data in a progression that, in authentic grounded theory research, may prove an extended process. As with initial open coding 'All hypothetical relationships proposed deductively during axial coding must be considered provisional until verified repeatedly against incoming data' (Corbin and Strauss, 1990: 13).

There is a further stage of abstraction addressed by selective coding. This is 'the process by which *all* categories are unified around a "core" category' (ibid., p. 14). Indeed, the value of a theory depends at least in large part, on 'a process of abstraction that takes place over the entire course of the research' (ibid., p. 15). The notion of a core category has value regardless of whether one adopts a grounded theory strategy. It can often be tapped by asking questions such as 'If my findings are to be conceptualized in a few sentences … what does all the action/interaction seem to be about? How can I explain the variation that I see between and among the categories?' (ibid., p. 14).

Poststructural interpretivism

There are numerous positions to which one can attach the label 'interpretive', indeed too many to risk omission by listing them here. Drisko (2013b) has a helpful representation of mainstream constructivist frameworks in their application to social work. Denzin has expounded his position over many years, with both overlap and development, but we draw on four expressions of his considered thinking and standpoint (Denzin, 1994, 1997, 2002; Denzin and Lincoln, 2005).

'In the social sciences there is only interpretation. Nothing speaks for itself' (Denzin, 1994: 500). Hence 'we do not study lived experience; rather we examine lived textuality' and 'the direct link between experience and text ... can no longer be presumed' (ibid., p. 33).

> Thus the mystery of experience. There is no secret key that will unlock its meanings. It is a labyrinth with no fixed origins and no firm center, structure, or set of recurring meanings. All that can be sought is a more fully grounded, multisensual, multiperspectival epistemology that does not privilege sight (vision) over the other senses, including sound, touch and taste. (Ibid., 1997: 36)

For Denzin, favourite metaphors to describe how this carries through to making sense of data are *bricoleur* and *montage*. He uses the first in different ways – of the role of the researcher (a 'quilt maker'); of the bringing together of different fields; different materials (therefore as mixed qualitative methods); and of the nature of research as a 'piecing together'. The term *montage* is taken from the world of narrative films and he often refers to the famous Odessa Steps sequence in *The Battleship Potemkin* to make his point. 'In montage, several different images are juxtaposed or superimposed on one another to create a picture.' It 'creates the sense that images, sounds and understandings are blending together, overlapping, forming a composite, a new creation' (Denzin and Lincoln, 2005: 3). Pursuing the quilt making metaphor, the researcher stitches, edits, and puts slices together to create a kind of unity, in which 'many different things are going on at the same time – different voices, different perspectives, points of view, angles of vision' (ibid., p. 5).

In pursuit of a good text the researcher is after truth and verisimilitude. By truth, Denzin refers to 'a commitment to post-Marxism and feminism with hope but no guarantees', which 'exposes how class, race and gender work their ways into the concrete lives of interacting individuals' (1997: 10). By verisimilitude, he deliberately adopts a term used in traditional, foundational ideas of validity. However, for Denzin each form – research reports, keynote addresses, committee reports, grant proposals, journal articles – 'has its own laws of genre, its own verisimilitude' (ibid., p. 11).

Truth and verisimilitude are clearly different from one another, such that it seems possible for a text to have truth but not verisimilitude and *vice versa*. Indeed, although Denzin says that 'the truth of a text must always be aligned with the verisimilitude it establishes', he goes on to conclude 'the truth of a text cannot be established by its verisimilitude. Verisimilitude can always be challenged ... Truth is political, and verisimilitude is textual' (ibid., pp. 11, 12). He uses the term 'deconstructive verisimilitude' in this context (ibid., p. 13).

Having taken this position, how does a critical interpretivist engage in 'data analysis'? Expressed as a general stance, Denzin places the focus of the research 'on those life experiences (epiphanies) that radically alter and shape the meanings persons give to themselves and their life projects' (Denzin, 1994: 510). The core of interpretation should be the personal experience stories subjects tell one another and 'the stories that are presented to the reader should be given in the language, feelings, emotions, and actions of those studied' (ibid., p. 511).

This perhaps sounds somewhat intangible and elusive. But Denzin does suggest a form of interpretive analysis that can be pursued by researchers. With Lincoln, he advocates triangulation, which is multi-method in focus and 'reflects an attempt to secure an in-depth understanding of the phenomenon in question. Objective reality can never be captured. We know a thing only through its representations. Unlike early formulations of triangulation, triangulation is not a tool or strategy of validation, but an alternative to validation.' It is 'best understood … as a strategy that adds rigor, breadth, complexity, richness and depth to any inquiry' (Denzin and Lincoln, 2005: 5). In practice the actual process seems not too far from most constructivist methods. Thus 'qualitative interpretations are constructed' (ibid., p. 26) and entail:

- Indexing – creating a field text consisting of field notes and documents.
- Developing a research text consisting of notes and interpretations based on the field text.
- This is then recreated as a working interpretive document 'that contains the writer's initial attempts to make sense of what he or she has learned' (p. 26).
- Finally, there is a 'public text' – which may take one or more of several forms.

Denzin also has taken a special interest in the application of his approach to fields such as social work, pointing out that there are particular issues for applied fields. For example, 'Action-oriented and clinically oriented qualitative researchers can also create spaces where those who are studied (the Other) can speak' (Denzin and Lincoln, 2005: 26; c.f. Denzin, 2002; Mohr, 1997).

However, we placed data analysis in inverted commas a moment ago for good reason. In sharp contrast to grounded theory it makes limited sense for critical interpretivists to speak of data as something that, through a process of coding and abstraction, is analysed. In this limited respect critical poststructuralism, along with some other critical theory, feminist and participatory frameworks, has echoes of grounded theory in refusing to separate fieldwork and analysis into distinct and temporally separate phases. But Denzin goes further. 'Interpretation is an art; it is not formulaic or mechanical' (1994: 502). Yet Denzin appears to acknowledge the importance of analysis when he concludes that critical theorists 'foreground praxis, yet leave unclear the methodological side of the interpretive process that is so central to the grounded theory and constructionist approaches' (ibid., p. 509). We return to the blurring of stages of research when dealing with qualitative writing forms in Chapter Sixteen.

Motifs of qualitative analysis

The two positions we have sketched above are complex and distributed over numerous articles, books and other sources. A rereading of the previous pages may help fix the key elements of each position. Notwithstanding these two relatively polarised analytic frameworks, the qualitative researcher will encounter similar exhortations from all quarters, almost homiletical in quality, to approach analysis with particular commitments in mind. Be alert to the presence of discourse, approach your analysis in ways that reflect the character of qualitative data, and – again and again – be reflexive. For some, this amounts to a claim for the relative superiority of qualitative research on the grounds that it 'respects the complexity of the social world' (Hammersley, 2008: 39).

We owe ideas of discourse to Foucault. The extracts from and summary notes in Example 11.3 illustrate Foucault's careful, even tentative approach.

EXAMPLE 11.3 | **Foucault on Discourse Under-Understood**

Among the much over-used and probably under-understood words that have wide currency in qualitative research, 'discourse' has high standing. Foucault lamented the 'equivocal meaning of the term *discourse*, which I have used and abused in many different senses' (Foucault, 2002: 120). He was always aware that it was a work in progress.

He defines discourse as 'a group of statements in so far as they belong to the same discursive formation'. However discourse 'does not form a rhetorical or formal unity, endlessly repeatable, whose appearance or use in history might be indicated ...' It is made up of 'a limited number of statements for which a group of conditions of existence can be defined'. By this he refers to fields of discourse and speaks of clinical discourse, psychiatric discourse, the discourse of natural history and so on. He wishes to use the term in this way 'to reveal a descriptive possibility' (ibid., p. 121).

So discourses are made up of statements and are practices that follow certain rules. 'A statement belongs to a discursive formation as a sentence belongs to a text, and proposition to a deductive whole' (ibid., p. 130).

Discourse in this sense is not an ideal, timeless form. The problem is not to ask oneself how and why it was able to emerge and become embodied at this point in time; it is, from beginning to end, historical – 'a fragment of history, a unity and discontinuity in history itself, posing the problem of its own limits, its divisions, its transformations, the specific modes of its temporality rather than its sudden irruption in the midst of the complexities of time' (ibid., p. 131). It is not a document but a 'monument', and is not something to be interpreted. In this connection he remarks 'it refuses to be "allegorical"' (ibid., p. 155). Rather like Kuhn's apparent understanding of a paradigm, one cannot easily stand outside it. Its 'archaeology' will demand much.

Hence we should not think of discursive practices as *psychological* (e.g. a conscious formulation of an idea or desire), or *rational* (an inference), or a case of more or less *competent speaking* (grammatical), but as statements falling within a discursive formation.

(Foucault, 2002)

Applications of Foucauldian analysis can be found in social work, and are important in the spread of interest in historical and archival research (c.f. Fraser and Gordon, 1994).

'Be reflexive'

Confessional accounts emerged in the 1970s as qualitative researchers became more methodologically self-conscious and felt less tied to conventional forms and the need to demonstrate their scientific credentials. The influence of narrative methods and feminist epistemology have shaped this development. We illustrated from Rapley's account of confessional interviewing styles in Chapter Seven. In this connection there is an often-made distinction between confessional and realist tales, that we develop in Chapter Sixteen (van Maanen, 2011). Ethnography for decades had been characteristically told as a realist tale, in which writers sought to make themselves invisible, although this was not universally the case. Clifford Shaw's 1920s life history, *The Jack-Roller* (Shaw, 1966), is a realist tale but Shaw is far from invisible. Confessional tales are not necessarily fallibilistic in tone. Seale (1999) remarks they can function to show grounds for having gained true *entrée*, as a reflexive methodological accounting, and as a means of gaining the reader's trust in the author.

Reflexive accounts can be found in those researchers who advocate that we should make our theoretical assumptions clear. Seale remarks 'it is clear that the word "theory" is here standing for many things, such as the values, prejudices or subconscious desires of the researcher, many of which are by definition not available for explanation by the person who has been influenced by them' (ibid., p. 163). In postmodern pleas for reflexivity and confessional accounts the authority of and trust in the writer is decentred. For Denzin, for example, a radical pluralism emerges, where 'polyphony and dialogue are the ideals, with problematic status accorded to the voice of the author' (ibid., p. 170).

Whichever position one takes 'Fieldwork is a site for identity work for the researcher' (Coffey, 1999: 115) and this is achieved through textual products. In an important early paper, Babcock spoke of the 'infinite variety' in that 'reflexivity appears in many different costumes on many different stages' (Babcock, 1980: 6). In a series of overlapping distinctions she suggests it may be:

- Private (e.g., journal keeping) or public (some form of shared experience).
- Singular and individual (e.g., contemplating oneself in a mirror) or plural and collective.
- Internal (e.g., a story within a story) or external (e.g., 'the once upon a time frame that tells us this is a play or story' p. 6).
- Implicit (e.g., as represented in a cultural custom) or explicit (field logs).
- Partial or total.

More simply, reflexive research has two senses. First, individual awareness that does not take at face value either members' accounts of their own activities or 'the typical practices of objectification used by academic researchers'. Second, 'Sensitivity to the operation of power and privilege both in the phenomena being studied and in the practices of the researcher'. The latter should be understood 'as socially instituted, not as personal failures' (Packer, 2011: 330). Babcock goes as far as to conclude that 'The only cure for subjectivity is reflexivity'

(Babcock, 1980: 11). Yet there is an epistemological paradox in efforts at reflexivity in that in trying to say something about oneself one confounds 'subject and object, seer and seen, self and other, art and life' (ibid., p. 5).

Ben-Ari and Enosh (2011) put forward a model for being reflexive (they actually say 'reflective') in qualitative social work research. Their argument is nuanced and developed. They bring together different levels of qualitative analysis and anchor them in relation to levels of reflection – observation, informants' accounts, text deliberation and contextualisation and reconstruction. To illustrate, they reproduce an observation fieldnote that reads:

> Looking over a beautiful Galilee valley, made up of scattered two-story stone buildings, with expansive lawns and meticulous gardens reminiscent of a well cared-for residential community … People are walking round dressed in jeans and brown work shirts. Only the small PA (Prison Authority) logo hints to the onlooker that they are, in fact, inmates of a prison.

The linked reflection reads:

> Conducting a research project in a prison facility, the researchers expect to see high walls, watchtowers, grey buildings, neglected surroundings, and facilities for a body search. However, upon entry, the researchers encounter the pastoral view of the site.

> The researchers experience a dissonance between the *pre-existing expectations* and the actual site. (Ben-Ari and Enosh, 2011: 160–1)

How, in the light of the preceding paragraphs, should we respond to frequently heard pleas, often linked to inductive analysis, to 'put aside researchers' own views and promote active listening and open-minded consideration in research interviewing, observations, and document analysis' (Gilgun, 2013: 111)? Tufford and Newman (2012) address this perennial challenge through the idea of bracketing – expressed at its simplest, the process by which qualitative researchers seek to *put aside preconceptions so that the true experiences of respondents are reflected in the analysis and reporting of research.*

However, despite a broad shared sense of the meaning of this term there remains a lack of consensus over what is to be held in abeyance. An example of how aspects of these commitments can be demonstrated may be borrowed from a helpful recommendation about preparing questions for a research interview. McCracken (1988) recommends that long qualitative interviews are preceded by the investigator reviewing his/her personal experience of the topic of interest. Eliciting such prior experience has two paradoxically 'opposite' effects. First, 'deep and long-lived familiarity with the culture under study has, potentially, the grave effect of dulling the investigator's powers of observation and analysis', but 'it also has the advantage of giving the investigator an extraordinarily intimate acquaintance with the object of study' (McCracken, 1988: 32). In so doing we should be ready to 'glimpse and systematically reconstruct a view of the world that bears no relation to our own', and 'come to the text with a certain disingenuous wonder, refusing to supply the assumptions and understandings' (ibid., 44). Such a cultural review, 'calls for minute examination of [our] experience. The investigator must inventory and examine the associations, incidents and assumptions that surround the topic is his or her mind ... the object is to draw out of one's own experience the systematic properties of the topic' (ibid., p. 32).

EXAMPLE 11.4 ⊣ **Cultural Review**

Suppose I am preparing to interview a woman having difficulties coping with caring for her 25 year old son who has serious learning disabilities and lives at home. A personal and cultural review will require me to do two things:

1. Make a list of the different topics that would need to be the focus of my self-inquiry for a cultural review.
2. Make a paragraph of notes for each of the topics in my list.

My list of topics might include

- Who have I cared for?
- My own feelings about being cared for by a close relative or partner.
- My reaction to carrying out personal care tasks.
- My feelings about the boundaries between family time and work time.
- My definition and use of free time.
- How I view '*free* time' compared to '*working* time'.
- Satisfactions gained from caring.
- How do I react when there are restrictions on my time?
- Daytime caring and evening caring.
- Weekday caring and weekend caring.
- My ideal balance between time alone and time with family.

Having made my list of headings, the next stage is to make notes under each heading. For example, I have included *my feelings about being cared for by a close relative or partner*. If I resent the thought that I may at some time have to face physical dependency on a close relative, then this may make me unreasonably negative towards the person who is caring. I have also listed *who have I cared for*? In cases where male family members have constrained a woman into a stereotypical caring role, she will be especially sensitive to the potential for discrimination that exists in the caring role in western societies.

In undertaking a cultural review we demonstrate reflexivity and render explicit what we know and do not know. We become 'autobiographically conscious of our own reactions to our work' (Clandinin and Connelly, 2000: 46).

Based on Shaw (2011b)

Miller and Crabtree undertook a study of the understanding and experience of pain, for which each member of the research team inventoried her or his own past pain incidents, associations and assumptions. They develop McCracken's original application in two ways, both of which may be useful in a social work context. First, they recommend that the discovery of cultural categories be expanded to include preliminary direct contact with individuals from the cultural group being studied. Second, in addition to the conceptualising value of the exercise, they argue that 'the self-exploration also prepares a reservoir of empathy for the researcher when the respondent shares similar thoughts and emotions' (Miller and Crabtree, 1992: 199).

A further connection should be made. One of Babcock's distinctions and forms of reflexivity was between internal (e.g., a story within a story) or external (e.g., 'the once upon a time frame that tells us this is a play or story'). This helpfully draws us to the inescapable connection between reflexivity and coding. In their illuminating discussion of 'narrative linkages' in interviews, Holstein and Gubrium (1995) talk about how narrative contexts shift in interviews, and how there are elements of narrative reflexivity in which participants convey, by their replies, that they see diverse contexts for interpreting life. They refer in this connection to 'indigenous coding'. 'In practice, both the interviewer and the respondent continuously engage in coding experience' (Holstein and Gubrium, 1995: 56). This 'active coding' 'takes place and unfolds as an integral part of the interview process, not just beforehand and afterward' (ibid., p. 57). An application of this idea is given in Example 11.5 Indigenous Coding, with emphasis added.

EXAMPLE 11.5 — Indigenous Coding

A probation officer describes an example of her work which had not gone well. A man had been placed on probation for an offence of threatening to kill his ex wife, which involved holding a knife to her throat. Once on probation he seemed to be doing 'amazingly well'. The probation officer was 'all set to take (the order) back to the court to ask for it to be revoked because I felt we'd made such an enormous amount of progress'. 'Then of course his ex-wife phoned me and … said that he'd never stopped drinking and bullying her'.

A question from the interviewer invites the probation officer to think in terms of certain evaluative options. In response to a question from the interviewer the probation officer refers to various analytic 'codes' for understanding her work. Some of the key terms are italicised in the following extract.

Interviewer: What was it about this case that you think you weren't doing well?

Probation Officer: (Sigh) The evidence was that I'd taken what the man had said very much at *face value*. I'm still not sure in retrospect whether I should have made more effort to follow up with his ex-wife. I mean *at the time* I was (sigh), I felt that actually offering her the information was sufficient, given that they weren't currently married, he wasn't currently living with her and that she had her *right to privacy* and not to be involved. There was also an issue of *confidentiality* about what he told me during the interviews, that obviously I wasn't going to be able to share that

> with his ex-wife without his permission. So I was, I mean basically I felt like a total mug, certainly in terms of effectiveness, not only totally ineffective but also possibly *worsened a bad situation* by *colluding* with this man in the belief that everything was actually all right, and *wasted a great deal of time* in *supposed counselling* sessions (laugh).
>
> Extract from research reported in
> Shaw and Shaw (1997/2012)

Anticipating and preparing for analysis

Having explored the general stances that shape how analysis is approached, we turn to more specific strategies and steps that call for critical imagination and implementation as part of foreseeing and preparing for analysis. Foreseeing and anticipating are not mentioned by accident. Throughout the research act we need to think and act in the light of how we expect to make sense of the subsequent data. Checking back to the part of the chapter on grounded theory, the interplay of fieldwork and analysis was seen as a defining characteristic of that approach, and Denzin's brand of critical interpretivism so deeply permeates the fieldwork and the analysis that it makes limited sense even to conceive of analysis as a stage of research.

Similar points can be made about perhaps all forms of qualitative research. Jacqueline Wiseman made the point clearly some forty years ago, when she referred to how the

> constant interplay of data gathering and analysis is at the heart of qualitative research. It is therefore difficult to discuss coding, processing, analysis, and writing without also discussing planning and data gathering … For me, with the possible exception of the early planning stages. All aspects of the research act are going on almost simultaneously. (Wiseman, 1974: 317)

But in this part of the chapter we focus more explicitly on the work that the researcher needs to undertake as a bridge between fieldwork and analysis. Keeping in mind the challenges of reflexive practice, the tasks we have in mind include field logs, field diaries, file-work, transcription, preliminary memoing and decisions regarding technology and software. We have dealt with coding in some detail in earlier parts of the chapter.

Fieldnotes, diaries and memos

In fieldwork, and perhaps especially in ethnography, decisions about fieldnotes are perhaps more important than any other. We have introduced them already in Chapter Ten. They are 'the textual place where we, at least privately, acknowledge our presence and conscience' (Coffey, 1999: 120). Lofland and Lofland have helpful remarks on this area. They describe fieldnotes as basically 'a more or less chronological log of what is happening to and in the setting and to and in the observer … For the most part, fieldnotes are a running description of events, people, things heard and overheard, conversations among people, conversations with people' (Lofland and Lofland, 2006: 93).

Given the endemic selectivity of fieldnotes, one way to reduce this is 'to complement the notes by diaries or day protocols written by the subjects under study in parallel with the researcher's own note-taking.' Another consideration is to include 'photos, drawings, maps and other visual materials' (Flick, 2006: 287). These may be as simple as layouts of fieldwork space, the physical location of people in that space, and any physical movements during the fieldwork period, but may also include digital images. How long should fieldnotes be? Bearing in mind that we assume a field log will be kept in research that is predominantly about planned asking of questions as well as in more ethnographically directed fieldwork, such notes will be longer in the latter case and the Loflands' rule of a minimum of 'at least a couple of single-spaced typed pages for every hour of observation' (Lofland and Lofland, 2006: 95) does not seem unreasonable. Lofland and Lofland distinguish mental notes, jottings and full fieldnotes, but for most researchers the use of mobile electronic devices opens new possibilities, and the Loflands' plea for 'cloistered rigor' (ibid., p. 92) as a means of recording as soon as possible becomes less difficult to achieve.

While not wishing to reinstate a naïve boundary between data and its interpretation, we do retain a distinction based on intentionality. There are occasions when our intention is, as far as lies in us, to record events, actions and interactions in as unmingled a way as possible. There are also occasions when we are quite aware that we are entertaining interpretive, analytic ideas. To make a clear distinction in fieldnotes between one and the other seems entirely reasonable advice. Lofland and Lofland imply the value of this distinction when they advise that 'the first step in taking fieldnotes is to evoke your culturally commonsensical notion of what constitutes a descriptive report' (ibid., p. 89), and add as a helpful general rule to 'stay at the lowest possible level of inference' (ibid., p. 93).

It may be helpful to employ this distinction through keeping a field log for the record and a research diary for puzzles, confusions, mistakes, any sense of a breakthrough, and reflections on matters of reflexivity, as well as more self-aware moments of provisional interpretation, although we counsel against an over-punctilious pursuit of this rule.

An interesting example of fieldnotes that includes interpretive and reflexive asides is given by Gerhard Riemann in his work on ethnographies of practice carried out with social work students in Germany (Riemann, 2005, 2011). His approach included asking students to keep ethnographic field notes. The examples he provides exemplify how fieldnotes oblige us to avoid taking the mundane for granted and sliding past the puzzling. They pose issues about the prevalence of unplanned incidents and how we respond to them; the nature of stigma; the ambiguous processes of becoming familiar with local circumstances of the clinic; and the occurrence of incongruity. They also compel us to recognise the emotional dimensions of fieldwork. Finally, they implicitly caution us against undue confidence regarding what counts as relevant for inclusion in fieldnotes. 'Later, certain details noted may begin to take on a "sociological importance", so decisions regarding what is deemed interesting or not can have a bearing on later interpretive – theoretical work' (Roberts, 2007: 68–9).

Transcription

As with all decisions about the recording and working with data, we should avoid treating transcription only as a series of technical judgements. Packer remarks, as have others, that we underestimate the difference between the recording and the transcription. There are numerous issues for transcribers – verbal features such as hesitations, pauses, false starts etc.; and non-lexical expressions – *ums* and *aaahs*. Capturing punctuation is difficult. The digital sound record is itself selective. Speech is being 'fixed' by writing. What is a fleeting event in time that disappears becomes fixing the 'said', and so it leaves a trace (Packer, 2011: 116). 'It is the temporality of discourse that makes fixing necessary' (ibid., p. 117). The move from speech to text also changes the relationship of discourse to the speaker. Asking what a text means is not the same as asking what the speaker meant. The said now comes to matter more than what the author meant to say. The move to text also changes the audience – not the person/s whom the speaker addressed but anyone who can read it. In Example 11.6 we suggest several everyday rules in response to some of the most frequently asked questions we have encountered.

EXAMPLE 11.6	**Everyday Rules for Transcribing – FAQs**

Is it possible to transcribe selectively? Almost always we would say 'No'. This is because unless you have very clear propositions that you are looking at, then selective *transcription* is in effect selective *analysis*, in which you are deciding what is important before you have properly looked at the data. Because you are working with qualitative material such as semi-structured interviews, this points to the probability that you do not have specific postulates in advance so do not know what will be relevant and what not.

Should the transcription be word for word? There are different levels of transcription. Parts of the interview that are clearly opening preambles or closing 'signing off' remarks can be left out, but that is about all. You need to decide what your transcription conventions will be. For a basic, minimum transcription these should include how you will:

- anonymise.
- Mark words or phrases you cannot hear.
- Mark words or phrases where you are not 100% sure what has been said.
- Deal with pauses; nonverbal communication, etc. Will it be important to reflect voice tone e.g., stresses, rise/fall of voice?
- Indicate overlapping speech.

(Continued)

(Continued)

You should include a 'glossary' of the conventions you have used. The most commonly used conventions have been developed in and borrowed from conversation analysis.

How should I format the page? The issue here is that you need to transcribe it so that it is useful as a tool for analysis. Our suggestions are:

1. If you are planning to work from hard copies, set the right-hand margin wide. This is so you can scribble notes in the margin at a later stage. By 'scribble' we have in mind either longhand or on screen, using the comment functions in word processing packages.
2. Add line numbers continuous, not page-by-page, throughout the text.
3. If working from hard copies, decide the line spacing you will use. We advise double spacing. This is so that you can make brief notes between lines.

I plan to use a computer assisted data analysis package. Should I use the package to develop my transcriptions? On the whole, our advice is to complete the data preparation outside the package. We have more to say about this later in the chapter.

Finally, it is time consuming and could take up to eight hours for every interview-hour. Even if you can afford to pay someone, we strongly advise that you undertake some yourself.

Technology

Computer Assisted Qualitative Data Analysis (CAQDAS) tends to be regarded with either unquestioning enthusiasm or scepticism and mistrust. Dey gives voice to the latter, although not adhering to it himself, when he remarks 'it is sometimes argued that the computer encourages "data fragmentation". Computer-based analysis can be likened to dissection – to the irony of trying to understand the living by dissecting the dead. Instead of studying the data in situ, the data are "fragmented" into bits and the overall sense of the data is lost' (Dey, 1993: 64). In contrast, Drisko claims that 'at the cutting edge, computer software offers whole new vistas for qualitative research, expanding the types of data it addresses and the forms through which knowledge is developed and communicated' (Drisko, 2013a: 284).

Drisko's recent survey of CAQDAS provides a wide-ranging introduction to its challenges and opportunities. He cautions that, 'Unlike statistical software, qualitative data analysis software does not "do" the analysis; it merely facilitates it ... The use of software in no way guarantees a meaningful or rigorous analysis. It may offer some modest overtones of thoroughness but these can be appearances only if the software is not used thoughtfully' (Drisko, 2013a: 287). He expresses this point more firmly - 'Computer software does not teach researchers the methods of qualitative research, nor enforce any particular method of analysis' (ibid., p. 287). This last point is perhaps too categorical. Grounded theory has been well served by software analysis packages, but narrative research less so. As Flick expresses it, the use of computer programmes 'has made the use of analytic techniques like theoretic coding more explicit and transparent' (2006: 354).

Turning to decisions about which package to use, the most helpful text is Lewins and Silver's book (2007). In deciding which packages to use they advise researchers to review their preferred style of working, the amount and kind of data they have, how central thematic coding is to their project, whether they need a variety of analysis tools, whether they are working solo or in a team, and what degree of institutional and peer support they will be able to draw on. 'All CAQDAS packages have pros and cons and the choice between them is necessarily based on different factors for different researchers, methodologies, data types, etc.' (Fielding et al., 2006). They also advocate that, even when a package is chosen, users should adopt imaginative and experimental approaches to their use. 'We resist the idea that there is a "right way" to use any given product.'

Nonetheless, it remains possible to draw good practice guidelines for preparing for and sequencing computer assisted qualitative analysis. Example 11.7 is based on, and in places quoting from, Drisko (2013a).

EXAMPLE 11.7	**Preparing for and Sequencing Computer Assisted Data Analysis**

1. Collect the electronic data files and make sure they have been proofed and are in final form, before copying any electronic files into the computer software.
2. Open the software and start a new 'project'.
3. 'Assign' the raw data files into the analysis software.
4. It is good practice to start each new project with a memo that documents your overall expectations, hopes and/or hypotheses. All such memos become part of the project file.
5. The coding process – 'marking meaningful passages and coding them is the single most time consuming part of qualitative data analysis.' Multiple coding options allow researchers to find approaches that best fit their analytic needs and personal styles.
6. Search for all instances of a word or concept, for which you will find a range of search functions.
7. Save and output coded materials. Computer software can save and output coded materials in many formats.
8. Use more advanced search functions, known as 'queries', to allow for exploration within already coded materials. 'Boolean queries allow for location of all passages with *both* one code *and* another, one code *or* another, or one code *but not* another. In this manner researchers may examine if relationships within coded materials fit certain existing or developing concepts and theories. Another form of query examines materials coded as superordinate and subordinate to each other, helping to explore and clarify hierarchical relationships among content and concepts. Still another form of query allows for the exploration of the proximity among content in coded passages.'
9. 'Filter' documents, meaningful passages and codes into subsets for analysis.
10. Visually portray relationships within the data. Software can establish links among codes, segments of data, documents and memos.
11. Once relationships are created, they can be displayed as 'network maps' portraying the content and relationships visually.

(Continued)

(Continued)

12. Consider direct analysis of images, audio and video.
13. Use where appropriate geographic location and imaging tools. 'Google earth images and maps may be linked to descriptions of neighborhoods or specific resources such as bus routes and locations of supermarkets. Here computer software allows very detailed location information using GPS coordinates as well as photographic images of specific locations.'

Based on and quoting from Drisko (2013a)

The key verbs in this process are search, link, code, query, annotate, map and network. But simply because such functions are available does not mean that they will necessarily be appropriate in a given project. This list has one draw-back, in that it implicitly limits the use of various devices to analysis, whereas as Flick demonstrates, there are numerous ways of using such devices in qualitative research (Flick, 2006: 343f), and we are naïvely modernist if we fail to understand that issues of technology have run through the whole history of social research (Lee, 2004).

The field is rapidly changing and has implications well beyond data analysis.

> The way we collect, retrieve, store and manage data will always be shaped by context including the historic moment, and our relationship to it … [A]s we move between various constructions (such as book as 'artefact' versus book as lending object, or Internet as study object versus functional tool) we change the nature of our own physical and social interactions with the object, with the environment, and with others. (Staller, 2010: 287)

Three developing challenges should be noted. First, publication and presentation forms have struggled to mirror these developments, and 'Research models and publication media and formats will have to expand and change to keep pace with these new tools' (Drisko, 2013a: 286). Some journals have moved to a compromise position of having adjunct sites where fuller material can be displayed, although the implications for future formats have yet to be realised. Second, computer software makes team-based qualitative research much more practical and, sometimes, makes it possible, including 'geographically dispersed, multi-site, group qualitative research' (ibid., p. 288). Finally, developments are opening up new opportunities for multimedia data analysis and display, although Drisko cautions that 'One picture or video may be worth a thousand words, but only if what it conveys is important and useful to realizing the researcher's purposes' (ibid., p. 290).

Having considered the significance and practice of fieldnotes, field diaries, memoing, transcription and coding, and recognised the particular technological contexts in which they take place, we turn our attention in the next chapter to the actual analytic process.

Taking it further

Locate and read the article on reflexivity by Babcock. Also reread the section in this chapter on reflexivity. Drawing on Babcock's five overlapping distinctions mentioned in this chapter, spend perhaps two hours reflecting in their light on a current or recent research project in which you have been involved.

Record your results in a confidential memo written to yourself.

TWELVE
Doing Qualitative Analysis

In Chapter Eleven we explored contrasting frameworks for qualitative analysis, but also those elements that are shared across different approaches. We considered ways in which we may anticipate and prepare for analysis. In this chapter we approach the details of doing analysis.

Following a reminder of the ambiguity that often surrounds talk of qualitative analysis, we outline and illustrate how analysis takes place within the range of fieldwork methods we discussed in Chapters Seven through Ten. We compare thematic and narrative analysis, and then consider ethnography and the analysis of texts and documents. We widen our scope slightly to include also visual methods and secondary qualitative analysis.

We draw the chapter to a close by glancing at the process by which we draw together analytic conclusions – a theme that will preoccupy us in particular ways in Chapter Thirteen.

Qualitative researchers have sometimes manifested an ambivalence about the idea of data analysis. Indeed, we placed inverted commas around the term on one occasion in Chapter Eleven. This is due in part to a tendency to view 'analysis' as *techne* in the restricted sense that it can be reduced to how-to rules that are pragmatically independent of the purposes of research. This fails to notice that the kind of research itself presupposes certain ways of explaining, such that any 'data', regardless of method, are in fact produced by the researcher. 'In this respect, the idea that we "collect" data is a bit misleading. Data are not "out there" waiting collection, like so many rubbish bags on the pavement ... (O)ur observations are concept-laden abstractions from the flow of experience – and we should be wary of taking these products of our thinking as enjoying an existence independent of it' (Dey, 1993: 16, 20).

We foresaw this point in the previous chapter, in talking about how analysis is anticipated and foreshadowed in the earlier stages of research. In addition, we will recognise in the final chapter that analysis is not over and done with as a once and for all stage of research. 'Fieldwork, at its core, is a long social process of coming to terms with a culture. It is a process that begins before one enters the field and continues long after one leaves it' (van Maanen, 2011: 117). 'Knowing a culture, even our own, is a never ending story' such that 'our analysis is not finished, only over' (ibid., pp. 119, 120). In Chapter Eleven we mentioned Holstein and Gubrium's reference to indigenous coding, as an activity which takes place and unfolds as an integral part of the interview process, not just beforehand or afterwards. Example 12.1 follows on from Example 11.5 to illustrate the interweaving of analysis and fieldwork. The interviewer also is seeking to promote the visibility of narrative linkages. Holstein and Gubrium go so far as to claim that 'the interviewer interpretively challenges the respondent to make sense of experience in relation to various subjective possibilities' (1995: 59). The question and answer sequence, which immediately follows the exchange in Example 11.5, illustrates the form this may take.

EXAMPLE 12.1 — **Analysis in Interviewing**

Interviewer:	Is part of the difficulty the difficulty itself of being able to interpret evidence, because what you said was there seemed to be lots of clues which you could reasonably be expected to interpret as meaning things are going well?
Probation Officer:	Yes.
Interviewer:	And suddenly one bit of evidence jeopardises all those other bits of evidence?
Probation Officer:	Yeah, I mean it's basically the one bit of evidence, the phone call from the ex-wife, put a completely different interpretation on everything else that had occurred.
Interviewer:	Is that something generally about interpreting work, the problem of interpreting evidence?
Probation Officer:	It's a difficulty in evaluating people's attitudes (laugh) because you're very much dependent on the information they volunteer and what they tell you. This guy chose for his own reasons to deliberately mislead. I mean needless to say he was impeccable about keeping his appointments, about being on time (laugh). He worked very hard to present a certain picture. As I say on the evidence I had available, I made one assessment that turned out to be completely false because of the evidence I didn't have access to, i.e., what was actually going on when he was visiting his ex-wife.

Answer to questions and stories told

Bearing in mind the dangers of treating analysis purely as a series of technical steps, we enter this field acknowledging, with Packer, that:

1. Understanding a text is always an active process.
2. Readers/researchers can never be free from preconceptions. Rather, we encounter a text within a horizon.

3. Understanding is always interested, not detached. It always involves 'application'.
4. No text has a single correct interpretation. 'The meaning of a text is an *effect* of reading it' (Packer, 2011: 97).
5. The encounter with a text can change the reader. 'We read, and we conduct research, to learn something' (ibid., p. 97).

While we have chosen to bring interviews and narratives together, we should remember that narratives, as Roberts finely develops (Roberts, 2002), are not solely a product of interviews. They may emerge from visual methods, documents and ethnographic accounts of one kind and another. We pick up these overlaps during the chapter.

Analyses of answers to questions asked and of stories told are sometimes presented as wholly distinct from one another. We may tend to take for granted that the respective natures of thematic and narrative analysis are different and straightforward. Themes are plural, narrative is singular; thematic analysis disaggregates the text into different meanings, while narrative analysis is holistic. There is *some* truth in both these contrasts. Likewise, it makes some degree of sense to say that in thematic analysis our interest lies in ideas from *within* cases compared across *different cases* as the unit of analysis, while in narrative research our interest is in comparing cases against each other *as a whole*. These distinctions do not exhaust ways we should think of answers and stories. We should also consider to whom the person is speaking (audience) and for what purpose.

A fifth analytic distinction sometimes made is between *what* is being said – the content – and *how* it has been said. The distinction is central to qualitative analysis, but mapping it onto thematic and narrative analysis is more problematic. There *is* often more focus on content in thematic analysis, and there *is* a lot of emphasis on how things are said in narrative. But on the whole we find this an unhelpful way of distinguishing between them. For example, it severely limits how we think about themes. Take the following example from a study by one of the authors, where a social worker who had done a small research project is reflecting on the difference between practice and research.

> I'm not good at interviews – sorry, you're now listening to me thinking out loud – I'm not very good at interviewing, never think I'm very good at interviewing people, which I've done a lot of times and again it's because I have this thing I have to follow and that I feel I'm not free to ask people … I'm terrified I'll forget something. It's more serious asking because – when you're a social worker it is gaining people's trust and then you go back, it's all a jigsaw, layers of things you find, so you don't have to find it out the first time. In this one I feel I have to find everything on this one interview and that has made me freeze. I found that difficult.

In terms of themes this could be 'coded' as social work interviews are more reliant on gaining the initial trust of the person, and also that they are like a 'jigsaw'. By contrast, in research interviews it is all or nothing. Given the occasional debates among social work writers about if and how social work interviews are similar to research interviews (one we touch on elsewhere in this book), this offers an interesting entry to the experience of practice/research relationships. But this does not exhaust how this passage can be understood, because central features of the social worker's speech are personal disclosure and reflexivity. We hear her saying, 'sorry, you're now listening to me thinking out loud'; 'I'm terrified'; 'I found that difficult'. So there is 'how?' as well as 'what?'

In general, we should recognise a range and diversity within qualitative analysis, but in doing so not make too absolute distinctions between thematic and narrative explorations. Indeed, the distinction between what is said and how it is said – or perhaps better the told and the telling – comes into its own when we think of how narratives have themes that draw our attention to the 'what' of the narrative. So how can we talk in terms of themes when we want to present narrative analysis? The main answer is that we need to keep the story intact by theorising *from the case* rather than from component themes or categories *across cases*. Mainstream thematic analysis is interested in cross-case analysis in terms of themes, and in so doing care is needed. The risk is that researchers rush to themes and forget the case, arising from a tendency to take themes too presumptively. Analysis is approached with the assumption that we know the themes because we have the data collection instrument.

It is often advisable as an initial step in qualitative analysis to forget the instrument and its implicit presupposed themes and look at the data. Otherwise one is drawn into the very misleading assumption that – in a way rather similar to the logic of surveys and questionnaires – the possibilities for analysis are entirely constrained by the instrument. While this is almost a *sine qua non* for surveys it is usually a disaster for qualitative analysis. This suggests one answer to the often-asked question of where one should start in analysing data. Start, we advise, by selecting an interview that you think had much to tell you, but which held some puzzles for you, and perhaps ran counter to how you had anticipated it would run. Then move to working on a contrary 'case' that you think will not easily fit with your tentative analytic ideas. There are two principles at stake here. Force yourself to examine the unexpected, the puzzling, and the incongruous. Look for apparent absurdities in the text and ask how they could have made sense to a reasonable person. Second, make yourself try to falsify, rather than search for expanding confirmatory notions. In doing so the researcher brings to the analysis:

- A sense of what the literature and one's own previous work tells us ought to be there in the data.
- A sense of how this topic is constituted in one's own experience.
- A 'glancing sense of what took place in the interview' (McCracken, 1988: 42).

Beginning by identifying key utterances in the text of a single interview, the analyst should be ready, quoting McCracken again, to 'glimpse and systematically reconstruct a view of the world that bears no relation' to their own view or that of the literature. This entails the cultivation of a 'mannered' reading of the text. 'Come to the text with a certain disingenuous wonder, refusing to supply the assumptions and understandings' (McCracken, 1988: 44). It will involve watching for whatever associations the text evokes in the reader, including those occasions when the evaluator recognises what is being said, not because the utterance has been successfully decoded, but because a sudden act of recognition has taken place' (ibid., p. 44). 'Categorizing the data is anything but mechanical, for it requires a continual exercise of judgement on the part of the analyst' (Dey, 1993: 132).

An illustration of thematic analysis of narratives is Williams' classic research on the genesis of chronic illness, to which we referred in Chapter Eight (Williams, 1984). We saw how he asked a delightfully simple question ('Why do you think you got arthritis?') which led to narratives that addressed the genesis of their arthritis, and in ways that were very different from the medical mainline account of hereditary predispositions. He took the already familiar idea of illness as disrupting biography, which prompted narrative reconstructions of their biographies.

Reading Williams' article (see Example 8.3) it is apparent that he has undertaken some 'cleaning' of the text. This is an area where there is some ambiguity in the literature. The blurring of research *genres* that we discussed in Chapter Three problematises the question of whether a transcript reproduces spoken words with fidelity. In a radical example of such 'cleaning' Catherine Phillips sketches a narrative from her own clinical practice as a social worker in an emergency department in an acute care hospital in Toronto. Drawn from multiple interactions, 'It has been assembled … to demonstrate two things: one, that clinical interactions are a series of social texts; and two, when studied closely, such interactions are replete with everyday acts of power that must be attended to in social work research into clinical practices … It is my hope that the writings of experience in this article can confront the fictions, fantasies, narratives, explanations, and signs that allow patients in pain a limited number of transgressions' (Phillips, 2007a: 201).

She is giving a form of autoethnography, which yields a very powerful piece of writing, made so in part by the process of editing. Yet in doing so the co-construction of the narrative, language as topic, and immediate contexts for talking all become less evident.

More on thematic analysis

Several important issues lie just below the surface in what we have so far discussed. How should we understand the relationship between the part and the whole in one or a number of interviews? How can we recognise a 'unit' of data? What is the relationship between different levels of analysis, as seen, for example in grounded theory's distinction between different kinds of coding? What makes a theme of importance?

In a fairly widely shared account of qualitative exploration, Dey proposes that '"Analysis" … involves breaking data down into bits, and then "beating" the bits together … The core of qualitative analysis lies in these related processes of describing phenomena, classifying it, and seeing how our concepts interconnect.' In so doing 'we transform our data into something it was not' (Dey, 1993: 31). 'Categories are created, modified, divided and extended through confrontation with the data' (ibid., p. 134). He accepts with slight reluctance the difficulties entailed in pleading for both abstraction and contextualisation:

> Once the data is categorized, we can examine and explore the data in our own terms. There is an irony inherent in this process, for in order to compare data within or between categories, we have to abstract the data from the context in which it is located. Without abstraction, comparison is not possible. And yet one of the most powerful injunctions of qualitative analysis is that data should be analysed in context. How can these contradictory requirements be reconciled? ... Unfortunately we cannot accomplish these requirements simultaneously. But the ability to see the data one way, and then another, is perhaps the nearest we can hope to come to coping with this paradox. (Dey, 1993: 13, 136)

The tension of category and context is close to that between abstraction and generalisation - *abstraction* ('the practice of dividing the whole into elements that are distinct from one another and from their original contexts') and *generalising* ('the practice of finding what is common or repeated among these elements') (Packer, 2011: 59). Packer is unequivocal in his criticism of the assumption that we can somehow split analysis into such distinct operations. He attacks grounded theory as proceeding by 'fracturing' into 'incidents'. 'But an interview is not made up of incidents. It is made up of verbal *descriptions* of incidents.' By treating them as the same, the incident is detached from its context, to find what is common. 'Fragmentation is abstraction in the service of generalization' (ibid., pp. 64, 65). The meaning we give to words follows from the context in which we use them, such that the process of abstraction silences the voice of the participant.

We are not sure that analysis leaves us quite without a port in the storm. We find it helpful to recall what Herbert Blumer long ago called 'sensitizing concepts' (Blumer, 1954). Contrasting his notion with a more traditional idea of concepts as defining something in an abstract way, he explains that

> A definitive concept refers precisely to what is common to a class of objects, by the aid of a clear definition in terms of attributes or fixed bench marks ... A sensitizing concept lacks such specification of attributes or bench marks and consequently it does not enable the user to move directly to the instance and its relevant content. Instead, it gives the user a general sense of reference and guidance in approaching empirical instances. Whereas definitive concepts provide prescriptions of what to see, sensitizing concepts merely suggest directions along which to look. (Blumer, 1954: 7)

He helpfully implies the consequences for analysis.

> What is common (i.e., what the concept refers to) is expressed in a distinctive manner in each empirical instance and can be got at only by accepting and working through the distinctive expression ... One moves out from the concept to the concrete distinctiveness of the instance instead of embracing the instance in the abstract framework of the concept. This is a matter of filling out a new

situation or of picking one's way in an unknown terrain. The concept sensitizes one to this task, providing clues and suggestions. (Blumer, 1954: 8)

These considerations relate to the question of what counts as a unit or 'bit' of data – an issue that also lay just below the surface in our discussion of CAQDAS in the last chapter. One way of thinking about this issue is to think of a 'bit' of data as a unit of meaning. This helpfully steers us away from thinking of grammatical coherent units, and also of logically coherent units. But this does not resolve the problem. A 'unit' means something that has singularity – it is an item or an element of something. But what we may see as a unit of meaning may of course have more than one meaning and also we should not assume that it is irreducible.

Decisions on units of data tie into choices about how data is transcribed. They also flow from adoptions of different methods. Narrative methods overlap with, for example, arts-based methods. Cynthia Poindexter (2002) reflects on two accounts related to the stigma associated with AIDS (Example 12.2). Alongside a range of analytic models for narrative research, she provides a 'rough content' version and a poem that allow comparison. The poem is in itself a form of analysis. 'In developing a poem, the researcher selects talk and re-forms it into a nontraditional re-presentation. The resulting poem may bring points to the fore, clarify and make the account more compelling, create a different effect, and engage the reader and listener, and tell us something about lived experience which we did not previously understand' (Poindexter, 2002: 71). The line breaks and, of course, the selection of material, suggest the writer's assumptions about elements and units of meaning.

| EXAMPLE 12.2 | Alternative Transcription and Units of Meaning |

Rough content

The other incident that happened to me, was not someone who knew me, but I went back, my father was a headmaster of a boys' school in Vermont and I went there for the 50th reunion of one of my cousins. But anyway, the minister there, the school had a minister come for every morning service, and afterwards we were walking back to have breakfast, it was early Sunday morning and I was with the minister's wife and she's, she had, we were talking about ministry stuff because my father's in the ministry and my, her husband had known of him and stuff, and she was saying they used to have a church down here in Massachusetts and they retired up here in Vermont, and then she said out of the blue she said, 'and it's getting so crowded up here, I thought the AIDS epidemic would take care of that', she said, and you know. And we'd just gone to, just celebrated communion service and talked about things to do with communion service and all that so I just said to her, 'You know, what you just said offends me, I have a son with AIDS' and she was just taken aback. Fortunately for me, there was two of the people at the 50th who were gay men, one of whom, both of whom had HIV, whom I naturally gravitated to, hadn't seen since forever and so forth. So I went and I said 'I can't quite believe what I heard' and I wanted someone to validate. [I: So you could share it.] Yes, validate because it was just mind-blowing to me that this had happened. So you never know where that kind of stuff will crop up, you've probably experienced some. [I: But it's enraging every single time.] It is. [I: And hard to explain.] So, those are the only two instances, everyone else was just wonderful.

Poem

Stuff Will Crop Up

The minister's wife said out of the blue

'it's getting so crowded up here,

I thought the AIDS epidemic would take care of that'

I just said to her,

'what you said to me offends me –

I have a son with AIDS.'

I can't quite believe what I heard –

It was just mind-blowing to me

that this had happened.

You never know where that kind of stuff will crop up.

Poindexter (2002)

The intertwining of different strands of qualitative research recurs at this point, in that questions of transcription and units of data and meaning carry through to decisions about how to quote from the data (Taylor, 2012). We make just one point here – that qualitative research papers tend to rely too heavily on brief snippets and extracts from transcripts. Once again, this is more than a distinction between thematic and narrative analysis. Thematic analysis often calls for more extended quotations. In Example 12.3 a social work academic is reflecting on the nature of a research network in which s/he is a member. While it would be possible to disaggregate the text into smaller 'bits', appreciation of the sense-making going on is enriched by the more extended passage (the extract has been heavily anonymised) and by regarding it as a single unit of meaning.

| EXAMPLE 12.3 | A Network of Researchers |

... well there's, there's a dynamic within the network which is applied versus basic if you like, or another way of putting it would be theoretically oriented versus practically oriented, and that's an important dynamic in the network. It's unresolved, and that's good, I mean it ought to be unresolved, because there isn't ... a way of saying that Aleksander's interest in

(Continued)

(Continued)

Marxist social policy for example, Marxist theory, is irrelevant to the question of whether or not a welfare to work possibly could work in the Netherlands. There should not be, and there never was I think in the network, a position on that, because it was clear that there were theoretical perspectives which people could offer which would inform the way in which practical application of research to policy would take place, and for me, keeping that unresolved, valuing people's theoretical contributions, without advancing theory over practical relevance was incredibly important.

There was a wonderful exchange in (city in one European country) where a guy called Mikael attended from (another European country), ... and Daniel gave a highly theoretical account of a particular development, and Mikael said at the end of this, 'But what use is this?', and the question was almost breaking the rules, because the point was it was, it was an offer from Daniel to expand an area of thinking, and it's for network members to consider how it might apply in their case, or be useful to them. There shouldn't have been a request to Daniel to say to any individual network member, 'And this is what it means for your country or your research project or your specific research interest.' But I think for me ... that was an interesting example of the dynamic within the network that holds some things together in tension all the time, in tension.

Extract from research in progress by Ian Shaw and Neil Lunt

We appreciated in Chapter Eleven how grounded theory works within a framework of different levels of analysis, via its coding scheme. Even when the researcher distances herself from the deductive aspects of researcher-supplied concepts, analysis perhaps inevitably works at different levels of generality. Hannah Jobling's research on Community Treatment Orders (Example 12.4) gives a clear example of how this may work.

| EXAMPLE 12.4 | Levels of Analysis – Community Treatment Orders |

Community Treatment Orders are used by mental health practitioners to impose conditions on how service users live in the community, once they have been discharged from compulsory hospitalisation. Conditions commonly relate to medication, engagement with professionals, residence and substance misuse. CTOs work by giving the practitioner power to recall the service user to hospital if they are deemed to be a risk to themselves or others and/or if they have broken the conditions of the CTO. This analytic framework was developed from detailed initial analysis of five diverse practitioner interview transcripts. The example gives four different kinds of text, ranging from the general theme, the five categories, sub-categories in two cases, and two instances of analytic text that provided the elements for the framework.

General theme: When Community Treatment Orders were judged to work or not – how did practitioners talk about CTO outcomes and what do they judge to be good or bad outcomes?

Category 1 – The nature of proof and causality
Category 2 – Corroboration by others
Category 3 – Balancing outcomes

Sub-categories

1. How practitioners managed the ethical discomfort that CTOs could engender.
2. The tangibility of effects the CTO might bring about and how they might be quantified.

Analytic note: It was believed to be easier to 'prove' the positive 'hard' impact of their use than the potentially negative 'soft' impact – "… so this piece of legislation is going to keep you in treatment, it's going to keep you well and we're very good at evaluating these risks. I think we're much less good at thinking about the other risk, actually what is the impact on a person of having somebody else telling you, this is what you must do …"

3. Who the CTO is supposed to be 'good' for.

Category 4 – The temporal nature of outcomes
Category 5 – The kinds of outcomes to which practitioners referred

Sub-categories

1. Ensuring treatment
2. Behavioural change
3. Lowering levels of restriction
4. Lowering levels of risk
5. Negative outcomes

Analytic note: Practitioners also talked in terms of negative outcomes including: the exacerbation of the revolving door cycle; the reinforcement of negative behaviour; the creation of dependency/passivity; negative psychological repercussions (such as an increase in feelings of stigma/fear of services); disengagement from services.

Extract from unpublished analytic memorandum, Hannah Jobling

More on narrative analysis

Consider the following extract from Mayer and Timms' *The Client Speaks* – the first major full-length study of how the experience of social work was recounted by those on the receiving end (Mayer and Timms, 1970). The fieldwork was done in the summer of 1969. 'Mrs Hunter' is telling the researcher how she came to decide to go to a social work agency then called the Family Welfare Association (FWA). She faced 'terrible debt' due to her husband's gambling, and could not face the strain and worry any longer.

I met a woman up at the laundry and I just was … oh I was desperate! I just burst out crying. I thought I was on my own actually, it was late at night. And a woman started talking to me, a complete stranger … I poured out my life to her. You know how you meet someone and you talk to them. She said she'd been to the FWA and she knew others who had been there too. After telling me her case, she said they were bound to help me – to give me financial help – that it was a dot on the cards … And I thought to myself, well, I *will* go.

Going back to our early distinction between the told and the telling, we can think of narrative as either *resource*, where the text is read for what it tells us about the subject matter of the story, and as *topic*, where the story tells us about the processes through which a life is constructed. Mrs Hunter's brief story can be understood in both of these ways. Accounts of how service users come to arrive at social work agencies are typically told and recorded as outcomes of people's interactions with professionals of one kind or another, and typically as the result – right or wrong – of judgements about service needs. This narrative yields a very different picture. But it also takes the form of what we may call a performative narrative, with dramatic *motifs* throughout. In this regard a narrative typically will have:

- A plot. The dynamic tension that holds the story together and moves it along.
- Episodes. Autobiographical events central to the story.
- Themes.
- Characters.
- A point of view from which the story is told.

We can also make some distinctions about the different forms narratives may take. Narratives may act as moral tales, as stories of survival in adversity, as autobiography, as a coming out story, or as a re-evaluation of the past. Denzin's suggestions about the significance of different kinds of epiphany, discussed in Chapter Thirteen, are relevant at this point.

There are, of course, interpretive challenges when working with narratives. Riessman refers to some of these in her reflections on the narrative given by Asha – a woman in South India who came to an infertility clinic (Riessman, 2001).

> First, they do not speak for themselves. Narrative excerpts require interpretation, expansion, and analysis – 'unpacking' to uncover and interpret the inevitable ambiguities contained in any form of language. Second, narratives are situated utterances. They unfold in particular interactions with particular listeners, and these contexts shape what is said, and what cannot be spoken ... Narrators do not tell *their* story, that is, reveal an essential self – but *a* story that shines light on certain aspects of identity, and leaves others in shadow ...Finally, narratives of personal troubles, such as infertility, are situated in cultural and historical time. (Riessman, 2001: 81)

Place, space and time

Becker long ago set himself to 'pull out and describe the basic analytic operations carried on in participant observation', and in so doing deal with what he saw as a weak area (Becker, 1970b: 26). Thinking of place and space affords opportunity, for example, to reflect afresh on social workers' day-to-day working environments. An illuminating example, using the field of network analysis within organisational research, can be found in a substantial national evaluation of a UK government initiative, the Children's Fund (University of Birmingham and Institute of Education, Edwards et al., 2006).

| EXAMPLE 12.5 | Organisational Space and Movement |

The Children's Fund was launched in November 2000 as part of the government of England's commitment to tackle disadvantage among children and young people. The programme aimed to identify at an early stage children and young people at risk of social exclusion, and make sure they receive the help and support they need to achieve their potential. It encouraged voluntary organisations, community and faith groups to work in partnership with local statutory agencies, and children, young people and their families, to deliver high-quality preventative services to meet the needs of communities.

The authors of the evaluation posed the rarely-asked question, how does knowledge 'move around', upstream and downstream, within an organisation? For example, between *levels*, between *strategy and practice*, and between different '*spaces*' or 'fields' within an organisation – e.g., between child protection teams and teams working with children with a disability? Sustaining a sense of place and movement, they suggest that three types of informal networks among practitioners were evident:

- New trails trodden for the first time between individual practitioners who recognised the benefits of a collaborative response to the social exclusion of a child.
- Networks which built on old networks and relationships but where there was evidence of the impact of the preventative intentions of the Children's Fund.
- Old established networks which were continued or resuscitated and where there was little evidence of the impact of the Children's Fund.

Edwards et al. (2006: 193)

They describe the first of these as 'light etchings or traces on a local landscape' (p. 193). This gives a sense of what they call 'boundary zones' – organisational 'spaces between services where practitioners could meet' (ibid., p. 193) but of limited space where strategy players and practice players could engage. 'Places where Board members and practitioners met to share ideas were relatively rare' (ibid., p. 202). In addition, 'Changes in social contexts were so complex and often so fast moving that keeping up was beyond the capabilities of individuals' (ibid., p. 215).

While this analysis yields rather different descriptions and explanations to those emerging from the various forms of verbal data considered in the previous pages, the challenges of analysis are not wholly different. Dey talks about the issues as follows:

The very quality of qualitative data – its richness and specificity – makes for problems when we try to make comparisons between observations. For what are we comparing? There are no standard categories in terms of which to compare observations. Indeed, there are no clear boundaries as to what constitutes an observation. (Dey, 1993: 101)

This, he suggests, poses 'two important questions. First, what is an observation? ... Second, how can an observation be judged similar to or related to some other observations? Why put a bit of data into one pile, but not into another?' (ibid., p. 101). Here are issues that are familiar to us from our previous discussion. First, what counts as a unit of observation, a 'bit' of data, and how do we recognise it? Second, how do we engage in the work of comparison – that work which 'has always been the backbone ... of good sociological thinking'? But of course 'finding two or more things that are alike in some important way yet different in other ways ...' (Becker, 2011: 185) sounds easier than it is. One recurrent reason for this happens when we are deceived into thinking that things named in similar terms (e.g., 'social worker') *are* the same, or that things with very different names (to take a familiar example from Goffman, prisons and long stay hospitals) *are* different.

Field notes, logs, diaries and *ad hoc* memos form grist to the analytic mill of ethnographers. Clandinin and Connelly suggest the more extensive value of such accounts when they advocate constant writing of field texts. 'So long as researchers are diligently, day by day, constructing field texts, they will be able to "slip in and out" of the experience being studied, slip in and out of intimacy' (Clandinin and Connelly, 2000: 82). Yet as we have seen in Chapter Eleven, these resources are not straightforward. There are at least three reasons for this. First, there is no way that an ethnographer can record everything that she observes – 'everything'. Second, it is not clear how plausible it is to suggest that an ethnographer can get both inside and outside a culture. Clandinin and Connelly refer in this connection to never fully getting it. 'The taken-for-grantedness is never exhausted and ... mystery is always just behind the latest taken-for-granted sense making' (p. 78). Third, field notes, though written as description, are interpretation. There is a form of dualism at work, inherent perhaps in the central idea of 'fieldwork' – that there are two components to ethnography, the field and the work, and hence both participation (entailing what is experience-near) and the observation (stemming from being in a different culture and seeking to understand what is experience-far). For the ethnographer time, space and voice are alike problematic.

When we turn to how ethnographers analyse their fieldwork records, we are face to face with just the same challenges of abstraction, context and generalising that we noted in dealing with thematic and narrative analysis. Packer extends his same worries to this new context. What is known about how ethnographers actually analyse fieldnotes suggests something 'alarmingly similar' (Packer, 2011: 240) to the process of abstraction and generalisation present in interview analysis. This may entail indexing by some sort of coding framework and then sorting topically, in ways that remove notes from the context and also presume that time is not important. Contrary to this, ethnographers' accounts 'function as instruments *to see* actions and events in a particular way ... [E]thnographers are involved in the same kind of work as the people they study: they are *making* order, *organizing* the complex details of everyday life in an orderly way that will be compelling to the people who read their accounts' (ibid., p. 241).[1] The ethnographer is 'an interested (in both senses of that word) sojourner' (Geertz, 1973: 20), and is a witness more than a member. One culture meets another. This same underlying point is expressed in a very different way by Manning in his intriguing work on *Freud and American Sociology* (Manning, 2005) when he concludes 'I believe that all autoethnography is an analysis of ... counter-transference' (p. 155).

This should not be read as a counsel of despair. Manning, for instance, warns against 'a groundless, indulgent subjectivism that blurs the line between sociology and short-story telling' (ibid., p. 156). To repeat what we said in the previous chapter, while not wishing to reinstate a naïve borderline between data and its interpretation, we do support a distinction based on intentionality. There are occasions when our intention is, as far as lies in us, to record events, actions and interactions in as unmingled a way as possible. There are also occasions when we are quite aware that we are entertaining interpretive, analytic ideas. To make a clear distinction when analysing fieldnotes between one and the other seems entirely reasonable advice. The sometimes too-easy accusations of dualism rarely offer an alternative way forward.

Documents, visual data and secondary analysis

By this time readers will have caught the drift of our approach, such that they will take on a self-driving navigation of the issues. Our general line is twofold. First, the core challenges and processes in qualitative analysis are shared between the various fieldwork methods, whether they be interviews, narratives, ethnography, visual methods, analysis of texts and documents or even secondary qualitative analysis. But the specifics of how these processes are recognised and carried through varies. We treat these issues more illustratively in the subsequent paragraphs. Second, the process of analysis cannot be split off from either what precedes or from what follows.

In the earlier chapter on 'Traces and deposits' we distinguished the meaning of documents at three levels. First, the intended content, or the meaning(s) the author intended to produce. Second, the received content – the meaning constructed by the audience. We noted that in each of these cases we must not treat documents as homogenous or singular in either their intended or received meanings. Third, there is the meaning constructed by the researcher. This recognises that the text may have meanings beyond the intentions. But this is 'transient and ephemeral'. 'As soon as a researcher approaches a text to interpret its meaning, he or she becomes a part of its audience.' Hence, 'textual analysis involves

---

[1]Packer's argument is a comprehensive case for a form of ontological realism, over against what he sees as the dualism of epistemic constructivism. For a detailed assessment of his argument see Shaw, 2013.

mediation between the frames of reference of the researcher and those who produced the text' (Scott, 1990: 31).

To repeat something we said in Chapter Nine, Scott draws together the distinctions into research practice advice when he concludes that 'we must recognise three aspects of the meaning of a text – three 'moments' in the movement of the text from author to audience' (Scott, 1990: 134). Distinguishing the meaning the author *intended* to produce and the *received* content, or the meaning constructed by the audience, we should not assume that there is just one intended or received meaning. Texts typically have multiple meanings. But there is also a third meaning of the text, as constructed by readers who were not members of the original intended audience. For example, a social worker may intend a community care contract to be a means of empowering service users. A line manager may see the same document as a more or less adequate protection of agency accountability. A subsequent reader may interpret it as reinforcing or challenging conventional gender roles. Texts may have meanings beyond their intentions. But as soon as a third party reads a text to interpret its meaning s/he becomes part of its audience.

This is a theme that we have had occasion to return to several times in this book. Take, for just one example, how the *motifs* of narrative research resonate with documents, particularly personal documents. When we hear the service user we need to distinguish the teller's story, the telling of the story, the life experience of people in the story, our experience of the story, and the wider audience of people who read our text or account. In consequence, the researcher operates 'in a forest of events and stories pointing inward and outward, and backward and forward' (Clandinin and Connelly, 1994: 418). As Clandinin and Connelly later went on to express it, narrative practitioners are 'walking in the midst of stories' in the two senses of being 'somewhere along the dimensions of time, place, the personal and the social' and also 'as in the middle of a nested set of stories – ours and theirs' (Clandinin and Connelly, 2000: 63). Roberts remarks to similar effect in his excellent book on biographical research that 'In studying the lives of others we are also researching and constructing ourselves … The "mere" recounting of a life itself may well alter the life perspectives of the researcher and the researched' (Roberts, 2002: 50, 23).

There has been much interest in *visual methods* in the opening years of this century. This is stimulated in part by blurring of the boundaries between the social sciences and the humanities, and partly by the opportunities offered by developments in technology. We deliberately take an example from visual methods in Example 12.6 that is drawn from a pre-internet, pre-digital age as a way of avoiding the expected and familiar but also to tacitly illustrate that visual methods are not as new as may be thought. Indeed, early scholars such as Malinowski and W.I. Thomas, writing almost a hundred years ago, regularly included drawings and photographs in their publications.

Research with children has been one area where visual methods have been widely and profitably used (e.g., Mitchell, 2010) but they have also been employed more extensively (Kearney and Hyle, 2004; Lorenz, 2010a). The connection with influence from the humanities is more widespread than visual methods. Creative and *arts-based methods* was the area where writers were most likely to claim that they were doing innovative research in a survey of journals in the first decade of the century (Wiles et al., 2010). In social work one of the main locations of arts-based approaches has been the journal *Qualitative Social Work*. Szto and colleagues (2005) explore poetry and photography, Wulff and others (2010) use drama in relation to racism, and Phillips (2007a) draws on innovative writing forms to depict social work in a hospital, and on the visual arts to talk about social workers' experience of loss and grief (Phillips, 2007b). Gallardo et al. (2009) draw on poetry and narrative to understand depression, and Poindexter (2002) likewise uses poetic forms of narrative when writing about HIV. Knowles and Cole (2008) have provided a comprehensive collection of work in this still developing area.

The analysis of such data connects in some ways with ethnographic fieldwork. An old example may help illustrate something of what is entailed.

| EXAMPLE 12.6 | Visual Images |

Take some genuinely good picture ... Using a watch with a second hand, look at the photograph intently for two minutes. Don't stare and thus stop looking; look actively. It will be hard to do, and you'll find it useful to take up the time by naming everything in the picture to yourself: this is a man, this is his arm, this is the finger on his hand, this is the shadow his hand makes, this is the cloth of his sleeve, and so on. Once you have done this for two minutes, build it up to five, following the naming of things with a period of fantasy, telling yourself a story about the people and things in the picture. The story needn't be true; it's just a device for externalising and making clear to yourself the emotion and mood the picture has evoked ...

When you have done this exercise many times, a more careful way of looking will become habitual. Two things result. You will realise that ordinarily you have not consciously seen most of what is in an image even though you have been responding to it. You will also find that you can now remember the photographs you have studied much as you can remember a book you have taken careful notes on.

In this extract from an interesting essay written in 1974, Howard Becker is talking to sociologists about photography. He is 'translating' between photography and sociology, without sentimental attachment to either. He suggests questions that the viewer should bring to the photograph that express in commonsense ways ideas that are present in most social work analyses – questions about what we might call status, norms, rules, common understandings, deviance, rule violations, sanctions or conflict resolution.

Turning briefly to secondary qualitative analysis, there is growing interest in re-using qualitative data, reflected in the establishment of the qualitative archive, Qualidata, by the ESRC in the UK (Heaton, 1998; Irwin and Winterton, 2011). Heaton refers to two fundamental methodological issues. 'The first is whether secondary analysis of qualitative studies is tenable, given that it is often thought to involve an inter-subjective relationship between the researcher and the researched … The second issue concerns the problem of where primary analysis stops and secondary analysis starts' (Heaton, 1998).

We hold in general terms to the older position that there are remaining differences between the analysis of primary and secondary sources. In a characteristically careful way, Hammersley concludes that 'terminologically speaking, the phrases 're-using' or 'reworking' data do not seem to be so problematic as to be without value. They mark a roughly defined, albeit not entirely clear-cut, distinction that may be of relevance on many occasions' (Hammersley, 2010: 2.5). His response in regard to the argument that secondary data raises issues of lack of fit and absence of context is that 'the problem is not unique to this sort of work, and is a matter of degree' (ibid., 3.4). Rather, 'Mediation, of some kind, is always involved. Even where we are able actively to generate data, for instance through going to observe in relevant situations or to interview informants, we will often not know all that we later decide we needed to know about the contexts in which the data were produced in order to interpret them soundly' (ibid., 3.5). Hence, 'the problem is not unique to re-using data, nor is it necessarily severe, but it is more likely to occur in that kind of work than in what are currently dominant forms of qualitative research, and it can be very difficult and sometimes impossible to handle' (ibid., 3.6).

Continuing questions

During this chapter we have moved back and forth between analytic tasks and decisions that are shared in broad terms when dealing with qualitative materials in any form, and analytic work that is specific to particular fieldwork strategies. In these concluding sentences we are again pointing to overarching questions. Who should be doing the analysis? What should we make of options for different forms of participatory analysis? How do questions of research ethics impinge on analysis? How should we move from the specifics of analysis to general conclusions? How are analytic conclusions reflected in the inscribing and writing of qualitative research?

We have taken these up from place to place in other chapters – ethics in Chapter Six; generalising in Chapter Five and elsewhere; writing in Chapter Sixteen; drawing conclusions to some extent in Chapter Sixteen. When drawing analytic conclusions, we are asking what does any qualitative analysis 'say'? How should we move from themes, conceptual illumination, spatial patterns, and so on, to wider conclusions regarding theory, practice, policy and power? For example, how do we decide what themes are important in developing more general analytic conclusions? The main cautionary tale is that we should not slip back into the logic of surveys where the prevalence of one theme over another generally affords it greater explanatory weight. 'Being empirically grounded does not mean that in a mechanical way there must always be empirical instances for every category. A category can be relevant empirically if it reveals something important about the data, even where empirical instances of that category are few or even non-existent' (Dey, 1993: 143f). This is reminiscent of Geertz's eminently quotable phrase about how 'small facts speak to large issues, winks to epistemology, or sheep raids to revolution' (Geertz, 1973: 23).

We have reached the end of the central and longest section of the book, and move in the final four chapters to broader questions that engage, among other things, with what we have called 'outer-science' questions such as relevance, justice, practice and utilisation. But Chapter Thirteen in some ways continues and expands the themes at the close of this chapter, addressing how we reach evaluative judgements.

Taking it further

As an exercise in developing visual analytic skills, the reader might select photographs they have taken of people or places, whether or not they are part of a research study. Checking out Becker's article. It can be downloaded from http://lucy.ukc.ac.uk/becker.html.[2]

Spend some unrushed time applying his questions to your photographs. Thoughts will flit across your mind. First, it is not easy. You need to study the photograph 'with the care and attention to detail one might give to a difficult scientific paper or a complicated poem' (Becker). This will help avoid simplistic assumptions about what the photographs are saying, or viewing them as holiday photos. Second, you may have come to doubt aspects of the photograph. For example, Becker – he is a stimulating guide here – quotes one of his sources as saying that 'the camera is a wonderful mechanism. It will reproduce, exactly, what is going on inside of your head!' Third, it may have prompted you to think that there may be more considered questions that can be brought to the kind of exercise you have just done. Indeed there will be.

---

[2] Accessed 20 June 2013.

PART III
The Purposes of Qualitative Social Work Research

PART III

THIRTEEN
Researching and Evaluating Interventions and Outcomes

We open the chapter with some considerations about central ideas about evaluation, outcomes, cause and what we have in mind in the evaluation context by 'qualitative'. We emphasise that evaluation should be distinguished from research in terms of purposes rather than methods.

The later parts of the chapter are more straightforward in structure and focus. We consider two general linked questions. First, are there particular inquiry designs that lend themselves especially to qualitative evaluation? Second, what methods of disciplined inquiry show special promise for qualitative evaluators and intervention researchers?

We assess the merits of simulations, longitudinal designs, indirect observation, change–process research, hermeneutic single case designs, and epiphanies.

We close the chapter with an illustrative case of the challenges for qualitative evaluation.

It has become almost axiomatic in social work and cognate fields of applied research to say that qualitative inquiry is geared to address *processes* whereas certain quantitative designs and methods are suited to assessing *outcomes*. It follows from this, so the convention goes, that central questions about whether, for example, a programme *works* – questions that on mainstream assumptions regarding evaluative research are the apogee of the evaluative mission – fall outside the competence of qualitative inquiry. There is sometimes more than a hint of disparagement of qualitative evaluation in this distinction, illustrated, for example, in Scriven's comment that formative evaluation focused on programme processes and improvement is in reality an interim version of summative evaluation, which provides information on 'mid-stream merit' (Scriven, 1997: 499). We are left with an impression of qualitative evaluation as an imprecise, ill-focused, descriptive, inductive exercise, strong on vicarious experience, but chronically at risk of failed credibility in the eyes of the people who count – the client.

In this chapter we set out reasons why we believe this divergence is mistaken. To go out on a limb somewhat, we reject the notion that qualitative methods can only answer descriptive questions. Also that it is subjective, studies experience not causes and generates, not tests, hypotheses. This is the view that 'qualitative research can *invent* hypotheses but can never *test* them, so it can never provide explanations' (Packer, 2011: 19).

To enable us to get inside these issues we start by teasing out the varying meanings of 'evaluation'.

Evaluation

The term 'evaluation' has three different senses which tend not to be sufficiently differentiated. These are:

- The process of doing a certain kind of inquiry – evaluation as *methodology*.
- The product of that inquiry in writing – evaluation as a written *account*.
- Making a *judgement* – evaluation as a considered determination.

The first two are readily familiar, although the relationship between method and account is more important than often realised. This is partly due to the problems we have discussed in the last two chapters that arise when different phases of inquiry are unduly split apart, and we talk about it once more when we discuss writing in Chapter Sixteen. But it is not possible to understand the purposes and processes of qualitative evaluation without also thinking of evaluating in a much wider sense of making a judgement. This brings us to more general debates in the social sciences about whether the researcher is only seeking to understand or also to explain, and linking to much wider issues of critical inquiry and in what sense evaluation and research include emancipatory purposes.

Consider the seven questions in Box 13.1. They are all about evaluation – that is, they are about the possible worth of policy or political initiatives, and/or welfare programmes. But in what ways are they different kinds of questions?

Box 13.1   Evaluation Questions

- Have the desired outcomes been attained and can they be attributable to the programme?
- Which parts of the programme worked well and which need improvement?
- How effective is the programme with respect to the organisation's goals, and to the beneficiaries' needs?
- How did the stakeholders experience the programme, either individually or co-constructively?
- Is this programme the most efficient choice between alternatives?
- In what ways are the premises, goals or activities of the programme serving to maintain or challenge power and resource inequities in society?
- How might the evaluation process challenge or possibly reinforce such structured inequities?

Jennifer Greene helps disentangle and connect these questions when she identifies four main positions in programme evaluation. She names these as post-positivism, pragmatism, interpretivism and critical or normative evaluation (Greene, 1994).

The typical evaluation questions addressed by *post-positivist*[1] evaluation are: Have the desired outcomes been attained and are they attributable to the programme? Is this programme the most efficient alternative? *Pragmatic* evaluations focus on questions such as: Which parts of the programme worked well and which need improvement? How effective is the programme with respect to the organisation's goals, and to the beneficiaries' needs? *Interpretivist* evaluation typically starts by asking how the stakeholders experience the programme, either individually or co-constructively. Finally, *critical*, normative evaluation addresses questions such as: In what ways are the premises, goals or activities of the programme serving to maintain power and resource inequities in society? How might the evaluation process challenge or even buttress these structured inequities?

Two inferences and one possible question seem to follow. The first inference is that evaluative questions are much wider and more diverse than we have tended to assume. We have been accustomed to thinking of evaluation as premised on programmes and policies being called on to yield evidence-based accountability. Long ago the tough-minded Cronbach and colleagues averred 'We are uneasy about the close association of evaluation with accountability. In many of its uses the word becomes an incantation and one that can cast a malign spell' (Cronbach et al., 1980: 133). 'Malign' in part because accountability in the strict sense of complete responsibility is only possible in a context of command. 'All too often, assignment of blame to individuals becomes the prime use of the accounts, while system improvement is forgotten' (ibid., p. 135). Such a demand has been a sign of discontent: 'those in charge of services are believed to be inefficient, insufficiently honest, or not self-critical' (ibid., p. 139). 'Accountability' thus falls heavily on the wrong person. 'Accountability is most demanded of those public servants condemned to farm rocky ground, under capricious weather conditions' (ibid., p. 137). The second inference is that assuming that either qualitative or quantitative methods and designs can answer some sorts of questions but not others (what can be called metaphorically a 'horses for courses' approach) is usually over-simple and unhelpful.

The question we have in mind is, if evaluation questions are so diverse, does this dissolve a cut and dried distinction between evaluation and research? Consolidating the ways research and evaluation sometimes have been distinguished, some have arrived at the various contrasts in Table 13.1.

---

[1] 'Post-positivist' is a term that needs care – as indeed with all compound expressions of this kind that start 'post-'. In some cases the force of the prefix 'post' is to emphasise *dis*continuity with what has gone before, as in the term 'postmodernism'. In other cases 'post' points to change yet continuity. Greene is using 'post-positivist' in this second sense.

Table 13.1　Unhelpful distinctions between evaluation and research

Evaluation	Research
Addresses practical problems	Addresses theoretical problems
Culminates in action	Culminates in description or explanation
Prescribes	Describes
Addresses short-term issues	Addresses long-term issues
Evaluation methods	Research methods
Is non-disciplinary	Is disciplinary
Includes insider evaluation	Is conducted by outsiders

On the whole we find these polarised contrasts neither informative nor helpful. For example, while there has been much attention to understanding the use of *evaluation* (it sometimes seems hard to find an issue of any major evaluation journal that does not include some discussion of the topic), there has been equally careful attention to the question of the use of *research*, and the debates do not seem all that different. This is a helpful point to make in the context of *social work* evaluation, because there has probably been more helpful work on social work *research* use than on evaluation use for social work (c.f. Cousins and Shulha, 2006; Ruckdeschel and Chambon, 2010; Walter et al., 2004).

But some kind of distinction does make sense – if mainly as a general tendency and orientation. Lincoln and Guba proposed perhaps the most powerful case for a strong distinction between evaluation and research (Lincoln and Guba, 1986). In a retrospective essay, Lincoln recalled that they came to the position that there are different forms of 'disciplined inquiry'. They concluded that research and evaluation are different forms of disciplined inquiry (along with what they called policy analysis) (Lincoln, 1990).

They define research as

> a type of disciplined inquiry undertaken to resolve some problem in order to achieve understanding or to facilitate action. (Lincoln and Guba, 1986: 549)

They define evaluation as

> a type of disciplined inquiry undertaken to determine the value (merit and/or worth) of some entity – the evaluand – such as a treatment, program, facility, performance, and the like – in order to improve or refine the evaluand (formative evaluation) or to assess its impact (summative evaluation). (Ibid., p. 550)

The value of this way of making the distinction, apart from the care with which the terms have been set out, is that the focus is on the *purpose* rather than the *practice* of research and evaluation. As Greene expresses it, 'Some vision of purpose is, at root, what guides all evaluation practice' (Greene, 1994: 539). In other words, we should not think of there being qualitative *research* methods and

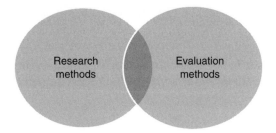

Figure 13.1 Methods portfolios in research and evaluation

different qualitative *evaluation* methods, but that evaluation shares the same large pool of methods with research, but has a characteristic emphasis on different kinds of purpose that will influence which methods are chosen in any particular project. The relationship of methods can thus be understood as in Figure 13.1. The whole area covered by both circles represents the full range of actual or possible inquiry methods. Each circle depicts a possible selection of methods employed in research or evaluation. The particular methods employed in any given instance will depend on the purpose of the inquiry, but in our conception are always drawn from a shared pool of actual and possible methods. For example, experimental designs have occasionally been used in wider social science research but are usually associated with evaluative studies. Conversely conversation analysis has rarely been used in evaluative studies (in practice the area of overlap will be much greater than implied by this diagram).

Five identifiable purposes of evaluation can be expressed as a general working rule (see Box 13.2).

Box 13.2   Working Rule – The Starting Point for Thinking About Whether to Undertake Evaluation and What Methods to Use is to be Clear About the Purpose/s of the Inquiry

1. Providing objective, impartial evidence for decision making; providing public accountability.
2. Generating or enhancing theory and knowledge about social policy, social problems and how best to solve them.
3. Instrumentally improving practice and organisational learning.
4. Highlighting the quality of lived experience and advancing practical wisdom and good practice.
5. Promoting justice/social change/social inclusion.

The point about the role of purpose is not, as such, especially novel, nor special to evaluation, and we should not assume that *research* never includes any of these value-based intentions. Silverman says of qualitative research that 'the multiple logics of qualitative research emerge from their relationships with the general purposes of research projects' (Silverman, 1997: 25). For example, one of us is engaged in a research project looking at how social workers communicate with children. The project includes an expectation that it will lead to enhanced knowledge about good practice. Qualitative evaluation divorced from purpose reinstates the instrumentalism of which quantitative evaluation sometimes has been guilty. On the other hand, evaluation defined exclusively in terms of ideology leaves us without strategy and short or medium term direction, and at risk of our own passions.

Choosing qualitative evaluation

We have begun to unravel conventional ways of thinking about the purpose and process of evaluation, and in doing so have implied that allocations of methods to problems only work at the more general level of how best to pursue wider purposes of inquiry. However, we do believe general criteria can be developed for choosing methods. Williams, for example (Box 13.3), collates a helpful list of criteria by which we may decide if a qualitative or naturalistic evaluation is appropriate (Williams, 1986).

Box 13.3   When to Choose Qualitative Evaluation

Williams says qualitative strategies will be appropriate in circumstances when one or more of the following apply:

1. Evaluation issues are not clear in advance.
2. Official definitions of the evaluand are not sufficient and insider ('emic') perspectives are needed.
3. 'Thick description' is required.
4. It is desirable to convey the potential for vicarious experience of the evaluand on the part of the reader.
5. Formative evaluation, aimed at improving the programme, policy or practice, is appropriate.
6. The outcome includes complex actions in natural settings.
7. Evaluation recipients want to know how the evaluand is operating in its natural state.
8. There is time to study the evaluand through its natural cycle. The true power of naturalistic evaluation is dissipated if there is not time to observe the natural functions of the evaluand in their various forms.
9. The situation permits intensive inquiry, without posing serious ethical obstacles.
10. The evaluand can be studied unobtrusively, as it operates, and in an ethical way.
11. Diverse data sources are available.
12. There are resources and consent to search for negative instances and counter evidence.
13. There is sufficient customer and end user agreement on methodological strategy.

Williams' list is helpful because it manages to be practical, thought provoking and relatively specific without losing value as a set of working rules. However, in

Example 13.1 we illustrate how the application of these criteria is not always straightforward. In addition we have provided a 'Taking it further' task at the end of the chapter, where you are invited to suggest your own assessment.

| **EXAMPLE 13.1** | **Electronic Records in Social Work with Children** |

The England and Wales government in the first decade of this century introduced an elaborate electronic recording system for all children assessed to be in need. Intended as both a conceptual framework and a method of practice, the aim was to support practitioners and managers in undertaking the key tasks of assessment, planning, intervention and review. It aimed to help them do this, in the government's words at the time, 'in a systematic manner, and to enable practitioners and managers to collect and use information systematically, efficiently and effectively'. It was based on a set of data requirements secured through 'exemplar' electronic formats for social work practitioners.

The evaluation team was tasked to advise on the local implementation and operation of the scheme in four pilot local authorities. The team opted for a mix of qualitative and structured methods including time-diaries; analysis of 'exemplar' records, focus groups, analysis of meeting records of local implementation groups; semi-structured, focus group and key informant interviews with managers, practitioners and service users.

Cross-referencing with William's list of criteria, the extensive qualitative aspects could be judged appropriate on the grounds that the following circumstances were satisfied:

- Insider ('emic') perspectives were needed, given the influence that diverse local stakeholders would have on the success or otherwise of the planned national roll-out of the policy innovation.
- Formative evaluation, aimed at improving the programme, policy and practice, appeared to be appropriate.
- The outworkings of the programme included complex actions in natural settings.
- There was sufficient time – three years – to study the workings of the 'system' (as it was called) through its natural cycle.
- Diverse data sources were available.

However, these assumptions were not equally shared between local stakeholders, the evaluation funders and the evaluation team. As a consequence, the eventual report became sensitive and controversial.

Causes, explanations and outcomes

The common view, as we have noted, is that if a social work researcher wishes to understand the causes and outcomes of practice and agency policy, then an experimental or quasi-experimental study design is called for. The evaluation writer, Stake, perhaps had this in mind when he remarked that 'to the qualitative scholar, the understanding of human experience is a matter of chronologies more than of cause and effect', and that 'the function of research is not ... to map and conquer the world but to sophisticate the beholding of it' (Stake, 1995: 39, 43).

In otherwise excellent qualitative texts the idea of cause either gets no mention (e.g., Coffey and Atkinson, 1996; Riessman, 2008), or is discussed only in order to critique its relevance (e.g., Denzin and Lincoln, 2000). But this has not always been the case. Early case study research in 1920s Chicago by Clifford Shaw and his colleagues was focused on an 'intensive study of a series of cases of male juvenile delinquents and a comparable series of non-delinquents living in the same urban communities' (Ernest Burgess papers. University of Chicago. Special Collections, Box 31, Folder 2). They believed that case study research was helpful to understand causative factors in delinquent behaviour, and described the research process as an accumulation of a mass of data to afford a 'complete and vivid picture of the interrelated factors ...'. Shaw also argued that it is only possible to understand the delinquent act in the total context of the community setting, and it is 'particularly the life history document' that 'reveals the process or sequence of events ...'.

Robert Park, the early Chicago sociologist, also took the view that case study was better equipped for causal understanding than statistical manipulation. Ada Sheffield (Sheffield, 1922) believed that 'case-work agencies ... will gradually become what may be described as social laboratories' where 'study of ... cases would go on simultaneously with treatment'. This would lead to more explicit discussion of 'causative factors' (ibid., p. 38). For those associated with the 1920s Chicago School of Sociology, 'theories must be theories about constellations of forces, not theories of individual causes', and 'the best way to discover such constellations of causes was by case study'. The scale of the work was too big to undertake at the aggregate level – 'only the eclectic combination of ethnography, statistics, life history, and organizational history could do full justice to the multiple layers of spatial and temporal contexts for social facts' (Abbott, 1999: 207).

Returning to the present, there is a range of qualitative writers and social theorists who retain a significant place for causal arguments in social research. In these following paragraphs we make the general case for thinking in this way. In the following section of the chapter we develop examples of how this can be done (e.g., Example 13.3).

Qualitative writers have often detected limits to the central claim to competence in causal matters of randomised controlled trials. Silverman, in his study of HIV counselling, complained of the ways in which what he calls the Explanatory Orthodoxy of counselling research led to a focus on either the causes or consequences of counselling. This approach 'is so concerned to rush to an explanation that it fails to ask serious questions about what it is explaining' (Silverman, 1997: 24), such that the phenomenon of counselling 'escapes'. Traditional formulations of causal inputs and outcomes need at the very least to be delayed until we have understood something of the 'how'. For sound evaluative reasons we will want to ask the explanatory 'why' questions. 'There is no reason not to, provided that we have first closely described how the phenomenon at hand is locally produced' (ibid., p. 35). Miller and Crabtree make a comparable point when they conclude that evidence-based medicine 'actually offers qualitative clinical investigators multiple opportunities for entering, expanding, challenging, and adding variety and honesty to this space. There is so much *missing evidence!'* (Miller and Crabtree, 2005: 613). Randomised controlled trials, for example, have been criticised by Cronbach and others on grounds of weak external validity (Cronbach et al., 1980) and very little information about context or ecological consequences. 'Read any RCT report, and the only voice you hear is the cold sound of the intervention and faint echoes of the investigator's biases' – 'the sound of thin hush' (Miller and Crabtree, 2005: 613).

Hugh England, in his discussion of *Social Work as Art*, analysed what constitutes a rounded description and appraisal of practice in terms not unlike Silverman's argument. He concluded that 'without adequate description there can be no possibility of evaluation' (England, 1986: 155). This is helpful for good practice because without such description we will not force our favourite assumptions to become probable inferences. He rightly insisted that social work practice 'must be subject to a description and analysis which can determine quality' (ibid., p. 139). It has to be described in such a way that it renders access to and evaluation of its strengths and weaknesses feasible. By making clear the links between understanding, action and effect, practitioners will be able to conclude whether they have plausibly and adequately helped (ibid., p. 154). For instance, social workers, service users, carers, colleagues, first line managers and others who are part of the change agent system, need to make explicit the 'inventories of evidential signs they regularly but unwittingly scan' (Erikson, 1959: 82) if understanding is to lead to change, and change lead to understanding. Inadequate work, England suggested, will fail to make clear the links between understanding and effect. It may identify objectives and outcomes, but offer no scope for linking the two. Even on occasions where service users' wellbeing improves, it will not be shown to be ultimately rooted in the worker's practice. We suggest ways in which this can be enacted later in the chapter.

The inadequacy of conventional outcome designs arises in part from the extreme difficulty of isolating inputs. Abrams' paper on the problems of measuring informal care summarised the position as follows:

> The resistance of informal social care to experimental evaluation has entirely to do with the problem of breaking down the intractable informality of the treatment; of reducing informal caring relationships to the sort of units, factors, events, variables, items needed if specifiable inputs are to be systematically related to specifiable outcomes. (Abrams, 1984: 2)

Service outcomes are not a phase but a consequence, product, or effect, either planned or unintended. They are associated with endings, whether of success, failure or ambiguity. As such they involve disengaging, giving a decent burial, conserving beneficial results, conducting various administrative tasks, evaluating the process and task achievements of the service users, and private and public aspects of evaluating the practitioner. Yet we are deeply mistaken to think that outcomes are *solely* manifested as endings. The consequences of practice, intended or otherwise, beneficial or harmful, are frequently idiosyncratic, in that they occur gradually, cyclically or separately in time from the period of intervention. Different stakeholders may have competing interests in outcomes. As Long moderately states it, 'evidence on effectiveness and outcomes ... provides an apparently value-neutral, rational approach.' But 'beneath the range of technical issues in assessing outcomes are political and social values that need to be explicit' (Long, 1994: 175). 'An outcome of health and social care is more than an end point; it involves a valuation of that end point' (ibid., p. 165).

In social work, knowledge of outcomes – especially of future ones – is not so much informative as advisory. 'Like the cry of the backseat driver: "You'll be in the ditch in a minute", such communications function more like *advice*. "Consider how you would like it if things turned out this way" ... To receive such communications about ourselves may in a sense be informative; but it does not confront us with the "take-it-or-leave it" claim to our assent which is the hallmark of objective knowledge. We can falsify it' (McKay, 1988: 140, 141).

Insofar as it is necessary to understand *individual* outcomes – and in many classroom, school-level, health interventions, criminal justice programmes and human services interventions understanding of such outcomes is often vital – then quantitative, standardised measures sometimes will be inappropriate. Take, for example, social work interventions that aim at some form of individual autonomy and independence. 'Independence' has different meanings for different people under different conditions, and 'What program staff want to document under such conditions is the unique meaning of the outcomes for each client.' 'Qualitative methods are particularly appropriate for capturing and evaluating such outcomes' (Patton, 2002: 158, 476).

Denzin's interpretive interactionism has also had an impact on thinking about service outcomes (Denzin, 1989). Mohr, for example, applies his argument to the evaluation of clinical outcomes in health research. She argues that '[i]nterpretive interactionism permits intensive scrutiny of the ramifications and outcomes of various interventions' (Mohr, 1997: 284). It can:

1. Sort out different ways problems are defined.
2. Show how patients experience care. What it is about interventions they find helpful or not, and in what circumstances.
3. Identify 'secondary causes' e.g., contexts, culture and the meanings patients bring.

'Strategic points for intervention can be identified by contrasting and comparing patients' thick descriptions and these can be used to change, to improve, or to negotiate and renegotiate interventions' (Mohr, 1997: 284). It is valuable when 'an outcome may not be readily apparent, and ... the intervention is something that only the patient and not the professionals can define' (ibid., p. 285). Hence, while qualitative evaluation cannot resolve the problems of causal conclusions any more than quantitative evaluation, it can assess causality 'as it actually plays out in a particular setting' (Miles and Huberman, 1994: 10).

Design and fieldwork strategies for qualitative evaluation

Earlier in the book we have addressed questions of qualitative research design and fieldwork methods in some depth. Our focus here is more limited. Are there particular decisions about research strategy – both planning and design and fieldwork – that can facilitate considerations of evaluation and outcomes? We open this section by rehearsing several general design decisions that directly or indirectly enrich understanding and explanation of social work intervention. These include case studies, simulations of one sort or another, qualitative longitudinal designs, and combinations of methods that yield bases for complementary knowledge claims. We continue the chapter with a series of more specific fieldwork logics and methods that expand these possibilities.

To return to a recurring theme throughout this book, it is important to avoid the tendency to 'technicalise' choices of research methods. In this context, we stress that decisions about designs and fieldwork carry with them prior assumptions and values. As Romm cogently expresses it, 'the process of attempting to "know" about the social world already is an intervention in that world which may come to shape its constitution' (Romm, 1995: 137). She proposes the formula 'comprehension = application'. This says more than application is *based on* comprehension but rather comprehension is 'inextricably tied to' application (Romm, 1996: 26). She believes that this formulation 'provides a way of challenging the (excessive) partiality which ensues, ironically, in the quest to ground knowledge in an impartial "inquiry" moment' (ibid., p. 28). She helpfully insists on 'not suppressing alternative ways of conceiving and seeing the world' and 'the need to be critical or suspicious of our intellectual assumptions' (ibid., p. 26). So our social work practice decisions 'can be defended only on the grounds that one has thought-and-acted having taken one's encounter with other arguments and possibilities seriously' (ibid., p. 27).

One general way of thinking about qualitative designs in the context of evaluation is to consider options that proceed through one or more committed qualitative *fieldwork strategies*, while doing so within a framework that borrows something of the logic of *designs* that seek to 'control' and compare. Maxwell openly advocates such strategies. 'The issues of quantification and of experimental manipulation are independent dimensions of research design' (2004: 252) – or as it had been expressed bluntly and long before by Campbell, 'experimental design can be separated from quantification' (Campbell, 1978: 197). Romm's point about research being an intervention in the world could, in principle be reflexively adopted by the researcher changing their intervention in the research as a way of observing possible contingent consequences. In field research 'the researcher's presence is always an intervention in some ways … and the effects of this intervention can be used to develop or test causal theories about the group or topic studied' (Maxwell, 2004: 252). The following paragraphs suggest just one approach to ways in which the researcher's intervention may be controlled and, if necessary, varied.

Simulations

We outlined the use of simulation methods in Chapter Seven, and they have particular value in evaluative designs where qualitative methods are merged with more structured design logic. We noted that Wasoff and Dobash used a promising innovatory method in their study of how a specific piece of law reform was incorporated into the practice of solicitors (Wasoff and Dobash, 1992, 1996). The use of simulated clients in solicitors' offices – 'natural' settings and known to the research participants – allowed them to identify practice variations that could be ascribed with greater confidence to differences between lawyers rather than to the artifacts of differences between cases. We do not know of qualitative applications of this method in social work evaluation. However, there is an instance where the logic has been used through more structured methods (Forrester et al., 2008). This study analyses 24 taped interviews between social workers and an actor playing a parent (a 'simulated client'). Two child protection scenarios with different levels of seriousness were used. Example 13.2 suggests a hypothetical example of how the method might be applied for evaluative purposes. Variations in social work practice in community care from one service user to another often will be due to real differences between service users. By 'holding the service user constant' through an extensive simulated script, an approximation to the logic of conventional evaluative designs can be achieved, but with the added depth of qualitative methods.

EXAMPLE 13.2 — **The Simulated Service User**

An evaluation team wishes to carry out a qualitative evaluation of decisions made by housing managers, medical staff and social workers regarding the allocation of care management packages. They want to compare how different professional groups employ discretion and judgement in dealing with complex cases.

As part of a wider selection of methods, evaluators using simulated clients prepare a small number of very detailed case histories designed to test the practice decisions under consideration.

A researcher takes on the role of the service user in the case history.

The housing manager, relevant medical staff and social workers each interview the 'service user' within the 'natural' setting of their work.

There are limitations to the application of simulation methods. The method needs additional resources to prepare the case material, perhaps to act the role of clients, and to reflect on the quite detailed material that results from transcriptions of the interviews. The cost is therefore likely to be relatively high, and it requires reasonably high levels of research skills. It will be clear from the brief description that the method could not be a tool for evaluating particular *cases*, but would focus on specific *kinds of practice*. However, the use of simulated clients has several things going for it, in addition to the general logic of comparison and 'control'. First, some researchers, especially insider researchers who have completed professional training programmes, are likely to be familiar with the 'family' of role playing methods from which it is drawn. Second, other methods are not always feasible for practical or ethical reasons. Simulated clients overcome the ethical problems of seeking the co-operation of genuine clients. Finally, they render practice visible.

Longitudinal qualitative evaluation and indirect observation

A rather different development in qualitative designs that brings potential for evaluative comparison was also introduced in Chapter Five – that of longitudinal qualitative designs. Maxwell argues that these designs 'can address one of the main objections against using qualitative case studies for causal inference – their inability to explicitly address the "counterfactual" of what would have happened without the presence of the presumed cause' (2004: 253). The value of longitudinal qualitative designs has gradually been recognised by government bodies, including for purposes of better understanding of outcomes.[2] In terms of its general logic in relation to outcomes, a longitudinal approach 'provides information about changes over time in the effects of the policy, programme or service under evaluation. The impacts of these interventions or processes are rarely static and are subject to change. A longitudinal research design is the most illuminating method by which to explore this change.' (Molloy and Woodfield, 2002: 16) They illustrate its application in a study of a policy programme known as New Deal for the Unemployed, designed to assist those aged twenty five and over to return to the labour market.

Reverting to Maxwell's advocacy of such studies, two important elements and ideas need picking out. First, the passing reference to case studies, and second, the notion of comparison. We noticed earlier that case studies were one of the earliest conceptions of research design in the work of Shaw, Burgess and colleagues at Chicago and how causal inference was a central rationale for that development. Patton represents a contemporary instance of such arguments when he declares that 'qualitative case studies offer a method for capturing and reporting individualized outcomes' (Patton, 2002: 158), elaborating the point when saying that '[w]ell-crafted case studies can tell the stories behind the numbers, capture unintended impacts and ripple effects, and illuminate dimensions of desired outcomes that are difficult to quantify' (ibid., p. 152).

The idea of comparison is more abstract, although one can readily grasp the point Maxwell is making when we think of longitudinal designs. We are inclined to connect notions of comparison with conventional intervention designs, yet Becker insists that 'comparison has always been the backbone, acknowledged or not, of good sociological thinking' (Becker, 2011: 185). He develops the argument

---

[2] For example, the Department for Work and Pensions in Britain sponsored the Working Paper by Molloy and Woodfield (2002) http://research.dwp.gov.uk/asd/asd5/WP7.pdf.

from the work of Goffman and, in detail, the neglected work of Everett Hughes – 'both masters of ... comparison' (ibid., p. 193). One way Becker advocates for approaching this task is through bringing together diverse qualitative methods. For example, direct observation can be followed by indirect observation of causal processes through interviews. Such rich data 'counter the twin dangers of respondent duplicity and observer bias by making it difficult for respondents to produce data that uniformly support a mistaken conclusion, just as they make it difficult for the observer to restrict his observations so that he sees only what supports his prejudices and expectations' (Becker, 1970a: 52).

EXAMPLE 13.3	**Indirect Observation of Parental Involvement in Play Therapy with Children**

Hill's study of parental involvement in play therapy with children illustrates this idea of indirect observation of causal processes. His primary focus was on the development of a qualitative understanding of causal relationships within the therapeutic dynamics, so as to understand what influences outcomes. He followed Maxwell's reference to 'indirect observation' of causal processes through interviews, while recognising that, in his agency context at least, 'social workers do not often use clearly articulated integrated theoretical frameworks for interventions' (Hill, 2012: 365, 371).

Nonetheless, by using qualitative research methods it has been possible to describe causal processes, and to identify factors that are indicative, or counter-indicative, of constructive parental involvement in children's therapy. It has been possible to describe the dynamics of successful helping processes, and to identify aspects of professional expertise and ways in which service users are active in shaping interventions. (Hill, 2012: 376f)

In Table 13.2 we reproduce his general conclusions regarding the indicators and counter-indicators for parental involvement.

'Mixed methods' has fashionable currency if too often apparently premised on the supposition that two or more methods will always work in congruent conjunction, and are always, almost by definition, better than one. While we do not find this enthusiasm invariably cogent nor necessarily persuasive (Schwandt, 2007), there are certainly justifications for making choices of diverse methods on the grounds of research purpose. The traditional idea of undertaking qualitative 'pilot studies' as precursors to a main quantitative study can still be observed as when guidance is given regarding the merits of carrying out first stage process evaluations. More radically, Webber offers a rare instance of this operating at extremes when he explores the potential lying in moving from ethnography to randomised controlled trials, as a means of assessing complex social interventions (Webber, 2014).

Having considered, by and large, more general strategies for structuring qualitative intervention studies, we flesh these out with several more specific examples of how this 'works' in practice.

Table 13.2   Indicators and counter-indicators of parental involvement

	Indications	Counter-indications
Including parents in therapeutic play	Children needing parents to feel secure.	Children needing privacy.
	The need to model play therapy to parents – filial therapy and Theraplay.	Parents may be too distressed
	The need to rebuild confidence in parenting – 'containment'.	Parents may need preparation before participating
	The need to work on parent–child relationships – feminist and family systems theory.	

Source: Hill (2012)

Change-process research

Focusing on causality 'as it actually plays out in a particular setting' (Miles and Huberman, 1994: 10) turns us to causal networks as they exist at the level of the individual case. In this connection Bill Reid's work on *change–process research* has been far too little exploited as a form of practice research that is neither straight-forwardly outcome nor process research. Reid did not, of course, reject the role of controlled experiments but concluded that 'practical and ethical constraints on experiments necessitate a reliance on the naturalistic study of these relations' (Reid, 1990: 130). This entails a focus on the processes of change during the period of contact between the professional helper and the client system. Rather than relying on aggregated, averaged summary measures of outcomes, this approach focuses on micro-outcomes.

A systemic view of intervention is at its root, in which professionals and service users are viewed in a circular, mutually influencing interaction. In this model 'conventional distinctions between intervention and outcome lose their simplicity' (Reid, 1990: 135). 'It then becomes possible to depict change–process research as a study of strings of intermixed … interventions and outcomes (ibid., p. 136). While Reid defended experiments throughout his career, he suggested a more naturalistic stance when he said that 'averages of process variables that are devoid of their contexts at best provide weak measures' (ibid., p. 137).[3] Two radical conclusions follow that have greater force because they do not come from an opponent of conventional evaluation:

- We cannot divide intervention and outcomes in any clear way.
- Conventional methods of evaluation do not work well when we try to evaluate a group, especially when that ignores context.

Change–process research has been primarily developed in psychotherapy (e.g., Elliott, 2010; Greenberg, 1986) The usual way of connecting the process of

---

[3] For an assessment and appreciation of Reid's important work see Shaw, 2004.

intervention and the outcome is to see the first as one kind of predictor of the second. A qualitative variant on this approach is to ask service users what they found helpful or unhelpful about the intervention. A difficulty with this approach, as Elliott points out (2010) is that people's judgements about causes of events are often wrong. The danger is that clients may make attributional errors, following cultural scripts about the effects and nature of therapy or simply mistakenly attributing to therapy changes that are actually the result of their own efforts independent of therapy. He suggests that we can still use 'helpful factors' approaches, perhaps in combination with interpretive single case methods, as described in the next section.

Reid seems to have envisaged a basically quantitative approach, where a micro-analysis of processes and outcomes was the core of the method. Others in the psychotherapy field, such as Greenberg, Elliott and Stiles, have developed methods within an interpretive, theory-building framework. What these methods have in common is a focus on important moments in therapy.

Hermeneutic single case designs

A different and interesting argument for using qualitative methods as a means of understanding micro-processes has been suggested by McLeod in a thoughtful assessment of the potential of qualitative methods for understanding outcomes of counselling. He suggests that qualitative interviews are more likely to elicit critical perspectives than questionnaires, arising from the 'demand characteristics' of extended interviews. 'In terms of producing new knowledge that contributes to debates over evidence-based therapy, it would appear that qualitative evaluation is better able to explore the limits of therapeutic *ineffectiveness*' (McLeod, 2001: 178). Combined with their potential for eliciting positive relations between intervention and outcome, he concludes, not unlike Patton, that 'Qualitative interviews appear to be, at present, the most sensitive method for evaluating the harmful effects of therapy and also for recording its greatest individual successes' (ibid., p. 179).

In subsequent work he and others have developed and tested 'hermeneutic single case efficacy designs' (McLeod, 2010; McLeod and Elliott, 2011; Stephen et al., 2011). They are addressing the question whether a researcher within the humanistic tradition can do single case (N=1) studies. They criticise N=1 studies for proceeding by simplifying and condensing data. N=1 research entails an image of the person as a passive object on which therapy has an impact. Reflecting ideas present in critical realism, McLeod follows others in distinguishing 'hard' causality and 'soft' causality. The latter is reached through a complex, nonlinear, recursive and interactive process. It is

> much more interesting to study the *individual trajectories* by which individuals 'occupy the space' of client-centered therapy, and engage in that complex interactive process, and subsequently come to the outcomes they achieve, than it is to try to 'manipulate the variables' in order to establish strict linear causal relationships. (McLeod, 2010: 139)

A helpful example of the application of this method can be read in Stephen and colleagues' account of 'Lucy' (Stephen et al., 2011).

Epiphanies

We have referred to Mohr's appreciation of Denzin's potential for understanding outcomes, and his idea of epiphany as especially stimulating in an evaluative context. We have also referred to 'helpful factors' approaches that focus on important moments. In each case we have suggested the relevance for evaluative research. Denzin explains epiphanies as a 'moment of revelation in a life' that may be major or minor, relived, or illuminative (Denzin, 1989: 47). They are 'interactional moments and experiences which leave a mark on people's lives … In them, personal experience is manifested' (ibid., p. 70). They are often moments of crisis that, if major, alter the fundamental meaning structures in a person's life. They may be routinised on one hand or unstructured and 'totally emergent' on the other where 'the person enters into them with few if any prior understandings of what is going to happen' (ibid., p. 71). Their meaning is, he suggests, always given retrospectively. They take, he proposes, four possible forms (ibid., p. 71):

1. A major event 'which touches every fabric of a person's life'.
2. A cumulative or representative event – 'eruptions or reactions to experiences which have been going on for a long period of time'.
3. Minor epiphany, 'which symbolically represents a major, problematic moment'.
4. Episodes whose meanings are given in the reliving of the experience.

For an example of how this may apply, refer back to Chapter Seven, and to Neander and Skott's cogent and insightful analysis of joint interviews with parents and identified 'important persons', suggesting how they make sense as reflections on – and constitutions of – kinds of epiphanies.

Closing reflections

In this chapter we have discussed the nature of evaluation questions, and suggested careful comparisons between evaluation and research in terms of the purposes rather than the methods of inquiry. We explored the general criteria for opting for qualitative strategies, and invite readers to pursue this further in the 'Taking it further' task below. We bridged an earlier discussion of causality with reflections on qualitative contributions to research on outcomes, before giving the latter parts of the chapter to a rehearsal of several general strategy decisions that directly or indirectly enrich understanding and explanation of social work intervention, for example case studies, simulations of one sort or another, qualitative longitudinal designs and combinations of methods that yield a basis for complementary knowledge claims. The usual way of thinking about complementary knowledge claims is by way of bringing together qualitative and quantitative data. While that may be helpful, a much under-rated opportunity lies with the use of complementary qualitative methods.

However, we resist any prescriptive confidence in qualitative methods as easy solutions to difficult questions of evaluation and outcomes. We illustrate this in conclusion through a plea to respect the 'rough ground' of practice (Example 13.4). Schwandt and Dahler-Larsen engage in an illuminating conversation regarding their encounters with resistance to evaluation programmes (Schwandt and Dahler-Larsen, 2006). Dahler-Larsen reflects on an attempted evaluation of a free school with a Christian tradition in Denmark. He suggests that some communities may be characterised by 'a substantive value ... which cannot be made the object of reform'.

In response Schwandt suggests a different interpretation, when drawing on a study of rehabilitation in a cardiology hospital. He poses what he views as 'the basic question of the justification for the evaluator's role to challenge and engage in critique' and says 'I am continually perplexed by this problem' (2006: 502). He reflects on the metaphor of 'rough ground' as 'signifying that evaluation cannot always smooth out the creases in the intricate, uneven fabric of social practices or iron out difficulties in the appraisal of the value of those undertakings' (ibid., p. 503). Practice is rough ground because 'different ideas of what constitutes good practice and a good practitioner always compete for attention and because the moral, the political and the instrumental are always intertwined', and the very idea of critically engaging tradition is 'placing oneself in a place of being vulnerable to changing one's own ways of thinking' (ibid., p. 504).

| EXAMPLE 13.4 | Respecting the 'Rough Ground' of Practice |

Dahler-Larsen

My proposition is ... that there are some basic ingredients in communities that define themselves in a particular way which make these communities incompatible with the idea of evaluation, at least at some level or for some issues some of the time ... I think that perhaps the reason why some communities resist evaluation is that they have sensed that evaluation is the capacity of asking exactly those questions that may threaten the very existence of the community. (p. 499).

Schwandt

Perhaps evaluators should listen more carefully and respond more prudently to voices in communities that are hesitant or sceptical about evaluation ... Perhaps beneath their apparent 'resistance' to evaluation, communities ... are saying that they do not regard evaluation as smoothing and fixing things but rather as an activity that touches the rough ground of their lives, values and practices that constitute the world as they know it, and live in it, in other words, their *community*.

Schwandt and Dahler-Larsen (2006: 504)

Taking it further

The following paragraphs reproduce a 'semi-fictionalised scenario' by Schwandt and Burgon set within a municipality in northern Norway.

Tasks

First, reread the suggested criteria for utilising qualitative evaluation methods given in Box 13.3. Critically assess this debate between Burgon and Schwandt in the light of those criteria.

Second, consider how the issues debated between these authors might transfer to contexts with which you are familiar.

'Municipal officials charged with the administration and coordination of rehabilitation services for individuals in the community are meeting with representatives of several medical and social services (hospital-based physicians, vocational rehabilitation workers, occupational health personnel, physiotherapists, nurses, social workers, etc.) and representatives of several advocacy groups for disabled people. This is the second in a series of several meetings organised by the municipality. The topic of discussion is how best to design an evaluation of rehabilitation. Norwegian policy has recently defined rehabilitation as a set of processes that are planned and limited in time, with well-defined goals and means; wherein several professions or social services co-operate in assisting individual users in their efforts to achieve the best possible functioning and coping capabilities, while also promoting their independence and participation in society. Two external evaluators have been invited to participate in the conversation to offer their advice and assistance in the design of the evaluation that will eventually be commissioned by the municipality.

The conversation, often quite heated at times, and generally dominated by the powerful voices of the medical professionals, ranges over the concerns of various groups – e.g., ensuring functional improvement, integration into the workforce, providing coordinated assistance, respecting the user's autonomy, tailoring services to individual needs, facilitating user empowerment, integration of disabled individuals into community life, and so on.

Evaluator 1:   I think the best way to address the evaluation issues here is to look carefully at the definition of rehabilitation as a process for service provision that has well-defined characteristics and well-defined categories of beneficiaries. What I suggest is that we begin by defining the key dimensions of various types of rehabilitation processes, including who is (and ought to be) involved, and how. We work towards developing a set of criteria for planning processes that can, in turn, be used as a template to examine whether they are effective and efficient in achieving intended outcomes for different types of beneficiaries. We want to get at the facts of the matter here, so to speak – what does planning entail; what is an adequate measure of cooperation among professionals in planning; how do we judge whether the intended outcomes of planning were achieved; how is the process related to variables like available time, resource constraints, service location, professional responsibilities, user needs and values, and so forth ...

Evaluator 2: I agree, in general, with the idea of looking at rehabilitation as a process. But I suggest we focus on portrayals of what various people involved in this 'process' actually experience. In other words, we might attempt to grasp the various actors' understandings of the meaning of rehabilitation and the ways in which they attach value to it. I suggest that we think in terms of the ways people involved in rehabilitation make sense of their experience with it. In other words, focus on understanding rehabilitation as a lived reality; how it is felt, experienced, undergone, made sense of, accomplished, and valued. Rather than orienting the evaluation around such notions as planning processes, service providers and beneficiaries, means and outcomes, and goals and variables, we might think in terms of meanings, norms, routines, rituals, interactions, deliberations, dilemmas, paradoxes, issues, and so forth – ideas that draw our attention to the immediacy and particularity of the experience of rehabilitation ...'

Schwandt and Burgon (2006: 98–9)

FOURTEEN
Social Justice

This chapter explores the relationship between social work research and social justice. It begins with a discussion of standpoints and notes the internationally agreed social work aim of promoting social justice. The chapter then introduces a number of qualitative research designs and methods particularly associated with social justice. These are participatory research designs, focus groups, deliberative methods, visual methods and other arts-based research, including ethnodrama. The chapter concludes with two points: the differences that may be introduced when the recipients of services become engaged in research and the importance of researching 'up' to fully understand power relations.

Debates about social justice and the positions that people may take in relation to it, such as feminist, Marxist, anti-racist, postmodern and emancipatory, are somewhat familiar to social work researchers with backgrounds in practice. Relationships with those who receive our services, and other marginalised groups in society are discussed and debated in practice and policy areas such as user involvement in policy development, direct payments to disabled people who purchase and manage their own services and the need to listen to often unheard voices such as young children and people living with dementia. In research, parallel debates have challenged the dominance of scientists and other academics in setting research questions, choosing research methods, extracting data *from* less powerful groups, interpreting the results and presenting them to other members of the academy. Power relations have been disrupted by moves to involve service users in research or for research agendas to be set and led by less powerful groups. In this chapter we offer a number of examples of methods and designs associated with research that aims to further social justice agendas. We begin, however, with discussing standpoints and their relationship with social justice.

Standpoints and approaches

In Chapter Two we discussed standpoint epistemologies and the role of the 'insider' in research relationships. Here we return to these debates and briefly trace how 'standpoints' have developed in social science research and how these relate to social justice in social work research.

> The social work profession promotes social change, problem solving in human relationships and the empowerment and liberation of people to enhance wellbeing ... Principles of human rights and social justice are fundamental to social work. (International Federation of Social Workers, 2012)

The passage above is taken from a definition of social work agreed by the International Federation of Social Workers in 2000. It can be seen that the international social work profession has no difficulty in taking a position regarding the aims of its work. For social work researchers, then, it may be seen as natural to adopt an overall aim for research that it should strive to promote social change and social justice. Is such a stand partisan? Might it lead to researcher bias in their analysis? It can be argued that unreflective bias is a risk in all research and that an important insight that arose from early standpoint researchers, such as feminist sociologists, was that 'objective' social science was itself heavily biased in favour of the white, middle-class male perspectives that dominated academia until relatively recently (Delamont, 2003; Stanley and Wise, 1983).

In the 1970s and 1980s feminist social scientists exposed some of the patriarchal assumptions in research designs and outputs of that era. For example they noted that the majority of research was conducted with men and boys, but that findings were often generalised to theorise about 'people' in a way that did not happen with research where participants were women and girls. Although, in fact, in the emerging social work research literature with service recipients, women as clients *were* being interviewed (Mayer and Timms, 1970), in the social sciences more generally there was little direct access to women's perspectives and experiences (Stanley and Wise, 1983). Such criticisms extended beyond the level of attention to women's experiences, however. The critique extended to the maintenance of power differences between participants and researchers, reinforced by data generation methods, analysis and the production of research outputs (Stanley and Wise, 1983). Early feminist social scientists thus paved the way for participant involvement in research from commissioning to dissemination, the development of accessible and culturally sensitive data generation methods and a heightened reflexivity on the part of researchers (Delamont, 2003).

Feminist research has laid the foundation for similar approaches in relation to other marginalised groups, and researchers and activists in other fields including childhood studies (James et al.,1998), queer studies (Ahmed, 2006), disability studies (Goodley, 2011) and indigenous approaches (D'Cruz and Jones, 2004) have drawn on the language of feminism or used it as a comparative standpoint. This has been given, by some, the broad term 'emancipatory research' (Alston and Bowles, 2003). According to Whitmore (2001: 84–5) there are four key elements to emancipatory research. These are:

1. A recognition that differing personal, social and institutional 'locations' (class, race, gender, disability, sexuality, professional status, etc.) affect how different parties experience and interpret the world and therefore it is impossible to carry out value free or neutral research;
2. An explicit attempt to question and challenge power relations in research, asking questions such as: Who creates knowledge? Who controls and conducts research? Who benefits from it?
3. A legitimatising of 'other' ways of knowing and of expressing that knowledge (often using alternative data collection and dissemination methods as discussed in this chapter);
4. The research is linked to action such as changing perceptions of oppressed groups or changing practices and policies. Researchers who work within such a framework are likely to place themselves in a 'transformative paradigm' as defined by Mertens and Ginsberg (2008).

Swigonski (1994) argues that feminist standpoint research is consonant with social work values due to the desire to place the experiences of marginalised groups at the centre of inquiry and then to interrogate the social structures that maintain processes of marginalisation. Feminist research has undergone many transformations and any short summary here risks over-simplifying some complex debates (Delamont, 2003). Post-structural and post-modern approaches reject the essentialising of women's experiences that may have been present in some earlier writings, instead exploring decentred and multiple identities (Gibson-Graham, 1994). These approaches controversially underplay analyses based on class and gender (Delamont, 2003). Similar debates have emerged in other areas, with, for example, authors in childhood studies rejecting simplistic dichotomies such as 'child – adult' and 'structure – agency' (Prout, 2005). In social work, too, we would argue against any assumption that service user/ recipient (or expert by experience, Preston-Shoot, 2007) perspectives can be 'uncovered' unproblematically nor that it is sufficient to simply aim to 'give voice' to marginalised groups (Wulf-Andersen, 2012). As we explained in Chapter Two, we see merit in the more muted strands of standpoint epistemologies which emphasise insider *privileged* rather than *monopolistic* claims to knowledge. In the next section we explore these issues further in the discussion about participatory methods.

Common forms of research designs and methods associated with social justice approaches

We do not believe that any method, design or paradigm is *necessarily* linked to social justice and would argue that any designs and methods in this book, and indeed it might be argued any quantitative methods, might be harnessed towards social justice objectives. Nonetheless, there are a number of research methods and designs that have been especially associated with social justice approaches, particularly those that attempt to involve marginalised groups in initiating and conducting research, and these are discussed next.

Participatory approaches and user-led research

Participatory approaches are increasingly common across the social sciences and public health research. Many pieces of research are labelled 'participatory' but it is clear that such approaches can be placed across a broad continuum (Holland et al., 2010). At one extreme, there are research studies that are entirely initiated, designed, carried out and disseminated by academic researchers who do not belong to the social group or share in the social experiences of those being researched. Such projects are sometimes labelled 'participatory' because the researched are enabled to express their views through more or less engaging methods, rather than, for example being simply measured or observed. At the other end of the continuum are projects initiated and led by non-academics: citizens, service users, residents, children and youth, for example, with at most facilitation and support from academic researchers. These are often labelled participatory action research (PAR), particularly when carried out with an aim of informing and stimulating change (Chataway, 1997; and see Chapter Five). In between there are a whole range of ways in which participants become involved in research processes, including being involved in steering groups and as trained peer researchers. A sticky problem in engaging in participative methods is the challenge of achieving genuine participation and avoiding tokenistic or superficial approaches (Kellett et al., 2004). Nonetheless, as Heath and Walker (2012) suggest, to place a value on the *level* of participation, with user-led research seen as the best or indeed only valid response to a desire to disrupt research hierarchies, is likely to be counter-productive. Wulf-Anderson (2012: 577) suggests that to focus on hierarchies of participation asks the wrong type of question if it 'focuses on the relation between the researcher and the researched and portrays differences of positions and interests as a problem to be solved rather than an interesting quality that must be propagated and accommodated'. She continues that it can also presume a homogeneity among participants that masks hierarchies of power and diversities that exist in all groups.

Community-based, participatory research projects have their roots in community development work and the methods indeed often overlap to such a great extent that it can be difficult (and may be unnecessary) to distinguish between participative practices in the communities and participative research in communities. Many community researchers (for example, McIntyre, 1997) draw inspiration from Paulo Freire's (1970) philosophy and methodology in Latin America, where he worked to facilitate marginalised groups' meaningful engagement in society. However, there are different styles in which community development practices and academia co-exist in participatory research. One central difference is the degree to which the research aims to bring participants into the academy or, alternatively, bring the academy into the participants' everyday lives and cultures. In the former, participants may be trained in formal research methods and act as peer researchers or be enabled to conduct their own research entirely (see Example 14.1). In the latter, the researcher works with participants' own preferred methods of understanding the world to explore an area of inquiry. This might be exemplified by some of the arts-based methods such as the pantomime in Example 14.5. Both approaches have merits (and there are many variants of these two approaches). Enabling participants to use established research methods on an equal basis gives credibility to research outputs in circles such as local and national governments and academia. Working with methods that fit with participants' forms of communication may be more engaging for participants and demands that audiences learn to respond to diverse forms of expression.

EXAMPLE 14.1   **Children as Peer Researchers**

Mary Kellett is a researcher with the Open University in the UK and has set up a children's research centre. This centre is dedicated to training and enabling children to act as peer researchers about issues that are important to them, and is relatively unusual in working with primary school aged children (under 12s) rather than older children and young people. In a paper co-written with three ten-year-old researchers (Kellett et al., 2004), two research reports written by the child researchers are included. One project reports on a survey of children's views of the impact of their parents' employment on home life and the other on social aspects of watching television. These were topics that the children were interested in and that they had hypotheses about, although these authors explain that their expectations were somewhat revised by the results (as is not unusual in social research). In the paper's conclusion the authors reflect on the advantages of this approach:

> Some might dismiss the research efforts of these children as simplistic and conclude that adults could have researched the topics much more extensively. This would be to miss several important points. Firstly, the children succeeded in getting responses from within their peer group in a way that may not have been possible for adult researchers because of power and generational issues. Secondly, their work adds to the body of knowledge about children and childhood from a genuine child perspective. Thirdly, the dissemination of research carried out by them and, importantly, owned by them, is an important vehicle for the child voice. Fourthly, the experience of participating as active researchers has been an empowering process. (Kellett et al., 2004: 341)

The advantages expressed by Kellett and her co-researchers, of different questions being asked by participant researchers, of their often superior ability to engage peers in research and the social and political advantages gained by the participant researchers themselves can easily be seen in research with adult groups in social work such as research co-produced or led by disabled researchers. Often, as seen in Kellett's research, two key rationales are provided. Firstly that the process is good – it is empowering – and secondly that it makes for better research – peer researchers can do better fieldwork and bring different insights. Barriers and difficulties have perhaps been less readily discussed in this relatively recent approach, where there may be seen to be a need to advocate for its acceptance by the wider research community. However some papers reflect on complexities in this field. Holland et al. (2010) discuss some of the ethical and practical complications of their participatory project with children in foster and kinship care, including issues of confidentiality and power imbalances within the participant group. Chataway (1997), in a discussion of the process of facilitating a participatory action research project in a divided Native Canadian community, discusses how classic PAR approaches were constraining in this context and that different approaches and compromises had to be developed throughout the project. Banks and Armstrong (2012) bring together a series of case studies from recent community-based participatory research projects that explore some of the ethical issues that arose and how they were worked with. Complicating factors that arose in some of the projects included the need to somehow bridge academic talk and writing and everyday communication styles and the risk of participatory research being proposed by funders whose assumptions may set up the research to focus on specific symptoms rather than causes of marginalisation.

The centre at Durham University that hosted Banks and Armstrong's work has produced a useful guide to planning a community-based participatory research project, highlighting the careful planning and negotiations that need to take place to prevent difficulties and misunderstandings (Centre for Social Justice and Community Action, 2012). They state that underlying ethical principles need to be based on mutual respect, equality and inclusion, democratic participation, a commitment to active, reciprocal learning, an aim to promote positive change, an expectation of collective action and a commitment to personal integrity, such as honest reporting of research results (ibid., p. 8). Such goals can be achieved more easily if at early stages there has been open discussion about roles and responsibilities, protocols for safety, confidentiality, informed consent and handling conflict, mutual understanding on ownership of results and how best to disseminate results and end the project.

Participatory approaches and ethics

Butler's (2002) code of ethics for social work research, which we introduced in Chapter Six, clearly links ethics, social justice and approaches to research design. The code suggests that social work research should aim to be emancipatory and that researchers should work in partnership with oppressed groups to set and implement research agendas. The code also suggests that 'where appropriate' research should be centred around the 'perspectives and lived experience of the research subject' (ibid., p. 245).

Research which allows service users and other excluded groups, whose perspectives are often unheard, to present their views first hand could indeed be seen to be ethical, although whether it is *more* ethical than other types of research is possibly a lazy assumption (Murphy and Dingwall, 2001). Indeed, some social work academics might argue that this type of research is now over-dominant, in the UK at least, and that there is a strong ethical imperative to put more research effort into establishing the effectiveness of interventions designed to help service recipients, because it is unethical to use practice methods that may cause harm (Sheldon and Macdonald, 2009). Others might argue that it does not matter what the research design and data generation method is, so long as service users have played a part in establishing research questions, distributing funding and designing research. Qualitative designs predominate in participative research (Holland, 2009) but there is no reason why participative frameworks should not result in designs that are primarily quantitative. McDonald and Kidney (2012) in a review of 37 journal articles about ethics and research with people with learning disabilities claim that the growing tendency for research collaborations between people with LD and academics offers the opportunity to strengthen the ethics of research in this field. Certainly service users can bring unique insights into ethical matters, as was seen in Example 5.2 in Chapter Five. Despite these ethical advantages of participatory designs, there are inevitably ethically difficult issues with which to engage. In Chapter Nine we highlighted the dilemmas faced by ethnographic researchers grappling with the level of approval needed from participants before publishing research findings. Confidentiality can also be an issue. Holland et al. (2010) were unable to engage participants in *cross-case* analysis, as much of the data produced in a participatory project with looked-after children had not been shared across the group. The young people were involved in analysing their own data, but this was only one stage of the analysis and restricted the ability of the project to be fully participative.

Data generation and representation in social justice approaches

Social justice approaches are associated with a wide range of data generation methods. Qualitative methods are, however, particularly associated with participative research and other designs that aim to promote social justice. Ann Oakley (1981) and other early feminist researchers used in-depth qualitative interviews to attempt to put researcher and researched on a more equal footing. There are many types of qualitative methods for data generation and representation that we could have included in this chapter on social justice but for reasons of space we choose to include four: focus groups, deliberative methods, visual research methods (particularly photovoice) and other arts-based methods (particularly ethnodrama). These take us on a journey from more familiar social science forms to the less familiar.

Focus groups with marginalised groups

Focus groups can be used as data generation with little sense of social justice as a research aim. They can be entirely planned and managed by a professional researcher and used to collect data from participants with no further involvement with the participants. This is an *extractive* model of research. Ways of conceiving and implementing focus groups have, however, begun to shift. Kamberelis and Dimitriadis (2005) capture aspects of these changes and believe that 'focus groups can be key democratic spaces during an age when such spaces are becoming increasingly elipsed and atomised.' They 'foreground the importance not only of content, but also of expression, because they capitalize on the richness and complexity of group dynamics. Acting somewhat like magnifying glasses, focus groups induce social interactions akin to those that occur in everyday life but with greater force' (Kamberelis and Dimitriadis, 2005: 903–4).

They argue that focus groups are of value for:

- Disclosing group dynamics.
- Showing the constitutive power of discourse.
- Filling in gaps from, for example, observation.
- Drawing out nuance and contradiction.
- Eliciting 'group resistance narratives' (p. 897).
- Inspiring self-interrogation.
- A pedagogical value of 'giving back'.
- Promoting collective memory.[1]

The majority of writers in this field have opposed the application of focus groups to anything other than research or formal evaluation purposes. In our view this always has been an unhelpful generalisation, and the diversified conception offered by Kamberelis and Dimitriadis opens up particular contributions to qualitative research on assessment, planning, intervention and outcomes. Exercises in problem setting, project development, anti-discriminatory practice, addressing work that has become 'stuck', consumer feedback exercises, and working with sensitive topics, are all ways in which focus groups have something to offer to social work research and practice.

Problem setting is often a central feature of early work in project development. 'Social research has not done well in reaching people who are isolated by the daily, exhausting struggles for survival, services and dignity' (Plaut et al., 1993: 216). Plaut and colleagues' account of the use of focus groups for community mobilisation among poor, white, politically conservative, rural communities illustrates how the method can lead to empowerment. Working as part of a larger project for community oriented primary health care, they organised extensive focus group work around small, subjectively identified, communities. Groups were asked to identify community health problems. A range of projects was initiated following the focus groups, and the groups became not only a source of data but 'a process for resident involvement in and legitimation of the project and its interventions' (Plaut et al., 1993: 206). They conclude that the focus group is useful, not only as a research instrument, 'but as a means whereby a community can recognise its needs within the framework of its own language and contexts, and mobilise accordingly' (ibid., p. 216–7).

The potential for empowering participants, and hence for anti-discriminatory evaluation, is also illustrated in Jarrett's (1993) work with black women at risk of

---

[1]We are drawing for this list on a workshop they facilitated at the 2010 Congress of Qualitative Inquiry at the University of Illinois, together with their contribution to Denzin and Lincoln, 2005.

long-term poverty, and outside traditional family patterns. Madriz (2003), writing as a 'Latina feminist' (p. 365), notes that focus groups are part of a collectivist rather than an individualistic model and provide much more than simply data for research. Focus groups with women of colour may facilitate their 'writing culture together' while they 'expose and validate women's everyday experiences of sub-jugation and their individual and collective survival and resistance strategies' (ibid., p. 364). She notes that the group situation may serve to minimise the power and voice of the researcher, and allow participants to share experiences, ask each other questions and develop 'collective testimonies' (ibid., p. 365).

Deliberative methods

Deliberative methods are used in public policy and in research to bring together policymakers, subject experts, service users and lay citizens to discuss and form conclusions about policies and other questions. Principles include listening care-fully to others' perspectives, respect for others' forms of expression and acknowledging other viewpoints (Barnes, 2005). Beresford (2010b) traces the roots of deliberation in the UK to the conservative governments of the 1980s and 1990s, with an emphasis on consumer choice and decrease in state powers, through a New Labour emphasis at the turn of the century on participation and public involvement. Meanwhile, citizens juries have been used in the USA and planning cells in Germany, since the 1970s and public participation through forms of deliberation are now common in health and other public policy settings world-wide (Abelson et al., 2003; Barnes, 2005). Lohmann and Lohmann (2010) note that early twentieth century social work pioneers, such as Jane Addams in Hull House, could also be seen as engaging in deliberative democracy in the open salon discussions she and others held in inner-city Chicago. House and Howe (1999: xix) point to the potential for using deliberative methods in evaluations to 'incorporate the views of insiders and outsiders, give voice to the marginal and excluded, employ reasoned criteria in extended deliberation, and engage in dialogical interactions with significant audiences and stakeholders in the evaluation.'

Deliberative methods share some similarities with focus groups in that they tend to involve participants discussing important questions in group settings, but there are some key differences. With most focus groups the data are gener-ated in the group setting but then analysed and conclusions drawn elsewhere, usually by the researcher (who may not have facilitated the focus group) although in more participative models the analysis and writing might include participants too. In some forms of deliberative inquiry, the data generation, analysis and concluding recommendations overlap and are carried out by the participants who relay their results to the policymakers (Evans and Kotchetkova, 2009). There are also overlaps with action research (see Chapter Five), but here again there are key differences in the role of the researcher. In action research the researcher is a co-producer of knowledge and an equal partner with par-ticipants. In deliberative inquiry the researcher is more of a behind-the-scenes facilitator and organiser (Evans and Kotchetkova, 2009). Certainly, in common with many of the methods discussed in this chapter, one effect is to disrupt the notion of researcher-as-expert and to promote the inclusion into public forums of those whose participation is often marginalised.

Despite these seemingly laudable aims there are a number of challenges in using deliberative inquiry in research and public policy formation. Firstly there is an issue of who is involved and who assigns their categorisation into a particular group. For example, as Barnes (2005) notes, 'older people' will also hold a range of other identities, gender, class, sexualities, ethnicities and race, etc. Evans and Kotchetkova (2009) found that the 'lay citizens' in their deliberative forum wished to recast themselves as 'friends of people living with diabetes'. Secondly, the choice of information to share to ensure that debate is considered and informed may well be in the hands of those in most power and careful consideration needs to be given to the form and content of information-sharing (Felt et al., 2013; House and Howe, 1999) and to the format of discussion (Barnes, 2005). Thirdly, even with careful planning, power dynamics may be played out in surprising ways. Evans and Kotchetkova (2009: 639) found, in their deliberative inquiry process about prioritising research and treatment funds for Type 1 diabetes, that the aim of encouraging everyone to listen carefully to each others' position and consider their point of view became superseded by a different dynamic: 'patients were granted, and then retained, the right to set the terms of the debate and, where necessary, used highly emotive language to suppress the concerns of others.' While they acknowledge that this may in some ways be a welcome departure from the dominant voice of 'experts', they suggest that the core aims of deliberative inquiry were undermined in this way.

Deliberative methods appear to have been used much more extensively in health policy settings than social work or social welfare settings, yet we see a potential for their use to promote debate about policy responses to a wide range of social work issues such as safeguarding children in neighbourhoods, youth offending, community provision for sex offenders and social care for older people. The method used by Felt and her colleagues in Example 14.2 shows the potential for promoting engaged debate through this method.

EXAMPLE 14.2	Imagine: Deliberative Research with Lay Citizens in Austria Using a Card Game Method

Felt and her colleagues (2013) facilitated a deliberative forum in Austria to enable lay citizens to discuss and debate the implications of nanotechnology (nano). 'The aim of our methodological approach was to create a space in which participants are encouraged to develop and negotiate individual and collective *imaginations* about nano. Imaginations are outcomes of imagination, which we understand as the ability and practice to relate and associate what is perceived as possible with what is seen as "given" or "real"' (p. 3).

The researchers took great pains to avoid setting up a dichotomy between experts and non-experts. This was achieved through avoiding having experts presenting 'facts about nano' at the beginning of the 4-hour session. Instead a short video introduced the topic, including the many layers of complexity associated with it, while participants took their seats. The rest of the session involved participants in a card game called IMAGINE. There were four stages. In each stage participants selected one or more cards from a pile and placed them on a board. The cards fell under four categories and each stage moved on to a different category of card: story cards, applications cards, issue cards and future cards. Thus participants moved from reading about people's experiences, to potential applications of new technologies, to issues such as ethics, responsibilities and policies and lastly to possible futures for the technologies. They were asked to explain and discuss their choices in a group at each stage.

The advantages reported by the researchers was that 'experts' such as scientists and policymakers were present only in the stories in the cards, allowing lay citizens to speak more freely. The card game format was familiar to many and gave everyone a chance to speak. The material on the cards ensured that everyone had something to say. They state that the structured technique worked well in Austrian society where there are low levels of participation and public engagement in policymaking.

This study does not fulfil the deliberative method norm of engaging different stakeholders together in one event, but the card game technique appears promising for promoting engagement in deliberation events.

Visual methods

Visual methods are not necessarily used with an aim of promoting social justice in research but they often are, and therefore some brief discussion of visual methods is warranted in this chapter, with a focus on the more participatory applications of visual methods such as PhotoVoice. Visual methods can include photography, drawing, collage-making, mapping, story-boards and video making. Visual materials may be used to elicit discussion and reflection (Bahn and Barratt-Pugh, 2011). They can be produced by participants as part of the exploration of a topic (Mannay, 2010) and they may be used to represent the results of research, such as through a film or exhibition (Sharpe, 2012). Russell and Diaz (2013) introduced visual images at the analysis stage of their research into lesbian identities, using photographs to illuminate and draw deeper meaning from the emerging codes and later to represent findings.

> In this study, photography serves the following purposes: (a) to make the invisible visible, (b) to symbolize conceptual codes, (c) to emit understanding and, (d) to add dimension to lesbian cultural experience ... Photography, as a method in the research process itself, occurred after theoretical codes emerged, an adjunct process not to collect data but to artistically represent the data. Participants identified the potential images they believed would best represent these codes. (Russell and Diaz, 2013: 437)

Spencer (2011: 1) argues that the social sciences have over-emphasised the written and spoken word and undervalued the visual world which is a central part of everyday lives. Visual methods, he argues, have a potential 'to provide a deeper and more subtle exploration of social contexts and relationships ... allowing us to see the everyday with new eyes'. Mannay (2010), who researched women's and daughters' experiences in the researcher's home community, used visual methods of self-directed photography, mapping and collage-making to enable her, and her participants, to see their familiar world in new ways (Example 14.3).

EXAMPLE 14.3 — **Magazine Clippings Collage**

PhotoVoice is a collective visual method that has explicit social justice aims (see http://www.photovoice.org/ for more information and online resources). Photographs, taken by participants, are also interpreted and given meaning by participants as co-researchers. Wang and Burris (1997) claim that this method allows members of communities to make explicit their experiences and concerns, to promote dialogue through discussing the images and their interpretation in groups and to represent their views to others such as the general public and policymakers. There is a clear social action element to this method.

EXAMPLE 14.4 — **Photo Voice and Brain Injury**

Laura Lorenz's work with brain injury survivors has much to offer qualitative researchers. 'One way to understand patients' perspectives on living with illness and experiencing healthcare is to carry out qualitative research that allows patients to share their experiences in an unstructured way' (Lorenz, 2010a: 863). She makes the case that participatory visual methods can serve as a useful reflection and teaching tool to help providers and patients listen to each other and to promote empathy, engagement, and mutual learning in the therapeutic relationship (Lorenz, 2010b). From 2006 to 2007, she carried out a study of lived experience with brain injury with six brain injury survivors who were accessing outpatient services in Boston, Massachusetts.

Laura Lorenz describes a study in which a brain tumour survivor, injured 17 years earlier (Judy), took photographs of her life with brain injury and discussed them with other brain injury survivors and the author. The photographs focused on in this article are of cookbooks ('lost identity' as chef), a box of medications ('these are my brain injuries'), her new garden ('the new Judy') and her keys in the freezer ('We as brain injured people put things in weird places'), and she gives fuller attention to the keys in the freezer. Of her study as a whole she says that visual metaphors became vehicles for voice as participants used PhotoVoice to make visible their brain injuries and their efforts to wrestle with the cognitive and emotional impacts and discover new purpose and meaning in life (Lorenz, 2010b).

'I did not select Judy … to be statistically representative. Rather, I selected her because she appeared to find participating in my study to be meaningful, and her story in turn seemed meaningful to me' (Lorenz, 2010a: 863).

A man's photographs depict his sense of frustration and confusion. They comprise cans in the sink ('the disorder that I'm living with right now'), a stuffed refrigerator ('nothing's where it belongs'), vegetables on display in a supermarket ('a supermarket is just utter confusion to me') and a nicely presented summer salad ('it just has a feeling in your mouth, like rubber').

Lorenz reflects that 'my choice of Judy as a case study raised a concern for me. Was I overly drawn to Judy as a hero in her quest for healing after brain injury? … Was I choosing to explore Judy's story because it fulfilled my personal need for a lived experience with brain injury that exemplified agency and enrichment?' Did, as she suspects, her '"transformative plot" lens' push her towards '"romanticizing" the "illness Quest" of Judy'? She cautions in this context that 'We must take care to avoid aggrandising Judy's visual data – the organised pill box and the beautiful garden – or minimising her verbal data, when she describes forgetting to take her medications and falling in her plants and crushing them' (Lorenz, 2010a: 871).

These cautions as to romanticising are valuable. 'What is the value of a scientific enterprise that is more concerned with being "right-on" than with being right?' (Dingwall, 1997b: 64).

Visual methods can be an excellent means to engage participants and co-researchers who may be alienated by written forms. For example, a group of Gypsy and Traveller children in England, who had low literacy levels, chose to explore and represent images of their communities through producing a photographic exhibition to be shown in a family theme park (Sharpe, 2012). On the other hand, Schaefer (2012) helpfully reminds us not to make assumptions about interests and abilities. In her participative study with young people in rural East Germany she found that several young people were initially anxious and reluctant to use video cameras, although for some this attitude changed through the research process.

Other arts-based research – fiction, poetry, dance and ethnodrama

Photography, as has been seen, has been used to promote participation, engender dialogue and represent participants' experiences and perspectives to others. Other arts forms are also increasingly commonly used for similar social justice aims. Critical, qualitative arts-based research is, according to Finley (2011: 435) 'a genre of research in which methodologies are emergent and egalitarian, local, and based in communal, reflective dialogue'. Finley places social change as central to her promotion of critical arts-based research, distancing herself from the many other uses to which the arts and humanities are used in social research.

Performance texts that arise from research are argued to be effective ways of raising awareness, encouraging empathy and highlighting the emotional aspects of social life. For these aims, they can be more effective than formal academic writing (Foster, 2013). Differing forms of representation are gradually becoming more acceptable. With the advent of digital visual images and online publication, photographs and other visual images are increasingly seen in academic journals, and other arts forms such as poetry and fiction are increasingly represented in journals such as *Qualitative Social Work*, *Qualitative Inquiry* and *Cultural Studies =Critical Methodologies*. Denzin (2013) has published an entire paper in the form of a play in *Qualitative Research* about the representation of Native Americans in a nineteenth century international travelling show and the social, cultural and political conditions that underlay their involvement. All of the analysis and discussion is contained in the play and there is no additional academic commentary.

Denzin's work is a dramatised product drawn from primary materials such as journals and paintings from the era. Poetry as a form of research dissemination often reformulates interview transcripts into poetic forms. There may be some rearrangements of order and some condensing of the prose, but the form represents participants' direct words made new in a different form. The following extract is from a much longer poem in an article by Wulf-Andersen (2012: 570) that discusses a participative project with young adults who have used social services. The poem relates Laura's story:

The Psychiatrist

And then I'm sent to the psychiatrist too
first there are conversations with mum, John and me
then they are just with me and John
and then my mum and John
and mum and me
and finally
it's just
me . . .

They were conversations about the course of the illness

as well as stuff that happens and what moves you . . .

But I thought it was a drag

because the psychiatrist asks you questions

that you have to answer

and that's annoying

I didn't get to ask him any questions

Wulf-Anderson used the poetic form to analyse the data, to discuss it with participants and to disseminate. Interestingly, while Laura loved the poem based on her data, another young person, Martin, disliked his. He did not like how his words sounded nor the free-form poetry that did not rhyme nor follow a structured meter. He contributed his own poem.

Other increasingly common forms of arts-based research are dance and ethnodrama. By typing 'Dance your PhD' into YouTube it is possible to see the winners of this annual competition, sponsored by the journal *Science*, where whole theses (including social science research) are conveyed most strikingly through dance. Ethnodrama is another performance medium that has emerged since the early 1990s (Mienczakawoski, 2001) and aims to convey experience alongside participants. Dramas are developed co-operatively as part of the data generation and analysis process. When performed to others, such as educators, policymakers, politicians and the lay public there may be an overt intent to stimulate reflection and learning (Foster, 2013; Mienczakawoski, 2001). Unlike some poetic forms of representation, which are often largely based on primary data (such as interviews and diaries), ethnodrama is often intentionally fictional.

EXAMPLE 14.5	**The Wizard of Us**

Dorothy: No, don't say that! I came down here because I believed there must be more to life and this isn't it! Listen, why don't you come with me back to the crossroads? There are other cities nearby. Let's go and visit them together and see where they lead to. If we stick together, then maybe we'll find a better place.

Scarecrow: Nah. I'm too tired and don't think I can be bothered. Think I'll just stay here and have a kip!

Dorothy: Oh, please! I really could do with some help … and it would be nice to have a friend.

Scarecrow: Really? Well … nobody ever asked me for my help before. They all thought I was too stupid! I suppose it wouldn't do any harm seeing what else is out there. Okay, I will. (Foster, 2013: 41).

(Continued)

(Continued)

Victoria Foster carried out a participative research project with the users of a Sure Start, neighbourhood based programme for families with young children. Six local women worked with the researcher to plan and carry out the research and finally to perform some of the findings. They explored local experiences of parenting and engagement with local services through a survey and creative methods such as poetry, short films and drama.

The project's after-school family drama group elected to put on a pantomime, as the form of theatre they were most familiar with. Foster had planned that this experience might lead to the group being prepared to work on more serious drama that displayed important issues emerging from the participatory research project. The group resisted this, not wanting to do anything so dreary and elected to stage another pantomime that included the most important findings from the research. Thus '*The Wizard of Us*' was developed, performed and filmed for the local community, professionals and policymakers and excerpts used as part of academic conference presentations.

Foster reflects that the drama had many advantages in that it was scripted and directed by local women, many reported that the experience of taking part had been personally transformative and gave a more rounded and positive view of local experiences than that often imposed by outsiders. On the other hand the researcher had some concern that the women chose only to portray the positive aspects of the Sure Start project, sidelining some negative aspects that emerged from the research, and that the drama, although well received, was largely ignored as part of the national Sure Start evaluation in comparison with the research project's more conventional outputs. Thus its effects were more apparent at the micro rather than the macro level.

Conclusion

In this chapter we have tried to show that social justice issues play a central role in qualitative social work research, just as they do in social work policies and practices. Although social justice aims can in theory be met through almost any research design or method, certain approaches have become particularly associated with social justice and we have highlighted some of these here. We end with two final observations, one about the nature of participatory research and the other about who should be engaged in social justice research.

Firstly, we need to be prepared to do some shifting of our expectations and agenda if we are going to genuinely involve service users and other potentially marginalised groups in our research. An approach that expects user collaborators to slot into our ways of working is not participative. As the examples in this chapter have shown, we need to be imaginative and flexible about how we may generate data, analyse and present findings. We also need to be prepared to share in agenda-setting. One of us (IS) was involved in supporting a research programme that funded projects bid for and led by mental health service users across the UK. Three things became clear. Research questions were different to those often raised by academic researchers and policymakers. They were more orientated towards rights and experiences than service delivery and practice. Definitions of good practice were different than those often used in academic led evaluations. Lastly, the user-researchers held powerful views about stigma and labelling, suggesting the need for careful use of terms and labels (Shaw, 2012c).

Secondly, social justice oriented research should not simply engage with the 'oppressed' or marginalised. This means that we are simply trying to understand one aspect of how power relations work in our society and also risks putting responsibility for change on the shoulders of the least powerful. McIntyre (1997: 19–20) studied the meaning of 'whiteness' with a relatively powerful group of middle class white teachers in the United States but with an aim of 'breaking the silence about what it means to be a white in our society (in order to) engage in dialogue about our racial identities, the meaning of whiteness and our positionalities as teachers, thereby fostering the development of critical consciousness'. Pease (2010: 109) sums up the advantages of this approach – 'Generally researchers study down rather than up ... Why do we focus on women who are disadvantaged as opposed to why men are overly advantaged? ... We need to interrogate privileged social locations ... and the ways that our research practice may unwittingly reproduce the exploitative relationships that we are challenging' (Pease, 2010: 109).

Taking it further

Having read the chapter, consider the following questions:

Design and methods: Do qualitative methods have greater natural affinity with social justice research aims than quantitative methods? Is participatory research more ethical than non-participatory research?

Validity: Do concerns with social justice mean that participatory designs should be assessed by different criteria than mainstream science?

Bias: What is the relationship (if any) between claiming a standpoint and being biased?

FIFTEEN
Qualitative Research
and Practice

> In this chapter we explore initially how we should begin thinking about the general relationship between practice and qualitative research, and then set out ways in which we can do so. In the first part of the chapter we map the kinds of knowledge involved. These include 'practical knowledge', common sense, tacit knowledge and expert knowledge. We take the linked ideas of reflective and reflexive work as an example.
>
> In the main part of the chapter we look at the mirrored questions of those forms of qualitative research that challenge and are challenged by practice, and forms of practice that challenge and are challenged by qualitative research. We go on from there to consider two arenas that in a less dualistic way may bring research and practice into a single whole. The first of these – what is happening when practitioners engage in qualitative research – is based on recent empirical work that suggests new ways of thinking about the nature and possibly *genre* of qualitative practitioner research. Finally, we outline and sketch examples of 'qualitative social work' – a form of practice that entails the 'translation' of qualitative methods as ways of doing social work. We present this as an ingredient of what we call sociological social work.

The relationship between various forms of disciplined inquiry and professional practice lies just below the surface of qualitative research. In a predecessor volume to the present one Hall and – with careful detail – White recorded how they held both insider and outsider roles in relation to their research participants (Hall, 2001; White, 2001). Hall 'arrived' as an outsider but became in different ways a partial insider. White started as an insider, yet found herself undergoing a fruitful, if potentially hazardous, process of de-familiarisation through which she became in some degree a marginal 'inside "out"' member. Scourfield (2001) focused on the research and practice relationship through his consideration of what it was like to interview expert professional social work interviewers.

Yet qualitative researchers sometimes appear to take a hands-off approach to explaining and making judgements. They favour a descriptive rather than prescriptive approach to values, and prefer that research should be 'oriented to understanding the case more or less as a whole, not for patching its pieces and fixing its problems' (Stake, 1991: 77). This stance goes back to the roots of qualitative research, which provide researchers with 'powerful disincentives to assert responsibility for more than their story. The applicability of the story to other contexts is a judgement left to others' (Greene, 1993: 40–1). Local relevance and the human story are regarded as the primary goals of qualitative research, and not generalisability.

This open-minded stance can give qualitative research in social work 'a *prima donna* image' (Simon, 1986: 52). 'In insisting that ethnographers have the freedom to define problems after they get into the field, ethnography's representatives inadvertently may do more to keep ethnography out of policy research than to keep pretenders out of doing ethnography' (ibid., p. 55). It is partly in response to such issues that writers such as Packer seek through qualitative inquiry to 'open our eyes to unnoticed aspects of human life and learning, unexplored characteristics of the relationship between humans and the world we inhabit, and unsuspected ways in which we could improve our lives on this planet' (Packer, 2011: 3). Hence qualitative research is not a set of techniques but a 'basis for a radical reconceptualization of the social sciences as forms of inquiry in which we work to transform our forms of life' (ibid., p. 3). He draws on Habermas' idea that inquiry should be motivated by an 'emancipatory' interest.

In this chapter we develop several of the themes in the previous chapter, and consider the inter-relationship between qualitative research and direct practice in social work.

Practice, knowledge and research

The ground needs some preliminary clearing, through awareness of the kinds of knowledge involved. These include practical knowledge, common sense, tacit knowledge and expert knowledge. It has become acceptable, for instance, to recognise the similarities as well as differences between lay and expert knowledge. The assumption that researchers possess expert knowledge that is different from and inherently superior to 'citizen science' has been extensively questioned. The conclusion has been widely reached that 'the products of systematic inquiry will not necessarily be better than the presuppositions built into traditional ways of doing things. It is a modernist fallacy to assume otherwise' (Hammersley, 1993: 438).

There has been much – welcome – attention given to diverse arguments for reflective learning and practice in social work, influenced among others by the work of Donald Schön. While Schön (1983) has little to say explicitly about social work, his distinction between reflecting *on* action and reflecting *in* action has entered the vocabulary of social work students. We can call this a strong version of 'internalist' approaches to giving an account of a belief. From this perspective we assume that we can find out what we are justified in believing primarily by a process of learned reflection, that this process is internal to our mind, at least to a significant degree, and it is a process we can consciously access.

None of these assumptions is without controversy. Taking the third assumption, *can* we always access our reflective processes? Common sense knowledge, for example, is often tacit knowledge. When we think of tacit knowledge in professional work, it can be defined as knowledge or abilities that can be passed between experts by personal contact, but cannot be or has not been set out or passed on in formal statements, diagrams, verbal descriptions or instructions for action (Collins, 2001). There are actions, judgements and recognitions that we accomplish spontaneously. We do not have to think about them prior to performance. We are often unaware of having learned to do them. While we may remember once being aware of the understanding necessary for the action, we typically are now unable to describe the knowing that our actions reveal. It has become 'thinking as usual' knowledge: 'Tacit knowledge exists in that time when action is taken that is not understood, when understanding is offered without articulation, and when conclusions are apprehended without an argument' (Altheide and Johnson, 1994: 492). Tacit knowledge is not limited to what goes on in an individual's mind. For example, sociologists of knowledge in practice have explored the ways in which practice is a social form: 'People in different social groups take different things to be certain knowledge but they are not aware of the social basis of their certainties' (Collins, 2001: 110). There is perhaps inevitable tension between tacit, implicit understanding and explicit, planned research-based practice. Evaluation writers Stake and Trumbull may seem to suggest as much when they argue that, 'For practitioners ... formal knowledge is not necessarily a stepping stone to improved practice ... We maintain that practice is guided far more by personal knowings' (1982: 5).

Needless to say, knowledge from reasoning or from experience does not exhaust kinds of knowledge. Thomas Schwandt (1997) distinguishes theoretical knowledge ('knowing that'), craft or skill knowledge ('knowing how'), and practical–moral knowledge ('knowing from'). For Schwandt, when we talk about 'application', something more is intended than the instrumental sense of practicality (as though a social work model of intervention or a finding about effectiveness could be applied like a 'tool') – that is, the more fundamental sense of making something relevant to oneself. This involves a particular kind of knowledge – 'knowing from within or practical–moral knowledge', which 'requires not cleverness in application but understanding' (Schwandt, 1997: 76). 'Practical–moral knowledge aims to actually move people, not simply give them good ideas' (Schwandt, 1997: 81). If being practical means having an impact, then 'practical' *per se* is neutral rather than a good thing. We can have bad as well as good practical research. We cannot determine in advance whether or not social work research will be practical.

'Not cleverness in application but understanding' – Schwandt's phrase opens up the question of expertise in social work, whether different kinds of expertise are reconcilable, and how we recognise expertise in others or perhaps in ourselves.

Take for example the perspectives of service users or policymakers. The phrase 'experts by experience' has, as we considered early in this book, sometimes been used by service users. For example, Beresford says that 'what distinguishes service user knowledge (or knowledges) and what is unique about it, is that it is based on direct experience' (Beresford, 2010a). Having said as much, we should not think of expertise simply or perhaps even primarily about what someone knows. Summerson Carr pursues 'the simple premise that expertise is something people do rather than something people have or hold' (Carr, 2010: 18; c.f. Collins and Evans, 2007). Also, we do not regard different categories of expertise as incommensurable. Beresford concurs. 'Service users are not suggesting that experiential knowledge is the only knowledge that should be valued or that it should be prioritised. What they have repeatedly expressed concerns about is the way that it has long been systematically excluded from social policy discussions and developments and from social research' (Beresford, 2010a).

Practice and research

Where does this leave us with regard to how we should approach the relationship between social work practice and qualitative research? It pays for a moment to listen in to someone talking about how she came to enter social work and research (Example 15.1).

EXAMPLE 15.1 — **Occupational Identity and Commitments**

'I wish I could say that I had burning ideals which brought me to social work, but in fact as a young person, like many others growing up in the 1960's, my choices were very much determined by my family, class and cultural circumstances. For an Australian-born Chinese woman, raised in a lower middle class environment, there was a strong imperative, as for many migrant families, to get a university education. For people of my Chinese heritage, this tended to be in the professions. For people of female gender, this tended to be in teaching or the caring professions. My choice was, in fact, teaching. My mother's preference was social work, so that is where I landed as a young 18 year old ...

I was fortunate to gain a social work teaching post quite early in my career, and thus set about fulfilling my own intellectual interests more closely. In fact, it was in this position that I gained the passion for social work I had originally lacked. I found the intellectual mission of social work to be as challenging as its practical mission ...

I felt many senior social work academics were dismissive of their social work heritage, and often identified with the (male-dominated) established professions/disciplines. For me then, my intellectual endeavor has also been a political one – it is also about carving out a distinctive, valued and legitimate place for social work practice, knowledge and research in the academic world.'

Fook (2012)

We pick up interesting strands in these recollections in a moment. While we do not believe we need aspire to a circumstance in which research (and researchers) and social work (and social workers) coexist in perfect amity, we would want to provoke a relationship between the two of intellectual reciprocity based on egalitarian respect. This is less commonly encountered than might be expected, due in part to an unhelpful – because narrowly conceived – conception of the relationship between research and practice, and an unduly deferential and sub-servient conception of the relationship between social science and social work. In both cases the tendency is to fall back on a rationalist position whereby 'sci-ence' has inherent bragging rights over 'practice'. Practice is always viewed as something that in a responsive way must be 'based on' research; social work is viewed as standing in a beneficiary, suppliant pose towards social science (Shaw, 2012c). The chronic forms of subordination – of 'practice' to 'theory', or 'research' to 'practice' – hide how social science and social work have enjoyed perhaps their more fruitful relationships when each has been at least as much interested in what practice has to say to ideas or research as *vice versa*. 'Knowing' and 'doing', or research and practice, are not two wholly distinct areas that need mechanisms to connect them, but are to a significant degree part and parcel of one another. We have no interest in downplaying analytical knowledge. Reid may have been correct when he concluded that 'flawed research may be better evidence than "low grade" practice wisdom' (Reid, 1994: 476). But we do hope to persuade social workers to abandon the polarised tensions between 'theory' and 'practice'.

Not that particular social work scholars and social scientists necessarily relate that way. Edith Abbott, encountered several times in this book for her role at Chicago early in the previous century, was, like not a few of her successors down the decades, prone to assert a rather dismissive stance towards sociology, in ways that perhaps account in part for the apparent immunity of social work scholar-ship to the creative flourishing of the Chicago School of Sociology. In one place she complained acerbically that

> Some of those whom I am tempted to call our 'near' social science friends – because of course I do not consider such persons scientific – insist that social research in the field of social treatment must be carried on *for* and not *by* social workers whose professional field is under discussion. They even say that their untrained students are more competent to use the records of social agen-cies, to say what these records do or do not mean, than are the social workers themselves … I do not say that every social worker is a gifted researcher. Alas, no – but of how many of our social science colleagues can this be said? (Abbott, 1931: 170–1)

Yet while conversations have sometimes been cut off before even starting, there are some helpful developments within disciplines that draw on qualitative research. First, one general response has been to set qualitative research in a framework of change. Thus Packer takes the position that 'The human sciences are motivated by a fundamental human interest in understanding one another in order to get things done' (Packer, 2011: 293). Romm develops the argument that 'the process of attempting to "know" about the social world already is an intervention in that world which may come to shape its constitution' (Romm, 1995: 137). She says that 'The view that theory is applied in practice and may be tested in that practice, can amount to an unreflected/unreflexive endorsement of a theoretical position' (Romm, 1996: 25). 'One is not just applying "findings", but intervening in the social discussion in a specific way, that is, in a way which authorises particular conceptions' (1995: 145).

A second – and much less often encountered – alternative is to seek to understand and theorise the practice/research relationship. One way of doing this was taken up some time ago by Becker and Carper in developing the idea of 'commitment' as part of an occupational identity and career. It seems a plausible assumption that occupational identity for social work academics and researchers will not be the same as that for practitioners. This simple notion points to an understanding of one reason why research/practice relations in social work are difficult – that separate occupational cultures exist and indeed become established as entailing a set of contrasting commitments.

Occupational identity can be seen as drawing on an occupational title and its associated ideology, commitment to task, and 'the kinds of organizations, and positions within them, in which one's future lies' (Becker and Carper, 1956/1970a: 183). Occupational titles, ideologies, the nature of tasks and kinds of organisations differ greatly for social work practitioners and academic faculty. Finally, 'occupational identities contain an implicit reference to the person's position in the larger society' (ibid., p. 186), for example to social class, social mobility and family. Several aspects of these elements can be read off from Fook's account (Example 15.1) of her entry to social work and research. It seems almost inevitable from this analysis that the expectation that research should have practical application will vary between and within each group.

Moreover, how practice and research are seen in social work should not be seen in a static way. Changes in identity occur *via* various mechanisms. These include 'the development of problem interest and pride in new skills, the acquisition of professional ideology, investment, the internalization of motives, and sponsorship' (Becker and Carper, 1956/1970b: 198). We also need to take into account that such change may produce *conflict* where an individual ends up with either one element of occupational identity incongruent with others or indeed the occupational identity in conflict with e.g., family and wider social identity (Becker and Carper, 1957/1970). Again, one can detect hints of this in Fook's story. We can reasonably hypothesise that making a commitment to engaging with research has costs for a social worker – it may violate expectations of occupational community, and lead to occupation change with risks e.g., abandoning earlier career 'investment.' It may entail costs such as loss of social network connections or status loss. The adjustment in career interests also may entail loss through unfitting oneself for other future positions. Becker takes from Goffman's analysis of face to face interaction the idea that a front – a 'safe face' – developed to support one identity, may be lost by a shift to a new identity. For example in social work, a commitment to advocacy on behalf of service users may be lost in research situations where stances of impartiality may be valued and expected. A further element is that what is valued varies in sub-cultures *within* a practice or academic community (Shaw and Norton, 2007). Finally, in social work the career move to university typically occurs after a lengthy period in practice, where such commitments have become established, and hence pressure to continue to act consistently with those will be considerable (c.f. Becker, 1970d: 285).

We have conceived of qualitative research as entailing a commitment to action and change. We have also emphasised the neglected importance of taking steps to understand and theorise the relationship between practice and research. These do not exhaust ways of enriching the practice/qualitative research relationship, and we return to the theme in Chapter Sixteen where we sketch recent interest in 'public sociology.' For now we look at the mirrored questions of those forms of qualitative research that challenge and are challenged by practice, and forms of practice that challenge and are challenged by qualitative research.

Interchange of forms of research and practice

Seeing 'research' and 'practice' as in some ways similar calls for a further piece of ground clearing. To develop a question we introduced in Chapter Two, is social work practice a form of inquiry – or more specifically of qualitative inquiry? Padgett's view is unequivocal. 'Qualitative research is incompatible with the practice mandate when the practitioner is also the researcher. I can see no satisfactory way to blend the two roles' (Padgett, 1998: 37). This is associated with her scepticism regarding advocacy roles in research. She laments the 'erosion of rigour that comes with the loss of critical distance' (ibid., p. 11). We have said sufficient to show that we believe this position is at best partial. There are three main points that should be made.

First, we reject straightforward conceptions of knowledge and its relationship to theory and action. This is largely a criticism of assumptions of technical rationality in the relation of research and practice. We have said sufficient about this already.

Second, we believe that the relationship between the practice of research and the practice of social work should be treated as an empirical matter rather than primarily a theoretical one (c.f. Kirk and Reid, 2002). It calls for what has been called in a different context, 'a careful and committed empiricism' (Barone, 1992: 145). There is now a growing amount of evidence that sheds light on how practitioners seek to make evaluative sense of their day-to-day practice. Broadly comparable conclusions have been drawn from fieldwork with social workers in American private agencies, the British Probation Service and practitioners with greatly varying amounts and kinds of professional experience (Elks and Kirkhart, 1993; Humphrey and Pease, 1992; Shaw and Shaw, 1997a, 1997b; Sheppard et al., 2000). Sheppard et al.'s work highlights the processes of critical appraisal and hypothesis generation in social work practice.

Third, there is what Riessman has called 'a sympathetic connection' between certain kinds of social work and qualitative kinds of data – 'talk, therapeutic conversation, agency records, narratives about experiences with organisations and macro systems' (Riessman, 1994: ix). The tie is proximate but neither universal, homogenous nor capable of straightforward transfer from one to the other. It requires methodological work, which one of us has described as involving 'counter-colonizing' and 'translating' (Shaw, 2011b). We saw in Chapter Two an interesting example of this by Lang. She considers 'differences in the data-processing strategies of social work practice and qualitative research and … how the two might be integrated' (Lang, 1994: 265). This concern with 'the correspondences and disjunctures between the activities of the qualitative researcher and the social work practitioner' (ibid., p. 266) was led by her concern 'to permit both knowing and doing to be derived from the same data' (ibid., p. 274). She advocates, for instance, a greater readiness on the part of social workers to remain in the inductive pattern of inquiry. In a plausible paradox she argues that 'existing theory must have a more provisional status, a less central locus … in order to open the possibility of theory building' (ibid., p. 276).

We are not convinced by arguments to the effect that research is one thing and practice is another and they should be kept separate. They are not one and the same, but neither can they be neatly disentangled. We talk again about this in relation to the idea of sociological social work below.

Having set out our stall, what do we have in mind when referring to forms of research and practice that are reciprocally challenging? On the part of research we are once more reminded of the stance taken by some, but not all, of the sociologists at Chicago in the 1920s. In exploring such mutually respectful *rapprochements,* there is a sense of unfinished business that emerges from reading Ernest Burgess. The realisation that he actively sought to engage with social work audiences has radical implications for contemporary cross-boundary activity (Burgess, 1923, 1927, 1928, 1930a; c.f. Shaw, 2009). In a rare more recent example, on the uses of ethnography (to which we hinted in an earlier chapter), Bloor argues from reviews of a street ethnography of HIV-related risk behaviour among Glasgow male prostitutes, and comparative ethnographies of eight therapeutic communities, that there are two ways in which ethnography might speak to the practitioner. He suggests that *first*, it may 'model' a service delivery that can be transferred to service providers. For example, 'ethnographic fieldwork, in its protracted and regular contacts with research subjects, has much in common with services outreach work' (Bloor, 1997: 227). From his therapeutic community studies, Bloor suggests the very act of comparative judgement can model helpful service practice. 'Rich description of particular kinds of therapeutic practice can assist practitioners in making evaluative judgements about their own practices' (ibid., p. 229). *Second*, ethnographers may, where appropriate, draw practitioners' attention to practices they think worth dissemination and further consideration. Bloor and McKeganey list seven practices which seemed to them to promote therapy in their original settings (Bloor and McKeganey, 1989), and which they discussed with the practitioners in the therapeutic communities. Incidentally, they point out the corresponding implications for ethnographers, in that

> any attempts to further exploit the evaluative potential of ethnography for a practitioner audience must be paralleled by a growth in ethnographic studies which focus on practitioners' work, not practitioners' conduct. (Bloor and McKeganey, 1989: 210)

Until that time, when 'citizens themselves commend the work of practitioners, then it is not the place of sociologists to murmur of false consciousness and demand resistance to pastoral care' (Bloor, 1997: 235). In a deceptively gentle later piece he concurs with and illustrates that the researcher has an obligation to bring about good. 'It is an obligation we all share in all social settings and that therefore stretches across the entire duration of a research project. And it is not an obligation we can ignore with impunity in the service of some higher calling such as scientific rigour' (Bloor, 2010: 20).

The argument could be developed in other areas. While careful judgement is called for in response to some arguments for participatory forms of data analysis (c.f. Shaw, 1999a: 177–9), such viewpoints do illustrate how research practices may in turn speak to and implicitly question forms of assessment in social work. The same inferences could be explored from work in the areas of deliberative evaluation (House and Howe, 1999), indigenous coding and member validation exercises. Example 15.2 allows us almost to listen in to Whitmore as she worked with young people in their evaluation of a drop-in service in Toronto (Whitmore, 2001).

| **EXAMPLE 15.2** | **Participatory Analysis with Young People** |

How to analyze and interpret all this information from so many different sources? More importantly, how could I fully engage the youth team members and even the broader youth population in such a complex and time consuming process?

I began by explaining the basic data analysis process: figuring out how to summarize and make sense out of mountains of information. This involved summarizing (frequencies) and comparing (cross tabs) for the quantitative data, and summarizing, picking out key words or phrases and developing themes and patterns for the qualitative data. Then we would look at how the parts 'fit' together to make a whole, using the analogy of a puzzle.

After photocopying each data set twice, and putting the original away for safe keeping, we divided into teams (two youth and one of the adults), each taking a data set. Each team read through the data and discussed their sense of the whole and some preliminary impressions of what respondents were saying. They then cut up each survey questionnaire, putting all answers to Q1 in one envelope, Q2 in another envelope, etc. The next step was to take all the answers to each question and sort them into piles of similar answers. Then, they named each pile. After a fairly intensive process, this produced a set of categories. Team members recorded these on flipcharts to share and discuss with the whole team.

> Lots of discussion ensued about what was meant by certain phrases, or how to interpret this or that comment, both in the small sub groups and whole team. These we were often able to clarify by referring back to the original interview or survey. As we compared the responses from each source, a set of overall themes gradually emerged. At the same time, we were developing a list of recommendations for change. It was a slow process, but as the results came into focus, so did our excitement about the possibilities for change at the Drop In. (Whitmore, 2001)

A final example of such reciprocal work between practice and research can be found in the social work thinking about reflective practice (and critical reflection) and qualitative thinking on reflexivity. While the two usually proceed without reference to one another (but see Fook, 2000), the connections are more than linguistic. Reflection is produced when practitioners encounter situations which are problematic and challenge the habits of routine practice. The key impetus in the application of these understandings to researching the development of practice has been the work of Donald Schön (1983) and his analysis of 'the death of technical rationality'.[1] The concept of the reflective practitioner is one in which there is an intimate and interactive relationship between thinking and action so that critical analysis of practice by practitioners becomes a form of action research. Reflection can give rise to a range of foci for research:

- Frame analysis – the making conscious of the assumptive frameworks that practitioners bring to practice, so that they can also consider alternatives that might lead to more effective reflection on action.
- Repertoire building – bringing together examples of good practice that can be used as resources for learning and the development of complex practice (for example, the kind of problem-based or case study learning exemplified by social work educators as part of the Enquiry and Action Learning approach).
- Research on methods of inquiry and over-arching theories – such as the use of instances of practice as ways of eliciting established methods of problem-solving, but also to examine alternative strategies – sometimes using structured methods such as critical incident analysis.
- Research on the process of reflection in action – exploring the process of reflection in order to understand more completely the nature of expertise and how it can be promoted.

While there are difficulties with the ideas of both reflection and reflexivity, it continues to be helpful to explore the value of the bridge between research and practice, offered by characterising the reflective research method, as following four stages in a cyclical process, consisting of experience, reflection, conceptualisation and action.

A potential limitation of the ways we have understood the practice/research interface so far is hinted at in how we have spoken. We have continued to accept 'practice' and 'research' as separate entities. The criticism that such approaches

---

[1] We acknowledge our debt to Nick Gould in the following passage (Shaw and Gould, 2001: 164–68).

are always prone to is that they reinforce dualistic, binary splits between action and thinking, mind and body, and so on. We find ourselves slightly uncomfortable with ways in which 'dualism' tends to be used as a kind of swearword, an intellectual stigma. This inference can be drawn from our outline earlier in this chapter of ways we can theorise different sets of occupational commitments. However, in the remaining part of this chapter we introduce two ways in which the bifurcation of practice and research can and should be to some degree dissolved. First, we draw on a qualitative analysis of practitioner research to consider whether in some instances it may better be seen as a distinct *genre* of social practice. Second, we return to the idea of sociological social work, and sketch an image of qualitative social work.

Practitioners doing research

Society's modes of producing knowledge and interrogating itself appear to be changing in the emerging 'knowledge economy,' and at the same time, public service communities look to research and evaluation knowledge for legitimation. The watchwords of the new knowledge-related practices include evidence-based practice, best practice, science-based practice, knowledge diffusion and management, getting research into practice, and collaboration. Research is becoming increasingly problem oriented and more socially open (Nowotny et al., 2001). A consequence of this is an increasing diversification of research-active actors and agencies. In these contexts Callon and Rabeharisoa (2003) distinguish between the 'confined research' of professional, dedicated research institutions and 'research in the wild' that emerges as concerned social groups, such as patient advocacy groups, begin to engage in knowledge practices that reach the public arena. This has echoes in debates about public sociology that we refer to in Chapter Sixteen. Indeed, Callon and Rabeharisoa suggested that the major distinction is not between those who do and do not have access to research practice but between different modes of organising and practising research. They characterise research in the wild as being marked by direct concern with the outcomes of research, researchers as both its subjects and objects, overlap between the production and appropriation of knowledge, personal stakes and incentives, and a research process that is one of identity formation.

McLeod defines practitioner research as 'research carried out by practitioners for the purpose of advancing their own practice' (McLeod, 1999: 8). This definition has much going for it. First, it includes a statement of purpose, and hence incorporates an implicit criterion for assessing the quality of research. It is not adequate to define practitioner research simply as research carried out by practitioners, without grounding it on a basis of purpose. Second, it makes explicit a practice rationale, rather than broader policy or academic rationales for research. Finally, it includes an implicit model of how practitioner research can be useful.

The idea that practitioners should be researchers is not a new idea. The clinical research model has honourable precedents in the work of doctors who trailed their vaccination methods on themselves, and in the clinical research of psychotherapists. There is also a parallel tradition of the teacher-as-researcher. The advocates of scientific practice in social work also have a history going back two centuries. Charles Loch spent much energy in the late nineteenth century arguing that social work is like science: 'It is science – the science of life – in operation – knowledge doing its perfect work' (quoted in Timms, 1968: 59).

Yet qualitative practitioner research is still often invisible in social work. McLeod describes what is missing as 'knowledge-in-context practitioner research' as against the scientific practitioner model (McLeod, 1999: 13). He identifies the key characteristics of such practitioner research as being '[b]orn out of personal experience and a "need to know"'. Its aim is to produce knowledge that makes a difference to practice, in which the investigator uses reflexive self-awareness throughout to gain access to implicit meanings. It is hence relatively limited in scope. It 'addresses the moral and ethical issues associated with the combination of researcher and practitioner roles, and with a process of inquiry into the experience of perhaps vulnerable or fragile informants'. The researcher retains ownership of the knowledge that is produced, and 'the findings represent subjective, personal knowing as well as objective, impersonal or "factual" knowledge'. The results are written and disseminated in ways consistent with the above principles (ibid., pp. 8, 9). We saw in Chapter Thirteen the work of Elliot, McLeod and others in developing hermeneutic case study designs that are crafted with the intention of providing a deeper exemplification of this form of inquiry that is almost entirely missing from the North American scientific practice movement (Shaw, 2006).

Our present interest in this field is in ways of bringing qualitative analysis to bear on whether it seems plausible to see practitioner research as a form of practice that sits creatively but uncomfortably between the established cultures of research and professional practice. If this argument can be made to hold water, we consequently doubt whether it is helpful to envisage all practitioner research as being either 'inside' or 'outside' practice or research. The understanding that seems best to depict the experience of practitioners is to see them, in their practitioner-as-researcher work, as possessing a sociality outside, or at least on the margins of, *both research and practice* – an uncomfortable but creative marginalisation marked by an identity that is neither research nor practice. We do not want to promote romantic claims that practitioner researchers bring a distinct epistemology or methodology (c.f. Cochran-Smith and Lytle, 1990), but a more provisional and nuanced position. In doing so we draw particularly on a study of networks of practitioner researchers sponsored by their Scottish children's agency (Shaw and Lunt, 2011, 2012).

The evidence is partly derived from the foci of their research. In a previous study of 42 practitioner researchers in Wales the central focus of all but one of the topics was classified as either 'service delivery' (29) or 'direct practice' (12). A very small number was linked in secondary or 'accidental' ways to service user concerns and one was related to training (Shaw and Faulkner, 2006). These research interests are starkly different from those of service users where issues are likely to include coping, identity, information needs, support needs, self-help, carers, women's issues and rights and opportunities. They are also different from qualitative research by university-based social work researchers (c.f. Shaw and Ramatowski, 2013).

But we want to push away from this, to capture the experience and nature of practitioner research in social work. It is familiar to think of research through roughly linear considerations – running vertically down through time. Differently, Shaw and Lunt encountered among the practitioner researchers a horizontal weft of analytic ideas regarding language, memory, moral accountability, ownership, meaning, value, and social work practice, which ran through every phase of their projects. This suggests that the elements of practitioner research have to be understood as interwoven, and bringing together and containing different career/life concerns that otherwise may remain scattered. We summarised these in Chapter One, and rehearse them here.

- Practitioner researchers engage with a language and culture that is strange yet potentially rewarding for practice and research. They find themselves located in a culture that lies between 'practice' and 'research' but is fundamentally shaped by and challenges both.
- Practitioner researchers are typically engaged in negotiating an uncertain world, which is at its heart an effort to learn what it's about.
- The location of practitioner research as lying both within and outside of core professional work poses difficult challenges of moral accountability for work within their practice cultures.
- Involvement in practitioner research stirs reflection on the meaning and value of professional work. For some practitioners this may be overly demanding in the context of the perceived constraints of their core work.
- The nature of practitioner research is something that emerges from the experience, rather than something that prescribes it in advance. It is only in the doing of practitioner research that its critical identity takes shape.

Shaw and Lunt (2012)

In Example 15.3 we overhear practitioners as they struggle to articulate some of the themes just given.

EXAMPLE 15.3 ┤ **Voices from Practitioner Inquiry**

'It's something that I haven't ever done before, so to be able to talk about, undertaking a piece of research or a study in this way, I quite like that, I quite like to be learning new things and we talked before about the language, the process and that was all new to me, and then being able to see it through and I'm quite excited at this point in time about getting it written and completed and that's about a sense of achievement for me.

It's opened up a whole range of things that I've never done before and so I would like to pursue maybe ways of combining the two, if that is possible, in a more proactive way, I don't ... know how even to go about that.

I kind of felt when I was doing the actual interviews that that was set around time that was convenient for children and young people but at other times I could, I felt – you know people – "you're doing your research again". Well it kind of felt like skiving to take too much time off.

I really wanted something for the kids who took part in that, you know this wasn't really necessarily something for me but it was more about the kind of process that they took part in and that feels like that's kind of disappeared and that it has been something more *corporate.*

I just kind of feel that it's almost like as if I'm not sure if I did it. Does that make sense? I kind of feel as if I've gone in, I've done it, I've come back out and it's not really been noticed.

It actually reminded me of how hard that can be sometimes for kids - and I don't pretend to remember this every day – but sometimes actually it allowed me to think, to be free of all the other things, the letters and phone calls and just thinking just generally how hard it must be to buzz the buzzer, to come to this building. That really came through for me when I did the research programme.

It opens up so many possibilities I had not thought of ... I think what I am and what I would like to be are different. I am a practitioner and that is my job, so that's what I have to do and I'm bound by the context of that because that is my income, that is my livelihood. I would like to be more of a researcher. It's opened up a whole range of things that I've never done before and so I would like to pursue maybe ways of combining the two.'

Shaw and Lunt (2012)

A notion: sociological social work

When suggesting what Riessman calls 'a sympathetic connection' between certain kinds of social work and qualitative data, we emphasised that making the connection requires methodological work, which we described as involving 'counter-colonising' and 'translating'. We want to suggest that the term 'sociological social work' will do helpful service here. 'Helpful' because it locates things in a bigger picture. That larger picture would entail a far more comprehensive strategy than we should develop here (c.f. Shaw, forthcoming). However, one element of sociological social work includes the development of a (qualitative) methodological practice (Shaw, 2011b).

Social work, throughout its time, has been tempted by what Burgess long ago described as an 'atomic view of the individual' (Burgess, 1928: 525). While the contrast with a *sociological* social work needs little stating, the fact that we have tracked back nine decades pulls to the surface once again a minor theme of this book, that social work has neglected the archaeology and genealogy essential, among other things, to a grasp of qualitative research. Sociology and social work began 'not as distinct fields but as part of a general impulse for social science that emerged out of the reform activism of the nineteenth century. What we today take for granted as the "natural" division of social science into separate disciplines, including sociology and social work, was a decades-long development out of that original impulse' (Lengermann and Niebrugge, 2007: 63).

Pauline Young's 1930s book on social work interviewing – significantly subtitled 'a sociological analysis' and dedicated to Ernest Burgess 'Teacher and Friend' – is unambiguously a practice text. Yet when she goes inside her vision for social work she speaks in a voice strange to social work, at least until sociological frameworks illuminated British and wider European social work for a period from the 1960s. It is her constant easy movement between what today would be seen as different, even dissonant, literatures that is so striking. Interviewing, she insists, 'is itself a phenomenon in the general field of social interaction, and the problems which it faces have to do for the most part with social situations' (Young, 1935: x). We repeat in Example 15.4 her eight tests of a successful interview that entail assumptions far distant from the psychiatric hegemony of some of the social work schools of her time:

EXAMPLE 15.4 — **Pauline Young on Tests of Social Work Interviewing**

'Have I rendered the interviewee articulate? ...

Have I seen and understood the interviewee's problems and position from his point of view?

Have I succeeded in learning his attitudes? ...

Did I enter his life?

Have I enlarged his social world? ...

Have I invaded the personality of the interviewee or secured his story against his will or his knowledge?

Did I secure important data ...?

Did I learn the cause of his behavior?

Did I impose my views or plans ...?'

Young (1935: 85–6)

It is worth pointing up a general strategy in how Pauline Young is expounding the conjunction between sociology and social work. Whereas the dominant convention, to this day, is for social workers to set out the value of research findings as a practice *resource*, Young talks primarily in terms of the value for practice of qualitative sociological *method*. We find this deeply helpful. As a consequence, 'countercolonising' requires practitioners to act upon research methods rather than simply apply them. 'Translation' raises issues of language and culture, and underscores the interpretative character of the process. Social workers need to develop a dialogic practice, both within social work and with methodologists. For example, Janesick's 'stretching' exercises for qualitative researchers are an example of work based on a learning rationale that provides a fertile basis for professional 'counter-colonising' and 'translating' (Janesick, 1998). The quality of 'methodological practice' will have an emergent, opportunistic and particularistic character. Whitmore's use of visual methods exemplifies this opportunist quality (Whitmore, 2001). To maximise the gains from this process social workers need to avoid remaining, too much, insiders. 'The familiar not only breeds contempt, it breeds darkness as well' (Eisner, 1988: xii). Furthermore, 'methodological practice' will have a participatory and collaborative character.

One of us has developed an extended case for and exemplification of such methodological practice (Shaw, 2011b). We suspect that most social workers when asked to give examples of qualitative methods would list interviews, focus groups, forms of observation and perhaps participatory methods or narrative methods. Yet, given simply in alphabetical order, the range of qualitative methods that are susceptible to translation for qualitative social work includes arts-based research, auto-ethnography, case studies, documents, ethnography, focus groups, interviews, life histories, narrative, participant observation, participatory inquiry, self-observation, simulation and visual methods.

Throughout this chapter we have traversed the landscape of qualitative research and of social work. While there has been a tendency to see these as two separate landscapes, we in fact see these as one landscape, if a rather cluttered one. We have suggested various ways in which it is possible to promote and exemplify a qualitative informed professional practice that is both challenged by, and in turn challenges, qualitative inquiry in its broadest conceptions. In doing so we have tried to exemplify how we think disagreement and debate should be handled – how practitioners and researchers ought to practise difficult conversations. In the final chapter we step back from face to face practice to review the wider consequences of qualitative research in social work.

SIXTEEN
The Consequences of Qualitative Research

In Chapter Fifteen we took the day-to-day practice of social workers as a reference point. In this final chapter we explore more broadly the consequences, career and influences of qualitative research. We immediately will see that, although this is far from straightforward, a qualitative approach to unwrapping the issues enriches our understanding. We open with a general outline of thinking about the 'impacts' of research, and broad ways in which qualitative research is socially relevant. A substantial part of the chapter is about the utilisation of qualitative research, through the lenses of different ways of modelling this process and also through empirical evidence from qualitative studies of research utilisation. This includes the significance of recognising that a qualitative research project has a 'natural life' or career.

We devote space to interesting developments in forms of writing in qualitative social work research and practice. While we have introduced this in a chapter about the consequences of qualitative research, it is a further example of the interweaving of practices and decisions throughout the qualitative research process. We conclude with several reminders regarding the limits of qualitative – indeed all – social research.

In this final chapter we explore the broad consequences, career and influences of qualitative research. These are, however, far from transparent or on the surface. This is due in large part to the outworking of ways in which all social research, even when small scale and unfunded, moves progressively into a wider social arena, where ownership claims are diffuse, and jurisdiction over its identity, uses and direction is shared and sometimes hotly disputed. After giving an anecdote about how a USA evaluation study that showed the lack of success of spelling drills led to the perverse irony of more spelling drills, Cronbach and colleagues remarks,

> Here we glimpse a significant generalisation: whether an evaluation is launched to promote a cause or to report neutrally on events, the measurement procedures and reports can have a wholly unanticipated influence on what happens next. (Cronbach et al., 1980: 27)

This can prove deeply unsettling, especially for someone new to the research experience. In Example 16.1 we hear again the voices of practitioners referred to in Chapter Fifteen (Example 15.3), but here expressing just that sense of disquiet.

EXAMPLE 16.1 — **Who Owns My Research?**

A number of participants experienced a strength of feeling about a project unfinished, and the sense that the wider agency programme had been foregrounded at the expense of their individual projects.

> I really wanted something for the kids who took part in that, you know this wasn't really necessarily something for me but it was more about the kind of process that they took part in and that feels like that's kind of disappeared and that it has been something more *corporate*.

> I ended up somehow presenting my research project three times to a public audience which I'm really, I am not really sure why. I kind of got into this situation where I did it at a staff conference and two other kinds of conferences and that felt like it ... it lost meaning for what it was about.

One consequence of this was a feeling of having muted voices or becoming invisible. Two pointed, almost poignant comments from a focus group will serve.

> I just kind of feel that it's almost like as if I'm not sure if I did it. Does that make sense? I kind of feel as if I've gone in, I've done it, I've come back out and it's not really been noticed.

> It's just I feel as if I've kind of gone in and done it and I go away to Edinburgh and I disappear every so often to do things like this and I come back but you know nobody's really aware of what I've done. And I kind of think that's a shame because it feels like it's been a major piece of work for me – for *me*. I think, I look at and I think I can't believe I actually did that but it feels like it's disappeared into the air somehow.

Shaw and Lunt (2012)

For reasons we develop further, later in the chapter, this suggests that a qualitative understanding of research utilisation deepens a broad conclusion that the inbuilt tendency of accountability models of evaluation to look for culpability when interventions do not deliver the goods is often badly off the mark. Kirk and Reid helpfully criticise 'practitioner-blame' responses that are premised on discussions of science as progress, science as having to struggle against 'organizational banality' and practitioners as subverting research and easily being threatened. They respond:

Omitted from these portraits of research is any suggestion that researchers' motives may extend beyond the good and worthy; that scientists are not strangers to aggrandizement or status seeking; that the research process itself can be subjective and biased, sometimes fatally so; or that researchers may have a personal, as well as a professional, stake in persuading practitioners to value their work. There is little recognition that scientific technology has limits or that what researchers have labored to produce may not be particularly usable. (Kirk and Reid, 2002: 190)

Drawing conclusions from research therefore is never straightforward. Work in the field of evaluation illuminates ways of thinking about this question.

Everyone agrees that information somehow informs decisions, but the relationship is not direct, not simple. Often the more important the decision, the more obscure the relationship seems to be. (House, 1980: 68)

House goes as far as to say that, 'subjected to serious scrutiny, evaluations always appear equivocal' (ibid., p. 72). He argues that evaluations can be no more than acts of persuasion. 'Evaluation persuades rather than convinces, argues rather than demonstrates, is credible rather than certain, is variably accepted rather than compelling' (ibid., p. 73). Researchers have too frequently underplayed the role of judgement and hence of argumentation. This has resulted in an unduly technical, methods-oriented analysis, an over-confidence in quantification, and a tendency to represent knowledge in an impersonal, objectified form. Those who fail to accept the 'compelling' conclusions drawn from evaluation are dismissed as irrational.

There have been several attempts to take a different approach to thinking through the reasoning process involved in constructing justified evaluative arguments. These typically emphasise the complex connection between evidence and conclusions, and commence from the differences between formal and informal reasoning, in ways that reflect the relationships between different kinds of knowledge we referred to in Chapter Fifteen. Whereas formal reasoning assumes a tight fit between the premises and conclusions within an argument, informal logic 'deals with ordinary, everyday language, where rules of inference are less precise and more contextual' (Fournier and Smith, 1993: 317). The key question is whether good but non-deductive reasoning is possible – i.e., reasoning that is not logically formal. 'The consensus among informal logicians is that there can be logically good, but nonvalid reasoning' (Blair, 1995: 73).

This philosophical argument has direct practice implications because much evaluative reasoning is non-deductive. For example, we may sometimes engage in good all-things-considered reasoning, where there are reaons for and against a point of view but where the pros outweigh the cons. The paper by House cited above falls into that category. Also, there has been growing acceptance of the circumstances in which it may be legitimate to reason from factual evidence to evaluative conclusions, where there can be no logical relation of implication for such an argument. Finally, informal logicians have concluded that much reasoning is dialectical. Reasons for a claim are seen as a move in an argument – an attempt to persuade offered as part of an actual or possible exchange between parties who differ.

Utilising qualitative social work research

These arguments should not excuse us from thinking about the consequences of qualitative research. As a way in, we look first at arguments, current at the time of writing, about the impact of research. We then consider the general case that can be made for the relevance of qualitative research, against critics who criticise its alleged weaknesses on that count. Having set those contexts we explore research utilisation.

'Impacts' of research

There have been loud claims as to the importance of planning for and prioritising research impacts. We accept the term for the sake of clarity, though we find the hard, percussive violence of the word uncomfortable. It has come to the fore in the UK perhaps more than most countries, through the twin drivers of an influential national quinquenniel assessment of research quality in universities and the criteria for grant allocation through the main research funding councils. The latter define impact as 'the demonstrable contribution that excellent research makes to society and the economy'.[1] Key aspects of this definition of research impact are that impact must be demonstrable and that one cannot have impact without excellence. The research councils express it as follows:

- 'We aim to achieve research impact across all our activities. This can involve academic impact, economic and societal impact or both:
- *Academic impact* is the demonstrable contribution that excellent social and economic research makes to scientific advances, across and within disciplines, including significant advances in understanding, method, theory and application.
- *Economic and societal impact* is the demonstrable contribution that excellent social and economic research makes to society and the economy, of benefit to individuals, organisations and nations.'

They distinguish the impact of social science research as:

i. *Instrumental*: influencing the development of policy, practice or service provision, shaping legislation, altering behaviour.
ii. *Conceptual*: contributing to the understanding of policy issues, reframing debates.
iii. *Capacity building*: through technical and personal skill development.

Determining the impact of social science research is not a straightforward task. Policy and service development is not a linear process, and decisions are rarely taken on the basis of research evidence alone. This makes it difficult to pin down the role that an individual piece of research has played. In a blog posting, two

---

[1]http://www.rcuk.ac.uk/kei/impacts/Pages/home.aspx

historians criticise what they see as the 'essentially paternalistic, top down approach to assessing whether a project will have value and relevance.'[2]

> In resisting being told how to do things from those above us within the university, research councils and government, we should also be wary of doing the same when we're working with those outside the academy … It is not the exchange of knowledge that is most effective in this case of a history or arts and humanities project, but the use of conversations to question the very foundations of how we practise within a professional sense. (King and Rivett, 2013)

They detect a general paradox that 'the current focus on achieving research impact that offers new possibilities for collaboration, and has allowed us to pursue our individual projects, can also limit innovation … It leads us into a focus on a more one-way form of dissemination from research to public(s) and those parts of partnerships that are measurable in terms of impact.'

Is qualitative research relevant?

Almost thirty years ago Janet Finch (1986) identified three reasons why qualitative research, especially in the policy field, had had little impact. The context of her arguments has dated, and she speaks only of the UK, but the underlying issues remain. First, from the perspectives of governments the utility of statistics and politically neutral 'facts' gives specious attractiveness to statistical and survey-based reports. Second, the Fabian model of the researcher–policymaker relationship had been dominant. Sidney and Beatrice Webb articulated and consolidated a model which became tied in to Labour Party policy, which in turn became the driver for social research. This entailed a social engineering model aimed at social justice through the Fabian belief in the 'inevitability of gradualness' and research which was both partisan and rigorous. This tradition inherited the assumption of politically unproblematic facts which would speak for themselves.

Third, social administration and sociology developed as separate disciplines in Britain (much as social work and sociology developed in institutionally separate locations in the USA). When qualitative methodology permeated sociology it was usually without a policy focus. There resulted an anti-quantitative thrust in sociology, and the empirical tradition within social policy research was one target of this attitude. British sociology came to have a well-nigh universal distaste for social reform. Taken as a whole these points help explain the perceived grounds for the criticism, sometimes heard, that qualitative research yields little of applied value. However, Hammersley (2000a) notes that there is a model of the practice/research relationship behind these criticisms that sits uneasily with

---

[2]http://blogs.lse.ac.uk/impactofsocialsciences/2013/07/08/engaging-people-in-making-history/?pfstyle=wp

the assumptions about the nature of the social world of qualitative research, *viz* an engineering model of providing techniques that work. In Example 16.2 we take Hammersley's argument as a model for thinking about the relevance of qualitative research.

| EXAMPLE 16.2 | **Hammersley on the Relevance of Qualitative Research** |

Hammersley (2000a) notes a model of the practice/research relationship behind criticism of the relevance of qualitative research that sits uneasily with the assumptions about the nature of the social world of qualitative research. The assumption is of an engineering model of providing techniques that work. The engineering model 'implies that research findings have inherent and determinate practical implications' (ibid., p. 393) − or at least should have. What is likely to be a more appropriate understanding is an enlightenment model that treats findings as more uncertain and unpredictable research and as 'providing resources that practitioners can use to make sense of the situations they face and their own behaviour, rather than telling them what is best to do' (ibid., p. 393).

In developing this case he draws on 'the fundamental insights of interactionism and phenomenology; notably, that the social world is complex and processual in character, so that there is a high level of contingency inherent in any course of action' (ibid., p. 400). He borrows from an earlier article to identify five different capacities that qualitative research brings for contributing to practice.

1. Appreciative

'The ability to understand and represent points of view which are often obscured or neglected' (Hammersley, 2000a: 394f). A problem with mainstream approaches to research use is that they are too closely aligned to a 'correctional' perspective, where the perspectives of the policy enforcement community come to dominate. This term suggests a helpful connection between research a generation or more ago on deviance, and how we should address research use in social work.

Qualitative researchers are sometimes accused of taking sides. But 'while partisanship is undoubtedly a danger in appreciative research, it is not automatically built into it' (ibid., p. 395). 'By contrast, partisanship is built into correctionalism, though this often remains invisible to correctionalists, since they identify their own viewpoint with the public good' (ibid., p. 396).

2. Designatory

To 'enable people to think consciously what they have been only half aware of' and thus 'finding the most illuminating language with which to describe people's experiences and actions'. Hence 'by providing a language which conceptualises the tacit knowledge on which teachers rely, qualitative researchers can aid the development of professional knowledge and skills' (Hammersley, 2000a: 396). This can be a way of rendering explicit forms of good practice.

3. Reflective

Holding up a mirror to the people's experience to see what is going on, rather than what is thought to be going on or wished.

(Continued)

(Continued)

4. Immunological

Hammersley here refers to 'the potential for research to immunise us against grandiose schemes of innovation, against raising expectations or setting targets too high; indeed against the "idolatry of the new" more generally' (ibid., p. 398).

5. Corrective

In contrast to point 1, he here refers to the 'correction of macro-theoretical perspectives, rather than of the world' (ibid., p. 399).

In summary, he takes the line that 'qualitative work in particular ... can remind politicians and policymakers that innovation may have unintended and unforeseen consequences; that what is an improvement is not always a matter of consensus (that there are always diverse perspectives); and that problems often cannot be solved by sheer act of will, by putting in more effort, or through trying to make practices "transparent"' (Hammersley, 2000a: 400).

Utilising qualitative research

In this part of the chapter we consider the utilisation of qualitative research first through the lenses of different ways of modelling this process and second through empirical evidence from qualitative studies of research utilisation. In some of what follows we are indebted to research and writing carried out in the evaluation community in the USA a generation or more ago, and which has rarely been surpassed.

Models of research utilisation

Hammersley made a distinction between engineering models of research use and enlightenment models. This distinction was developed in the 1970s through the work of Carol Weiss in the USA and Martin Bulmer in the UK. The conventional rational assumption about the utilisation of research was that research led to knowledge, which in turn provided a basis for action of an instrumental, social engineering kind. The historical roots of this view are deep (Finch, 1986). Weiss was not the first to question the legitimacy of this view, but her significance lies in the empirical underpinnings, explanatory cogency, and plausibility that she conveys. With her colleagues she interviewed 155 senior officials in federal, state and local mental health agencies. Officials and staff used research to provide information about service needs, evidence about what works, and to keep up with the field. However, it was also used as a ritualistic overlay, to legitimise positions, and to provide personal assurance that a position held was the correct one. At a broader conceptual level it helped officials make sense of the world. For all these purposes, 'It was one source among many, and not usually powerful enough to drive the decision process' (Weiss, 1980: 390; c.f. Patton, 1988; Weiss, 1988). As for direct utilisation,

> Instrumental use seems in fact to be rare, particularly when the issues are com-
> plex, the consequences are uncertain, and a multitude of actors are engaged in
> the decision-making process, i.e., in the making of policy. (Weiss, 1980: 397)

Research use was also reflected in officials' views of the decision-making process. Decisions were perceived to be fragmented both vertically and horizon-
tally within organisations, and to be the result of a series of gradual and
amorphous steps. Therefore, 'a salient reason why they do not report the use of
research for specific decisions is that many of them *do not believe that they make
decisions*' (ibid., p. 398). Hence the title of her paper – 'Knowledge Creep and
Decision Accretion'. This provided the basis for her argument that enlightenment rather than instrumental action represents the characteristic route for
research use.

Writing in that same period of fruitful thinking about research utilisation,
Bulmer added the idea of empirical utilisation, which entails 'a conception of
social research involving the production of accurate data – meticulous, precise,
generalisable – in which the data themselves constitute an end of the research'
(Bulmer, 1982: 31). This echoes Finch's reference to the Fabian research tradition in the UK where the task of social research is to produce facts for use.
Bulmer associated this with the tradition leading back through Peter Townsend
and David Donnison to Richard Titmuss and then to Rowntree and Booth.

A more elaborated array of kinds of uses, and one geared more to social work
practice, has been given by Kirk and Reid (2002), when they distinguish instrumental, enlightenment, conceptual, persuasive, and methodological utilisation,
as well as indirect use mediated through, for example, research-based models.
We have seen examples of methodological use and indirect use in the previous
chapter when we discussed qualitative social work and Bloor's suggestions for
how ethnography might model intervention.

Walter et al. (2004) set their approach to research use in an organisational
context, and identified three different ways of thinking about and developing the
use of research in social work and social care. They insist they are not mutually
exclusive. The *research-based practitioner* is about the individual having a personal commitment to use research by keeping up to date with research and
applying it to practice. The capacity of practitioners and more senior staff to
access and interpret research is one barrier to this model. In the *embedded
research model* the responsibility lies with policymakers and managers to embed
research in the systems and processes of service delivery, through standards and
procedures. Finally, the *organisational excellence model* relies on social work
organisations developing a research-minded culture. This includes creating partnerships with local universities to adapt research findings to local contexts and
encourage a learning culture in agencies.

Each one of these approaches to research utilisation shares the assumption
that research utilisation should not be viewed as a one-way, end of project, act
of 'dissemination' but one of active utilisation. In Example 16.3 Cronbach turns
this into a prescription for good research practice.

EXAMPLE 16.3	Lee Cronbach on Tellable Stories

The evaluator faces a mild paradox. 'All research strives to reduce reality to a tellable story', but 'thorough study of a social problem makes it seem more complicated' (Cronbach et al., 1980: 184). Their resolution of this paradox lies in the aphorism that comprehensive examination does not equal exhaustive reporting. 'When an avalanche of words and tables descends, everyone in its path dodges' (ibid., p. 186).

The main criterion is the extent to which relevant people learn from the evaluator's communications. Therefore the evaluator should seek constant opportunity to communicate with the policy shaping community throughout the research. They believe that 'much of the most significant communication is informal, not all of it is deliberate, and some of the largest effects are indirect' (ibid., p. 174). Their recommendations are:

- Be around.
- Talk briefly and often.
- Tell stories. Always be prepared with a stock of anecdotes regarding the evaluation.
- Talk to the manager's sources.
- Use multiple models of presentation.
- Provide publicly defensible justifications for any recommended programme changes. These will be very different from scientific arguments.

Cronbach is strongly opposed to holding on until all the data is in and conclusions are firm. Influence and precision will be in constant tension, and if in doubt we should always go for influence. Live, informal, quick overviews, responsiveness to questions, the use of film and sound clips, and personal appearances, are the stuff of influence. The final report thus acts as an archival document. 'The impotence that comes with delay ... can be a greater cost than the consequences of misjudgement.'

Cronbach et al. (1980: 179)

From what we have seen so far we can deduce two working rules about research utilisation. First, use is premised on assumptions about research audiences. Second, use stems from assumptions about the purpose of research. We glance in the following paragraphs at evidence from qualitative studies of utilisation, where these two rules are further grounded and elaborated.

What do we know about utilisation?

Weiss' framework was based on empirical work. Kirk and Reid observe to the same effect that '[t]he bottom line for research utilization is what actually happens in the field among practitioners' (Kirk and Reid, 2002: 194). In a mixed qualitative study of social work research in British universities, Shaw and Norton came across statements by universities that aspired to capture the essence of their approach to social work research (Shaw and Norton, 2007). Here are two examples:

Our raison d'être (is) to improve policies and services for service users and carers ... provide products that will help to translate research findings into policy and practice. (University I)

> [Our approach] brings together conceptual, methodological and theoretical creativity and innovation but in a way which is empirical and has clear practice implications … Our long-standing, overall philosophy has been to encourage an approach to social work research which makes a significant contribution to *theory, policy* and *practice* and which is *multidisciplinary* in nature. (University II)

The second university is making what looks much more like a *discipline* claim, unlike the first. University I's gaze is outward to the world of policies and services. It is more obviously 'applied', whereas University II is more apparently interested in the world of ideas.

When individuals spoke to the researchers regarding their own research there was a pervasive cluster of differences – between *rigour* and *relevance, inner science* and *outer science* criteria, *practice* and *theory*. Compare, for example, these two contrasting remarks:

> If I haven't worked out how what I want to say … relates to something that I would see as a sort of improvement in human well-being then I wouldn't write the article – full stop.

> If it's methodologically poor research that has a large impact then I would judge it as not useful because it's actually influenced moves in the wrong direction. It's added to confusion and misunderstanding and bad policy rather than the reverse.

For some, academic rigour holds greatest importance, while to others it is the extent to which the work addresses and offers solutions to current issues in social work, and academic rigour is secondary. Some prioritise research that develops theory, while others prioritise a direct link with practice. The involvement of users as partners and co-producers in the research process was often seen as the litmus test of distinctively social work research.

> … It was the methodology because it wasn't just about writing, it was about actually involving people in what the writing was going to say.

However, the standing of this as a fundamental mark of quality was not agreed within the social work community.

> I think we're beginning to make user involvement a kind of, a test for quality and I think that is extremely poor methodology. I think what you have to do, just as with anything else, is justify user involvement as part of the methodology.

This was one of the areas where deep-seated debates emerged within the study, ranging from those who would probably place 'value-for-people' and 'value-for-use' above strictly epistemological and knowledge-building standards, to those who believe that such extrinsic, outer-science quality criteria may not always be appropriate criteria for a particular piece of research. Our own position is that 'inner' and 'outer' science criteria of use and quality are both indispensable, and they should be brought to bear on any given research project or output.

We remarked at the opening of this chapter that research projects have a life and a career that is not in the control of the researcher. 'Once a manuscript is released and goes public ... the meanings writers may think they have frozen into print may melt before the eyes of active readers' (van Maanen, 2011: 25). Judgements of quality and usefulness are never final – they are always 'in-the-making'. It has become almost a mundane commonplace to talk of narrativity in regard to some kinds of research data, but in this case it is central to understanding the quality and usefulness of social work research. The participants in the series of workshops, group interviews, case studies and interviews within this study crafted and hammered out accounts and stories, such that the data was replete with them. As people tell stories of the quality of their and others' research, those to whom they are told are more than neutral hearers. They are audience and become characters in their stories (Clandinin and Connelly, 1994). Focus group members shared and actively honed estimations of quality in the research of others, including on occasion others present in the group. All this suggests the dynamic character of quality, such that 'we never establish quality once and for all' (Stake and Schwandt, 2006: 405).

Writing qualitative research

'The ethnographer "inscribes" social discourse; he writes it down. In so doing he turns it from a passing event, which exists only in its own moment of occurrence, into an account, which exists in its inscriptions and can be reconsulted' (Geertz, 1973: 20). In doing so one is trying to 'rescue the "said" of such discourse from its perishing occasions and fix it in perusable terms' (ibid., p. 20). Writing is interwoven with every moment of qualitative research. Writing is not something that happens as a final account of analysis but happens throughout, through fieldnotes, transcriptions and memos. 'Fieldwork is a site for identity work for the researcher ... [T]his identity work is achieved through the textual products of ethnography' (Coffey, 1999: 115). Fieldnotes are 'the textual place where we, at least privately, acknowledge our presence and conscience.' They are 'a way of documenting our personal progress' (ibid., p. 120). 'Fixing' involves inscribing events, for 'human action involves *events* that are fleeting but are fixed in everyday life, in official records and other kinds of registration' (Packer, 2011: 223). As a consequence 'Research ... includes not only the interaction between the researcher and the issue, but also the interaction between the researchers and their potential readers' (Flick, 2006: 406).

The written form of the previous paragraph conveys familiar hallmarks of academic writing, especially through citing respected sources. Despite occasional departures, we have written much of this book in that familiar writing voice. In these last few pages we consider what, with little exaggeration, may be referred to as a revolution in approaches to social science writing, especially by qualitative writers. This is an area where social work has been active, perhaps most frequently in the USA. Stanley Witkin, during the tenure of his editorship of the journal *Social Work* in the opening years of the century, was most prominent through his editorials and invited articles. The journal *Qualitative Social Work* has provided a prominent platform for innovative forms of writing. Individual scholars such as Karen Staller have ventured fruitfully into the field. For example, she creatively challenges conventions of journal writing in an article that takes the form of an exchange between author, editors and reviewers (Staller, 2007) and she reflects on that and other experiences in Chapter Three (Example 3.2).

Various points need making by way of preamble. First, a self-conscious concern with writing qualitative research is not new. We noted earlier in the book Pauline Young's comments on her relationship with the sociologist Robert Park in her 'Dr. Robert Park as a Teacher.' For example, 'He insisted that his students carefully examine each sentence and see if "the words march along". He would say "*You* are not writing for professors; train yourself to write for the general public."' Second, a significant element in more recent developments has been the mutual influence between ethnography and aesthetics (Atkinson, 2013). But we should not think this is a question of introducing rhetoric into writing where it previously did not exist. 'Style is just as much a matter of choice when the experimentalist writes in a self-conscious, hyper-realistic, attention-grabbing dots-and-dashes fashion – where, for instance, ellipses are used to simulate (and stimulate) the effect of a … missed heartbeat – as when the traditionalist falls back on the neutral pale-beige, just-the-facts fashion of scientific reporting' (van Maanen, 2011: 5). Third, writing is usually not a choice between one and another kind. Tales of one sort are often nested in tales of another sort. Finally, 'once a manuscript is released and goes public … the meanings writers may think they have frozen into print may melt before the eyes of active readers' and 'different categories of readers will display systematic differences in their perceptions and interpretations of the same writing' (van Maanen, 2011: 25).

What is it that is being eschewed in such developments? There are *genres* of writing – loose sets of criteria for a category of composition. The term is often used to categorise literature and speech, but is also used for any other form of art or utterance, and relates to the history of ideas about rhetoric. Classic distinctions of *genre* in literature are those between prose, drama and poetry. When applied to academic writing it includes recognition of ways it is associated with a tradition and a community, with a distinctive style, and forms of expression and vocabulary. The characteristics of this distinctive style, when evident in mainstream academic writing include exactness, clear linkages between different aspects of what is written, seriousness of tone, and transparency, for example through the notion of replicability.

Perhaps the most influential characterisation of forms of writing is van Maanen's *Tales of the Field* (van Maanen, 2011). His distinction between realist and confessional tales has entered the literature, although these are but two of seven distinct *genres* he identifies. 'Of all the ethnographic forms … realist tales push most firmly for the authenticity of the cultural representations conveyed by the text' (ibid., p. 45). They are marked by authorial invisibility – 'a studied neutrality characterizes the realist tale' (ibid., p. 47). They also have a documentary style of minute detail, yet in qualitative writing one that may suggest presence. Realist texts convey interpretive omnipotence. But however interpretive authority is achieved '[r]ealist tales are not multivocal texts where an event is given meaning first one way, then another, and then still another. Rather a realist tale offers one meaning and culls its facts carefully to support that reading' (ibid., p. 52f.). Example 16.4 offers an example of such documentary style that also conveys something of authorial presence through extracts from Edith Abbott's housing research in 1930s Chicago.

EXAMPLE 16.4 — **Realist Writing in 1930s Chicago**

There are graphic descriptions of the different chosen neighbourhoods. For example, 'To get a picture of a cross-section of the West Side, it is easy to follow one of the north and south streets and go over the bridge over the river's "south branch" straight ahead to the bridge over the "north branch"' (Abbott, 1936: 77). Of the Old Lumber Yards district she says 'Dilapidation was everywhere. The cellars, even the first floors, were damp because of the grading up of streets and alleys from three to seven feet above the level of the yards. The walls of the cellars and the floors of the first stories were often decayed and musty, with the water draining down about the foundations ... Floors were warped and uncertain, plumbing generally precarious ... window panes broken or entirely gone, doors loose and broken, plaster caked and grimy, woodwork splintered and long unvarnished' (ibid., p. 80).

It is apparent from this that she sometimes talks as if she is walking the districts as when she says '[r]eturning to the busy Halsted Street thoroughfare, one came to ...' (ibid., p. 85), and '[l]eaving the Lithuanian colony a journey was made around to the back of the great Stock Yards area ... the area usually referred to as "back of the yards", where very congested and insanitary conditions are still to be found.' This yields a frequent sense of presence, as in 'Looking down the narrow passageways, numerous frame shacks are to be seen on the rear of the lots' (ibid., p. 130).

Abbott (1936)

Confessional tales are marked by personalised authority where 'The omnipotent tone of realism gives way to the modest, unassuming style of one struggling to piece together something reasonably coherent out of displays of initial disorder, doubt and difficulty' (van Maanen, 2011: 75). 'The attitude conveyed is one of tacking back and forth between an insider's passionate perspective and an outsider's dispassionate one' (ibid., p. 77). 'Confessional accounts … can be understood as attempts to deal with problems of trust … If only the writer were able to confess all … sufficient information and empathy will be generated to believe his or her story' (Seale, 1999: 165). 'The implied story line of many a confessional tale is that of a fieldworker and a culture finding each other and, despite some initial spats and misunderstandings, in the end, making a match' (van Maanen, 2011: 79). Example 16.5 conveys this last point through Elizabeth Whitmore's account of participatory analysis with young people in Toronto (Whitmore, 2001).

EXAMPLE 16.5	A Confessional Account of Participatory Writing

We first listed all the different ways that we could report what we had learned. These ranged from the usual written report to interactive presentations with the Drop In service users, and seminars and demonstrations to other audiences.

It was totally unrealistic to expect the youth, most of whom had not finished high school, to write a detailed formal report (needed for the agency Board and also for the funders). So how to engage the youth in drafting the written report, if I was to do the actual writing? I had faced this dilemma before ... and this time, I wanted to devise a process that would result in real ownership of the product by everyone on the team.

Team members began by brainstorming the various parts of the report and then bit by bit, the content – all recorded on flipcharts, of course. I then drafted these into a narrative, which the group then went over (and over and over ...) One youth, after proclaiming that she did not read and this was boring anyway, pointed out a number of misspelled words and factual errors in one of the drafts – "This is not spelled right. That is wrong!" We did eight drafts of the report and in the end, the youth fully understood and identified with the results. The youth themselves produced as many pieces of the report as possible – cover, index, graphics, charts and tables, appendices. They were deservedly very proud of the final product.

We also did a number of presentations, in which the youth took the lead. We spent quite a bit of time preparing for the first one – a public presentation about our process to the local social work professional association – which got an enthusiastic response. Thereafter, their stage jitters gradually diminished with each one. They presented to the agency board, to the AGM, did a workshop with the wider population of Drop In service users and were guest speakers at a university seminar.

Perhaps the most interesting reporting mechanism was 'The Kit' – a guide for other youth evaluators interested in how to do their own evaluations. 'The Kit' was designed and produced entirely by the youth team members, who collectively brainstormed the contents – 'what we did', 'how we did it' and 'tips' (lessons learned) – and then divided up the work. It is the youths' representation of what they learned; its style, content and graphics speak to young people. The result is a boisterous, colourful guide, full of life, energy and humour.

Whitmore (2001)

Not all alternatives to realist writing take the form of experimental writing forms. And some experimental writing forms have a clear realist intent. Over half a century ago C. Wright Mills was arguing for what he called sociological poetry. 'It is a style of experience and expression that reports social facts and at the same time reveals their human meanings. As a reading experience, it stands somewhere between the thick facts and thin meanings of the ordinary sociological monograph and those art forms which in their attempts at meaningful reach do away with the facts, which they consider as anyway merely an excuse for imaginative construction' (Mills, 2008: 34). Bloor's 'Rime of the Globalised Mariner' is a pointed use of one manifestation of the form. He borrows the form and metre of Coleridge's *Rime of the Ancient Mariner* to describe and analyse the social situation of the globalised mariner. 'The paper aims to be a piece of "public sociology" and (in seeking to appeal in as vivid a manner as possible) is written in a style that

Wright Mills called "sociological poetry"' (Bloor, 2013: 30). 'The narrative covers deficiencies in seafarer training, reductions in crew numbers, the consequent long hours and seafarer fatigue, and the failure of global governance of the industry' (ibid., p. 30). Example 16.6 is an extract from the text.

EXAMPLE 16.6 | **The Rime of the Globalised Mariner – Sociological Poetry**

'I had no wish to work on ships –
Filipinos know it's hard –
Mouths were many, jobs were scarce,
From birth my life was marr'd.

The Mariner telleth of early hardships and how he and his parents were cheated by the maritime colleges and the crewing agents.

'From green island homes we travel,
As mariner, nurse, or maid,
And remit to our loved ones
The pittance we get paid.

'Father scraped up money
For training college fees –
A scam of the local senator,
Whose throat I'd gladly seize.

Filipino maritime training institutions are often controlled by persons with powerful political connections.

'The college had no equipment,
Just endless, pointless drill,
No qualifications either –
The news made my father ill.

The academic training often follows a military model and is of poor quality. And it does not qualify cadets for certificates of seafarer competency without additional practical experience – 'sea time'. Most colleges fail to arrange 'sea time' for their cadets.

Extract from Bloor, 2013

Bloor's allusion to public sociology makes a point link. Relationships between professions, the academy and the world have been the focus of a debate that began in sociology in the first decade of the century regarding 'public sociology'. Michael Burawoy set it going with his 2004 presidential address to the American Sociological Association (Burawoy, 2005). Central to his argument, he laments an 'antagonistic interdependence among four types of knowledge: professional, critical, policy, and public' (ibid., p. 4. By 'professional' he here means 'profession' as discipline science work). 'Public sociology brings sociology into a conversation with publics, understood as people who are themselves involved in conversation' (ibid., p. 7). This includes an '*organic public sociology* in which the sociologist works in close connection with a visible, thick, active, local and often counterpublic' (ibid., p. 7), where sociologists are working with 'a labor movement, neighborhood associations, communities of faith, immigrant rights groups, human rights organizations.' 'Between the organic public sociologist and a public is a dialogue, a process of mutual education' (ibid., p. 8).

This far from exhausts the range of writing forms that has currency. We noted poetic forms in narrative research in Chapter Twelve, and Witkin's remarks about 'living a constructionist life' in Chapter Three. Other instances range from the relatively simple switch to second person speech that directly addresses someone (e.g., Shaw, 2013) to writing forms that reflect space and movement in the organisation of the text on the page (Martin, 2007).

We should not think of writing *genres* as unchanging. For example, the use of the first person singular and the active voice have both become more acceptable within mainstream qualitative writing. Furthermore, even within a single piece of traditional academic writing there are different forms, for example between the 'factual' and the 'theoretical.' In addition, we should not overdo the distinction between how traditional sciences are done and written about and how the human sciences are done and written about. Interviewed for the BBC, Roald Hoffman, the theoretical chemist, remarked 'The language of science is incredibly interesting; it's a natural language under strain' (Wolpert and Richards, 1997: 24). He said of chemistry, 'I love it. I like the subject, its position in between, its compromise between simplicity and complexity ... [B]eauty is in the reality of what's out there, residing at the tense edge where simplicity and complexity contend' (ibid., pp. 20, 21).

There has been tendency to treat van Maanen's account in romantic Orwellian terms – realist tales bad, confessional tales good. But he insists that 'it is important not to judge realist tales too harshly ... Realist ethnography has a long and by-and-large worthy pedigree' (van Maanen, 2011: 54). He warns against denying the 'matters covered in a classic realist tale because one prefers a lurid confessional or breezy impressionist tale', and insists 'we need more not fewer ways to tell of culture' (ibid., p. 140). *All* writing is performative, but 'experimental writing cannot be a substitute for a clear sense of *why* one conducts ethnographic fieldwork and *who* one writes for' (Packer, 2011: 239). Atkinson is sharply critical of some forms of ethnographic writing including autoethnography and 'so-called ethnographic fiction'. 'It is too facile, stylistically speaking. It includes far too much emphasis on the feelings and personal experiences of the actual or implied narrator' (Atkinson, 2013: 32). Mills was speaking of a particular book but his words perhaps can be extended slightly when he calls for 'the self-discipline of the craftsman of experience' and regrets authors' writing that 'often gets in the way of what he would show you' (Mills, 2008: 35).

Uses and limits of qualitative research

Where does this leave us? In the first place, we should not be precious about our theories. Too much time spent discussing theory is paralysing. We need to defend social work against attacks, and hence need those people who pursue 'philosophical and methodological worry as a Profession' (Becker, 1993: 226). But while we still have to do theoretical work, it should not be regarded a higher form of intellectual activity and thus 'especially virtuous' (ibid., p. 221). There are some circumstances where theory has been overemphasised. For example, emancipatory researchers, especially some of those whose work is underpinned by neo-Marxism, should not feel too aggrieved by Lather's vigorous insider warnings against theoretical imperialism – the 'circle where theory is reinforced by experience conditioned by theory' (Lather, 1986b: 261). 'Theory is too often used to protect us from the awesome complexity of the world' and

> In the name of emancipation, researchers impose meanings on situations rather than constructing meaning through negotiation with research participants. (Ibid., pp. 267, 265)

Too often, 'one is left with the impression that the research conducted provides empirical specificities for more general, *a priori* theories' (Lather, 1986a: 76). One of van Maanen's 'tales' added latterly is 'formal tales' told in order to build, test and analyse theory and where 'theory is sovereign'. He cautions that 'there is more than a little theology involved whenever people are said to be acting on the basis of unseen and unknown forces.' Hence 'fieldworkers must tread softly when telling formal tales, for in the end, all representations are contestable. Formal tales alone cannot protect us from the wind' (van Maanen, 2011: 131). However, while it has to be recognised that theory 'constrains practice in certain ways (by outlining options for appropriate action) ... at a certain point theoretical "knowledge" (however fragile) must be brought to bear in order that action may ensue' (Romm, 1995: 164).

Lather's remarks point to our second conclusion – that at their worst 'scientific concepts can reinforce a vast array of dangerous or hateful political and moral agendas' (Jacob, 1992: 495). Hence, 'It is incumbent on the knower to be aware continually of partiality, and it is incumbent on the knower as intervener to attempt to instil such an awareness in the consciousness of participants (by requiring them to listen to the position of "the enemy")' (Romm, 1995: 163) and being able to hear and remember bad news.

Third, we should not retreat into the bunker to protect ourselves against the demand that theory and critique must go hand in hand. We have seen that when theory/practice relationships are viewed as the failure of practitioners to apply the theories developed by those who are engaged in empirical and theoretical pursuits, this distorts reality. To regard theory and practice problems as breakdowns in communication that afflict practitioners is to fail to recognise that practical problems of this kind occur in the course of any theoretical undertaking. To assume that they can somehow be identified and tackled in theory and then 'applied' in practice tends to conceal how they are generated out of practice. As Parton reminds us, practice informs the development of theory as much as, if not more than, *vice versa* (Parton, 2000).

Fourth, we should concur with Hall in the predecessor volume to this book, when he questions the idea that research is either 'academic' or 'applied'. He remarks that 'one can see what is meant by this distinction … but all social research, inasmuch as it is about and results from an engagement with the social world, is "applied"' (Hall, 2001: 58).

Finally, our vision of the relationship between social work and research must never be utopian – but it must always be radical. It may have been Einstein who said that '[t]hings should be made as simple as possible, but not any simpler'. Qualitative theory and research should persistently entice us with glimpses of the possibility of seeing the world differently. The impact of theory will perhaps be greatest where the ideas have sufficient 'fit' with the issues professionals encounter on an everyday basis, while at the same time providing an alternative framework within which to understand these issues.

In our consideration of generalisation in qualitative research we have implicitly questioned strong versions of relativism in social research. It is true that 'in effect you have to be a relativist if you are going to study any historical moment in science' (Jacob, 1992: 500). But this willing suspension of belief as an attitude of mind should not be confused with relativism – that combination of 'intuitionism and alchemy' (Geertz, 1973: 30).

> Science can be socially framed, possess political meaning, and also occasionally be sufficiently true, or less false, in such a way that we cherish its findings. The challenge comes in trying to understand how knowledge worth preserving occurs in time, possesses deep social relations, and can also be progressive … and seen to be worthy of preservation. (Jacob, 1992: 501)

Taking it further

Reread Example 16.2 on the relevance of qualitative research.
Working in pairs or small groups, and gaining access to the journal *Qualitative Social Work*, explore how far you can go in matching examples of social work research to each of Hammersley's five 'capacities' for relevance and use. For example, why do you think we identify the following as a good example of the 'designatory' capacity of qualitative research?

Neander, K. and Skott, C. (2006) 'Important meetings with important persons: Narratives from families facing adversity and their key figures', *Qualitative Social Work*, 5(3): 295–311.

Neander, K. and Skott, C. (2008) 'Bridging the gap – the co-creation of a therapeutic process: Reflections by parents and professionals on their shared experiences of early childhood interventions', *Qualitative Social Work*, 7(3): 289–309.

As you undertake this work keep brief notes of different writing *genres* that you notice within the journal.

References

Archives

University of Chicago, Special Collections Research Center. Chicago School of Civics and Philanthropy. Records Box 2 Folder 7. Preliminary Report of the Committee Appointed by the Trustees of the Chicago School of Civics and Philanthropy, 15, April 1914.

University of Chicago, Special Collections Research Center. Department of Sociology. Interviews with Graduate Students of the 1920s and 1930s.

University of Chicago, Special Collections Research Center. Ernest Burgess papers.

University of Chicago, Special Collections Research Center. Queen, S.A. (nd) *Sixty Years of American Sociology as Viewed by a Participant Observer*. Stuart Alfred Queen. Papers.

University of Chicago, Special Collections Research Center. Robert Ezra Park. Collection.

University of Chicago, Special Collections Research Center. Social Science Research Committee University of Chicago. Department of Economics. Records, 1912–1961.

References

Abbott, A. (1999) *Department and Discipline: Chicago Sociology at One Hundred*. Chicago: University of Chicago Press.

Abbott, E.A. (1931) *Social Welfare and Professional Education*. Chicago: University of Chicago Press.

Abbott, E.A. (1936) *The Tenements of Chicago, 1908–1935*. Assisted by Sophonisba P. Breckinridge, and other associates in the School of Social Service Administration of the University of Chicago. Chicago: University of Chicago Press.

Abelson, J., Forest, P., Eyles, J., Smith, P., Martin, E. and Gauvin, F. (2003) 'Deliberations about deliberative methods: Issues in the design and evaluation of public participation processes', *Social Science and Medicine*, 57(2): 239–251.

Abrams, P. (1984) 'Evaluating soft findings: Some problems of measuring informal care', *Research, Policy and Planning*, 2(2): 1–8.

Adam, B. (1990) *Time and Social Theory*. Cambridge: Polity Press.

Adam, B. (1995) *Timewatch: The Social Analysis of Time*. Cambridge: Polity Press.

Adam, B. (2004) *Time*. Cambridge: Polity Press.

Adler, P.A. and Adler, P. (2002) 'Do university lawyers and the police define research values?', in W.C. van den Hoonaard (ed.), *Walking the Tightrope: Ethical Issues for Qualitative Researchers*. Toronto: University of Toronto Press.

Ahmed, S. (2006) *Queer Phenomenology*. Durham, NC: Duke University Press.

Al-Janabi, H., Coast, J. and Flynn, T.N. (2008) 'What do people value when they provide unpaid care for an older person? A meta-ethnography with interview follow-up', *Social Science and Medicine*, 67(1): 111–121.

Allet, N., Keightley, E. and Pickering, M. (2011) 'Using self-interviews to research memory', Realities toolkit #16, Morgan Centre for the Study of Relationships and Personal Life, University of Manchester. Available at: http://www.socialsciences.manchester. ac.uk/morgancentre/realities/index.html.

Al-Makhamreh, S.S. and Lewando-Hundt, G. (2008) 'Researching "at home" as an insider/outsider: Gender and culture in an ethnographic study of social work practice in an Arab society', *Qualitative Social Work*, 7(1): 9–23.

Alston, M. and Bowles, W. (2003) *Research for Social Workers*, 2nd edn. London: Routledge.

Altheide, D. and Johnson, J. (1994) 'Criteria for assessing interpretative validity in qualitative research'. in N.K. Denzin and Y.S. Lincoln (eds), *Handbook of Qualitative Research*, Newbury Park: Sage.

Andrews, M., Squire, C. and Tamboukou, M. (eds) (2008) *Doing Narrative Research*. London: SAGE Publications.

Ashman, L.L.M. and Duggan, L. (2009) 'Interventions for learning disabled sex offenders', *Cochrane Database of Systematic Reviews*, Issue 1. Art. No.: CD003682. DOI: 10.1002/14651858.CD003682.pub2.

Atkins, S., Lewin, S., Smith, H., Engel, M., Fretheim, A. and Volmink, J. (2008) 'Conducting a meta-ethnography of qualitative literature: Lessons learnt', *BMC Medical Research Methodology*, 8: 21.

Atkinson, D. (2005) 'Research as social work: Participatory research in learning disability', *British Journal of Social Work*, 35(4): 425–434.

Atkinson, P. (2009) 'Ethics and ethnography', *21st Century Society*, 4(1): 17–30.

Atkinson, P. (2013) 'Ethnographic writing, the Avant Garde and a failure of nerve', *International Review of Qualitative Research*, 6(1): 19–35.

Atkinson, P. and Delamont, S. (1993) 'Bread and dreams or bread and circuses? A critique of case study research in evaluation', in M. Hammersley (ed.), *Controversies in the Classroom*. Buckingham: Open University Press.

Atkinson, P. and Delamont, S. (2006) 'Editors' introduction: Narratives, lives, performances', in P. Atkinson and S. Delamont (eds), *Narrative Methods, Volume 1: Sage Benchmarks in Social Research Methods*. London: SAGE Publications.

Atkinson, P., Coffey, A., Delamont, S., Lofland, J. and Lofland, L. (eds) (2001) 'Editorial introduction', *Handbook of Ethnography*. London: SAGE Publications.

Attree, P.M. (2004) 'Growing up in disadvantage: A systematic review of qualitative evidence', *Child: Care, Health and Development*, 30(6): 679–689.

Attree, P.M. and Milton, B. (2006) 'Critically appraising qualitative research for systematic reviews: Defusing the methodological cluster bombs', *Evidence and Policy: A Journal of Research Debate and Practice*, 2(1): 109–126.

Babcock, B.A. (1980) 'Reflexivity: Definitions and discriminations', *Semiotica*, 30(1/2): 1–14.

Bagnoli, A. (2009) 'Beyond the standard interview: The use of graphic elicitation and arts-based methods', *Qualitative Research*, 9(5): 547–570.

Bahn, S. and Barratt-Pugh, L. (2011) 'Getting reticent young male participants to talk: Using artefact-mediated interviews to promote discursive interaction', *Qualitative Social Work*, published online.

Bampton, R. and Cowton, C.J. (2002/2008) 'The e-interview', *Forum Qualitative Sozialforschung/Forum: Qualitative Social Research*, 3(2), Art. 9. Available at: http://nbn-resolving.de/urn:nbn:de:0114-fqs020295.

Banks, S. and Armstrong, A. (2012) *Ethics in Community-based Participatory Research*. Durham: Durham University Centre for Social Justice and Social Action. Available at: http://www.dur.ac.uk/resources/beacon/CBPRethicscasesrevisedDec2012.pdf. Accessed 10 February 2013.

Barbour, R.S. (2001) 'Checklists for improving rigour in qualitative research: A case of the tail wagging the dog?', *British Medical Journal*, 322(7294): 1115–1117.

Barbour, R. (2007) *Doing Focus Groups*. London: SAGE Publications.

Barnes, M. (2005) 'The same old process? Older people, participation and deliberation', *Ageing and Society*, 25(2): 245–259.

Barone, T. E. (1992) 'Beyond theory and method: A case of critical story telling', *Theory into Practice*, 31 (2): 142–146.

Barter, C. and Renold, E. (1999) 'The use of vignettes in qualitative research', *Social Research Update*. Available at: http://sru.soc.surrey.ac.uk/SRU25.html. Accessed February 2014.

Barter, C. and Renold, E. (2000) '"I wanna tell you a story": Exploring the use of vignettes in qualitative research with children and young people', *Social Research Methodology*, 3(4): 307–323.

Bates, S. and Coren, E. (2006) *The Extent and Impact of Parental Mental Health Problems on Families, and the Acceptability, Accessibility and Effectiveness of Interventions.* Children and Families' Services Systematic Map Report 1, Social Care Institute for Excellence. Available at: http://www.scie.org.uk/publications/map/map01.pdf. Accessed 25 July 2013.

Becker, H.S. (1960/1970) 'Notes on the concept of commitment', in H. Becker (ed.), *Sociological Work.* New Brunswick, NJ: Transaction Books.

Becker, H.S. (1970a) 'Fieldwork evidence', *Sociological Work: Method and Substance.* New Brunswick, NJ: Transaction Books.

Becker, H.S. (1970b) 'Problems of inference and proof in participant observation', *Sociological Work: Method and Substance.* New Brunswick, NJ: Transaction Books.

Becker, H.S. (1970c) 'Whose side are we on?', *Sociological Work: Method and Substance.* New Brunswick, NJ: Transaction Books.

Becker, H.S. (1970d) 'The self and adult socialization', *Sociological Work: Method and Substance.* New Brunswick, NJ: Transaction Books.

Becker, H.S. (1974) 'Photography and sociology', *studies in the Anthropology of Visual Communication,* 1(1): 3–26.

Becker, H.S. (1993) 'Theory: The necessary evil', in D. Flinders and G. Mills (eds), *Theory and Concepts in Qualitative Research: Perspectives from the Field.* New York: Teachers College, Columbia University Press.

Becker, H.S. (1998) *Tricks of the Trade.* Chicago: The University of Chicago Press.

Becker, H.S. (2011) 'The art of comparison: Lessons from the master, Everitt C. Hughes', in C. Hart (ed.), *The Legacy of the Chicago School of Sociology.* Poynton, UK: Midrash Publications.

Becker, H.S. and Carper, J. (1956/1970a) 'The elements of identification with an occupation,' in H. Becker (ed.), *Sociological Work: Method and Substance.* New Brunswick, NJ: Transaction Books.

Becker, H.S. and Carper, J. (1956/1970b) 'The development of identification with an occupation', in H. Becker (ed.), *Sociological Work: Method and Substance.* New Brunswick, NJ: Transaction Books.

Becker, H.S. and Carper, J. (1957/1970) 'Adjustment of conflicting expectations in the development of identification with an occupation', in H. Becker (ed.), *Sociological Work: Method and Substance.* New Brunswick, NJ: Transaction Books.

Ben-Ari, A. and Enosh, G. (2011) 'Processes of reflectivity: Knowledge construction in qualitative research', *Qualitative Social Work,* 10(2): 152–171.

Benney, M. and Hughes, E.C. (1956) 'Of sociology and the interview', *American Journal of Sociology,* 62(2): 137–142.

Beresford, P. (2010a) 'Re-examining relationships between experience, knowledge, ideas and research: A key role for recipients of state welfare and their movements', *Social Work and Society,* Vol. 8. Available at: http://www.socwork.net/sws/article/view/19/56. Accessed February 2014.

Beresford, P. (2010b) 'Service users and social policy: Developing different discussions, challenging dominant discourses', in I. Greener and S. Holden (eds), *Social Policy Review 22: Analysis and Debate in Social Policy, 2010.* Bristol: The Policy Press.

Berger, L. (2001) 'Inside out: Narrative autoethnography as a path toward rapport', *Qualitative Inquiry,* 7(4): 504–518.

Blair, J.A. (1995) 'Informal logic and reasoning in evaluation', in D.M. Fournier (ed.), *Reasoning in Evaluation: Inferential Links and Leaps.* New Directions for Evaluation, No. 68. San Francisco: Jossey-Bass.

Bloor, M. (1978) 'On the analysis of observational data: A discussion of the worth and uses of inductive techniques and respondent validation', *Sociology*, 12(4): 545–552.

Bloor, M. (1997) 'Addressing social problems through qualitative research', in D. Silverman (ed.), *Qualitative Research: Theory, Method and Practice*. London: SAGE Publications.

Bloor, M. (2010) 'Commentary: The researcher's obligation to bring about good', *Qualitative Social Work*, 9(1): 17–20.

Bloor, M.J. (2013) 'The rime of the globalised mariner: In six parts (with bonus tracks from a chorus of Greek shippers)', *Sociology*, 47(1): 30–50.

Bloor, M. and McKeganey, N. (1989) 'Ethnography addressing the practitioner', in J. Gubrium and D. Silverman (eds), *The Politics of Field Research: Sociology Beyond Enlightenment*. Newbury Park: SAGE Publications.

Bloor, M., Frankland, J. and Thomas, M. (2001) *Focus Groups in Qualitative Research*. London: SAGE Publications.

Bloor, M., Fincham, B. and Sampson, H. (2007) *Qualiti (NCRM) Commissioned Inquiry Into the Risk to Well-being of Researchers in Qualitative Research*. Qualiti, Cardiff University School of Social Sciences. Available at: http://www.cardiff.ac.uk/socsi/qualiti/CIReport.pdf. Accessed February 2014.

Bloor, M., Fincham, B. and Sampson, H. (2010) 'Unprepared for the worst: Risks of harm for qualitative researchers', *Methodological Innovations Online*, 5(1): 45–55.

Blumer, H. (1954) 'What is wrong with social theory?', *American Sociological Review*, 18(1): 3–10.

Boden, R., Epstein, D. and Latimer, J. (2009) 'Accounting for ethos or programmes for conduct? The brave new world of research ethics committees', *The Sociological Review*, 57(4): 727–749.

Boelen, W.A.M. (1992) 'Street corner society: Cornerville revisited', *Journal of Contemporary Ethnography*, 21(1): 11–51.

Bogolub, E. (2010) 'The obligation to bring about good in social work research: A new perspective', *Qualitative Social Work*, 9(1): 9–15.

Bond, M. (1990–1991) '"The centre, it's for children": Seeking children's views as users of a family centre', *Practice*, 7(2): 53–60.

Booth, A., Papaioannou, D. and Sutton, A. (2012) *Systematic Approaches to a Successful Literature Review*. London: SAGE Publications.

Bornat, J. and Bytheway, B. (2012) 'Working with different temporalities: Archived life history interviews and diaries', *International Journal of Research Methodology*, 15(4): 291–299.

Bourdieu, P. (1977) *Outline of a Theory of Practice*. Cambridge: Cambridge University Press.

Bradbury, H. and Reason, P. (2003) 'Action research: An opportunity for revitalizing research purpose and practices', *Qualitative Social Work*, 2(2): 155–175.

Brante, T. (2011) 'Professions as science-based occupation', *Professions and Professionalism*, 1(1): 4–20.

Broadhurst, K., Wastell, D., White, S., Hall, C., Peckover, S., Thompson, K., Pithouse, A. and Davey, D. (2010) 'Performing "initial assessment": Identifying the latent conditions for error at the front-door of local authority children's services', *British Journal of Social Work*, 40(2): 352–370.

Brown, J.D. and Wissow, L.S. (2009) 'Discussion of sensitive health topics with youth during primary care visits: Relationship to youth perceptions of care', *Journal of Adolescent Health*, 44(1): 48–54.

Bulmer, M. (1982) *The Uses of Research*. London: Allen and Unwin.

Burawoy, M. (2005) 'For public sociology', *American Sociological Review*, 70(1): 4–28.

Burgess, E.W. (1923) 'The interdependency of sociology and social work', *Journal of Social Forces*, 1(4): 366–370.

Burgess, E.W. (1927) 'The contribution of sociology to family social work', *The Family*, October: 191–193.

Burgess, E.W. (1928) 'What social case records should contain to be useful for sociological interpretation', *Social Forces*, 6(4): 524–532.

Burgess, E.W. (1930a) 'The cultural approach to the study of personality', *Mental Hygiene*, 14(April): 307–325.

Burgess, E.W. (1930b) 'The value of sociological community studies for the work of social agencies', *Social Forces*, 8(4): 481–491.

Burgess, R. (1984) *In the Field*. London: Allen and Unwin.

Burke, T.K. (2007) 'Providing ethics a space on the page: Social work and ethnography as a case in point', *Qualitative Social Work*, 6(2): 177–195.

Butler, I. (2002) 'A code of ethics for social work and social care research', *British Journal of Social Work*, 32 (2): 239–248.

Butler, I. and Drakeford, M. (2011) *Social Work on Trial: The Colwell Inquiry and the State of Welfare*. Bristol: The Policy Press.

Butler, I. and Williamson, H. (1994) *Children Speak: Children, Trauma and Social Work*. London: Longman.

Butler, I. and Williamson, H. (1996) '"Safe?" Involving children in child protection', in I. Butler and I. Shaw (eds), *A Case of Neglect? Children's Experience and the Sociology of Childhood*. Aldershot: Avebury.

Bywaters, P. and Ungar, M. (2010) 'Health and well-being', in I. Shaw, K. Briar-Lawson, J. Orme and R. Ruckdeschel (eds), *Sage Handbook of Social Work Research*. London: SAGE Publications.

Callon, M. and Rabeharisoa, V. (2003) 'Research "in the wild" and the shaping of new social identities', *Technology in Society*, 25(2): 193–204.

Campbell, D. (1978) 'Qualitative knowing in action research', in M. Brenner and P. Marsh (eds), *The Social Context of Methods*. London: Croom Helm.

Campbell, D. (1979) 'Degrees of freedom and the case study', in T. Cook and C. Reichardt (eds), *Qualitative and Quantitative Methods in Evaluation Research*. Beverly Hills: SAGE Publications.

Campbell, R., Adams, A.E., Wasco, S.M., Ahrens, C.E., and Sefl, T. (2009) 'Training interviewers for research on sexual violence: A qualitative study of rape survivors' recommendations for interview practice', *Violence Against Women*, 15(5): 595–617.

Carey, M. (2009/2013) *The Social Work Dissertation*. Maidenhead: Open University Press.

Carey, M. (2012) *Qualitative Research Skills for Social Work: Theory and Practice*. Aldershot: Ashgate Publishing.

Carr, E.S. (2010) 'Enactments of expertise', *Annual Review of Anthropology*, 39: 17–32.

Carr, E.S. (2011) *Scripting Addiction: The Politics of Therapeutic Talk and American Sobriety*. Princeton, NJ: Princeton University Press.

Castleden, H., Garvin, T. and Huu-ay-aht First Nation (2008) 'Modifying photovoice for community-based participatory indigenous research', *Social Science and Medicine*, 66(6): 1393–1405.

Cedersund, E. (1999) 'Using narratives in social work interaction', in A. Jokinen, K. Juhila and T. Poso (eds), *Constructing Social Work Practices*. Aldershot: Ashgate Publishing.

Centre for Social Justice and Community Action (2012) *Community Based Participatory Research*, Centre for Social Justice and Community Action, Durham University, https://www.dur.ac.uk/resources/beacon/CBPREthicsGuidewebNovember2012.pdf. Accessed 21 January 2014.

Chambon, A. (2008) 'Social work and the arts: Critical imagination', in J.G. Knowles and A. Cole (eds), *Handbook of the Arts in Qualitative Research: Perspectives, Methodologies, Examples*. Thousand Oaks: SAGE Publications.

Chambon, A., Johnstone, M. and Winckler, J. (2011) 'The material presence of early social work: The practice of the archive', *British Journal of Social Work*, 41(4): 625–644.

Chase, S.E. (2005) 'Narrative inquiry: Multiple lenses, approaches, voices', in N.K. Denzin and Y. Lincoln (eds), *Sage Handbook of Qualitative Research*. Thousand Oaks: SAGE Publications.

Chataway, C.J. (1997) 'An examination of the constraints on mutual inquiry in a participatory action research project', *Journal of Social Issues*, 53(4): 747–765.

Chelimsky, E. (1997) 'Thoughts for a new evaluation society', *Evaluation*, 3(1): 97–118.

Cicourel, A.V. (1964) *Method and Measurement in Sociology*. New York: Free Press.

Cicourel, A.V. (1985) 'Text and discourse', *Annual Review of Anthropology*, 14: 159–185.

Clandinin, D.J. and Connelly, F.M. (1994) 'Personal experience methods', in N. Denzin and Y. Lincoln (eds), *The Sage Handbook of Qualitative Research*. Thousand Oaks, CA: SAGE Publications.

Clandinin, D.J. and Connelly, F.M. (2000) *Narrative Inquiry*. San Francisco: Jossey-Bass.

Clark, A. and Emmel, N. (2010) 'Using walking interviews', Realities Toolkit #13. Available at: http://www.socialsciences.manchester.ac.uk/morgancentre/realities/toolkits/walking-interviews/index.html. Accessed 21 January 2014.

Clark, C. (2006) 'The moral character of social work', *British Journal of Social Work*, 36(1): 75–89.

Clark, T. (2008) 'We're over-researched here! Exploring accounts of research fatigue within qualitative research engagements', *Sociology*, 42(5): 953–970.

Cochran-Smith, M. and Lytle, S. (1990) 'Research on teaching and teacher research: The issues that divide', *Educational Researcher*, 19(2): 2–22.

Cocks, A. (2006) 'The ethical maze: Finding an inclusive path towards gaining children's agreement to research participation', *Childhood*, 13(2): 247–266.

Coffey, A. (1999) *The Ethnographic Self*. London: SAGE Publications.

Coffey, A. and Atkinson, P. (1996) *Making Sense of Qualitative Data*. London: SAGE Publications.

Collins, H. (2001) 'What is tacit knowledge?', in T. Schatzki, K. Cetina and E. von Savigny (eds), *The Practice Turn in Contemporary Theory*. London: Routledge.

Collins, H. and Evans, R. (2002) 'The third wave of science studies: Studies of expertise and experience', *Social Studies of Science*, 32(2): 235–296.

Collins, H.M. and Evans, R. (2007) *Rethinking Expertise*. Chicago: University of Chicago Press.

Collins, J.A. and Fauser, B.C.J.M. (2004) 'Editorial: Balancing the strengths of systematic and narrative reviews', *Human Reproduction Update*, 11(2): 103–110.

Colucci, E. (2007) '"Focus groups can be fun": The use of activity-oriented questions in focus group discussions', *Qualitative Health Research*, 17(10): 1422–1433.

Corbin, J. and Morse, J.M. (2003) 'The unstructured intensive interview: Issues of risk and reciprocity when dealing with sensitive topics', *Qualitative Inquiry*, 9(3): 335–354.

Corbin, J. and Strauss, A. (1990) 'Grounded theory research: Procedures, canons and evaluative criteria', *Qualitative Sociology*, 13(1): 3–21.

Corden, A., Sainsbury, R., Sloper, P. and Ward, B. (2005) 'Using a model of group psychotherapy to support social research on sensitive topics', *International Journal of Social Research Methodology*, 8(1): 151–160.

Cortazzi, M. (2001) 'Narrative analysis in ethnography', in P. Atkinson, A. Coffey, S. Delamont, J. Lofland and L. Lofland (eds), *Handbook of Ethnography*. London: SAGE Publications.

Cousins, J. B and Shula, L. M. (2006) 'A comparative analysis of evaluation utilization and its cognate fields of inquiry' in I. Shaw, J. Greene and M. Mark (eds), *Sage Handbook of Evaluation*. London: Sage Publications.

Craig, G., Corden, A. and Thornton, P. (2000) *Safety in Social Research*. Social Research Update, Issue 20. Sociology Department: University of Surrey. Available at: http://sru.soc.surrey.ac.uk/SRU29.html. Accessed 21 January 2014.

Crang, M. and Thrift, N. (eds) (2000) *Thinking Space*. New York: Routledge.

Crombie, I.K. (1996) *The Pocket Guide to Critical Appraisal*. London: BMJ Publishing.

Cronbach, L., Ambron, S., Dornbusch, S., Hess, R., Hornik, R., Phillips, D., Walker, D. and Weiner, S. (1980) *Toward Reform of Program Evaluation*. San Francisco: Jossey-Bass.

Crow, G. and Edwards, R. (2012) 'Perspectives on working with archived textual and visual material in social research', *International Journal of Research Methodology*, 15(4): 259–262.

Curran, T. (2010) 'Social work and disabled children's childhoods: A Foucauldian framework for practice transformation', *British Journal of Social Work*, 40 (3): 806–825.

Darlington, Y. and Scott, D. (eds) (2002) *Qualitative Research in Practice: Stories from the Field*. Buckingham: Open University Press.

Davies, M. and Kelly, E. (1976) 'The social worker, the client and the social anthropologist', *British Journal of Social Work*, 6(2): 213–231.

D'Cruz, H. (2004) *Constructing Meanings and Identities in Child Protection Practice*. Melbourne, Australia: Tertiary Press.

D'Cruz, H. and Jones, M. (2004) *Social Work Research: Ethical and Political Contexts*. London: SAGE Publications.

de Boer, M.E., Hertogh, C.M., Dröes, R.M., Riphagen, I.I., Jonker, C. and Eefsting, J.A. (2007) 'Suffering from dementia – the patient's perspective: A review of the literature', *International Psychogeriatrics*, 19(6): 1021–1039.

Deeb, H.N. and Marcus, G.E. (2011) 'In the green room: an experiment in ethnographic method at the WTO', *PoLAR: Political and Legal Anthropology Review*, 34 (1): 51–76.

Delamont, S. (2003) *Feminist Sociology*. London: SAGE Publications.

Delamont, S. (2007) 'Arguments against auto-ethnography', *Qualitative Researcher*, Issue 4, 2–4. Available at: http://www.cardiff.ac.uk/socsi/qualiti/QualitativeResearcher/QR_Issue4_Feb07. Accessed 21 January 2014.

de Montigny, G.A.J. (1995) *Social Working: An Ethnography of Front-line Practice*. Toronto, Ontario: University of Toronto Press.

Denscombe, M. and Aubrook, L. (1992) '"It's just another piece of schoolwork": The ethics of questionnaire research on pupils in schools', *British Educational Research Journal*, 18(2): 113–131.

Denzin, N.K. (1989a) *Interpretive Biography*. Newbury Park: SAGE Publications.

Denzin, N.K. (1989b) *The Research Act in Sociology*. New York: McGraw Hill.

Denzin, N.K. (1994) 'The art and politics of interpretation', in N.K. Denzin and Y. Lincoln (eds), *Handbook of Qualitative Research*. Thousand Oaks: SAGE Publications.

Denzin, N.K. (1997) *Interpretive Ethnography*. Thousand Oaks: SAGE Publications.

Denzin, N.K. (2002) 'Social work in the seventh moment', *Qualitative Social Work*, 1(1): 25–38.

Denzin, N.K. (2013) 'The Travelling Indian Gallery, Part Two', *Qualitative Research*. Published online before print. Available at: http://qrj.sagepub.com/content/early/2013/01/11/1468794112468477.abstract. Accessed 21 January 2014.

Denzin, N.K. and Lincoln, Y. (2000) (eds) *Sage Handbook of Qualitative Research*. Thousand Oaks: SAGE Publications.

Denzin, N.K. and Lincoln, Y. (2005) 'The discipline and practice of qualitative research', in N.K. Denzin and Y. Lincoln (eds), *Sage Handbook of Qualitative Research*. Thousand Oaks: SAGE Publications.

Department for Constitutional Affairs (2007) *Mental Capacity Act 2005: Code of Practice*. London: The Stationery Office.

Dey, I. (1993) *Qualitative Data Analysis: A User-friendly Guide for Social Scientists*. London: Routledge.

Dickson-Swift, V., James, E., Kippen, S. and Liamputtong, P. (2006) 'Blurring boundaries in qualitative health research on sensitive topics', *Qualitative Health Research*, 16(6): 853–871.

Dickson-Swift, V., James, E., Kippen, S. and Liamputtong, P. (2008) 'Doing sensitive research. What challenges do qualitative researchers face?', *Qualitative Research*, 7(3): 327–353.

Dingwall, R. (1977a) '"Atrocity stories" and professional relationships', *Sociology of Work and Occupations*, 4(4): 371–396. Reprinted in P. Atkinson and S. Delamont (eds), (2006) *Narrative Methods, Volume 1: Sage Benchmarks in Social Research Methods*. London: SAGE Publications.

Dingwall, R. (1997b) 'Accounts, interviews and observations', in G. Miller and R. Dingwall (eds), *Context and Method in Qualitative Research*. London: SAGE Publications.

Dingwall, R. (1997c) 'Conclusion: The moral discourse of interactionism', in G. Miller and R. Dingwall (eds), *Context and Method in Qualitative Research*. London: SAGE Publications.

Dingwall, R. (2008) 'The ethical case against ethical regulation in humanities and social science research', *21st Century Society: Journal of the Academy of Social Sciences*, 3(1): 1–12.

Dinitto, D.M., Busch-Armendariz, N.B., Bender, K., Woo, H., Tackett-Gibson, M. and Dyer, J. (2008) 'Testing telephone and web surveys for studying men's sexual assault perpetration behaviors', *Journal of Interpersonal Violence*, 23(10): 1483–1493.

Dixon-Woods, M., Bonas, S., Booth, A., Jones, D.R., Miller, T., Sutton, A.J., Shaw, R.L., Smith, J.A. and Young, B. (2006) 'How can systematic reviews incorporate qualitative research? A critical perspective', *Qualitative Research*, 6(1): 27–44.

Doyle, L.H. (2003) 'Synthesis through meta-ethnography: paradoxes, enhancements, and possibilities', *Qualitative Research*, 3(3): 321–344.

Draucker, C.B., Martsoff, D.S. and Poole, C. (2009) 'Developing distress protocols for research on sensitive topics', *Archives of Psychiatric Nursing*, 23(5): 343–350.

Drisko, J. (2013a) 'Qualitative data analysis software: An overview and new possibilities', in A.E. Fortune, W.J. Reid and R.L. Miller, Jr. (eds), *Qualitative Research in Social Work*. New York: Columbia University Press.

Drisko, J. (2013b) 'Constructivist research in social work', in A.E. Fortune, W.J. Reid and R.L. Miller, Jr. (eds), *Qualitative Research in Social Work*. New York: Columbia University Press.

Easton, P. (2012) 'Identifying the evaluative impulse in local culture: Insights from West African proverbs', *American Journal of Evaluation*, 33(4): 515–523.

Edens, J.F. and Epstein, M. (2011) 'Voluntary consent in correctional settings: Do offenders feel coerced to participate in research?', *Behavioral Sciences and the Law*, 29(6): 771–795.

Edwards, A., Barnes, M., Plewis, I. and Morris, K. (2006) *Working to Prevent the Social Exclusion of Children and Young People: Final Lessons from the National Evaluation of the Children's Fund*. DfES Research Report, 734. London: DfES.

Edwards, G. (2010) *Mixed-method approaches to social network analysis*. Discussion Paper. NCRM: http://eprints.ncrm.ac.uk/842/1/Social_Network_analysis_Edwards.pdf. Accessed 21 January 2014.

Eisenhandler, S.A. (2008) 'The rose and the thorn: Some ethical dilemmas in a qualitative study of older adults', *Journal of Religion, Spirituality and Aging*, 20(1–2): 63–76.

Eisenhardt, K.E. (1989) 'Building theories from case study research', *The Academy of Management Review*, 14(4): 532–550.

Eisner, E.W. (1988) 'Educational connoisseurship and criticism: Their form and functions in educational evaluation', in D.M. Fetterman (ed.), *Qualitative Approaches to Evaluation in Education: The Silent Revolution*. New York: Praeger.

Eisner, E.W. (1991) *The Enlightened Eye: Qualitative Inquiry and the Enhancement of Educational Practice*. New York: Macmillan.

Elks, M. and Kirkhart, K. (1993) 'Evaluating effectiveness from the practitioner's perspective', *Social Work*, 38(5): 554–563.

Elliott, J. (2005) *Using Narrative in Social Research*. London: SAGE Publications.

Elliott, R. (2010) 'Psychotherapy change process research: Realizing the promise', *Psychotherapy Research*, 20(2): 123–135.

Ellsberg, M. and Heise, L. (2002) 'Bearing witness: Ethics in domestic violence research', *Lancet*, 4: 1599–1604.

Emerson, R.M., Fretz, R.I. and Shaw, L.L. (2001) 'Participant observation and fieldnotes', in P. Atkinson, A. Coffey, S. Delamont, J. Lofland and L. Lofland (eds), *Handbook of Ethnography*. London: SAGE Publications.

Emmel, N. and Clark, A. (2009) 'The methods used in Connected Lives: Investigating networks, neighbourhoods and communities', *Real Life Methods, The Manchester/Leeds Node of the ESRC National Centre for Research Methods*. Available at: http://eprints. ncrm.ac.uk/800/. Accessed 21 January 2014.

England, H. (1986) *Social Work as Art*. London: Allen and Unwin.

Enosh, G. and Buchbinder, E. (2005) 'Strategies of distancing from emotional experience: Making memories of domestic violence', *Qualitative Social Work*, 4(1): 9–32.

EPPI-Centre (2007) *EPPI-Centre Methods for Conducting Systematic Reviews* (updated 2010), Evidence for Policy and Practice Information and Co-ordinating Centre, Institute of Education, London. Available at: http://eppi.ioe.ac.uk/cms/LinkClick.aspx ?fileticket=hQBu8y4uVwI%3D&tabid=88. Accessed 21 January 2014.

Erikson, E. (1959) 'The nature of clinical inference', in D. Lerner (ed.), *Evidence and Inference*. Illinois: Free Press.

Eskelinen, L. and Caswell, D. (2006) 'Comparison of social work practice in teams using a video vignette technique in a multi-method design', *Qualitative Social Work*, 5(4): 489–503.

ESRC (2010) *Framework for Research Ethics*. Swindon: ESRC. Available at: http:// www.esrc.ac.uk/_images/Framework-for-Research-Ethics_tcm8-4586.pdf. Accessed 21 January 2014.

Evans, R. and Kotchetkova, I. (2009) 'Qualitative research and deliberative methods: promise or peril?', *Qualitative Research*, 9(5): 625–643.

Felt, U., Schumann, S., Schwarz, C. and Strassnig, M. (2013) 'Technology of imagination: a card-based public engagement method for debating emerging technologies',

Qualitative Research. Published online before print, January 2013. Available at: http://qrj.sagepub.com/content/early/2013/01/04/1468794112468468.abstract. Accessed 21 January 2014.

Ferguson, H. (2011) *Child Protection Practice*. Basingstoke: Palgrave.

Fielding, N., Lewins, A., Silver, C. and Lee, R. (2006) *Methods Briefing 15: Computer Assisted Qualitative Data Analysis*. Available at: http://www.ccsr.ac.uk/methods/publications/documents/CAQDAS.pdf. Accessed 21 January 2014.

Finch, J. (1986) *Research and Policy: The Uses of Qualitative Methods in Social and Educational Research*. London: Falmer Press.

Finch, J. (1987) 'The vignette technique in survey research', *Sociology*, 21(1): 105–114.

Fincham, B., Scourfield, J. and Langer, S. (2008) 'The impact of working with disturbing secondary data: Reading suicide files in a coroner's office', *Qualitative Health Research*, 18(6): 853–862.

Finley, S. (2011) 'Critical arts-based inquiry: The pedagogy and performance of a radical, ethical aesthetic', in N.K. Denzin and Y. Lincoln (eds), *Sage Handbook of Qualitative Research*. Thousand Oaks: SAGE Publications.

Fisher, M., Qureshi, H., Hardyman, W. and Homewood, J. (2006) *Using Qualitative Research in Systematic Reviews: Older People's Views of Hospital Discharge*. London: Social Care Institute for Excellence. Available at: http://www.scie.org.uk/publications/reports/report09.pdf. Accessed 21 January 2014.

Flick, U. (2006) *An Introduction to Qualitative Research*. London: SAGE Publications.

Flick, U. (2007) *Designing Qualitative Research*. London: SAGE Publications.

Floersch, J. (2002) *Meds, Money, and Manners: The Case Management of Severe Mental Illness*. New York: Columbia University Press.

Flyvbjerg, B. (2006) 'Five misunderstandings about case-study research,' *Qualitative Inquiry*, 12 (2): 219–245.

Fook, J. (2000) 'Reflexivity as method', in J. Daly and A. Kellehear (eds), *Annual Review of Health Social Sciences*. Palliative Care Unit, La Trobe University, Bundoora.

Fook, J. (2012) 'Professional voices from the field: A story', in T. Maschi and R. Youdin (eds), *Social Worker as Researcher: Integrating Research with Advocacy*. Boston: Pearson.

Forrester, D., Kershaw, S., Moss, H. and Hughes, L. (2008) 'Communication skills in child protection: How do social workers talk to parents?', *Child and Family Social Work*, 13(1): 41–51.

Forsberg, H. and Vagli, Å. (2006) 'The social construction of emotions in child protection case-talk', *Qualitative Social Work*, 5 (1): 9–31.

Fortune, A. (1994) 'Commentary: Ethnography in social work', in E. Sherman and W. Reid (eds), *Qualitative Research in Social Work*. New York: Columbia University Press.

Fortune, A., Reid, W.J. and Miller, R. Jr. (eds) (2013) *Qualitative Research in Social Work*. New York: Columbia University Press.

Foster, V. (2013) 'Pantomime and politics: The story of a performance ethnography', *Qualitative Research*, 13(1): 36–52.

Foucault, M. (2002) *The Archaeology of Knowledge*. London: Routledge.

Fournier, D. and Smith, N. (1993) 'Clarifying the merits of argument in evaluation practice', *Evaluation and Program Planning*, 16(4): 315–323.

Franklin, C.S., Cody, P.A. and Ballan, M. (2010) 'Reliability and validity in qualitative research', in B. Thyer (ed.), *The Handbook of Social Work Research Methods*. Thousand Oaks: SAGE Publications.

Fraser, N. and Gordon, L. (1994) 'A genealogy of dependency: Tracing a key word of the US Welfare State', *Signs*, 19(2): 309–336.

Freire, P. (1970) *Pedagogy of the Oppressed*. New York: Continuum Books.

Gabb, J. (2008) *Researching Intimacy in Families*. Basingstoke: Palgrave Macmillan.

Gabb, J. (2009) 'Researching family relationships: A qualitative mixed methods approach', *Methodological Innovations Online*, 4(2): 37–52. Available at: http://www.methodologicalinnovations.org.uk/wp-content/uploads/2013/11/4.-Gabb-final-August-9-09.pdf. Accessed 21 January 2014.

Gallardo, H., Furman, R. and Kulkarni, S. (2009) 'Explorations of depression: Poetry and narrative in autoethnographic qualitative research', *Qualitative Social Work*, 8(3): 287–304.

Geertz, C. (1973) *The Interpretation of Cultures*. New York: Basic Books.

Geertz, C. (1983) *Local Knowledge*. New York: Basic Books.

Gibbs, A. (1997) 'Focus groups', Social Research Update #19, Department of Sociology, University of Surrey. Available at: http://sru.soc.surrey.ac.uk/SRU19.html. Accessed 21 January 2014.

Gibson, L. (2010) 'Using email interviews', Realities Toolkit #09. Available at: www.manchester.ac.uk/realities. Accessed 1 February 2014.

Gibson-Graham, J.K. (1994) '"Stuffed if I know!": Reflections on post-modern feminist social research', *Gender, Place and Culture: A Journal of Feminist Geography*, 1(2): 205–224.

Giddens, A. (1993) *New Rules of Sociological Method*. Stanford: Stanford University Press.

Gilgun, J. (1994) 'A case for case studies in social work research', *Social Work*, 39(4): 371–380.

Gilgun, J. (2013) 'Grounded theory, deductive qualitative analysis and social work research and practice', in A.E. Fortune, W.J. Reid and R.L. Miller, Jr. (eds), *Qualitative Research in Social Work*. New York: Columbia University Press.

Gilmour, R. and Cobus-Kuo, L. (2011) 'Reference management software: A comparative analysis of four products', *Issues in Science and Technology Librarianship*, Summer. http://www.istl.org/11-summer/refereed2.html. Accessed 21 January 2014.

Goldstein, H. (1994) 'Ethnography, critical inquiry and social work practice', in E. Sherman and W.J. Reid (eds), *Qualitative Research in Social Work*. New York: Columbia University Press.

Goodley, D. (2011) *Disability Studies*. London: SAGE Publications.

Gough, D., Thomas, J. and Oliver, S. (2012) 'Clarifying differences between review designs and methods', *Systematic Reviews*, 1: 28. Available at: http://www.systematicreviewsjournal.com/content/1/1/28. Accessed 21 January 2014.

Gredig, D. and Marsh, J.C. (2010) 'Improving intervention and practice', in I. Shaw, K. Briar-Lawson, J. Orme and R. Ruckdeschel (eds), *The Sage Handbook of Social Work Research*. London: SAGE Publications.

Greenberg, L.S. (1986) 'Change process research', *Journal of Consulting and Clinical Psychology*, 54(1): 4–9.

Greene, J. (1990) 'Three views on the nature and role of knowledge in social science', in E. Guba (ed.), *The Paradigm Dialog*. Newbury Park: SAGE Publications.

Greene, J. (1993) 'The role of theory in qualitative program evaluation', in J. Flinders and G. Mills (eds), *Theory and Concepts in Qualitative Research*. New York: Teachers College Press.

Greene, J. (1994) 'Qualitative program evaluation: Practice and promise', in N.K. Denzin and Y. Lincoln (eds), *Handbook of Qualitative Research*. Thousand Oaks: SAGE Publications.

Greene, J. and Caracelli, V. (1997) *Advances in Mixed Method Evaluation: The Challenge and Benefits of Integrating Diverse Paradigms*. New Directions for Evaluation, No. 74. San Francisco: Jossey-Bass.

Greene, J.C., Sommerfield, P. and Haight, W.L. (2010) 'Mixing methods in social work research', in I. Shaw, K. Briar-Lawson, J. Orme and R. Ruckdeschel (eds), *The Sage Handbook of Social Work Research*. London: SAGE Publications.

Greenhalgh, T. and Peacock, R. (2005) 'Effectiveness and efficiency of search methods in systematic reviews of complex evidence: Audit of primary sources', *BMJ*, 331:1064, bmj.38636.593461.68.

Guba, E. (1990) 'The alternative paradigm dialog', in E. Guba (ed.), *The Paradigm Dialog*. Newbury Park: SAGE Publications.

Gubrium, J.F. and Holstein, J.A. (1998) 'Narrative practice and the coherence of personal stories', *Sociological Quarterly*, 39(1): 163–187.

Gubrium, J.F. and Holstein, J.A. (2002) *Sage Handbook of Interview Research: Context and Method*. Thousand Oaks: SAGE Publications.

Gubrium, J.F., Buckholdt, D.R. and Lynott, R.J. (1989) 'The descriptive tyranny of forms', *Perspectives on Social Problems*, 1(2): 195–214.

Guillemim, M. and Gillam, L. (2004) 'Ethics, reflexivity and "ethically important moments" in qualitative research', *Qualitative Inquiry*, 10(2): 261–280.

Hakim, C. (2000) *Research Design*. London: Routledge.

Hall, A. (1974) *The Point of Entry*. London: Allen and Unwin.

Hall, C. (1997) *Social Work as Narrative*. Aldershot: Ashgate Publishing.

Hall, C. and White, S. (2005) 'Looking inside professional practice: Discourse, narrative and ethnographic approaches to social work and counselling', *Qualitative Social Work*, 4(4): 379–390.

Hall, C., Slembrouck, S. and Sarangi, S. (2006) *Language Practice in Social Work: Categorisation and Accountability in Child Welfare*. London: Routledge.

Hall, T. (2001) 'Caught not taught: Ethnographic research at a young people's accommodation project', in I. Shaw and N. Gould (eds), *Qualitative Research in Social Work*. London: SAGE Publications.

Hall, T. (2004a) *Better Times Than This*. London: Pluto Press.

Hall, T. (2004b) 'Through a glass darkly: Undercover in low-pay Britain and America', *Sociology*, 38(3): 623–630.

Hall, T., Lashua, B. and Coffey, A. (2008) 'Sound and the everyday in qualitative research', *Qualitative Inquiry*, 14(6): 1019–1040.

Hammersley, M. (1992) *What's Wrong With Ethnography?* London: Routledge.

Hammersley, M. (1993) 'On the teacher as researcher', *Educational Action Research*, 1(3): 425–445.

Hammersley, M. (1995) *The Politics of Social Research*. London: Sage Publications.

Hammersley, M. (2000a) 'The relevance of qualitative research', *Oxford Review of Education*, 26(3/4): 393–405.

Hammersley, M. (2000b) *Taking Sides in Social Research*. London: Routledge.

Hammersley, M. (2008) *Questioning Qualitative Inquiry*. London: SAGE Publications.

Hammersley, M. (2010) 'Can we re-use qualitative data via secondary analysis? Notes on some terminological and substantive issues', *Sociological Research Online*, 15(1)5. Available at: http://www.socresonline.org.uk/15/1/5.html. Accessed 21 January 2014.

Hammersley, M. and Atkinson, P. (2007) *Ethnography*. London: Routledge.

Hammersley, M. and Gomm, R. (1997) 'Bias in social research', *Sociological Research Online*, 2(1). Available at: http://www.socresonline.org.uk/2/1/2.html. Accessed 21 January 2014.

Hannigan, B. and Allen, D. (2013) 'Complex caring trajectories in community mental health: Contingencies, divisions of labor and care coordination', *Community Mental Health Journal*, 49(4): 380–388.

Hart, C. (1998) *Doing a Literature Review*. London: SAGE Publications.

Harvey, W.S. (2011) 'Strategies for conducting elite interviews', *Qualitative Research*, 11(4): 431–441.

Hayes, D. and Devaney, J. (2004) 'Assessing social work case files for research purposes', *Qualitative Social Work*, 3(3): 313–333.

Healy, D., Harris, M., Cattell, D., Savage, M., Chalasani, P. and Hirst, D. (2005) 'Service utilization in 1896 and 1996: Morbidity and mortality data from North Wales', *History of Psychiatry*, 16(1): 27–41.

Heath, S. and Walker, C. (2012) 'Introduction', in S. Heath and C. Walker (eds), *Innovations in Youth Research*. Basingstoke: Palgrave Macmillan.

Heath, S., Charles, V., Crow, G. and Wiles, R. (2007) 'Informed consent, gatekeepers and go-betweens: Negotiating consent in child and youth orientated institutions', *British Educational Research Journal*, 33(3): 403–417.

Heaton, J. (1998) *Secondary Analysis of Qualitative Data*. University of Surrey: Social Research Update, 22. Available at: http://sru.soc.surrey.ac.uk/SRU22.html. Accessed 21 January 2014.

Hedin, L., Höjer, I. and Brunnberg, E. (2012) 'Jokes and routines make everyday life a good life: On 'doing family' for young people in foster care in Sweden', *European Journal of Social Work*, 15(5): 613–628.

Held, V. (2006) *The Ethics of Care: Personal, Political, and Global*. Oxford: Oxford University Press.

Hesse-Biber, S. (2010) 'Qualitative approaches to mixed methods practice', *Qualitative Inquiry*, 16(6): 455–468.

Hill, A. (2012) 'Help for children after child sexual abuse: Using a qualitative approach to design and test therapeutic interventions that may include non-offending parents', *Qualitative Social Work*, 11(4): 362–378.

Hill, A. and Shaw, I. (2011) *ICT and Social Work*. London: SAGE Publications.

Hirst, D. and Michael, P. (2003) 'Family, community and the 'idiot' in mid-nineteenth century North Wales', *Disability and Society*, 18(2): 145–163.

Holland, J., Thomson, R. and Henderson, S. (2006) *Qualitative Longitudinal Research: A Discussion Paper*, Families and Social Capital ESRC Research Group, London: South Bank University. Available at: http://www.lsbu.ac.uk/ahs/downloads/families/familieswp21.pdf. Accessed 21 January 2014.

Holland, S. (2009) 'Listening to children in care: A review of methodological and theoretical approaches to understanding looked after children's perspectives', *Children and Society*, 23(3): 226–235.

Holland, S. (2011) *Child and Family Assessment in Social Work Practice*. London: SAGE Publications.

Holland, S. (2012) 'Trust in the community: Understanding the relationship between formal, semi-formal and informal child safeguarding in a local neighbourhood', *British Journal of Social Work*. First published online 1, August. Available at: http://bjsw.oxfordjournals.org/content/early/2012/08/01/bjsw.bcs118.abstract. Accessed 21 January 2014.

Holland, S. and Crowley, A. (2013) 'Looked after children and their birth families: using sociology to explore changing relationships, hidden histories and nomadic childhoods'. *Child and Family Social Work*, 18 (1): 57–66.

Holland, S., Renold, E., Ross, N. and Hillman, A. (2008) 'The everyday lives of children in care: Using a sociological perspective to inform social work practice', in B. Luckock and M. Lefevre (eds), *Direct Work: Social Work with Children and Young People*. London: BAAF.

Holland, S., Renold, E., Ross, N.J. and Hillman, A. (2010) 'Power, agency and participatory agendas: A critical exploration of young people's engagement in participative qualitative research', *Childhood*, 17(3): 360–375.

Holland, S., Burgess, S., Grogan-Kaylor, A. and Delva, J. (2011) 'Understanding neighbourhoods, communities, and environments: New approaches to social work research', *British Journal of Social Work*, 41(4): 689–707.

Hollway, W. and Jefferson, T. (2000) 'Biography, anxiety and the experience of locality', in P. Chamberlayne, J. Bornat and T. Wengraf (eds), *The Turn to Biographical Methods in Social Science*. London: Routledge.

Holstein, J.A. and Gubrium, J.F. (1995) *The Active Interview*. Thousand Oaks, CA: SAGE Publications.

Hopman, M., de Winter, M. and Koops, W. (2013) 'The hidden curriculum of youth care interventions: A case study', *Children and Youth Services Review*, 35(2): 237–243.

House, E. (1980) *Evaluating with Validity*. Beverley Hills: SAGE Publications.

House, E. (1991a) 'Evaluation and social justice: Where are we now?', in M. McLaughlin and D. Phillips (eds), *Evaluation and Education: At Quarter Century*. Chicago, IL: Chicago University Press.

House, E. (1991b) 'Realism in research', *Educational Researcher*, 20(6): 2–9.

House, E. (1993) *Professional Evaluation*. Newbury Park: SAGE Publications.

House, E. and Howe, K. (1999) *Evaluation and Values*. Thousand Oaks: SAGE Publications.

Hubbard, G. (2000) 'The usefulness of indepth life history interviews for exploring the role of social structure and human agency in youth transitions', *Sociological Research Online*, 4(4). Available at: http://www.socresonline.org.uk/4/4/hubbard.html. Accessed 21 January 2014.

Huberman, A.M. and Miles, M.B. (1994) 'Data management and analysis methods' in N. K. Denzin and Y. S. Lincoln (eds) *Handbook of Qualitative Research*. Newbury Park: Sage.

Hugman, R. (2010) 'Social work research and ethics', in I. Shaw, K. Briar-Lawson, J. Orme and R. Ruckdeschel (eds), *The Sage Handbook of Social Work Research*. London: SAGE Publications.

Humphrey, C. and Pease, K. (1992) 'Effectiveness measurement in the probation service: A view from the troops', *Howard Journal*, 31(2): 31–52.

Humphreys, L. (1975) *Tearoom Trade: Impersonal Sex in Public Places*. New Jersey: Aldine Transaction.

International Federation of Social Workers (2012) *Definition of Social Work*. Available at: http://ifsw.org/policies/definition-of-social-work. Accessed 21 January 2014.

Inwood, J. and Martin, D. (2010) 'Exploring spatial (dis)locations through the use of roving focus groups', *Qualitative Researcher*, 12: 5–7.

Irwin, S. and Winterton, M. (2011) *Debates in Qualitative Secondary Analysis: Critical Reflections*. Timescapes Working Paper Series No. 4. Available at: http://www.timescapes.leeds.ac.uk/assets/files/WP4-March-2011.pdf. Accessed 20 June 2013.

Jacob, M.C. (1992) 'Science and politics in the late twentieth century', *Social Research*, 59(3): 487–503.

James, A., Jenks, C. and Prout, A. (1998) *Theorising Childhood*. Cambridge: Polity Press.

Janesick, V.J. (1998) *"Stretching" Exercises for Qualitative Researchers*. Thousand Oaks: SAGE Publications.

Jarrett, R. (1993) 'Focus group interviewing with low income minority populations', in D.L. Morgan (ed.), *Successful Focus Groups: Advancing the State of the Art*. Newbury Park: SAGE Publications.

Jaycox, L.H., McCaffrey, D.F., Ocampo, B.W., Shelly, G.A., Blake, S.M., Peterson, D.J., Richmond, L. and Kub, J.E. (2006) 'Challenges in the evaluation and implementation of school-based prevention and intervention programs on sensitive topics', *American Journal of Evaluation*, 27(3): 320–336.

Jenkins, N., Bloor, M., Fischer, J., Barney, L. and Neale, J. (2010) 'Putting it in context: The use of vignettes in qualitative interviewing', *Qualitative Research*, 10(2): 175–198.

Jensen, T., Gulbrandsen, W., Mossige, S., Reichelt, S. and Tjersland, O.A. (2005) 'Reporting possible sexual abuse: A qualitative study on children's perspectives and the context for disclosure', *Child Abuse and Neglect*, 29(12): 1395–1413.

Jimenez, L. and Walkerdine, V. (2011) 'A psychosocial approach to shame, embarrassment and melancholia amongst unemployed young men and their fathers', *Gender and Education*, 23(2): 185–199.

Johnson, R. B., Onwuegbuzie, A. J., and Turner, L. A. (2007) 'Toward a definition of mixed methods research', *Journal of Mixed Methods Research*, 1(2): 112–133.

Jovchelovitch, S. and Bauer, M. W. (2000) 'Narrative interviewing', in M.W. Bauer and G. Gaskell (eds), *Qualitative Researching with Text, Image and Sound: A Practical Handbook*. London: SAGE.

Juhila, K. and Pösö, T. (1999) 'Negotiating constructions: Rebridging social work research and practice in the context of probation work', in A. Jokinen, K. Juhila and T. Pösö (eds), *Constructing Social Work Practices*. Aldershot: Ashgate Publishing.

Kamberelis, G. and Dimitriadis, G. (2005) 'Focus groups: Strategic articulations of pedagogy, politics, and inquiry', in N.K. Denzin and Y. Lincoln (eds), *Handbook of Qualitative Research*. Thousand Oaks: SAGE Publications.

Kane, G.A., Wood, V.A. and Barlow, J. (2007) 'Parenting programmes: A systematic review and synthesis of qualitative research', *Child Care, Health and Development*, 33(6): 784–793.

Karnieli-Miller, O., Strier, R. and Pessach, L. (2009) 'Power relations in qualitative research', *Qualitative Health Research*, 19(2): 279–289.

Kearney, K.S. and Hyle, A.E. (2004) 'Drawing out emotions: The use of participant-produced drawings in qualitative inquiry', *Qualitative Research*, 4(3): 361–382.

Kellett, M., Forrest (aged ten), R., Dent (aged ten), N. and Ward (aged ten), S. (2004) '"Just teach us the skills please, we'll do the rest": Empowering ten-year-olds as active researchers', *Children and Society*, 18(3): 329–343.

King, L. and Rivett, G. (2013) 'Engaging people in making history'. Available at: http://blogs.lse.ac.uk/impactofsocialsciences/2013/07/08/engaging-people-in-making-history/?pfstyle=wp. Blog posting 8 July 2013.

Kirk, S. and Reid, W.J. (2002) *Science and Social Work*. New York: Columbia University Press.

Kitchen, H.A. (2002) 'The Tri Council on Cyberspace: Insights, Oversights and Extrapolations', in W. C. van den Hoonaard (ed.), *Walking the Tightrope: Ethical Issues for Qualitative Researchers*. Toronto: University of Toronto Press.

Kitsuse, J.I. and Cicourel, A. (1963) 'A note on the uses of official statistics', *Social Problems*, 11(2): 131–139.

Kitzinger, J. (1994) 'Focus groups: Method or madness?', in M. Bolton (ed.), *Challenge and Innovation: Methodological Advances in Social Research on HIV/AIDS*. London: Taylor and Francis.

Knowles, J.G. and Cole, A. (2008) *Handbook of the Arts in Qualitative Research: Perspectives, Methodologies, Examples*. Thousand Oaks: SAGE Publications.

Kulkarni, S., Bell, H., Beausoleil, J., Lein, L., Angel, R. and Mason, J.H. (2008) 'When the floods of compassion are not enough: A nation's and a city's response to the evacuees of Hurricane Katrina', *Smith College Studies in Social Work*, 78(4): 399–425.

Labov, W. (1972) *Language in the Inner City: Studies in the Black English Vernacular*. Oxford: Blackwell.

Lang, N. (1994) 'Integrating the data processing of qualitative research and social work practice to advance the practitioner as knowledge builder: Tools for knowing and doing', in E. Sherman and W.J. Reid (eds), *Qualitative Research in Social Work*. New York: Columbia University Press.

Langhinrichsen-Rohling, J., Arata, C., O'Brien, N., Bowers, D., and Klibert, J. (2006) 'Sensitive research with adolescents: Just how upsetting are self-report surveys anyway?', *Violence and Victims*, 21(4): 425–444.

Lashua, B.D. (2006) '"Just another native?" Soundscapes, chorasters, and borderlands in Edmonton, Alberta, Canada', *Cultural Studies <=> Critical Methodologies*, 6(3): 391–410.

Lather, P. (1986a) 'Issues of validity in openly ideological research', *Interchange*, 17(4): 63–84.

Lather, P. (1986b) 'Research as praxis', *Harvard Educational Review*, 56(3): 257–277.

Laurier, E., Lorimer, H, Brown, B., Jones, O., Juhlin, O., Noble, A., Perry, M., Pica, D., Sormani, P., Strebel, I., Swan, L., Taylor, A.S., Watts, L. and Weilenmann, A. (2008) 'Driving and passengering: notes on the ordinary organisation of car travel', *Mobilities*, 3 (1): 1–23.

Lee, R. (2004) 'Recording technologies and the interview in sociology, 1920–2000', *Sociology*, 38(5): 869–889.

Lee, R. (2008) 'David Riesman and the sociology of the interview', *The Sociological Quarterly*, 49(2): 285–307.

Lengermann, P. and Niebrugge, G. (2007) 'Thrice told: Narratives of sociology's relation to social work', in C. Calhoun (ed.), *Sociology in America: A History*. Chicago: University of Chicago Press.

Lewins, A. and Silver, C. (2007) *Using Software in Qualitative Research*. London: SAGE Publications.

Lincoln, Y. (1990) 'The making of a constructivist: A remembrance of transformations past', in E. Guba (ed.), *The Paradigm Dialog*. Newbury Park: SAGE Publications.

Lincoln, Y. and Guba, E. (1986) 'Research, evaluation and policy analysis: Heuristics and disciplined inquiry', *Policy Studies Review*, 5(3): 546–565.

Lofland, J. and Lofland, L. (2006) *Analyzing Social Settings*. Belmont: Wadsworth.

Lohmann, R.A. and Lohmann, N. (2010) 'Deliberation, dialogue and deliberative democracy in social work education and practice', in R.A. Lohmann and J. van Til (eds), *Resolving Community Conflicts and Problems*. New York: Columbia University Press.

Long, A. (1994) 'Assessing health and social outcomes', in J. Popay and G. Williams (eds), *Researching the People's Health*. London: Routledge.

Longhofer, J. and Floersch, J. (2012) 'Critical realism: Science and social work', *Research on Social Work Practice*, 22(5): 499–519.

Longhofer, J. and Floersch, J. (2013) *Qualitative Methods for Practice Research*. New York: Oxford University Press.

Long-Sutehall, T., Sque, M. and Addington-Hall, J. (2010) 'Secondary analysis of qualitative data: A valuable method for exploring sensitive issues with an elusive population?', *Journal of Research in Nursing*, 16(4): 335–344.

Lorenz, L.S. (2010a) 'Discovering a new identity after brain injury', *Sociology of Health and Illness*, 32(6): 862–879.

Lorenz, L.S. (2010b) *Brain Injury Survivors: Narratives of Rehabilitation and Illness*. Boulder, CO: Lynn Rienner Publishers.

Lorenz, W. (2007) 'Practising history: Memory and contemporary professional practice', *International Social Work*, 50(5): 597–612.

Macdonald, G. (2003) *Using Systematic Reviews to Improve Social Care*, SCIE Reports No. 4. London: Social Care Institute for Excellence. Available at: http://www.scie.org.uk/publications/reports/report04.pdf. Accessed 21 January 2014.

Macdonald, G. and Popay, J. (2010) 'Evidence and practice: The knowledge challenge for social work', in I. Shaw, K. Briar-Lawson, J. Orme and R. Ruckdeschel (eds), *The Sage Handbook of Social Work Research*. London: SAGE Publications.

Madriz, E. (2003) 'Focus groups in feminist research', in N.K. Denzin and Y.S. Lincoln (eds), *Collecting and Interpreting Qualitative Materials*. Thousand Oaks, CA: SAGE Publications.

Mancini, M.A. (2011) 'Understanding change in community mental health practices through critical discourse analysis', *British Journal of Social Work*, 41(4): 645–667.

Mannay, D. (2010) 'Making the familiar strange: Can visual research methods render the familiar setting more perceptible?', *Qualitative Research*, 10(1): 91–111.

Manning, P. (2005) *Freud and American Sociology*. Cambridge: Polity Press.

Markham, A. and Buchanan, E. (2012) *Ethical Decision-Making and Internet Research: Recommendations from the AoIR Ethics Working Committee* (Version 2.0). Available at: http://aoir.org/reports/ethics2.pdf. Accessed 21 January 2014.

Marsh, P. and Fisher, M. (2005) *Developing the Evidence Base for Social Work and Social Care Practice*. London: Social Care Institute of Excellence.

Marshall, C. and Rossman, G.B. (2011) *Designing Qualitative Research*. Thousand Oaks, CA: SAGE Publications.

Martin, M.C. (2007) 'Crossing the line: Observations from East Detroit, Michigan, USA', *Qualitative Social Work*, 7(4): 465–475.

Mason, J. (2002) *Qualitative Researching*. London: SAGE Publications.

Mason, J. and Davies, K. (2009) 'Coming to our senses? A critical approach to sensory methodology', *Qualitative Research*, 9(5): 587–603.

Massey, D. (1991) 'A global sense of place', *Marxism Today*, June: 24–29.

Maxwell, J.A. (2004) 'Using qualitative methods for causal explanation', *Field Methods*, 16(3): 243–264.

Maxwell, J.A. (2005) *Qualitative Research Design: An Interactive Approach*. Thousand Oaks: SAGE Publications.

Maxwell, J.A. (2012) *A Realist Approach to Qualitative Research*. Thousand Oaks: SAGE Publications.

Mayer, J.E. and Timms, N. (1970) *The Client Speaks*. London: Routledge and Kegan Paul.

Mayes, R. and Llewellyn, G. (2012) 'Mothering differently: Narratives of mothers with intellectual disability whose children have been compulsorily removed', *Journal of Intellectual and Developmental Disability*, 37(2): 121–130.

McCracken, G. (1988) *The Long Interview*. Newbury Park: SAGE Publications.

McDonald, K.E. and Kidney, C.A. (2012) 'What is right? Ethics in intellectual disabilities research', *Journal of Policy and Practice in Intellectual Disabilities*, 9: 27–29.

McIntyre, A. (1997) *Making Meaning of Whiteness: Exploring Racial Identity with White Teachers*. Albany: State University of New York.

McIvor, G. (1995) 'Practitioner research in probation', in J. McGuire (ed.), *What Works? Reducing Offending*. New York: Wiley.

McKay, D. (1988) 'Value free knowledge: Myth or norm?' in D. McKay (ed.), *The Open Mind and Other Essays*. Leicester: Inter-Varsity Press.

McKeganey, N., MacPherson, I. and Hunter, D. (1988) 'How "they" decide: Exploring professional decision making', *Research, Policy and Planning*, 6(1): 15–19.

McLeod, J. (1999) *Practitioner Research in Counselling*. London: SAGE Publications.

McLeod, J. (2001) *Qualitative Research in Counselling and Psychotherapy*. London: SAGE Publications.

McLeod, J. (2010) *Case Study Research in Counselling and Psychotherapy*. London: SAGE Publications.

McLeod, J. and Elliott, R. (2011) 'Systematic case study research: A practice-oriented introduction to building an evidence base for counselling and psychotherapy', *Counselling and Psychotherapy Research*, 11(1): 1–10.

McLeod, J. and Thomson, R. (2009) *Researching Social Change: Qualitative Approaches*. London: SAGE.

McMahon, A. (1998) *Damned if you Do, Damned if You Don't*. Aldershot: Ashgate Publishing.

Meadows-Oliver, M. (2003) 'Mothering in public: A meta-synthesis of homeless women with children living in shelters', *Journal for Specialists in Pediatric Nursing*, 8(4): 130–136.

Mendis, K. (2009) 'Collecting data from mothers who have experienced childhood family violence with the use of a feminist methodology', *Qualitative Social Work*, 8(3): 377–390.

Mertens, D.M. and Ginsberg, P.E. (2008) 'Deep in ethical waters: Transformative perspectives for qualitative social work research', *Qualitative Social Work*, 7(4): 484–503.

Mertens, D.M. and Hesse-Biber, S. (eds) (2013) *Mixed Methods and Credibility of Evidence in Evaluation*. New Directions for Evaluation, 138. San Francisco: Jossey-Bass.

Merton, R.K. (1971) 'Social problems and sociological theory', in R. Merton and R. Nisbet (eds), *Contemporary Social Problems*. New York: Harcourt Brace Jovanovich, Inc.

Merton, R.K. (1972) 'Insiders and outsiders: A chapter in the sociology of knowledge', *American Journal of Sociology*, 78(1): 9–47.

Merton, R.K. (1987) 'The focused interview and focus groups: Continuities and discontinuities', *Public Opinion Quarterly*, 51(4): 550–556.

Merton, R.K. and Kendall, P.L. (1946) 'The focused interview', *American Journal of Sociology*, 51(6): 541–557.

Messerschmidt, J. (2000) 'Becoming "real men": Adolescent masculinity challenges and sexual violence', *Men and Masculinities*, 2(3): 286–307.

Middleton, D. and Hewitt, H. (2000) 'Biography and identity: Life story work in transitions of care for people with profound learning difficulties', in P. Chamberlayne, J. Bornat and T. Wengraf (eds), *The Turn to Biographical Methods in Social Science*. London: Routledge.

Mienczakowoski, J. (2001) 'Ethnodrama: performed research – limitations and potential', in P. Atkinson, A. Coffey, S. Delamont, J. Lofland and L. Lofland (eds), *Handbook of Ethnography*. London: SAGE Publications.

Miles, M. and Huberman, A. (1994) *Qualitative Data Analysis: An Expanded Sourcebook*. Thousand Oaks: SAGE Publications.

Miller, G. (1997) 'Contextualizing texts: Studying organizational texts', in G. Miller and R. Dingwall (eds), *Context and Method in Qualitative Research*. London: SAGE Publications.

Miller, W. and Crabtree, B. (1992) 'Depth interviewing: The long interview approach', in M. Stewart, F. Tudiver, M. Bass, E. Dunn and P. Norton (eds), *Tools for Primary Care Research*. Newbury Park, CA: SAGE Publications.

Miller, W.L. and Crabtree, B.F. (2005) 'Clinical research', in N.K. Denzin and Y. Lincoln (eds), *Sage Handbook of Qualitative Research*. Thousand Oaks: SAGE Publications.

Mills, C.W. (2008) 'Sociological poetry' in J. Summers (ed.), *The Politics of Truth: Selected Writings of C Wright Mills*. Oxford: Oxford University Press.

Mitchell, F., Lunt, N. and Shaw I. (2010) 'Practitioner research in social work: A knowledge review' *Evidence and Policy* 6 (1): 7–31.

Mitchell, W. (2010) '"I know how I feel": Listening to young people with life-limiting conditions who have learning and communication impairments', *Qualitative Social Work*, 9(2): 185–203.

Mohr, W.K. (1997) 'Interpretive interactionism: Denzin's potential contribution to intervention and outcomes research', *Qualitative Health Research*, 7(2): 270–286.

Molloy, D. and Woodfield, K. with Bacon, J. (2002) *Longitudinal Qualitative Research Approaches in Evaluation Studies*. Working Paper 7. London: Department of Work and Pensions.

Moran-Ellis, J. (1997) 'Close to home: The experience of researching child sexual abuse', in M. Hester, L. Kelly and J. Radford (eds), *Women, Violence and Male Power: Feminist Activism, Research and Practice*. Buckingham, Philadelphia: Open University Press.

Morris, S.M. (2001) 'Joint and individual interviewing in the context of cancer', *Qualitative Health Research*, 11(4): 553–567.

Morrison, E.W. and Milliken, F.J. (2003) 'Speaking up, remaining silent: The dynamics of voice and silence in organizations', *Journal of Management Studies*, 40(6): 1353–1358.

Morse, J. (1991) 'Approaches to qualitative–quantitative methodological triangulation', *Nursing Research*, 40(2): 120–123.

Mulder, S.S., Rance, S., Suárez, M.S. and Condori, M.C. (2000) 'Unethical ethics? Reflections on intercultural research practices', *Reproductive Health Matters*, 8(15): 104–112.

Munro, E. (2011) *The Munro Review of Child Protection: Final Report*. London: Department for Education: http://www.official-documents.gov.uk/document/cm80/8062/8062. pdf. Accessed 21 January 2014.

Munro, E.R., Holmes, L. and Ward, H. (2005) 'Researching vulnerable groups: Ethical issues and the effective conduct of research in local authorities', *British Journal of Social Work*, 35(7): 1023–1038.

Murphy, E. and Dingwall, R. (2001) 'The ethics of ethnography', in P. Atkinson, A. Coffey, S. Delamont, J. Lofland and L. Lofland (eds), *Handbook of Ethnography*. London: SAGE Publications.

Neander, K. and Skott, C. (2006) 'Important meetings with important persons: Narratives from families facing adversity and their key figures', *Qualitative Social Work*, 5(3): 295–311.

Neander, K. and Skott, C. (2008) 'Bridging the gap – the co-creation of a therapeutic process: Reflections by parents and professionals on their shared experiences of early childhood interventions', *Qualitative Social Work*, 7(3): 289–309.

Noblit, G.W. and Hare, R.D. (1988) *Meta-Ethnography: Synthesizing Qualitative Studies*. London: Sage.

Nowotny, H., Scott, P. and Gibbons, M. (2001) *Re-thinking Science: Knowledge and the Public in an Age of Uncertainty*. Cambridge: Polity.

Nygren, L., Khoo, E. and Hyvönen, U. (2006) *The Travelling Idea of LAC: Conditions for Moulding a Systematic Approach in Child Welfare into Three National Contexts: Australia, Canada and Sweden*. Paper to the 7th Looked After Children Conference, Sydney, Australia, 15 August.

Oakley, A. (1981) *Subject Woman*. London: Martin Robertson.

Odedahl, T. and Shaw, A.M. (2002) 'Interviewing elites', in J.F. Gubrium and J.A. Holstein (eds), *Sage Handbook of Interview Research: Context and Method*. Thousand Oaks: SAGE Publications.

Orme, J., Ruckdeschel, R. and Briar-Lawson, K. (2010) 'Challenges and directions in social work research and social work practice', in I. Shaw, K. Briar-Lawson, J. Orme and R. Ruckdeschel (eds), *Sage Handbook of Social Work Research*. London: SAGE Publications.

Oxford Compact Thesaurus (2005) Oxford: Oxford University Press.

Packer, M. (2011) *The Science of Qualitative Research*. New York: Cambridge University Press.

Padgett, D.K. (1998/2008) *Qualitative Methods in Social Work Research*. Thousand Oaks: SAGE Publications.

Palmer, V. M. (1928). *Field Studies in Sociology: a Student's Manual*. Chicago: University of Chicago Press.

Parton, N. (2000) 'Some thoughts on the relationship between theory and practice in social work', *British Journal of Social Work*, 30(4): 449–463.

Parton, N. (2008) 'Changes in the form of knowledge in social work: From the "social" to the "informational"', *British Journal of Social Work*, 38(2): 253–269.

Parton, N. and O'Byrne, P. (2000) *Constructive Social Work*. Basingstoke: Macmillan.

Paterson, B., Gregory, D. and Thorne, S. (1999) 'A protocol for researcher safety', *Qualitative Health Research*, 9(2): 259–269.

Patterson, W. (2008) 'Narratives of events: Labovian narrative analysis and its limitations', in M. Andrews, C. Squire and M. Tamboukou (eds), *Doing Narrative Research*. London: SAGE Publications, pp. 22–40.

Patton, M. (1988) 'The evaluator's responsibility for utilization', *Evaluation Practice*, 9(1): 5–24.

Patton, M. (2002) *Qualitative Research and Evaluation Methods*. Thousand Oaks: SAGE Publications.

Pawson, R. and Tilley, N. (1997) 'An introduction to scientific realist evaluation', in E. Chelimsky and W. Shadish (eds), *Evaluation for the 21st Century*. Thousand Oaks: SAGE Publications.

Pearson, G. (2009) 'The researcher as hooligan: Where "participant" observation means breaking the law', *International Journal of Social Research Methodology*, 12(3): 243–255.

Pease, B. (2010) 'Challenging the dominant paradigm: Social work research, social justice and social change', in I. Shaw, K. Briar-Lawson, J. Orme and R. Ruckdeschel (eds), *The Sage Handbook of Social Work Research*. London: SAGE Publications.

Pezalla, A.E., Pettigrew, J. and Miller-Day, M. (2012) 'Researching the researcher-as-instrument: An exercise in interviewer self-reflexivity', *Qualitative Research*, 12(2): 165–185.

Phillips, C. (2007a) 'Pain(ful) subjects: Regulated bodies in medicine and social work', *Qualitative Social Work*, 6(2): 197–212.

Phillips, C. (2007b) 'Untitled moments: Theorizing incorporeal knowledge in social work practice', *Qualitative Social Work*, 6(4): 449–466.

Phillips, C. and Shaw, I. (2011) 'Innovation in social work research' *British Journal of Social Work*, 41 (4): 609–624.

Phillips, D. (1990) 'Postpositivistic science: Myths and realities', in E. Guba (ed.), *The Paradigm Dialog*. Newbury Park: SAGE Publications.

Pike, N. (2012) *'The Theory Doesn't Work Here': An Exploratory Study of Practice in a 52-Week Residential Special School*. Thesis submitted in partial fulfilment of the requirements for the Doctorate in Social Work, School of Social Sciences, Cardiff University. Available at: http://orca.cf.ac.uk/45084/. Accessed 21 January 2014.

Pithouse, A. (1998) *Social Work: The Social Organisation of an Invisible Trade*. Aldershot: Avebury.

Pithouse, A. and Atkinson, P. (1988) 'Telling the case', in N. Coupland (ed.), *Styles of Discourse*. London: Croom Helm.

Plaut, T., Landis, S. and Trevor, J. (1993) 'Focus groups and community mobilisation', in D.L. Morgan (ed.), *Successful Focus Groups: Advancing the State of the Art*. Newbury Park: SAGE Publications.

Plummer, K. (1997) 'Introducing Chicago sociology,' in K. Plummer (ed.), *The Chicago School: Critical Assessments Vol I, A Chicago Canon?* London: Routledge.

Poindexter, C. (2002) 'Meaning from methods: Representing narratives from an HIV affected caregiver', *Qualitative Social Work*, 1(1): 59–78.

Popper, K. (1989) *Conjectures and Refutations: The Growth of Scientific Knowledge*. London: Routledge and Kegan Paul.

Preston-Shoot, M. (2007) 'Whose lives and whose learning? Whose narratives and whose writing? Taking the next research and literature steps with experts by experience', *Evidence and Policy*, 3(3): 343–359.

Prior, L. (2003) *Using Documents in Social Research*. London: SAGE Publications.

Prior, L. (2004) 'Documents', in C. Seale, G. Gobo, J.F. Gubrium and D. Silverman (eds), *Qualitative Research Practice*. London: SAGE Publications.

Prout, A. (2005) *The Future of Childhood: Towards the Interdisciplinary Study of Children*. London: Falmer Press.

Punch, K.F. (2000) *Developing Effective Research Proposals*. London: SAGE Publications.

Queen, S.A. (1928) 'Social interaction in the interview: An experiment', *Social Forces*, 6(4): 545–558.

Rabenhorst, M.M. (2006) 'Sexual assault survivors' reactions to a thought suppression paradigm', *Violence and Victims*, 21(4): 473–481.

Rambo, C. (2007) 'Handing IRB an unloaded gun', *Qualitative Inquiry*, 13(3): 353–367.

Rapley, T. (2004) 'Interviews', in C. Seale, G. Gobo, J.F. Gubrium and D. Silverman (eds), *Qualitative Research Practice*. London: SAGE Publications.

Reed-Danahay, D. (2001) 'Autobiography, intimacy and ethnography', in P. Atkinson, A. Coffey, S. Delamont, J. Lofland and L. Lofland (eds), *Handbook of Ethnography*. London: SAGE Publications.

Rees, S. (1979) *Social Work Face To Face*. New York: Columbia University Press.

Reid, W. (1990) 'Change-process research: A new paradigm?', in L. Videka-Sherman and W. J. Reid (eds), *Advances in Clinical Social Work Research*. Silver Spring, MD: NASW Press.

Reid, W.J. (1994) 'Reframing the epistemological debate', in E. Sherman and W.J. Reid (eds), *Qualitative Research in Social Work*. New York: Columbia University Press.

Renold, E., Holland, S., Ross, N.J. and Hillman, A. (2008) 'Becoming participant: Problematising "informed consent" in participatory research with young people in care', *Qualitative Social Work*, 7(4): 427–447.

Ridley, D. (2008) *The Literature Review: A Step-by-Step Guide for Students*. London: SAGE Publications.

Riemann, G. (2005) 'Ethnographies of practice–practicing ethnography', *Journal of Social Work Practice*, 19(1): 87–101.

Riemann, G. (2011) 'Self-reflective ethnographies of practice and their relevance for professional socialisation in social work', *International Journal of Action Research*, 7(3): 1–32.

Riessman, C.K. (1993) *Narrative Analysis*. Newbury Park, CA: SAGE Publications.

Riessman, C.K. (ed.) (1994) *Qualitative Studies in Social Work Research*. Thousand Oaks: SAGE Publications.

Riessman, C.K. (2001) 'Personal troubles as social issues: A narrative of infertility in context', in I. Shaw and N. Gould (eds), *Qualitative Research in Social Work*. London: SAGE Publications.

Riessman, C.K. (2008) *Narrative Methods for the Human Sciences*. Thousand Oaks: SAGE Publications.

Riessman, C.K. and Quinney, L. (2005) 'Narrative in social work: A critical review', *Qualitative Social Work*, 4(4): 391–412.

Rivlin, A., Marzano, L., Hawton, K. and Fazel, S. (2012) 'Impact on prisoners of participating in research interviews related to near-lethal suicide attempts', *Journal of Affective Disorders*, 136(1–2): 54–62.

Roberts, B. (2002) *Biographical Research*. Buckingham: Open University Press.

Roberts, B. (2007) *Getting the Most Out of the Research Experience*. London: SAGE Publications.

Robinson, V. (1930) *A Changing Psychology in Social Case Work*. Chapel Hill, NC: University of North Carolina Press.

Rodriguez, N. and Ryave, A. (2002) *Systematic Self Observation*. Thousand Oaks: SAGE Publications.

Romm, N. (1995) 'Knowing as an intervention', *Systems Practice*, 8(2): 137–167.

Romm, N. (1996) 'Inquiry-and-intervention in systems planning: Probing methodological rationalities', *World Futures*, 47(1): 25–36.

Ronander, K. (2010) 'The restorative dynamics of walking', *Qualitative Researcher* Issue 12. pp. 3–5.

Rosenbaum, A. and Langhinrichsen-Rohling, J. (2006) 'Meta-research on violence and victims: The impact of data collection methods on findings and participants', *Violence and Victims*, 21(4): 404–409.

Rosenbaum, A., Rabenhorst, M.M., Reddy, M.K., Madhavi, K., Fleming, M.T. and Howells, N.L. (2006) 'A comparison of methods for collecting self-report data on sensitive topics', *Violence and Victims*, 21(4): 461–471.

Ross, N.J., Renold, E., Holland, S. and Hillman, A. (2009) 'Moving stories: Using mobile methods to explore the everyday lives of young people in public care', *Qualitative Research*, 9(5): 605–623.

Ruch, G. (2013) '"Helping children is a human process": Researching the challenges social workers face in communicating with children', *British Journal of Social Work*. First published online. Available at: http://bjsw.oxfordjournals.org/content/early/2013/03/24/bjsw.bct045.abstract. Accessed 21 January 2014.

Ruckdeschel, R. and Chambon, A. (2010) 'The uses of social work research', in I. Shaw, K. Briar-Lawson, J. Orme and R. Ruckdeschel (eds), *The Sage Handbook of Social Work Research*. London: SAGE Publications.

Ruckdeschel, R with Shaw, I (2013) 'Reflections on editing a qualitative journal' *Qualitative Social Work*, 12 (6): 750–764.

Ruckdeschel, R., Earnshaw, P. and Firrek, A. (1994) 'The qualitative case study and evaluation: Issues, methods and examples', in E. Sherman and W.J. Reid (eds), *Qualitative Research in Social Work*. New York: Columbia University Press.

Russell, A.C. and Diaz, N.D (2013) 'Photography in social work research: Using visual image to humanize findings', *Qualitative Social Work*, 12(4) 433–453.

Sainsbury, E. (1975) *Social Work With Families*. London: Routledge.

Sainsbury, E., Nixon, S. and Phillips, D. (1982) *Social Work in Focus*. London: Routledge.

Salmon, P. and Riessman, C.K. (2008) 'Looking back on narrative research: An exchange', in M. Andrews, C. Squire and M. Tamboukou (eds), *Doing Narrative Research*. London: SAGE Publications.

Satyamurti, C. (1981) *Occupational Survival: The Case of the Local Authority Social Worker*. Oxford: Basil Blackwell.

Savin-Baden, M. and Major, C.H. (2013) *Qualitative Research: The Essential Guide to Theory and Practice*. Abingdon: Routledge.

Schaefer, N. (2012) 'Using video in a participatory multi-method project on young people's everyday lives in East Germany: A critical reflection', in S. Heath and C. Walker (eds), *Innovations in Youth Research*. Basingstoke: Palgrave Macmillan.

Scheff, T. (1997) 'Part/whole morphology: Unifying single case and comparative methods', *Sociological Research Online* 2.3.1. Available at: http://www.socresonline.org. uk/2/3/1.html. Accessed 21 January 2014.

Schwab, J. (1969) 'The practical: A language for the curriculum', *School Review*, November: 1–23.

Schwandt, T. (1997) 'Evaluation as practical hermeneutics', *Evaluation*, 3(1): 69–83.

Schwandt, T.A. (2001/2007) *Dictionary of Qualitative Inquiry*. Thousand Oaks: SAGE Publications.

Schwandt, T.A. and Burgon, H. (2006) 'Evaluation and the study of lived experience', in I. Shaw, J. Greene and M. Mark (eds), *Sage Handbook of Evaluation*. London: SAGE Publications.

Schwandt, T.A. and Dahler-Larsen, P. (2006) 'When evaluation meets the "rough ground" in communities', *Evaluation*, 12(4): 496–505.

SCIE (2010) *SCIE Systematic Research Review Guidelines*, 2nd edn, Social Care Institute for Excellence. Available at: http://www.scie.org.uk/publications/researchresources/ rr01.pdf. Accessed 24 July 2013.

Scott, J. (1990) *A Matter of Record*. Cambridge: Polity Press.

Scott, S. (1998) 'Here be dragons: researching the unbelievable, hearing the unthinkable. a feminist sociologist in uncharted territory', *Sociological Research Online*, 3 (3) http:// www.socresonline.org.uk/3/3/1.html. Accessed 21 January 2014.

Scourfield, J. (2001) 'Interviewing interviewers and knowing about knowledge', in I. Shaw and N. Gould (eds), *Qualitative Research in Social Work*. London: SAGE Publications.

Scourfield, J. (2003) *Gender and Child Protection*. Basingstoke: Palgrave Macmillan.

Scourfield, J. and Coffey, A. (2006) 'Access, ethics and the (re)construction of gender: The case of researcher as suspected "paedophile"', *International Journal of Social Research Methodology*, 9(1): 29–40.

Scourfield, J., Fincham, B., Langer, S. and Shiner, M. (2012) 'Sociological autopsy: An integrated approach to the study of suicide in men', *Social Science and Medicine*, 74(4): 466–473.

Scriven, M. (1997) 'Truth and objectivity in evaluation', in E. Chelimsky and W. Shadish (eds), *Evaluation for the 21st Century*. Thousand Oaks: SAGE Publications.

Seale, C. (1999) *The Quality of Qualitative Research*. London: SAGE Publications.

Sharland, E. (2012) 'Systematic review', in M. Gray, J. Midgley and S.A. Webb (eds), *The Sage Handbook of Social Work*. London: Sage.

Sharpe, D. (2012) 'Young people and policy research: Methodological challenges in CYP-led research', in S. Heath and C. Walker (eds), *Innovations in Youth Research*. Basingstoke: Palgrave Macmillan.

Shaw, C. (1966) *The Jack-Roller*. Chicago: Chicago University Press.

Shaw, C., Brady, L-M. and Davey, C. (2011) *Guidelines for Research with Children and Young People*. London: NCB.

Shaw, I. (1999a) *Qualitative Evaluation*. London: SAGE Publications.

Shaw, I. (1999b) 'Seeing the trees for the wood: The politics of practice evaluation', in B. Broad (ed.), *The Politics of Research and Evaluation in Social Work*. Birmingham: Venture Press.

Shaw, I. (2004) 'William J. Reid: An appreciation', *Qualitative Social Work*, 3(2): 109–115.

Shaw, I. (2006) 'Human services', in I. Shaw, J. Greene and M. Mark (eds), *Sage Handbook of Evaluation*. London: SAGE Publications.

Shaw, I. (2008) 'Ethics and the practice of qualitative research', *Qualitative Social Work*, 7 (4): 400–414.

Shaw, I. (2009) 'Rereading *The Jack-Roller*: Hidden histories in sociology and social work', *Qualitative Inquiry*, 15 (7): 1241–1264.

Shaw, I. (2010) 'Logics, qualities and quality in social work research', in I. Shaw, K. Briar-Lawson, J. Orme and R. Ruckdeschel (eds), *The Sage Handbook of Social Work Research*. London: SAGE Publications.

Shaw, I. (2011a) 'Social work research: An urban desert?', *European Journal of Social Work*, 14(1): 11–26.

Shaw, I. (2011b) *Evaluating in Practice*. Aldershot: Ashgate Publishing.

Shaw, I. (2012) 'Is social work research distinctive?', *Social Work Education*, 26(7): 659–669. Reprinted in I. Shaw (2012) *Practice and Research*. Aldershot: Ashgate Publishing.

Shaw, I. (2012a) 'Ways of knowing in social work', in M. Gray and S. Webb (ed.), *Social Work Theory and Methods*. London: SAGE Publications.

Shaw, I. (2012b) 'The positive contributions of quantitative methodology to social work research: A view from the sidelines', *Research on Social Work Practice*, 22(2): 129–134.

Shaw, I. (2012c) *Practice and Research*. Aldershot: Ashgate Publishing.

Shaw, I. (2012d) 'Serendipity, misfires and occasional patterns: A career in social work research', in I. Shaw (ed.), *Practice and Research*. Aldershot: Ashgate Publishing.

Shaw, I. (2013) 'Angels and devils the following day', *Qualitative Social Work*, 12(2): 234–44.

Shaw I. and Gould, N. (2001) *Qualitative Social Work Research*. London: Sage Publications.

Shaw, I. and Clayden, J. (2009) 'Technology, evidence and professional practice: Reflections on the Integrated Children's System', *Journal of Children's Services*, 4(4): 15–27.

Shaw, I. and Faulkner, A. (2006) 'Practitioner evaluation at work', *American Journal of Evaluation*, 27(1): 44–63.

Shaw, I. and Lunt, N. (2011) 'Navigating practitioner research', *British Journal of Social Work*, 41(8): 1548–1565.

Shaw, I. and Lunt, N. (2012) 'Constructing practitioner research', *Social Work Research*, 36(3): 197–208.

Shaw, I. and Norton, M. (2007) *Kinds and Quality of Social Work Research in Higher Education*. London: Social Care Institute for Excellence. Available at: http://www.scie.org.uk/publications/reports/report17.asp. Accessed 21 January 2014.

Shaw, I. and Norton, M. (2008) 'Kinds and quality of social work research', *British Journal of Social Work*, 38(5): 953–970.

Shaw, I. and Shaw, A. (1997/2012) 'Game plans, buzzes and sheer luck: Doing well in social work', *Social Work Research*, 21(2): 69–79. Reprinted in I. Shaw (2012) *Practice and Research*. Aldershot: Ashgate Publishing.

Shaw, I., Bell, M., Sinclair, I., Sloper, P., Mitchell, W., Dyson, P., Clayden, J. and Rafferty, J. (2009) 'An exemplary scheme? An evaluation of the Integrated Children's System', *British Journal of Social Work*, 39(4): 613–626.

Shaw, I. and Ramatowski, A. with Ruckdeschel, R. (2013) 'Patterns, designs and developments in qualitative research in social work: A research note', *Qualitative Social Work*, 12 (6) 732–749.

Shea, S.M. (2012) 'The permanency plan game show: An intersubjective case study of a foster care child and her caregivers', *Psychoanalytic Social Work*, 19(1–2): 54–69.

Sheffield, A.E. (1922) *Case-study Possibilities: A Forecast*. Boston: Research Bureau on Social Case Work.

Sheldon, B. and Macdonald, G. (2009) *A Textbook of Social Work*. Oxon: Taylor and Francis.

Sheppard, M., Newstead, S., Di Caccavo, A. and Ryan, K. (2000) 'Reflexivity and the development of process knowledge in social work: A classification and empirical study', *British Journal of Social Work*, 30(4): 465–88.

Shostak, M. (1981) *Nisa, the Life and Words of a !Kung Woman*. Cambridge, MA: Harvard University Press.

Sieber, J.E. and Tolich, M.B. (2013) *Planning Ethically Responsible Research*. Thousand Oaks, CA: SAGE Publications.

Silverman, D. (1997) *Discourses of Counselling: HIV Counselling as Social Interaction*. London: SAGE Publications.

Simon, E.L. (1986) 'Theory in education evaluation, or, what's wrong with generic-brand anthropology?', in D. Fetterman and M. Pitman (eds), *Educational Evaluation: Ethnography in Theory, Practice and Politics*. Newbury Park: SAGE Publications.

Smart, C. (2007) *Personal Life*. Cambridge: Polity.

Smith, D.B. (2005) 'The limits of positivism revisited', in A. Bilson (ed.), *Evidence-based Practice in Social Work*. London: Whiting and Birch.

Smith, M. (2010) 'Victim narratives of historical abuse in residential child care: Do we really know what we think we know?', *Qualitative Social Work*, 9(3): 303–320.

Smith, R. (2011) *Whose Method is it Anyway? Researching Space, Setting, and Practice*. Cardiff School of Social Sciences Working Paper Series, Working Paper 135. Available at: http://www.cardiff.ac.uk/socsi/resources/wp135.pdf. Accessed 21 January 2014.

Spencer, S. (2011) *Visual Research Methods in the Social Sciences: Awakening Visions*. London: Routledge.

Squire, C., Andrews, M. and Tamboukou, M. (2008) 'Introduction: What is narrative research?' in M. Andrews, C. Squire and M. Tamboukou (eds), *Doing Narrative Research*. London: SAGE Publications.

Stacey, J. (1988) 'Can there be a feminist ethnography?', *Women's Studies International* 11 (1): 21–27.

Stake, R. (1991) 'Retrospective on "The countenance of educational evaluation"', in M. Mclaughlin and D. Phillips (eds), *Evaluation and Education at Quarter Century*. Chicago: University of Chicago Press.

Stake, R. (1995) *The Art of Case Study Research*. Thousand Oaks: SAGE Publications.

Stake, R.E. (2004) *Standards-based and Responsive Evaluation*. Thousand Oaks: SAGE Publications.

Stake, R.E. and Schwandt, T.A. (2006) 'On discerning quality in evaluation', in I. Shaw, J. Greene and M. Mark (eds), *Sage Handbook of Evaluation*. London: SAGE Publications.

Stake, R. and Trumbull, D. (1982) 'Naturalistic generalizations', *Review Journal of Philosophy and Social Science*, 7 (1): 1–12.

Staller, K. (2007) 'Metalogue as methodology', *Qualitative Social Work*, 6(2): 137–157.

Staller, K. (2010) 'Technology and inquiry: Future, present and past', *Qualitative Social Work*, 9(2): 285–87.

Staller, K. M (forthcoming) 'What remains? Heroic stories in trace materials', in Stanley L. Witkin (ed.), *Narrating Social Work Through Autoethnography*. NY: Columbia University Press.

Staller, K.M. and Mafile'o, T. (2010) 'Community', in I. Shaw, K. Briar-Lawson, J. Orme and R. Ruckdeschel (eds), *Sage Handbook of Social Work Research*. London: SAGE Publications.

Stanley, L. and Wise, S. (1983) *Breaking Out: Feminist Consciousness and Feminist Research*. London: Routledge and Kegan Paul.

Stephen, S., Elliott, R. and MacLeod, R. (2011) 'Person-centred therapy with a client experiencing social anxiety difficulties: A hermeneutic single case efficacy design', *Counselling and Psychotherapy Research*, 11(1): 55–66.

Stevenson, O. and Adey, C. (2010) 'Toy tours: Reflections on walking-whilst-talking with young children at home', *Qualitative Researcher*, 12: 8–10.

Stewart, D.W., Shamdasani, P.M. and Rook, D.W. (2007) *Focus Groups: Theory and Practice*. Thousand Oaks: SAGE Publications.

Sukarieh, M. and Tannock, S. (2013) 'On the problem of over-researched communities: The case of the Shatila Palestinian Refugee Camp in Lebanon', *Sociology*, 47(3): 494–508.

Sung-Chan, P. and Yeung-Tsang, W. (2008) 'Bridging the theory-practice gap in social work education: A reflection on an action research in China', *Social Work Education*, 27(1): 51–69.

Swain, J., Heyman, B. and Gillman, M. (1998) 'Public research, private concerns: Ethical issues in the use of open-ended interviews with people who have learning difficulties', *Disability and Society*, 13(1): 21–36.

Swigonski, M.E. (1994) 'The logic of feminist standpoint theory for social work research', *Social Work*, 39(4): 387–393.

Szto, P., Furman, R. and Langer, C. (2005) 'Poetry and photography: An exploration into expressive/creative qualitative research', *Qualitative Social Work*, 4(2): 135–156.

Tadd, W., Woods, R., O'Neill, M., Windle, G., Read, S., Seddon, D., Hall, C. and Bayer, T. (2012) *PEACH: Promoting Excellence in All Care Homes*, Panicoa. Available at: http://www.panicoa.org.uk/sites/assets/Tadd_PEACH_report.pdf. Accessed 21 January 2014.

Taylor, C. and White, S. (2001) 'Knowledge, truth and reflexivity: The problem of judgement in social work', *Journal of Social Work*, 1(1): 37–59.

Taylor, S. (2012) '"One participant said ..." The implications of quotations from biographical talk', *Qualitative Research*, 12(4): 388–401.

Terrell, J. and Staller, K. (2003) 'Buckshot's Case: Social work and death penalty mitigation in Alabama', *Qualitative Social Work*, 2(1): 7–23.

Thomas, J. and Holland, S. (2010) 'Representing children's identities in core assessments', *British Journal of Social Work*, 40(8): 2617–2633.

Thomas, W.I. and Thomas, D. S. (1928) *The Child in America*. New York: Alfred A. Knopf.

Thompson, R. and Holland, J. (2005) '"Thanks for the memory": Memory books as a methodological resource in biographical research', *Qualitative Research*, 5(2): 201–219.

Thrasher, F.M. (1927) *The Gang: A Study of 1313 Gangs in Chicago*. Chicago: University of Chicago Press.

Tilley, L. and Woodthorpe, K. (2011) 'Is it the end for anonymity as we know it? A critical examination of the ethical principle of anonymity in the context of 21st century demands on the qualitative researcher', *Qualitative Research*, 11(2): 197–212.

Timms, N. (1968) *The Language of Social Casework*. London: Routledge and Kegan Paul.

Trigger, D., Forsey, M. and Meurk, C. (2012) 'Revelatory moments in fieldwork', *Qualitative Research*, 12(5): 513–527.

Trinder, L. (2000) 'Reading the texts: Postmodern feminism and the "doing" of research', in B. Fawcett, B. Featherstone, J. Fook and A. Rossiter (eds) *Practice and Research in Social Work: Postmodern Feminist Perspectives*. London: Routledge.

Tronto, J. (1994) *Moral Boundaries: A Political Argument for an Ethic of Care*. New York: Routledge.

Tufford, L. and Newman, P. (2012) 'Bracketing in qualitative research', *Qualitative Social Work*, 11(1): 80–96.

Turner, M. and Zimmerman, W. (1994) 'Acting for the sake of research', in J. Wholey, H. Hatry and K. Newcomer (eds), *Handbook of Practical Program Evaluation*. San Francisco: Jossey-Bass.

Turney, D., Platt, D., Selwyn, J. and Farmer, E. (2012) *Improving Child and Family Assessments: Turning Research into Practice*. London: Jessica Kingsley Publishers

Ungar, M. and Nicholl, G. (2002) 'The harmony of resistance: Qualitative research and ethical practice in social work', in W.C. van den Hoonaard (ed.), *Walking the Tightrope: Ethical Issues for Qualitative Researchers*. Toronto: University of Toronto Press.

Uprichard, E. (2013) 'Describing description (and keeping causality): The case of academic articles on food and eating', *Sociology*, 47(2): 368–382.

US Department of Health and Human Services (2012) *Human Research Protections Frequent Questions*. Available at: http://answers.hhs.gov/ohrp/categories/1566. Accessed 5 October 2012.

van den Eynden, V., Corti, L., Woollard, M., Bishop, L. and Horton, L. (2011) *Storing and Managing Data: A Guide for Researchers*. UK Data Archive, University of Essex. Available at: http://www.data-archive.ac.uk/media/2894/managingsharing.pdf. Accessed 21 January 2014.

van den Hoonaard, W.C. (2002) (ed.) *Walking the Tightrope: Ethical Issues for Qualitative Researchers*. Toronto: University of Toronto Press.

van Maanen, J. (1988/2011) *Tales of the Field: On Writing Ethnography*. Chicago: University of Chicago Press.

Verd, J.M. and Porcel, S. (2012) 'An application of qualitative Geographic Information Systems (GIS) in the field of urban sociology using ATLAS.ti: Uses and Reflections', *Forum Qualitative Sozialforschung / Forum: Qualitative Social Research*, [S.l.] 13(2): <http://www.qualitative-research.net/index.php/fqs/article/view/1847/3373> Accessed 21 January 2014.

Walkerdine, V., Lucey, H. and Melody, J. (2002) 'Subjectivity and qualitative method', in T. May (ed.), *Qualitative Research in Action*. London: SAGE Publications.

Walter, I., Nutley, S., Percy-Smith, J., McNeish, D. and Frost, S. (2004) *Improving the Use of Research in Social Care Practice*. London: Social Care Institute for Excellence.

Wang, C. and Burris, M.A. (1997) 'Photovoice: Concept, methodology, and use for participatory needs assessment', *Health, Education and Behaviour*, 24(3): 369–387.

Ward, J. (2008) 'Researching drug sellers: An "experiential" account from "the field"', *Sociological Research Online*, 13(1): 14. Available at: http://www.socresonline.org.uk/13/1/14.html. Accessed 21 January 2014.

Waruszynski, B.T. (2002) 'Pace of technological change: Battling ethical issues in qualitative research', in W.C. van den Hoonaard (ed.), *Walking the Tightrope: Ethical Issues for Qualitative Researchers*. Toronto: University of Toronto Press.

Wasoff, F. and Dobash, R. (1992) 'Simulated clients in "natural" settings: Constructing a client to study professional practice', *Sociology*, 26(2): 333–349.

Wasoff, F. and Dobash, R. (1996) *The Simulated Client: A Method for Studying Professionals Working with Clients*. Aldershot: Avebury.

Wastell, D., Peckover, S., White, S., Broadhurst, K., Hall, C. and Pithouse, P. (2011) 'Social work in the laboratory: Using microworlds for practice research', *British Journal of Social Work*, 41(4): 744–760.

Webb, E.J., Campbell, D.T., Schwartz, R. and Sechrest, L. (1966) *Unobtrusive Measures*. Chicago: Rand McNally.

Webber, M. (2011) *Evidence-based Policy and Practice in Mental Health Social Work*. Exeter: Learning Matters.

Webber, M. (2014) 'From ethnography to randomised controlled trial: An innovative approach to developing complex social interventions', *Journal of Evidence Based Social Work*, 11(1–2): 173–82.

Weiss, C. (1980) 'Knowledge creep and decision accretion', *Knowledge, Creation, Diffusion, Utilization*, 1(3): 381–404.

Weiss, C. (1988) 'If programme decisions hinged only on information', *Evaluation Practice*, 9(1): 15–28.

White, S. (1998) 'Time, temporality and child welfare', *Time and Society*, 7(1): 55–74.

White, S. (1999) 'Examining the artfulness of "risk talk"', in A. Jokinen, K. Juhila and T. Posö (eds), *Constructing Social Work Practices*. Aldershot: Ashgate Publishing.

White, S. (2001) 'Auto-ethnography as reflexive inquiry: The research act as self-surveillance', in I. Shaw and N. Gould (eds), *Qualitative Research in Practice*. London: SAGE Publications.

White, S., Hall, C. and Peckover, S. (2009) 'The descriptive tyranny of the common assessment framework: Technologies of categorization and professional practice in child welfare', *British Journal of Social Work*, 39(7): 1197–1217.

Whitmore, E. (2001) '"People listened to what we had to say": Reflections on an emancipatory qualitative evaluation', in I. Shaw and N. Gould (eds), *Qualitative Research in Social Work*. London: SAGE Publications.

Whittemore, R. and Knafl, K. (2005) 'The integrative review: Updated methodology', *Journal of Advanced Nursing*, 52(5): 546–553.

Whyte, W.F. (1955) *Street Corner Society*. Chicago: University of Chicago Press.

Whyte, W.F. (1992) 'In defence of *Street Corner Society*', *Contemporary Ethnography*, 21 (1): 52–68.

Wiles, R., Pain, H. and Crow, G. (2010) *Innovation in Qualitative Research Methods: A Narrative Review*. ESRC National Centre for Research Methods. Available at: http://eprints.ncrm.ac.uk/919/1/innovation_in_qualitative_research_methods.pdf. Accessed 24 July 2013.

Williams, D.D. (1986) 'When is naturalistic evaluation appropriate?', in D.D. Williams (ed.), *Naturalistic Evaluation*. New Directions in Program Evaluation, No. 30. San Francisco: Jossey-Bass.

Williams, G. H. (1984) 'The genesis of chronic illness: narrative re-construction', *Sociology of Health and Illness*, 6(2): 175–200.

Williams, M. (2003) *Making Sense of Social Research*. London: SAGE Publications.

Williams, R. (1976) *Keywords: A Vocabulary of Culture and Society*. London: Fontana.

Wilson, J. and While, A.E. (1998) 'Methodological issues surrounding the use of vignettes in qualitative research', *Journal of Interprofessional Care*, 12(1): 79–87.

Winokur, M., Holtan, A. and Valentine, D. (2009) 'Kinship care for the safety, perma-nency, and well-being of children removed from the home for maltreatment', Campbell Systematic Reviews, 1. www.campbellcollaboration.org/lib/download/666. Accessed 21 January 2014.

Winter, K. (2011) *Building Relationships and Communicating With Young Children*. London: Routledge.

Wiseman, J.P. (1974) 'The research web', *Journal of Contemporary Ethnography*, 3(3): 317–328.

Witkin, R. (1994) 'Running a commentary on imaginatively relived events: A technique for obtaining qualitatively rich discourse', *British Journal of Sociology*, 45(2): 265–285.

Witkin, S. (2000a) 'Noticing', *Social Work*, 45(2): 101–103.

Witkin, S. (2000b) 'Writing social work', *Social Work*, 45(5): 389–394.

Witkin, S.L. and Saleebey, D. (2007) *Social Work Dialogues: Transforming the Canon in Inquiry, Practice and Education*. Alexandria, VA: Council on Social Work Education.

Wolcott, H. (1990) 'On seeking – and rejecting – validity in qualitative research', in E.E. Eisner and A. Peshkin (eds), *Qualitative Inquiry and Education*. New York: Teachers College Press, Columbia University.

Wolpert, L. and Richards, A. (1997) *Passionate Minds: The Inner World of Scientists*. Oxford: Oxford University Press.

Wulf-Andersen, T. (2012) 'Poetic representation: Working with dilemmas of involvement in participative social work research', *European Journal of Social Work*, 15(4): 563–580.

Wulff, D., St. George, S., Faul, A.C., Frey, A. and Frey, S. (2010) 'Drama in the academy: Bringing racism to light', *Qualitative Social Work*, 9(1): 111–127.

Xenitidou, M. and Gilbert, N. (2009) *Innovations in Social Science Research Methods*. Guildford, University of Surrey.

Yin, R.K. (2009) *Case Study Research*, 4th edn. Thousand Oaks: SAGE Publications.

Yoshihama, M. (2002) 'Breaking the web of abuse and silence: Voices of battered women in Japan', *Social Work*, 47(4): 389–400.

Young, P.V. (1929) 'Sociological concepts as an aid to social work analyses', *Social Forces*, 7(4): 497–500.

Young, P.V. (1935) *Interviewing in Social Work: A Sociological Analysis*. New York: McGraw Hill.

Zeller, R. (1993) 'Focus group research on sensitive topics – setting the agenda without setting the agenda', in D.L. Morgan (ed.), *Successful Focus Groups: Advancing the State of the Art*. Thousand Oaks: SAGE Publications.

Name Index

Subject Index

Abuse – *see also substance abuse* 25, 26, 28, 72, 104, 107–09, 110, 151, 178

Access 64, 87, 90, 106, 111, 143, 145, 160, 170f, 185–6.

Action research 34, 52, 91–2, 264, 266, 269, 287

Actor's perspective 16

Advocacy research – *see Justice*

Analysis – *see qualitative analysis*

Anonymisation 97, 102, 106, 116–7, 118, 166, 193, 215

Anthropology 9, 12, 47, 58, 157, 166, 182f

Applied research 48, 57, 241

Archives – *see also documents* 13, 47, 52, 93, 96–7, 113, 165–7, 170, 176–9, 202, 208, 235, 312

Art, art-based research – *see also film, poetry* 52–3, 158, 235, 261, 267, 274–6

Audience – *See also utilisation* x, 44, 50, 84, 98, 124, 153–4, 155, 159, 162, 167, 169, 171, 174, 215, 233f, 302, 304

Autobiography 14, 176–7, 191, 230

Autoethnography 102, 110, 120, 192, 224, 233, 309

Bias 11, 74, 89, 110, 123, 191, 249, 254, 267, 277, 296

Biography – *see also autobiography, autoethnography* 14, 87, 111, 148–9 155f, 160f, 162, 175, 224

Blurred genres – *see also genre* 47, 48, 49, 224.

Bricoleur 206

CAQDAS 194, 216–8

Carers 23, 69, 81, 111, 115, 162, 302

Case studies ix, 7, 8, 18, 34, 41, 49, 50, 88–90, 112, 116, 118–9, 150f, 176, 248, 253, 266, 273, 289

Cases – *see social work cases*

Cause 29–33, 42, 43, 160, 228, 247–50, 253f, 254f, 256

Change-process research 255–6

Chicago – *see also history* viii, 7, 17, 19, 43f, 47, 148, 176f, 201f, 248, 269, 282, 285, 306

Children 8, 23, 26, 36f, 71, 72, 74, 85–6, 87, 92, 96, 106, 113f, 115, 118f, 126, 132, 133, 144, 156f, 163f, 172–3, 178, 180, 195, 198, 231, 234f, 3247, 254–5, 265, 273, 291

Clients – *see service users*

Coding, indigenous coding – *see also qualitative analysis* 69, 97, 194, 203, 205, 212–3, 217, 271

Cohort studies 8, 75, 92

Common-sense – *see knowledge*

Communication 46, 85–6, 114, 124, 140, 143, 215, 250, 266, 302

Community 20, 23, 28, 33, 34, 52, 56, 93, 99, 116f, 141, 148, 167, 186, 192f, 200, 248, 258–9, 264, 266, 268, 273

Comparison 14, 169, 134, 167, 204f, 225, 231, 232, 253f

Concepts 6, 29f, 113, 193, 204–5, 217, 220, 228f, 271, 287, 297, 299, 301, 310
sensitising concepts 225–6

Constructivism 7, 48f, 123, 139, 154, 160, 171, 175, 176, 178, 207, 218

Contexts of research 5, 17f, 88, 138, 149, 151, 194–98, 212, 230, 236, 248, 255, 272

Conversation 9f, 29, 53, 111f, 124–5, 129, 141f, 145, 149, 159, 187f, 214, 259, 274f

Conversation analysis 197, 216, 245

Counselling 25, 45, 126, 213, 248, 256

Covert research 101, 106, 110, 135, 137, 192–3

Cultural review 83, 210–12

Culture 5, 6, 7, 8, 32, 47, 113, 115, 137, 138, 145, 152 170, 182, 183, 210, 220, 232f, 290, 292, 306, 309

Dance – *see arts-based research*

Databases 64, 66, 71–4

Decision making 14–15, 26, 52, 56, 136, 301

Deduction 39, 86, 204, 205, 208

Description – *see also thick description* 27, 32, 41, 86, 116, 139, 172, 188, 196, 199, 214, 225, 244, 249, 280, 285, 306

Design of qualitative research 29, 34, 52, 59, 68, 71f, 75, 76, 80–100, 111, 135, 166,